The End of the Middle Ages?

England in the Fifteenth and Sixteenth Centuries

THE FIFTEENTH CENTURY SERIES

Advisory Editor: Ralph A. Griffiths, Professor of Medieval History, University of Wales, Swansea

THE FIFTEENTH CENTURY SERIES is a tribute to the vitality of scholarly study of the later Middle Ages (and especially of the fifteenth century) and to the commitment of Alan Sutton (now Sutton) Publishing to make its conclusions widely available. This partnership, which Charles Ross did so much to encourage, has been extraordinarily productive in the quarter-century since the pioneering colloquium on 'The Fifteenth Century, 1399–1509: Studies in Politics and Society' was held in Cardiff and presided over by S.B. Chrimes. The proceedings of that colloquium, edited by S.B. Chrimes, C.D. Ross and R.A. Griffiths, were published in 1972 (and reprinted in 1995). Since 1979 Alan Sutton Publishing has published a number of papers, invited especially from younger scholars and discussed at further colloquia, which have become a notable feature of the academic landscape in Britain. Aside from the encouragement given to talented young historians, noteworthy features of these volumes are the breadth of topics addressed, the novelty of approaches adopted, and the participation of scholars from North America and the European Continent. The volumes have proved influential and informative, and there is good reason to include further volumes in this major new series, both to recognize the achievements of the present generation of fifteenth-century historians and to consolidate the interest in later medieval history which they had undoubtedly generated.

This sixth volume in THE FIFTEENTH CENTURY SERIES arises from a conference held at Aberystwyth in 1996. Drawing attention towards the end of the century, its aim is to re-examine the extent and varieties of social and political change in a period long thought to mark the boundary between medieval and modern. The seven contributors explore different areas of activity – from religion to warfare, from language to economic growth – and the editor offers a historiographical introduction and some concluding suggestions.

◇ THE FIFTEENTH CENTURY SERIES No. 6 ◇

THE END OF THE MIDDLE AGES?

ENGLAND IN THE FIFTEENTH AND SIXTEENTH CENTURIES

EDITED BY
JOHN L. WATTS

SUTTON PUBLISHING

First published in the United Kingdom in 1998 by
Sutton Publishing Limited · Phoenix Mill
Thrupp · Stroud · Gloucestershire · GL5 2BU

British Library Cataloguing in Publication Data
A catalogue record for this book is available from the British Library

ISBN 0-7509-1828-4

 ™ ALAN SUTTON™ and SUTTON™ are the
trade marks of Sutton Publishing Limited

Typeset in 10/15pt Baskerville.
Typesetting and origination by
Sutton Publishing Limited.
Printed in Great Britain by
WBC Ltd, Bridgend.

CONTENTS

Contributors

Simon Adams is Senior Lecturer in History at the University of Strathclyde. He holds a Leverhulme Research Fellowship for 1997/8.

G.W. Bernard was educated at Reading School and St Catherine's College, Oxford, where he gained his doctorate, later published as *The Power of the Early Tudor Nobility: A Study of the Fourth and Fifth Earls of Shrewsbury* (Brighton, 1985). His publications include *War, Taxation and Rebellion in Early Tudor England: Henry VIII, Wolsey and the Amicable Grant of 1525* (Brighton, 1986) and, as editor, a collection of essays on *The Tudor Nobility* (Manchester, 1992). Since 1980 he has taught at the University of Southampton, where he is a Reader in the Department of History.

R.H. Britnell teaches medieval history at Durham University. He is the author of *The Close of the Middle Ages? England 1471–1529*, published in 1997.

Clifford S.L. Davies' interests have been primarily in late fifteenth-century and Tudor history, with English relationships with the European powers a recurring theme. 'Henry V', however, is for him a gingerly step into new territory, undertaken in the hope that perspective may compensate in part for lack of first-hand expertise.

Jean-Philippe Genet is maître de conférences at the University of Paris I (Sorbonne) and co-director, with Ezio Ornato, of the CNRS/Paris I Laboratoire 'Culture, Politique et Société en Europe au Moyen Age'. He has published *Four English Political Tracts of the Later Middle Ages* (1977) and *Le Monde au Moyen Age* (1991), and has been, with Wim Blockmans, the general editor of *Origins of the Modern State*, a major cooperative project of the European Science Foundation.

Steven Gunn is fellow and tutor in modern history at Merton College, Oxford. His publications include *Charles Brandon, Duke of Suffolk, c. 1484–1545* (1988), *Cardinal Wolsey: Church, State and Art* (1991) and *Early Tudor Government, 1485–1558* (1995). He is currently researching the councillors and courtiers of Henry VII, and war and society in early Tudor England.

Colin Richmond is author of *John Hopton: A Fifteenth-century Suffolk Gentleman* (1981) and has completed the first two volumes of a three-volume study of the Paston family in the fifteenth century. He is now, after thirty-three years there, Professor Emeritus at the University of Keele.

John L. Watts has recently moved from Aberystwyth, where the conference which spawned this collection was held, to Corpus Christi College, Oxford. He has published a book called *Henry VI and the Politics of Kingship* (1996) and various articles on the ideological and institutional frameworks of politics in later medieval England.

ABBREVIATIONS

BIHR	*Bulletin of the Institute of Historical Research*
BJRL	*Bulletin of the John Rylands Library*
CAD	*A Descriptive Catalogue of Ancient Deeds in the Public Record Office*, 6 vols (1890–1915)
CClR	*Calendar of the Close Rolls*
CFR	*Calendar of the Fine Rolls*
CPR	*Calendar of the Patent Rolls*
EcHR	*Economic History Review*
EHR	*English Historical Review*
HJ	*Historical Journal*
HR	*Historical Research*
HMC	Historical Manuscripts Commission
JMH	*Journal of Medieval History*
LP	*Letters and Papers, Foreign and Domestic, of the Reign of Henry VIII*, eds J.S. Brewer, J. Gairdner and R.H. Brodie, 2nd edn, 23 vols in 38 (HMSO, 1862–1932)
NottMS	*Nottingham Medieval Studies*
RP	*Rotuli Parliamentorum*, 6 vols (n.p., n.d.)
TRHS	*Transactions of the Royal Historical Society*
VCH	*Victoria County History*

Note: Place of publication for all books cited is London unless otherwise specified

Introduction: History, the Fifteenth Century and the Renaissance

John L. Watts

Almost forty years before he wrote the introduction to the first of these collections of fifteenth century conference proceedings, S.B. Chrimes was grappling with the problem of how to capture and express the 'character' of fifteenth-century England.[1] For him and for his contemporaries, pioneers in the field to which this series is devoted, it was a problem that struck with particular force: the fifteenth century was little known and even less appreciated. As the dreary rump of one era, and the chaotic preamble of another, it stood little chance of being explored in depth, still less seen in its own terms. For us today, the perspective is rather different: we have come to know a great deal about fifteenth-century England, and the few scholars who were prepared to take its history seriously in the 1930s and '40s have left behind them an extensive progeny. As the volume of research has expanded, attempts have been made to re-conceive the period: to challenge its traditional boundaries of 1399 and 1485; to shift the historiographical focus from political to social history; to take more account of positive features, such as the spread of literacy and learning, the rise in peasant living standards, the interest in public order, or the creativity of responses to the economic slump.[2]

---

[1] S.B. Chrimes, 'Sir John Fortescue and his Theory of Dominion', *TRHS*, 4th ser., 17 (1934), 117–47.

[2] C.L. Kingsford, *Prejudice and Promise in Fifteenth-Century England* (Oxford, 1925), had pointed the way even before Chrimes wrote (see C. Carpenter, ed., *Kingsford's Stonor Letters and Papers, 1290–1483* (Cambridge, 1996), pp. 10–14, for a discussion). Note also the preface of E. Power and M.M. Postan, eds, *Studies in English Trade in the Fifteenth Century* (1933), which pointed to a very different fifteenth century from the one familiar to political historians. E.F. Jacob, with his background in the study of European history and political ideas, also brought fresh perspectives to the study of the

Yet somehow, even now, the problem of characterizing fifteenth-century England remains. Rosemary Horrox has recently observed that its historians still write as if they feel obliged to 'rescue' their subject from its one-time reputation, and this suggests that there continues to be a clearer sense of what the fifteenth century is not than of what it is.[3] We would probably all agree that the old picture of medieval systems declining into corruption and disarray is wrong, but there is no consensus (and few leads) on any alternative vision of the times. In a way, perhaps, this is only to be expected: more detailed knowledge, changing academic tastes and doubts about many traditional interpretative categories have conspired to make us wary of dealing in terms like the 'character' of an age. On the other hand, the resulting lack of definition has played a part in prompting calls for a new kind of constitutional history, while several discussions of the historiography of the fifteenth century have suggested that, if the 'character' of the age has not been dealt with explicitly in modern writing, more subliminal characterizations have nonetheless been influential.[4]

This last is a point worth pursuing. We may reject the language of 'character' or 'spirit of the age'; we may insist that society is too complex to be represented

---

fifteenth century in the 1920s and '30s: see, in particular, his essay, '"Middle Ages" and "Renaissance"', *Essays in the Conciliar Epoch* (Manchester, 1943), 170–84, which celebrates the moves towards a more 'social' understanding of the period. Full-length revisionist treatments along these lines began to appear around 1970: J.R. Lander, *Conflict and Stability in Fifteenth-Century England* (1969); F.R.H. du Boulay, *An Age of Ambition* (1970); C.S.L. Davies, *Peace, Print and Protestantism, 1450–1558* (1977).

[3] R. Horrox, *Fifteenth-Century Attitudes* (Cambridge, 1994), p. 1.

4 For this theme in arguments in favour of a new kind of constitutional history, see: C. Carpenter, 'Fifteenth-Century English Politics', *HJ*, 26 (1983), 963–7; R.E. Horrox (using rather different language), 'Local and National Politics in Fifteenth-Century England', *JMH*, 18 (1992), 391–403; E. Powell, 'After "After McFarlane": the Poverty of Patronage and the Case for Constitutional History', in D.J. Clayton et al., eds, *Trade, Devotion and Governance* (Stroud, 1994), 1–16; J.L. Watts, *Henry VI and the Politics of Kingship* (Cambridge, 1996), ch. 1. For comment on how the fifteenth century has, in practice, been characterized by historians, see these same sources, and also C. Carpenter, *Locality and Polity* (Cambridge, 1992), pp. 5–6; C.F. Richmond, 'After McFarlane', *History*, 68 (1983), 46–60; M.A. Hicks, 'Idealism in Late Medieval English Politics', *Richard III and his Rivals* (1991), 41–59; C. Carpenter, 'Political and Constitutional History: Before and After McFarlane', in A.J. Pollard and R.H. Britnell, eds, *The McFarlane Legacy* (Stroud, 1995).

by any single description, let alone by its published ideals; we may express unhappiness at the whole notion of 'periods' or 'ages', as owing much more to the ingenuity of historians than to the realities of the past. But if we want to interpret the past at all, we have to classify it, and our choice is really between doing this explicitly or implicitly. The common preference is to adopt the second approach and to feel that thereby we place fewer obstacles between ourselves and the telling of what really happened. Whatever advantages may lie in this way of doing things, however, it involves a certain sleight of hand. Ignoring classificatory systems and ideas does not altogether destroy them, and when from time to time we inspect our heuristic assumptions, we often find they are as crude and misleading as the ones more openly exposed in older writing: our late-modern uncertainty is only a partial protection against glibness and error. Some assumptions we may hold as explicit beliefs – the perception that politics is normally 'personal' in the later middle ages, for example – though we do not necessarily spend much time reflecting on these.[5] Many more, perhaps, are implicit and brought out into the open only by our critics. Some assumptions we hold as individuals, and then we usually are explicit, but many (such as the one above) are the products of common training.[6] Our tendency, in a quarter of British history which remains relatively unselfconscious, is to deal with these interpretative structures in relation to specific instances of their use, but since such structures do not simply and straightforwardly arise out of the evidence, there may be something to be said for exploring them head-on.

   In one particular area of the interpretation of the fifteenth century, there is a well-established precedent for this kind of activity: for want of a better term, we might call it the issue of the Renaissance, using that word to mean the various

---

[5] For example, G.L. Harriss, ed., *Henry V. The Practice of Kingship* (Oxford, 1985), pp. 9–10; B.P. Wolffe, *Henry VI* (1981), p. 25; R. Horrox, 'Personalities and Politics', A.J. Pollard, ed., *The Wars of the Roses* (Basingstoke, 1995), 89–109, p. 89; Watts, *Henry VI*, p. 363. The question of what 'personal' actually means, or of what we might miss by looking at things in this way, is less commonly considered.

[6] The work of K.B. McFarlane, so fundamental in the formation of three 'generations' of later medieval historians, is surely one major point of origin for this particular interpretative approach: Carpenter, *Locality and Polity*, pp. 3–4.

breaks with the 'medieval' past which were traditionally supposed to have occurred in the decades around 1500. Until quite recently, almost everybody who wrote on the fifteenth century felt obliged to make some comment on this question as a necessary first step in discussing the events and processes of the period. Chrimes himself was responding to this tradition with his comments on the difficulty of characterizing the fifteenth century: the problem was not 'the so-called transitional aspect of the period, for every century is transitional'; rather, it was the mixture of 'conservatism' and 'anticipation' running through many of the socio-political, cultural and intellectual trends of the time.[7] His words are a good illustration of the scepticism which was already becoming prevalent about the claims made on behalf of the Renaissance: where once scholars had engrossed all that was progressive in earlier centuries and pronounced it the work of 'forerunners', now, in the early decades of the twentieth century, they were finding so many medieval roots for supposedly new phenomena such as classicism, humanism and individualism that the emphasis was reversed and the 'medievalness' of many fifteenth- and sixteenth-century forms was widely proclaimed.[8] Against this background, a concern to define terms like 'Middle Ages' and 'Renaissance' became fashionable, and alongside it an interest in tracing the history of such terms and exploring the implications of their usage.[9]

[7] Chrimes, 'Sir John Fortescue', pp. 117–18. Note Larry Poos' witty observation that 'transitional era' is 'a phrase historians commonly employ to indicate that they understand what had gone before and what came after much better than what was going on in between' (*A Rural Society after the Black Death: Essex 1350–1525* (Cambridge, 1991), p. 1).

[8] W.K. Ferguson, *The Renaissance in Historical Thought. Five Centuries of Interpretation* (Cambridge, Mass., 1948), p. ix and chs 10 and 11.

[9] Ferguson, *Renaissance in Historical Thought*, is the most substantial treatment of the historiography of the Renaissance (chs 1 and 3 deal with the emergence of the term, and see pp. 291–2 for the beginning of initiatives to explore the history of its usage in the 1900s). Note also N. Edelman, 'The Early Uses of Medium Aevum, Moyen Age, Middle Ages', in his *The Eye of the Beholder: Essays in French Literature* (Baltimore and London, 1974), 58–81 (this was originally published in 1938 and includes a discussion of earlier treatments of the terminological problem); H. Weisinger, 'The Renaissance Theory of the Reaction Against the Middle Ages as a Cause of the Renaissance', *Speculum*, 20 (1945), 461–7; T.E. Mommsen, 'Petrarch's Conception of the Dark Ages', *Speculum*, 17 (1942), 226–42; Jacob, '"Middle Ages" and "Renaissance"'; G. Barraclough, 'Medium Aevum: Some Reflections on Medieval History and on the Term "The Middle Ages"', *History in a Changing World* (Oxford, 1957), 54–63.

By 1920, when Johan Huizinga wrote his lecture on 'The Problem of the Renaissance', the inappropriateness of traditional views on the division between medieval and modern was already apparent in almost every sphere.[10] And yet, in the famous book on the *Waning of the Middle Ages*, which he wrote about the same time, Huizinga was reluctant to abandon the old model:

> The Renaissance, when studied without preconceived ideas, is found to be full of elements which were characteristic of the medieval spirit in its full bloom. Thus it has become nearly impossible to keep up the antithesis, and yet we cannot do without it, because Middle Ages and Renaissance by the usage of half a century have become terms which call up before us, by means of a single word, the difference between two epochs, a difference which we feel to be essential, though hard to define, just as it is impossible to express the difference between a strawberry and an apple.[11]

Huizinga's predicament, it may be argued, has not gone away. It is clear in Chrimes' comments, quoted above: would he even think in terms of a problematic mixture of old and new in fifteenth-century thought, if this were not the fifteenth century and the ghost of transition still incompletely exorcized? It is also clear in the recurrent attempts of general histories – Lander in 1969, Loades in 1974, Davies in 1977, Du Boulay in 1981 and Thomson in 1983 – to break the stranglehold of 1485 (English history's own Renaissance, as we shall see below).[12] These attempts have been broadly successful at the level of explicit statement, but – as Steven Gunn has recently observed – the old division is perpetuated by a gulf of understanding between 'later medieval' and 'early

---

[10] Printed in his *Men and Ideas. History, the Middle Ages, the Renaissance* (1960), 243–87.

[11] J. Huizinga, *Waning of the Middle Ages* (Harmondsworth, 1955), p. 262, quoted in Ferguson, *Renaissance in Historical Thought*, p. 373.

[12] Lander, *Conflict and Stability*; D.M. Loades, *Politics and the Nation, 1450–1660* (1974); Davies, *Peace, Print and Protestantism*; Du Boulay, *Age of Ambition*; J.A.F. Thomson, *The Transformation of Medieval England, 1370–1529* (Harlow, 1983). Davies, pp. 11–13, and Du Boulay, pp. 11–16, discuss the question of periodization directly. For 1485 as the obvious location for the Renaissance in England, see D. Hay, *The Renaissance in its Historical Background* (Cambridge, 1961), pp. 12–13.

modern' historians, even when these people are writing about the same later
fifteenth century.[13] It is not that anyone now expects to find clear turning points
in the time of the Yorkists or early Tudors – though their absence continues to be
worthy of remark[14] – but rather that historians are not agreed about what
paradigms to evoke in dealing with the fifteenth century, and with its second half
in particular. In the absence of up-to-date structural discussion, they are not sure
how to characterize the period. More than a hundred years ago, Stubbs
suggested that, from 1485, history 'must be written or read from a new standing
point'.[15] His own had been the thirteenth century, perhaps; the standing points of
today's historians, if Gunn is right, are, on the one hand, the McFarlanite 'Later
Middle Ages' (an imagined space stretching roughly from Edward I to Henry VIII)
and, on the other, the Eltonian sixteenth century, with its centre in the 1530s.[16]
Neither of these really carries conviction as an adequate account of the later
fifteenth or early sixteenth centuries; no less than McFarlane in the 1930s and
Elton in the 1950s, we need something new.

Clearly enough, any new framework must rest on perspectives and a
periodization which are inspired by the times themselves, but here we
encounter a problem: this period was apparently one of flux. We may have
demolished totalizing narratives such as the Renaissance or the myth of 1485,

---

[13] S.J. Gunn, *Early Tudor Government, 1485–1558* (Basingstoke, 1995), pp. 2–8, and see also his review
of Carpenter, *Locality and Polity*, which memorably describes 1471–1509 as the 'earthquake zone' on a
'fault-line of mutual incomprehension' (*HJ*, 35 (1992), 999–1003, p. 999). Carpenter explores the point
further in 'Henry VII and the English Polity', in B.J. Thompson, ed., *The Reign of Henry VII* (Stamford,
1995), pp. 11–30, esp. pp. 11–16. It is interesting to note that literary scholars have recently become
preoccupied with the strength and institutional entrenchment of a 'medieval'/'Renaissance' divide in
the study of their discipline: see L. Patterson, 'On the Margin: Post-Modernism, Ironic History, and
Medieval Studies', *Speculum*, 65 (1990), 87–108; D. Aers, A Whisper in the Ear of Early Modernists. . .',
Culture and History, 1350–1600 (Detroit, Mich., 1992), 177–202.

[14] Note, for example, the opening line of Benjamin Thompson's introduction to *The Reign of Henry VII*
(Stamford, 1995): 'The reign of Henry VII used to be thought of as a turning-point in English history.'

[15] W. Stubbs, *Constitutional History*, vol. 3 (Oxford, 1878), p. 5.

[16] For McFarlane's urbanely qualified identification of 1290–1536 as a 'period' with 'a sort of
unity', see *The Nobility of Later Medieval England* (Oxford, 1973), pp. 5–6 and (with slightly different
dates) 268–9.

but we continue to be aware of all kinds of changes, going on in various spheres of life, around the turn of the century. We are not quite sure what to make of these and yet if we are going to find new ways of characterizing the period we shall need some kind of assessment of their relative and collective significance. One way of tackling this, perhaps, is to draw together historians from either side of the now-invisible (but still influential) 'Renaissance' divide and compare notes. We need to talk about what happened in the decades either side of 1500, and we need to explore how those happenings are understood and described by 'medievalists' on the one hand, and by 'early modernists' on the other. Was this a time detached from the 'Middle Ages' which are so familiar to half of us, even if it does not really belong with the 'early modernity' understood by the other half?

These were the underlying aims of the colloquium held at Aberystwyth, in July 1996, under the same title as this book. The eight speakers were asked to consider whether it was possible, or appropriate, to talk of significant change in the patterns, norms or attitudes prevalent in their own particular spheres of interest during the period c.1450–1550. Were there distinctive shifts from 'old' (or 'medieval') to 'new' (or 'modern', or 'early modern')? Where in the period, if at all, were watersheds to be found? The speakers were not bound to consider these questions at a general level: some of them chose to do so, others have dealt with specific episodes, or processes, or individuals. Equally, they were not obliged to deal in terms like 'Renaissance' or 'Middle Ages', though many of them have critical asides to offer about such terminologies and most have made links between the forms of the period in question and those of the times before or after. Seven of the eight papers are printed below.[17] As an introduction, I thought it might be helpful to survey the historiography of systemic change around the end of the fifteenth century, to consider some of the reasons why this way of seeing the period has been so persistent and to discuss some of their implications. At the end of the volume – and partly in response to a question from the floor

---

[17] Sadly, other commitments prevented Richard Marks from preparing his stimulating paper for publication. Its title was 'Around Bosworth: the Gentry and Visual Culture, c. 1480–1550', and its main focus was on the changing style of tombs and private chapels.

which went something like 'So when did the Middle Ages end, then, Richard?' –
there is a short conclusion, drawing together points made by the contributors and
making one or two further suggestions.

The tradition of a turning point at the end of the fifteenth century is, to a large extent,
the product of two grand narratives. One, much the grander, is the idea of the
Renaissance (in which, historiographically speaking, the Reformation forms a kind of
sub-set).[18] The other, a more local tale, though not without its analogues in other
countries, is the myth of national redemption at the hands of the Tudors. Other
narratives have confirmed and extended these – most notably, perhaps, the Marxian
account of the transition from feudalism to capitalism – but, as products of the
fifteenth century itself, the Renaissance and the Tudor myth have a certain priority. It
is hard to say which of them has been more influential in shaping the historiography of
England, or indeed to identify which came first: in many ways, they owe their power,
and their focus on the end of the fifteenth century, to the way in which they interlock.
Their history is well known, but it may be useful to rehearse its outlines here.

The Renaissance is an idea which began more or less in its own times. Vasari, in
his *Lives of the Painters* (1550), is normally credited with being the first to talk of a
'*rinascita*' in the field of the arts, but the notion of a rebirth of culture and indeed of
learning is clearly apparent long before, both in Italy, where this rebirth is supposed
to have started in the fourteenth century, and in the north and west of Europe,
where it began to take off in the latter half of the fifteenth.[19] From Petrarch onwards,
the metaphor spread that an age of light was replacing an age of darkness – literally
the 'Dark Ages' from the later seventeenth century when this term and other
familiar designations such as 'medieval', 'Middle Ages', 'antiquity', and 'modern'
were developed by the dictionary-writer Cellarius and his contemporaries.[20] The

---

[18] For the Reformation viewed as the religious dimension of the Renaissance, see R. O'Day,
The Debate on the English Reformation (1986), p. 133; Huizinga, 'Problem of the Renaissance', p. 268;
and also Ferguson, *Renaissance in Historical Thought*, pp. 74–7, 100, 177, 263, 284–6.

[19] Edelman, 'Early Uses of Medium Aevum', p. 59; Ferguson, *Renaissance in Historical Thought*, chs 1,
3 (note that 'renascantur bonae litterae' appears more than once in Erasmus' writings: ibid., p. 43).

[20] Mommsen, 'Petrarch's Conception of the Dark Ages', p. 227: Ferguson, *Renaissance in Historical
Thought*, pp. 73, 75; Edelman, 'Early Uses of Medium Aevum', pp. 63, 65.

original and central features of this age of light were, of course, its intellectual and artistic enterprises, but it soon acquired other characteristics. It is often said that Burckhardt's *Civilisation of the Renaissance* (1860) was the first work to assert the impact of the new culture in all areas of experience, and particularly in politics, but the tendency of the Renaissance idea to spread to other spheres was becoming apparent long before this.[21] For example, the Christian humanists of the early sixteenth century – and even more the Protestant reformers – added a religious dimension to the theme of rebirth: the darkness of the previous age was not only a matter of bad art and bad Latin, it was also a spiritual darkness, and the interconnectedness of these themes for contemporaries was captured in the many sixteenth- and seventeenth-century denunciations of the 'age of monks'.[22] Later, seventeenth- and eighteenth-century writers added new politics, new technologies and new discoveries to the Renaissance cocktail.[23] While historians before Burckhardt mainly used the actual term 'Renaissance' in a narrow sense – to express a cultural phenomenon – it seems reasonable to suggest that the concept of a sharp and fruitful break with the past was already shaping the understanding of a much wider range of activity. The location of this break might vary somewhat in time or place or theme, and as 'modernity' got longer and longer, analysts began to wonder if the Renaissance was actually more an age than a boundary,[24] but the general message is fairly clear as far as the middle ages are concerned. They ended sharply as society made a great leap forward, and – for everywhere except Italy – the end came sometime around 1500.

It is in its broader sense that the Renaissance idea has most profoundly affected English historiography. In a body of writing dominated by the themes of politics and

---

[21] Ferguson, *Renaissance in Historical Thought*, pp. 73–5, 179; Hay, *Renaissance in Historical Background*, p. 12.

[22] Ferguson, *Renaissance in Historical Thought*, pp. 29, 42, 46, 48; Weisinger, 'Renaissance Theory of the Middle Ages', pp. 462–3. M. McKisack, *Medieval History in the Tudor Age* (Oxford, 1971), p. 22, provides a wonderful English example of invective against 'monkery'.

[23] Ferguson, *Renaissance in Historical Thought*, p. 75; and see also below, at n. 26. It seems likely that some at least (or at some level) were conscious of a political Renaissance in the later fifteenth and early sixteenth century itself: see below, and also D. Hay, 'Did Politics Change in the Late Middle Ages and Renaissance?', in H. Mayr-Harting and R.I. Moore, eds, *Studies in Medieval History Presented to R.H.C. Davis* (1985), 297–307.

[24] For example, Barraclough, 'Medium Aevum', p. 57; Hay, *Renaissance in Historical Background*, pp. 15–24.

government, the 'Renaissance' so-called has typically appeared as a cultural symptom of the general emancipation from medieval norms which characterizes the Tudor age; only in studies of English literature has the term had much prominence, and in that context its epicentre has been the end of the sixteenth century, not its beginning.[25] Even so, a belief in sweeping change around 1500 has generally been a prominent feature of English writing. The English Renaissance, it appears, is essentially a governmental one, and if it was most famously coined in the nineteenth century as the 'New Monarchy', it is clear that the notion as a whole has a much longer pedigree.[26] In the introduction to his *First Part of the History of England* (1613), for example, Samuel Daniel wrote of the age of the Tudors in the following terms:

> A time not of that virility as the former, but more subtle, and let out into wider notions, and bolder discoveries of what lay hidden before. A time wherein began a great improvement of the sovereignty, and more came to be effected by wit than the sword. . . . The opening of a new world, which strangely altered the manner of this [one], enhancing both the rate of all things, by the induction of infinite treasure, and opened a wider way to corruption, whereby princes got much without their swords. . . . Ledger ambassadors first employed abroad for intelligences. Common banks erected, to return and furnish moneys for these businesses. Besides strange alterations in the state ecclesiastical; religion brought forth to be an actor in the greatest designs of ambition and faction. . . .[27]

Here, the sense of widespread innovation is mapped onto the coming of a particular dynasty (in the preface to a book which planned to carve up history along regnal lines: two 'sections' covering the beginning to 1485, a third planned to cover the Tudors).[28]

---

[25] For all these points, see Ferguson, *Renaissance in Historical Thought*, pp. 268–9.

[26] For 'New Monarchy', see McFarlane, *Nobility*, pp. 282–7; A. Goodman, *The New Monarchy, England, 1471–1534* (Oxford, 1988), pp. 1–8.

[27] Quoted in J.P. Kenyon, *The History Men*, 2nd edn (1993), p. 12.

[28] S. Daniel, *The First Part of the History of England* (1613), ff. A2v–A3v. Note that the 'sections' were divided 'according to the periods of those ages that brought forth the most remarkable changes' (f. A3r). These 'periods' (boundary lines?) were thus to be 1154, 1485 and 1603. Daniel himself never got beyond 1377, though the second section was carried by another author up to 1485 (Kenyon, *History Men*, p. 11).

We may be far away from the Rankean vision of Burckhardt, in which politics was central to the development of 'civilization' (*Kultur*), but the connections between a new dynasty, a new politics and a new world are quite clearly signalled. These connections, perpetuated in the tendency of leading eighteenth- and nineteenth-century histories to break at 1485,[29] owed much to the propaganda disseminated by the Tudors: the second of the grand narratives which has shaped the fate of the fifteenth century.

Sir Geoffrey Elton once described 'the England which Henry VII came to rule' as marked by 'an unstable social structure thriving on disorder and lawlessness, and . . . the rapidly increasing weakness of the crown'; but an England presented in such terms is really the product of accumulated propaganda, in which Henry VII's court writers played a particularly formative role.[30] Polydore Vergil's *Anglica Historia*, which proved to be the model – and sometimes the text – for much of the rest of Tudor historiography, was written with the intention of justifying and celebrating Henry VII's acquisition of the throne.[31] Vergil's work reached back to the very beginnings of English history, but at 1399 its structure subtly changes: the reign-by-reign format which has dominated since 1066 is succeeded by a comparatively continuous account of the ensuing eighty-six years, which makes the fifteenth century into a self-contained period.[32] Building on the Yorkist dogma that the wrong of 1399 had produced decades of disorder before its requital in 1461, Vergil produced a more sophisticated and extensive tale in which dynastic struggle and the ebbs and flows

[29] Hume, for example, originally began his *History of England* in 1603, but subsequently pushed back to 1485, perceiving that the authoritarian rule of the Tudors and Stuarts had begun with Henry VII. A single volume later appeared on the period 55 BC to 1485. Catherine Macaulay, Hume's main rival, wrote on 1603–89, but Hallam's *Constitutional History*, which seems to have succeeded Hume's as the main account, ran from 1485 to 1820. See Kenyon, *History Men*, pp. 49–52, 57, 70. The primacy of 1485 must have been confirmed for the new age of university history by Stubbs' decision to end there: see above, n. 15.

[30] G.R. Elton, *England Under the Tudors* (1955), pp. 1, 2.

[31] *The Anglica Historia of Polydore Vergil*, ed. and tr. D. Hay, Camden Society, 3rd ser., 74 (1950), pp. xx, xxix, xxxiv, xxxix; McKisack, *Medieval History in Tudor Age*, pp. 98–9, 105.

[32] Hay, *Anglica Historia*, p. xxx. The book-per-reign format continues, but continuous themes shape the narrative: Richard II's lack of an heir and the resulting discord; divine retribution; the mounting factiousness of the people.

of the Hundred Years War had combined to produce a cult of disobedience among the people, which it was Henry VII's divinely appointed role to repress. For Vergil, Henry was the re-founder of the republic:

> he was someone who thought that he should devote all his time and energy to the right ruling of the republic [res publica], bearing in mind that he had been called to power by the English people for that purpose, and that it was therefore of the greatest importance to him to ensure that his realm should once again flourish in laws, institutions and manners alike, and that everyone's hopes of a better future might be reborn. And Henry laid the foundation of this kind of government from the beginning.[33]

The idea of a political re-foundation in 1485 was thus present from the very start, and Tudor historiographical technique ensured that it remained, along with the sense of 1399–1485 as a distinct and ghastly backdrop against which the glories of the Tudor age could be set.[34] Bacon's *History of the Reign of King Henry VII* (1622), which also relied on Vergil (via Hall) and presented the king as the genius restorer of peace and order, propelled the myth of 1485 into the modern age: only in 1892 was Bacon superseded as the standard account.[35] While Henry VIII's reign pursued a historiographical trajectory which was partly independent – either as an age of bloody tyranny, or as the starting-point for the Reformation – there was also a marked tendency to seek the roots of his 'Tudor despotism' in the restoration of authority under Henry VII.[36] So it was that the Tudor age enjoyed

---

[33] Ibid., p. 7n. I am grateful to Robin Osborne for his help with the translation.

[34] Kenyon, *History Men*, pp. 4, 7–8. Hall's *Union of the Two Noble and Illustrious Families of Lancaster and York* (1548) took the unification and dramatization of 1399–1485 a stage further, of course: McKisack, *Medieval History in Tudor Age*, pp. 105, 107, 110.

[35] Hay, *Anglica Historia*, p. xx; S.B. Chrimes, 'The Reign of Henry VII', in S.B. Chrimes, C.D. Ross and R.A. Griffiths, eds *Fifteenth-Century England* (Manchester, 1972), pp. 67–85, at pp. 67–8. Bacon had very little to say about the period before 1485, however, and a brief reference to Edward IV, on p. 7, comments on the effectiveness of his 'mild and plausible' rule in the 1470s: J.R. Lumby, ed., *Bacon's History of the Reign of King Henry the VII* (Cambridge, 1876).

[36] For example Chrimes, 'Reign of Henry VII', p. 68 (Busch); Kenyon, *History Men*, p. 50 (Hume); A.F. Pollard, *Henry VIII* (1902), p. 28ff.

more than dynastic coherence (despite the very considerable fluctuations in religious policy) and the groundwork for the idea of 'New Monarchy' was firmly laid. This, when it emerged, diminished the importance of 1485 a little, by including Edward IV and Richard III alongside Henry VII,[37] but – as we shall see – the idea of a turning point survives a considerable amount of stretching in its boundaries. The fourteen years of strong, or efficient, or illiberal government before Bosworth were easily accommodated, as (in the long run) have been the pyrotechnic achievements of the third decade after Henry VII's death.

A third formulation has had a more equivocal role in shaping approaches to the later fifteenth century. This is the standard model of the middle ages, with its subdivisions into 'early', 'central' (or 'high', a more revealing usage) and 'late'.[38] The 'Middle Ages' themselves, as we have seen, are a product of the Renaissance idea, but the tendency to subdivide them must be a later development, related perhaps to the rehabilitation of medieval culture which arrived with the romantic movement.[39] In any event, its tendency is clear: it is to make the 'High Middle Ages' – a period conventionally running from roughly 1000 to 1300 – into the epitome of 'medieval' civilization, so that the institutions of this period are taken both as the hallmarks of what it is to be 'medieval' and also (as if there were not already enough circularity in this approach) as being in their fullest 'health', or 'bloom', in this period.[40]

---

[37] Goodman, *New Monarchy*, p. 1.

[38] For examples, see G. Leff, *History and Social Theory* (Univ. of Alabama, 1969), pp. 134–5, 148–9; R. Southern, *Western Society and the Church in the Middle Ages* (1970), ch. 2.

[39] Ferguson, *Renaissance in Historical Thought*, ch. 5.

[40] Patterson, 'On the Margin', pp. 92–3. Note how this colours the discussion of contests and conflicts, which appear as abundantly in the 'high' middle ages as in the later period. In Leff's periodization, for example, 950–1300 is 'the quintessential or archetypal Middle Ages when all that was most distinctive of medieval civilisation reached fruition before disequilibrium set in. Struggle and conflict there were in plenty, but they were the struggle and conflict of growth rather than disintegration and disarray'. These more negative forms of conflict appear between 1300 and 1550, which is 'the period of the breakdown of the main forms of medieval civilisation' (p. 148). We might wish to consider whether later conflicts represented a new kind of growth (unrelated to the papacy, which seems to be the centrepiece of the traditional periodization), or whether earlier ones represented the decay of earlier structures. It is interesting that while the fifteenth-/sixteenth-century 'Renaissance' has generally been treated with scepticism by modern historians, ideas of twelfth-/thirteenth-century 'fullness' or 'growth', or of an eleventh-/twelfth-century 'great leap forward' have survived comparatively intact.

The consequence for the 'Late Middle Ages' is well known: it is to be an age of 'decline', of 'waning' (in Huizinga's famous phrase), of 'unrest' (in R.W. Southern's), in which 'medieval' institutions lost force and relevance.[41] Despite challenges at the peripheries, the model retains some influence, both in historical literature and in the formation of medieval historians. Its results for the period under consideration here are ambivalent, however. On the one hand, it may work against the traditional boundaries between 'medieval' and 'early modern'. If the later middle ages are considered as a period of slow degeneration of medieval ideals and institutions, then the way is open to consider the forms of (say) the sixteenth century as part and parcel of this development – and this has been a common path, especially because of the vogue for seeking out the continuities between 'medieval' and 'Renaissance' culture. Meanwhile, in a more positive version of the same approach, degeneration might be rewritten as 'transformation', and then the dominant watershed becomes 1300, and the fourteenth and fifteenth centuries become part of a 'Renaissance (or early modern) period'.[42] On the other hand, the sense that the 'Middle Ages' are centred in the twelfth and thirteenth centuries affects the training and interests of 'medieval' historians and probably contributes to a view that any time in which the forms of the classic middle ages become hard to discern is not 'medieval' and needs to be read in a different way.[43]

---

[41] Southern, *Western Society and Church*, p. 44.

[42] One obvious example of this outcome is the Oxford Modern History School, which divides its three papers of British history at 1330 and 1685, ensuring that the middle paper is dominated by historians with research interests in the sixteenth and seventeenth centuries, while the early paper is taught by 'proper' medievalists (though the enormous distinction of Oxford Anglo-Saxon historians means that the centre of gravity in this area is earlier than it might otherwise be). See also Barraclough, 'Medium Aevum: Some Reflections', where the new periodization he proposes reproduces the normal assumptions and chronology of the early/high middle ages division, before moving on to a third period, 'the "Middle Ages" of Europe' (1300–1789) and a fourth ('modern', 1789 onwards): pp. 61–3.

[43] Patterson, 'On the Margin', pp. 101–8, offers some highly diverting comment on the formation of 'medievalists' and the pitfalls of 'medievalism'. Although his remarks are directed mainly at the (essentially literary and American) discipline of 'medieval studies', they raise issues which British medieval historians will find familiar.

The idea that the middle ages came to an end in or around 1485 thus rested on substantial historiographical foundations. This must explain something of the confidence and fullness with which it was stated in the great histories of the first age of professional history; and that statement, in turn, must explain something of its enduring influence. Since the early years of the twentieth century, however, it has come under sustained attack from practically all directions.[44] As we have seen, medieval precedents have been found for classically 'Renaissance' phenomena, whether these are intellectual and cultural (classicism, humanism, individualism, natural science) or social and political (mercantile capitalism, absolutism, *Realpolitik*, bureaucracy). At the same time, the medievalism of Renaissance poetry, or philosophy, or art, or religion has been widely noted. In the history of this period, as of others once seen as transitional, continuity has been a more popular theme than change. The importance of the Italian Renaissance for the rest of Europe has been questioned, and the so-called 'diffusionist thesis' challenged (though if this last cuts against an international and integrated Renaissance, it positively encourages the identification of 'national' Renaissances).[45] Other 'renaissances' have been found: literary and cultural awakenings in the twelfth century, or the ninth; a 'scientific revolution' in the seventeenth. It begins to appear that renaissance is a recurrent condition, either of human society, or – more probably – of historians' efforts to capture it.[46] And the sense that the modern age began with Petrarch and Dante, or Machiavelli and Luther, has lost most of its credibility – though the arrival of postmodernity may have given it a shot in the arm. In all, the Renaissance has lost its distinctiveness as a watershed, and if the identification of a 'Renaissance period' has helped to keep the label on the middle of the second millennium, in other ways it is a recognition that the idea of a single great turning point no longer carries conviction.[47]

---

[44] See Ferguson, *Renaissance in Historical Thought*, chs 10 and 11, for most of the points made in this paragraph.

[45] R. Porter and M. Teich, eds, *The Renaissance in National Context* (Cambridge, 1992), introduction.

[46] A.C. Spearing, *Medieval to Renaissance in English Poetry* (Cambridge, 1985), p. 1.

[47] Hay, *Renaissance in Historical Background*, makes a particularly explicit case for a Renaissance period: pp. x, 1, 25 (and see pp. 185–6 for its subdivision into 'phases'). Huizinga, 'Problem of the Renaissance', seems to have been groping after the notion of a period instead of a watershed in 1920: pp. 281–7.

These developments, together with others more closely related to its own particular conditions, have had a complex effect on the historiography of England in this period. On the whole, of course, continuity has had the upper hand, and the 'Renaissance' centred on 1485 has been in retreat. As elsewhere, this is partly the result of greater knowledge of the later middle ages. Increased attention has been paid to areas which had been comparatively peripheral in the construction of the '1485' narrative: the structure of political society, for example, which was much the same in the fifteenth and sixteenth centuries, or at least changed very slowly;[48] the economy, which had a different chronology, shaped by the plagues and peasant movements of the later fourteenth century and the price-rise and demographic recovery of the early sixteenth century;[49] the state of the pre-Reformation Church, which was found to be less moribund and more royally directed than had been realized.[50] But the trend in favour of continuity has also profited from revisionism in the old heartland of political history. Here, the most influential single step was surely Elton's conception of a 'Tudor Revolution in Government', which preserved the notion that dramatic change took place within the Tudor period, but transferred it to the 1530s and re-coined it as the birth of the modern state.[51] The resulting emphasis on continuity between the world of fifteenth-century government and that of Henry VII and Wolsey has found wide acceptance. Indeed, historians have differed from Elton mainly in

[48] This was a point particularly emphasized by McFarlane – see e.g. *Nobility*, ch. 8 and pp. 283–5 – though note also Davies, *Peace, Print and Protestantism*, pp. 317–20.

[49] For some remarks on the historiography of the later medieval English economy, see J. Hatcher, 'England in the Aftermath of the Black Death', *Past and Present*, 144 (Aug. 1994), pp. 3–35, at pp. 3–5. The alternative chronology is perceptible in e.g. Du Boulay, *Age of Ambition*, pp. 13–16, and M.H. Keen, *English Society in the Later Middle Ages* (1990), p. 5ff. On the other hand, R.H. Britnell's essay, below, shows how older works of economic history were influenced by the sense of a new beginning in the period around 1500.

[50] See, for example, C. Haigh, 'The Recent Historiography of the English Reformation', *The English Reformation Revised* (Cambridge, 1987), pp. 19–33, pp. 22–4 for modern historians' views on the health of the pre-Reformation Church; and D. Hay, 'The Church of England in the Later Middle Ages', *Renaissance Essays* (1988), pp. 233–48, for recognition of the extent of royal control before the Reformation.

[51] Usefully discussed in a few pages by Goodman, *New Monarchy*, pp. 6–8.

refusing to see the 1530s as revolutionary and instead extending the case for continuity into the age of Cromwell and beyond. Administrative development under the Tudors has been presented as a slow and incremental process, in which neither the 1530s nor the reign of Henry VII was especially distinctive.[52] At the same time, the recovery of royal power in the later fifteenth century has often been taken as nothing more fundamental than the arrival of stronger kings and/or better times following one of the medieval monarchy's periodic crises.[53] Since the Wars of the Roses now extend well into the reign of Henry VII (and, in more than one account, their consequences shape the character of a distinct period of government running from 1471 to 1529), the hegemony of 1485 is well and truly broken.[54] Even so, as these somewhat contradictory trends suggest, the picture has become a complex one; and in areas of history where the case for a time of change was most strongly made – politics and government, art and literature, ideas and manners – something of the old understanding remains in place.

[52] This seems to be the main implication of both C. Coleman and D. Starkey, eds, *Revolution Reassessed* (Oxford, 1986), and the so-called 'Evolution–Revolution' debate in *Past and Present*, 25, 29 and 31 (1963–5). In his conclusion to the former, Starkey maintains the idea of turning points, but argues that they are spread throughout the fifteenth and sixteenth centuries, that there were often several for each part of the government, and that they differed from institution to institution (p. 199). Note that Elton, without abandoning his view in essentials, did accept in 1964 that there was probably more continuity in administrative development than he had originally allowed: 'The Tudor Revolution: a Reply', *Past and Present*, 29 (Dec. 1964), 26–49, at pp. 26, 42. For the latest treatment of the 1530s, which goes well beyond the question of administrative development, see C.S.L. Davies, 'The Cromwellian Decade: Authority and Consent', *TRHS*, 6th ser., 7 (1997), 177–95.

[53] See especially McFarlane, *Nobility*, pp. 283–7, but also C.D. Ross, *Edward IV* (1974), pp. 420–6, and S.B. Chrimes, *Henry VII* (1972), pp. 319–22, both of which stress the personal aims and abilities of the kings themselves in shaping the fortunes of their governments.

[54] For an emphasis on the continuation of serious political difficulties beyond Stoke, see e.g. Carpenter, 'Henry VII and the Polity', pp. 16–18; I. Arthurson, *The Perkin Warbeck Conspiracy, 1491–99* (Stroud, 1994), pp. 3, 213; D. Luckett, 'Crown Patronage and Political Morality in Early Tudor England: the Case of Giles, Lord Daubeney', *EHR*, 110 (1995), 578–95. For a distinctive kind of government, 1461–1529, see G.L. Harriss, 'Medieval Government and Statecraft', *Past and Present*, 25 (1963), 8–39, pp. 25–34, and also, in a slightly different conception, Goodman, *New Monarchy*, pp. 78–81.

We are back at the point at which we began this historiographical discussion. What has happened is that empirical research has destroyed the old models at a formal level and as total explanations, but no alternative account of equivalent explanatory value has emerged. The triumph of 'continuity' marks the defeat of the old narratives, but it does not adequately express what we have found. No one would deny that changes of some kind were taking place in this period (after all, both continuities and changes must be present in a given context for the observer to be able to detect either), and support for continuity actually turns out to be support for a continuum of slow change – in ideas and language, in political, social and institutional forms, in economic activity – albeit a continuum in which the reigns of the Yorkist and early Tudor kings do not especially stand out. At the same time, this 'slow' change is often contrasted with the exceedingly 'fast' change presupposed by the Eltonian revolution and not (for example) the sort of slowness with which parliament developed into a recognizable form between the 1230s and the 1370s. In other words, the quarrel with Elton among sixteenth-century historians distorts the representation of what may appear to medievalists a period of relatively rapid alteration.[55] The essays in *Revolution Reassessed*, for example, leave us with the sense of a fairly dramatic transformation of English government between the 1490s and the 1560s, even if this is explicitly not the work of the 1530s alone. Meanwhile, since even slow change is relatively absent from discussions of the later medieval polity – say 1360 to 1460 – the succeeding period continues to stand out.[56] Such convulsions as did occur in the century before 1460 – and these could be dramatic, of course – have mainly been presented as the short-lived products of circumstance, but deciding where to draw the line between what is circumstantial and what is fundamental is not easy.

---

[55] As Elton himself observed, in relation (appropriately enough) to the Renaissance, 'the question is whether historians have not fallen into the error of opposing outright denial to an untenable outright assertion': *England Under the Tudors*, p. 430.

[56] G.L. Harriss, 'Political Society and the Growth of Government in Late Medieval England', *Past and Present*, 138 (Feb. 1993), 28–57, presents the period from 1300 to 1450 as one of steady growth, but most of the innovations he refers to fall before the end of Edward III's reign and the overall impression created is one of consolidation.

One reason why the later middle ages appear comparatively static is that late medievalists generally prefer to follow McFarlane in refusing to see circumstantial alterations in political arrangements as the symptoms of systemic change.[57] The alterations of the later fifteenth century have sometimes been approached in a similar way, but it is important to remember that 'circumstances' as large and prolonged as the Wars of the Roses could have had far-reaching effects, whether or not they had far-reaching causes: the 'recovery' of the later fifteenth century could not simply be a return to pre-crisis norms, as (on the whole) the 'recovery' of the 1410s and 1420s has been taken to be.[58] Perhaps we need to pay more attention to the possibility of significant change within the classic period of the later middle ages, but this would not altogether remove the problem of how to evaluate the responses made by both governments and society to the troubles of the mid-fifteenth century. Elton argued that Henry VII (and Henry VIII, initially) restored authority without departing from the 'household system' of the middle ages and with a conventional enough programme of restoring royal rights.[59] Later medieval historians have found both of these supposedly traditional modes of rule to be innovative, or at least untypical.[60] The question is what weight to give to novelties of this kind.

Other factors make for a nagging sense of change too. For one thing, a historiographical legacy of such awesome dimensions is hard to dispel, even with decades of academic scholarship devoted to this end. Big histories – of the state or of the nation, for example – tend to begin with the sixteenth century, or to deal scantily with the period beforehand, presenting it at best as a kind of pre-

---

[57] This attitude is clear in McFarlane's handling of both the 'New Monarchy' thesis and the 'Lancastrian Constitutional Experiment': *Nobility*, pp. 282–7; *Lancastrian Kings and Lollard Knights* (Oxford, 1972), pp. 78–9ff.

[58] For the 1410s and '20s viewed in this way, see e.g. G.L. Harriss, *Henry V. The Practice of Kingship* (Oxford, 1985), p. 209. Carpenter, *Locality and Polity*, chs 16 and 17, is distinctive among 'McFarlanite' works in arguing that the Wars of the Roses provoked a major change in the structures of rule.

[59] *The Tudor Revolution in Government* (Cambridge, 1962), chs 1.2 and 1.3; 'Henry VII: Rapacity and Remorse', *HJ*, 1 (1958), 21–39.

[60] Harriss, 'Medieval Government', pp. 24–34; Carpenter, 'Henry VII and the Polity', p. 16 *et seq.*; J.L. Watts, '"A Newe Ffundacion of is Crowne": Monarchy in the Age of Henry VII', in Thompson, ed., *Reign of Henry VII*, pp. 31–53, at pp. 35–6.

history.[61] Popular histories tend to preserve the old divisions of time, reproducing a much sharper sense of the gap between 'medieval' Yorkists and 'early modern' Tudors than can be found in academic writing. The challenge to the traditional way of seeing things only really flourishes in the small and specialized enclave of the academic study of the fifteenth century and even here, and to some extent *because* of specialization, it flourishes only as a challenge: there is no consensus in favour of an alternative grand vision, as perhaps there cannot be. Meanwhile, as we have seen, the historical sausage factory continues to produce 'medievalists' and 'early modernists', whose different learning and different agendas perpetuate the sense of change (never more so, perhaps, than when they are insisting on continuities across the great divide). If periods are a necessary evil, the dream of a fifteenth-century period which includes Henry VII as well as Henry IV, or of a 1450–1550 period which is constructed from its own norms and not those of the Tudor end remains largely unrealized – despite the pioneering efforts of individual historians. Many possible discursive and institutional reasons for this have now been surveyed: it is an open question whether they are more important than other familiar factors, such as the major changes in the evidence available to historians as we move from the fifteenth century to the sixteenth, or the impact on England of the emergence of a new European states-system.[62] And perhaps things really were significantly different; perhaps the end of the fifteenth century was indeed a time in which a concatenation of changes brought the end of what it makes sense to call a system, or a set of systems, and their replacement by another. We do not really know; or rather, we cannot really say.

[61] For example, D. Held *et al.*, eds, *States and Societies* (Oxford, 1983), an Open University reader claiming to offer 'a comprehensive selection of the major writings in the field', has no coverage of the period before 1500 whatsoever. Although interest in medieval nationalism is growing, the major treatments of national identity ignore the middle ages: e.g. E.J. Hobsbawm, *Nations and Nationalism Since 1780*, Canto edn (Cambridge, 1991) ('the "nation" . . . belongs exclusively to a particular, and historically recent, period': p. 9); B. Anderson, *Imagined Communities*, revised edn (1991), in which the middle ages are a period when 'the dynastic realm appeared for most men as the only imaginable "political" system' (p. 19).

[62] For the importance of changes in the evidence, see e.g. Carpenter, 'Henry VII', pp. 12–14 (though, as she points out, Henry VII's reign is anomalous in this regard, the main 'Tudor' record series not really beginning until after it). For the impact of the international situation, see Cliff Davies' article, below.

The existence of changes in the decades around 1500 is not in dispute, as we have seen: what matters – from the point of view of discussing the question of a watershed – is their weight, the extent to which they are concentrated and related, and the proportion of them which can be considered lasting. This is not a question which any of the contributors to this volume has chosen to tackle directly, but, in various ways, their essays bear upon it. Here is not the place to consider their conclusions, but it may be helpful to introduce some of the themes they are exploring, and the differing approaches they have taken to the business of measuring and assessing the evidence for change.

In a throwaway comment early in the *Waning of the Middle Ages*, Huizinga appears to link the Renaissance above all with the emergence of 'new modes of expression'.[63] Against a background of renewed interest in the role played by language and other modes of expression in shaping political and social interaction, this is an idea of some force. The changing languages of politics and political theory have attracted quite a lot of attention from historians of our period, and, given the self-consciousness of Renaissance writers and the prominence of publicist literature in what it is tempting to call the 'self-fashioning' of the period, this must be an important area to examine if we want to address larger questions of socio-political change. On the one hand, we shall want to know whether political language was indeed changing, and if so in what ways and to what extent? On the other hand, we shall want to consider the significance of these changes: do they contribute to real changes in the political environment, or are they merely epiphenomenal? Jean-Philippe Genet sets out a method for attacking the first question, making a case for the use of quantificatory methods in an area where qualitative analysis can easily degenerate into anecdotalism. Most of the other contributors have something to say about the second, but it is perhaps Colin Richmond who tackles the question most directly, with a paper which responds critically to the recent preoccupation of some fifteenth-century historians with political ideas and rhetoric.

The other essays subject familiar aspects of the traditional narrative of transformation to close scrutiny. Richard Britnell deals with the late fifteenth-

---

[63] Huizinga, *Waning*, p. 54.

century and early sixteenth-century economic scene, which, notwithstanding the
relative detachment of social and economic history, has been presented in terms
strikingly similar to those of the political story: mid-century slump; late-century
recovery. Steven Gunn and Simon Adams revisit the well-known story of how the
Tudors displaced the ancient nobility with the service of lesser men. Gunn looks
in detail at the career and political influence of one of Henry VII's most
important agents, Sir Thomas Lovell. Adams reaches across the historiographical
boundary to reconsider the affinity of the Elizabethan Earl of Leicester in the
light of the work of later medievalists on magnates and their connections. George
Bernard reconsiders the relationship between popular piety and organized
religion, which has been such an important theme in explanations of the
Reformation. By focusing on pilgrimage in the early sixteenth century, he is able
to explore both the intensity of orthodox religious feeling and the consequences
for churchmen of their efforts to provide for it. Finally, Cliff Davies looks at the
sphere of war and international relations, where recognition of the continuity of
chivalric ambition has tended to supplant the older tale of a shift towards
Realpolitik. With this and other narratives in mind, he compares the French wars
of Henry V and Henry VIII and asks how we should regard the differences
between them.[64]

---

[64] I should like to thank Christine Carpenter, Cliff Davies, Steve Gunn and Benjamin Thompson
for reading and commenting on a draft of this introduction.

1

New Politics or New Language? The Words of Politics in Yorkist and Early Tudor England

Jean-Philippe Genet

In some ways, language is the most important of social institutions. Words may be uttered in widely different circumstances, with different intentions, and they may be received and understood in an infinite variety of ways – they may even be misunderstood, and misunderstood intentionally. They nevertheless provide the medium through which people communicate and come to terms between themselves, whether for private or public purposes. They are not to be severed from actions, since most actions are decided, described, or enforced through words; other means of communication – gesture, music, space control, display of forms and colours and so on – are only supplementary to them.[1] Some of the words spoken or written in the past have come down to us. We historians call them 'sources', and it is upon these so-called sources that we rely to construct a coherent vision and understanding of the past periods which we are studying: say, for instance, Yorkist and early Tudor times.

However, when we do this, we tend to forget that we are dealing primarily with words belonging to an irretrievably lost language. We usually transform the words into ideas, or concepts. These seem to acquire a life of their own, as in the history of ideas; and the history of political thought too often tends to be a history of ideas, with the consequent difficulty that it is useless to the political historian, who is therefore in danger of being limited to the detail, the day-to-day

---

[1] More on this in J.Ph. Genet, 'Histoire et système de communication au Moyen Age', in J.Ph. Genet, ed., *L'histoire et ses nouveaux publics* (Paris, 1997), pp. 9–26.

working of the political machinery, while losing the sense of the structure, the way in which the whole political system was perceived, accepted, criticized, or even (at some level) refused by political society at large.

The trouble is that the study of 'language' confronts us with methodological difficulties of all kinds. The traditional history of ideas remains manageable to the historian of political societies: if he may disagree with some lofty generalizations and the general impression that ideas seem to be transmitted from an author to another like influenza, he can nonetheless adapt and pick up whatever seems to be of some use to him. Thanks to Quentin Skinner's stimulating approach and methodological improvements,[2] the benefits which could be expected have accrued, while the method remains clear. On the other hand, to try to reach the language through the words themselves implies three different and enormously time-consuming tasks, and I must frankly admit from the start that I am no linguist and that therefore I have a very restricted view of what such an enterprise demands.

1. We reach language through 'discourse'; or, rather, language is made up of discourses. Discourse is language as it is spoken or written by a given person (that is, a person who has received a specific education, occupies a precise place in society, has a profession, or whatever), in a given occasion (addressing a specific audience, in certain circumstances, at a precise moment, and so on). We need to establish what these discourses are.

2. The discourse is made of words, chosen among all other possible words which could have conveyed a similar meaning. We must have a precise knowledge of these words: that is, both of those which were used and of those which could have been chosen and were left aside. This implies that we must start from a purely lexicological study, constructing specific dictionaries for each type of discourse, or for each type of subject, after assembling all the existing texts in a corpus.

---

[2] Q. Skinner, *The Foundations of Modern Political Thought* (Cambridge, 1978).

3. To reach the actual meaning of a word, we must move from the paradigmatic approach of lexicology to the syntactic approach of semantics: that is, the study of the words through the contexts in which they are used.

To sum up the tasks involved in the study of language, then, we must differentiate the different kinds of discourse; then assemble the texts relevant to each kind of discourse in a corpus, and carry out a lexicological study of each corpus; and finally, we must make a semantic study of each word in accordance with the corpus in which it is to be found. Obviously, these tasks are impossible to achieve – indeed, impossible to conceive – without the help of a computer, but that is not the subject with which I intend to deal here, and I shall try in the following pages to keep the purely methodological and technical aspects of this kind of research to a minimum. I shall therefore concentrate upon the first two tasks: the differentiation of discourses on the one hand and the lexicological study on the other, leaving the semantic study for another occasion.

In attempting to survey what I consider to be the field of political language, I shall delineate six broad areas, themselves divided into several units. It must be clear that these areas and units are not separated by hermetically closed borders: they communicate. It must also be made clear that these divisions have been adapted to the situation prevailing between about 1450 and 1520. The six areas are: political speeches; political poetry; books and tracts intended for the moral edification of kings and nobility alike; political theology and religious writings with political connotations; law; and academic commentaries on political texts (Aristotle, St Augustine, Giles of Rome). In the present study the last three areas will be left aside. Law is a highly technical field and though the concepts of language and discourse may prove as useful in exploring it as they are elsewhere (not to mention the fact that the influence of legal language pervades other fields), the supposed technical precision of the language probably makes it unnecessary to invest the time and energy required by the method described above. The same is to a certain extent true of theology and academic commentaries, as long as they are written in Latin: we are dealing in these three cases with highly professional discourses where paradigmatic choice and semantic variation are easier to discover by a normal reading of the texts. Though I shall not apply the same method to these three fields (or rather subfields),[3] I shall give a very brief survey of their production.

As regards law, it may be useful to mention that this period is remarkable for the regular appearance, besides the Year Books, of the first tracts on the *Prerogativa Regis*: Thomas Frowyke's reading of 1496 and Brown's reading (before 1500), both for the Inner Temple, and Robert Constable's in 1495 for Lincoln's Inn.[4] Another production of the time, and one of the very few English canon law tracts to have had the distinction of being printed (in 1512), is the *De Justitia et sanctitate belli per Julium pontificem secundum in scismatibus*, written by a canon of Westminster, James Whystons, who received his training in canon law at Bologna.[5] These are apparently new beginnings, but the obscurity which still surrounds the Inns of Court in the fifteenth century, despite their importance, may remind us of the need to be cautious about overestimating the differences between the last decade of the fifteenth century and Fortescue's times.

Political theology, once the most important area of English political thought, appears to have been strikingly deserted by the second half of the fifteenth century.[6] After all, the Yorkists were prominent in suppressing Pecock's writings,

---

[3] See P. Bourdieu, *Les Règles de l'Art. Genèse et Structure du Champ Littéraire* (Paris, 1992), pp. 165–200 and for a useful presentation 'Pour une science des oeuvres', in P. Bourdieu, *Raisons Pratiques. Sur la théorie de l'action*, new edn (Paris, 1996), pp. 59–97.

[4] Constable's lecture is printed in S.L. Thorne, *Prerogativa Regis: tertia lectura Roberti Constabli* (New Haven, 1949). There are three extant manuscripts of Frowyke's *Reading on Prerogativa Regis for the Inner Temple* (1496): see B. Putnam, *Early treatises on the practices of the Justices of the Peace in the fifteenth and sixteenth centuries* (Oxford, 1924), pp. 129–32 and S.L. Thorne, *Prerogativa*, p. xlix–l. On the household in which he was brought up, see A.F. Sutton and L. Visser-Fuchs, 'The making of a minor London Chronicle in the Household of Sir Thomas Frowyk (died 1485)', *The Ricardian*, 10, 126 (Sept. 1994), 86–103. Brown was a reader at the Inner Temple *c.* 1500; his *Reading on Prerogativa Regis* is in MS. Cambridge UL Hh 3 6, ff. 55–70; see Putnam, *Early treatises*, pp. 148–9.

[5] James Whystons (d. 1512), a Bologna D.Cn.L. and a canon of St Stephen's, Westminster: Andrea Ammonio appended a poem to the *De iusticia et sanctitate belli*, printed by Pynson in 1512 (STC 25585); see A.B. Emden, *A Biographical Register of the University of Cambridge to 1500* (Cambridge, 1963), p. 636 (*BRUC* hereafter).

[6] J.Ph. Genet, 'Ecclesiastics and Political Theory in Late Medieval England: the End of a Monopoly', in B. Dobson, *The Church, Politics and Patronage in the Fifteenth Century* (Gloucester, 1984), pp. 23–44.

and it was at Thomas Bourgchier's instance that John Bury directed his *Gladium Salomonis* against the Bishop of Chichester.[7] Another Lancastrian bishop, the former Carmelite Stanbury (or Stanbridge), who became Bishop of Hereford,[8] had even less success, since his works have altogether disappeared and are known to us only through a disapproving John Bale, who found them *fere papistica*. The orthodox Walter Hunt was simply rearranging Thomas Netter's demonstration against Lollardy in his *De precellentia Petri* and his *De paupertate Christi*.[9] This last title proves that at least some of the ashes of the old quarrel were still warm, and they were rekindled in 1464 by a sermon preached at St Paul's by another Carmelite, Henry Parker,[10] who was attacked by the chancellor of Salisbury, William Ive, and defended by a fellow friar, John

---

[7] Reginald Pecock (d. ?1460), an Oxford D.Th. and Bishop of Chichester from 1450 to 1459, preached a resounding sermon at St Paul's Cross in defence of the episcopacy in 1447, which was answered by John Milverton, O. Carm., William Goddard, OFM and John Bury, OESA. The controversy prompted Archbishop Stafford to ask Pecock to develop his views, which led to the writing of *The repressor of overmuch blaming the clergy*, written in 1449 but published in 1455 only. The conclusions of the sermon are summed up in *The folewer to the Donet*, ed. E.V. Hitchcock, EETS, OS 164 (1924), p. 108. John of Bury (d. 1476), an Oxford D.Th. who became Prior of the Austin Friars for England, wrote his *Gladium Salomonis* at the Yorkist Bourchier's request: extracts are printed in Pecock, *The repressor of overmuch blaming the clergy*, ed. C. Babington, Rolls Series (1860), II, pp. 575–613. See A.B. Emden, *A Biographical Register of the University of Oxford to AD 1500*, 3 vols (Oxford, 1959), I, p. 329 (*BRUO* hereafter).

[8] John Stanbury or Stanbridge (d. 1474), O. Carm., an Oxford D.Th., was Henry VI's confessor and chaplain. None of his works (*De dote Ecclesiae, De potestate summi pontificis quoad leges humanas, De differentia potestatum ecclesiasticarum*) survives, but John Bale has *incipits* for all of them. See *BRUO*, III, pp. 1755–6.

[9] On Walter Hunt, O. Carm. (d. 1478), an Oxford DD who was Cardinal Kempe's chaplain, see *BRUO*, II, pp. 986–7; M. Harvey, 'Harley Manuscript 3049 and two Quaestiones of Walter Hunt, O. Carm.', *Transactions of the Architectural and Archaeological Society of Durham and Northumberland*, new ser., 6 (1982), 45–7; Hudson, A. *The Premature Reformation* (Oxford, 1988), 454–5. MS. London B.L. Harley 3049, given by Prior William Ebchester to Durham Cathedral Library in 1458, contains his *De praecellentia Petri* (the manuscript contains two important related works, *De dominio Apostolorum* by the Paris master Francis de Mayronnes and Pierre d'Ailly's *De Potestate Papae*) and his *De predestinatis*.

[10] Henry Parker (d. 1470), O. Carm., a Cambridge B.Th., preached at Paul's Cross on evangelical poverty (hence the *De Christi Paupertate* attributed to him by Bale?): see *BRUC*, p. 442.

Milverton.[11] But that was all. There were, however, some warnings of the struggles to come. In 1515 Richard Kidderminster roused the hostility of Parliament by preaching at St Paul's Cross against the act of 1512, which had strictly reduced benefit of clergy. Henry Standish, a Franciscan who was soon to become a Bishop of St Asaph, replied in defence of the laity and this exchange started a controversy which ended with the submission of the Convocation and of the Clergy.[12] But, on the whole, this period is one of the very few in English medieval and modern history when religious elements play virtually no part in the political debates of the time.

As regards the academic commentaries, which are also linked with the *Miroir* tradition through the academic (or, indeed, monastic) *tabulae* which often accompanied them, very few were produced at this time.[13] Even if the commentary on Aristotle's *Politics* was always more a Paris speciality than an Oxbridge one,[14]

---

[11] On Ive (d. 1486), an Oxford DD who became Headmaster of Winchester College and Chancellor of Sarum, see *BRUO*, II, pp. 1008–9. His *Lectiones de Mendicitate Christi* are in Oxford, Bodleian Library, MS. Lat. Theol. e 25, and John Bale also attributes to him a *De dominio Christi*. John Milverton (d. 1487), prior of the Carmelite convent in London in 1464–5, an Oxford D.Th.; all information about his works and his two controversial sermons – sermon *De Paupertate Christi*, preached 23 December 1464, and the sermon *Contra quemdam episcopum* (Reginald Pecock?) – derive from John Bale: cf. *BRUO*, II, pp. 1284–5 and note 7 above. On the quarrel, see F.R.H. Du Boulay, 'The Quarrel between the Carmelite Friars and the Secular Clergy of London', *Journal of Ecclesiastic History*, 6 (1955), 156–74.

[12] Richard Kidderminster, OSB (d. 1531), an Oxford D.Th., was abbott of Winchcombe from 1488 to 1525. I do not know if the text of his 1515 sermon at St Paul's Cross survives. Henry Standish (d. 1535), OFM, an Oxford D.Th., was Bishop of St Asaph from 1518. See *BRUO*, IV, pp. 533–44.

[13] On the *De Regimine Principum* (and on the authors mentioned in relation with it), see Ch. Briggs, 'Late Medieval Texts and Tabulae: The Case of Giles of Rome's De Regimine Principum', *Manuscripta* (Nov. 1993.), 253–75. Several English clerics of the later Middle Ages have been credited by John Leland and John Bale with the tabulation of endless lists of classical or academic works (a good example is the Carmelite Alan of Lynn, d. 1423) and even John Whethamstede has spent much time making such *tabulae* (some of which look more like excerpt collections): see for instance those in London B.L. Arundel MS. 11. This is a genre in itself and it needs a proper study as such. But the interest in it seems to decline at the end of the century.

[14] Ch. Flüeler, 'Die Rezeption der <<Politica>> des Aristoteles an der Pariser Artistenfakultät im 13. und 14. Jahrhundert', in J. Miethke, *Das Publikum politischer Theorie im 14. Jahrhundert* (Münich, 1992), pp. 127–51 and *Rezeption und Interpretation der aristotelischen Politica im späten Mittelalter*, 2 vols (Amsterdam and Philadelphia, 1992).

from this period we only have a commentary on Aristotle's *Ethics* attributed to Robert Hacumblene, provost of King's College, while the already-mentioned John Milverton wrote a commentary on the *De Civitate Dei*; this is indeed very little compared to what Oxford and Cambridge had previously produced.[15]

This does not mean that academics and clerics played no part in politics. But they were only individuals, if prominent ones, among those who delivered public speeches, orations, and sermons – the first of the three areas to be studied here. This area may in its turn be roughly divided into two groups: on one side, there are the formal orations, usually written and delivered in Latin, which are a new product of the age. Here, the early humanists were quick to establish themselves as the best practitioners: John Gunthorpe's speeches, delivered when he was ambassador in Spain and at the marriage of Charles the Bold with Margaret of York,[16] and John Russell's speech to Charles delivered in 1470 are the first examples of the new standards applied to the traditional legatine speech; Russell's speech was eventually printed (probably at Bruges) in 1477.[17] Others followed: William Selling's ambassador's speech to Innocent VIII in 1487, John Blythe's chancellor's speech at the visit of Henry VII to Cambridge, John Fisher's speech to Henry VII to thank him for what he had done for the same university in 1507,[18]

---

[15] Robert Hacumblene (d. 1528), a Cambridge DD, spent his whole life at Cambridge in King's College: a fellow in 1474, he became Provost in 1509. The *Commentarius in Aristotelis Ethica* in Cambridge King's College 11, bears the mention 'Quod Hacumblen'. See *BRUC*, p. 278. On Milverton, see note 11 above.

[16] John Gunthorpe (d. 1498), a Cambridge BD and Dean of Wells; his *Orationes Legatinae* are in Bodleian Library Bodley 587, ff. 73–93. See *BRUO*, II, p. 837 and *BRUC*, pp. 275–7, and R. Weiss, *Humanism in England in the Fifteenth Century*, 3rd edn (Oxford, 1967).

[17] John Russell (d. 1494), an Oxford D.Cn.L., was successively Bishop of Rochester (1476–80) and Lincoln. His speech when presenting the Garter to Charles the Bold at Bruges in 1470 was printed, probably by William Caxton in 1477, either at Bruges or at Westminster. His speech to the Bishop of Utrecht at the Utrecht Conference is still unpublished (MS. London B.L. Additional 48006, ff. 10–11). See below.

[18] William Selling (d. 1494), OSB, was a Bologna D.Th. who became Prior of Christ Church, Canterbury. His *Capita orationis legati R. Henrici ad Papam post matrimonium cum Elisabetha filia Edwardi IV*, addressed to Innocent VIII in 1486 is printed from MS. London B.L. Cotton Cleopatra E 3 in U. Balzani, 'Un' Ambasciata inglese a Roma', *Archivio della Societa Romana di Storia Patria*, III (1880), pp. 175–211 at pp. 196–207. See *BRUO*, III, pp. 1666–7, W. Schirmer, *Der englische Fruhhumanismus*

Pietro Griffo's speech for Henry VII, printed in 1509,[19] and the diplomatic speeches of Cuthbert Tunstall and Richard Pace are all examples of this new literary genre.[20]

On the other side, we find those speeches which were intended to have a more immediate effect on the listeners, and hence on the course of events. They are less formal, and here another problem appears: were they prepared and written? Or were they delivered on the spot, spoken without being written? We might call these 'virtual texts', since most of them do not exist any more in manuscripts. Some of these 'virtual texts' have been recorded, however, and although there may be a distance between the speech as it was uttered on the one hand, and the written version on the other, we may use the record. For instance, we know that

---

(Leipzig, 1931), pp. 154–62 and Weiss, *Humanism in England*, pp. 153–9. John Blythe (d. 1499), a Cambridge DCL, was Bishop of Salisbury from 1493 and Cambridge Chancellor 1494–8. His speech for the visit of Henry VII is in MS. Oxford B.L. Bodley 12; extracts are printed in J. Gairdner, *Letters and Papers Illustrative of the Reigns of Richard III and Henry VII*, Rolls Series, (1863), I, pp. 422–3; on Blythe, see *BRUC*, p. 68. John Fisher (d. 1535), a Cambridge DD, is better known as a political author for his tracts in defence of the validity of Queen Catherine of Aragon's marriage to Henry VIII. His *Oratio habita coram illustrissimo Rege Henrico Septimo* (1506) is in MS. Oxford B.L. Bodley 13 and printed in John Leland, *Itinerary*, 2, pp. 95–102. See J. Rouschausse, *La vie et l'oeuvre de John Fisher, évêque de Rochester, 1469–1535* (Nieuwkoop and Angers, 1972), pp. 18–19, for an analysis of this speech; on the divorce, G. Bedouelle and P. Le Gal, *Le 'Divorce' du Roi Henry VIII, Etudes et Documents* (Genève, 1987).

[19] Pietro Griffo (d. 1516), a friend of Ammonio and Colet, later Bishop of Forli, was papal collector in England in 1509–12 and used this opportunity to write an interesting history of this office, *De Officio Collectoris in Regno Anglie*, the original of which is Vaticano Ottobon. lat. 2948. He wrote an *Oratio (quam erat habiturus P. Gryphus ad Henricum VII Anglie Regem ni immatura regis mors prevenisset)*, printed by R. Pynson in 1509 (STC 12413), dedicated to the king's secretary, Thomas Ruthal, who asked Griffo to have the text printed: see D. Hay, 'Pietro Griffo, an Italian in England, 1506–1512', *Italian Studies*, 2 (1939), 118–28.

[20] Richard Pace (d. 1536), a Padua student, had several of his diplomatic speeches printed or circulated : his *Conclusiones de Veniis Pontificum et consilio de bello* were printed in 1517, since Erasmus sent a copy to Sir Thomas More; the *Oratio Richardi Pacei in pace nuperime composita* was printed by Pynson in 1518 (STC 19081A); see *BRUO*, III, p. 1417. Cuthbert Tunstall (d. at ninety-five in 1559), a Padua doctor in utroque, was successively Bishop of London (1522–30) and Durham (1530–59). His speech for the betrothal of Princess Mary, the daughter of Henry VIII, to the dauphin, *Cutheberti Tunstalli in laudem matrimonii oratio*, was printed by Pynson in 1518 (STC 24320) and reprinted the following year in Basle. He also preached the opening sermon for the 1523 Parliament, in the place of Thomas Wolsey (*Journal of the House of Lords*, I, lxxv). See *BRUO*, III, pp. 1913–15.

public sermons were preached in support of Edward IV by George Neville in 1461, and in support of Richard III by Ralph Shaw and Thomas Penketh,[21] but we have only Neville's text.[22] This problem arises particularly in relation to parliamentary speeches: during the whole period we lack satisfactory texts for the chancellor's opening sermon, since from 1423 onwards the summary was in Latin and, for the period under examination here, these texts are usually very short, or even totally lacking for most of the late Lancastrian and early Yorkist periods – far from the near-complete French texts we have for Adam de Houghton and Simon Sudbury in the late fourteenth century and the very complete Latin summaries we have for some of John Stafford's speeches in the earlier Lancastrian period. We have to be content with the bare bones, in Latin, of the parliamentary speeches of Alcock,[23] Chedworth, Morton,[24] and Warham.[25]

[21] Thomas Penketh (d. 1487), an Austin Friar, a Cambridge D.Th. He is credited by John Bale with a commentary on Augustine's *De Civitate Dei*. Ralph Shaw (d. 1484), a Cambridge B.Th. who became a canon of St Paul's in 1477 and the brother of Sir Edmund Shaw, Lord Mayor of London, is said to have accepted to preach in favour of Richard at Paul's Cross on 22 June 1483, but to have died soon after from the remorse to have pleaded for such a cause: H. Ellis, *Polydore Vergil's English History*, Camden Society, XXIX (1844), pp. 183–5. See *BRUC*, pp. 519–20, and C.A.J. Armstrong, *The Usurpation of Richard III* (1936).

[22] George Neville (d. 1476), an Oxford MA, became Bishop of Exeter at the age of twenty-four in 1456, then Archbishop of York in 1465. His parliamentary speeches are mentioned in *RP*, V, 373 (1460), 461 (1461), 496 (1463); his 1470 speech is mentioned by John Warkworth only. His speech at St Paul's in 1461 is printed in C.L. Scofield, *The Life and Reign of Edward the Fourth* (1923), I, p. 151; he had a little earlier (7 April) written a letter to the papal legate, Francesco Coppini (*Calendar of State Papers and Manuscripts relating to English Affairs . . . Venice . . . Northern Italy* (1864), I, pp. 99–100). See *BRUO*, II, pp. 1347–9.

[23] John Alcock (d. 1500), a Cambridge D.C.L, was successively Bishop of Rochester (1472–6), Worcester (1476–86) and Ely (1486–1500) and twice Chancellor of England, in 1475 and in 1485–7. His published works are mainly devotional tracts, printed between 1496 and 1502 by Wynkyn de Worde and R. Pynson. In 1472 he was deputized by the Chancellor and Bishop of Bath and Wells, Robert Stillington, to pronounce the opening sermon for the Parliament. His theme is announced, but not specified in the rolls (*RP*, VI, 3).

[24] John Morton (d. 1500), an Oxford DCL, Archbishop of Canterbury from 1486: his sermons are in *RP*, VI, 385 (1487), 409 (1488), 440 (1491), 458 (1495), 509 (1497). On Morton, see *BRUO*, II, pp. 1318–20.

[25] William Warham (d. 1532), an Oxford DCL, was Archbishop of Canterbury from 1503 onwards. His parliamentary speeches are in the *Lords Journal*, I, 3 (1510), 10 (1512), and 18 (1515).

On the other hand, we have two parliamentary speeches in English, which appear to be virtually complete: Robert Stillington's speech in 1467[26] and Thomas Rotherham's speech in 1474, a copy of which found its way into a Canterbury Cathedral letter-book.[27] To this meagre group may be added the two Speakers' speeches: William Allington's in 1472[28] and James Strangeways's in 1461.[29] Finally, there are the three drafts by John Russell.[30] We can complement these with other texts, most of which are not technically speeches: for instance, the letters sent by Richard, Duke of York, to the king and to the Archbishop of

[26] Robert Stillington (d. 1491), an Oxford DCL, was Bishop of Bath and Wells from 1466 onwards. His 1467 parliamentary speech is in *RP*, V, 622–3; on Stillington, see *BRUO*, III, pp. 1777–8, and on the speech, see S.B. Chrimes, *English Constitutional Ideas in the Fifteenth Century* (Cambridge, 1936), pp. 121–2.

[27] Thomas Rotherham (d. 1500), maybe an Oxford D.Th., was Bishop of Rochester (1468–72), of Lincoln (1472–80) and Archbishop of York (1480–1500). In Aberystwyth the *communis opinio* was that this speech had been delivered by John Alcock, on the grounds that he was deputed to give the chancellor's address at the time of Stillington's illness at the opening of Parliament. However, the speech in question is apparently from July 1474, and J.B. Sheppard attributes it to Rotherham, arguing that he was by then chancellor and that he had been admitted to Canterbury's confraternity, which provides a motive for the otherwise unexplained presence of such a speech in a Canterbury letter book. But I am quite ready to admit that this is not conclusive. The speech is printed from MS. Canterbury Cathedral N, f. 265a, in Sheppard, *Literae Cantuarienses*, Rolls Series (1889), III, pp. 274–85. See *BRUO*, III, pp. 1593–6, which shows that he had a magnificent library of Italian incunabulas.

[28] William Allington (d. 1479), a Cambridgeshire gentleman, was the grandson of a namesake, also Speaker of the Commons! His 1472 speech is printed in *RP*, VI, 8–9. See J.S. Roskell, *The Commons and their Speakers in English Parliaments, 1376–1523* (Manchester, 1965), pp. 283–9; *idem*, 'William Allington of Bottisham, Speaker in the Parliaments of 1472–5 and 1478', *Proceedings of the Cambridge Antiquarian Society*, 52 (1959), 43–55.

[29] Sir James Strangeways (d. 1480), a Yorkshire knight, the son of a Judge of the Common Pleas, was one of Warwick's retainers. His speech is printed in full in *RP*, V, 462–3. See Roskell, *The Commons and their Speakers*, pp. 271–5 and 364–5; *idem*, 'Sir James Strangeways of West Herlsey and Whorlton', *Yorkshire Archaeological Journal*, 39 (1958), 455–82.

[30] The drafts of the intended 1483 speeches for the opening of Parliament are in MS. London B.L. Vitellius E 10, printed by Chrimes, *English Constitutional Ideas*, pp. 168–78, 179–85, 186–91, to be compared with *RP*, VI, 237. On Russell, see *BRUO*, III, pp. 1609–11. For his alleged part in the continuation of the Crowland Chronicle, see N. Pronay and J. Cox, *The Crowland Chronicle Continuations 1459–1486* (1986), and A.J. Pollard, 'Review Article: Memoirs of a Yorkist Civil Servant', *The Ricardian*, 96 (1987), 380–5.

Canterbury in 1455; the appeal from William Burley to hand the protectorship to Richard and Richard's acceptance of the same year; and other manifestos from the period of the Wars of the Roses. To my knowledge, very little remains for the early Tudor period, when we lose the advantages of the *Rolls of Parliament* and have to be content with the *Lords' Journals*.

Another group of texts appears at first sight to be a haphazard collection. It is what at an earlier date could have been described as the 'Mirrors for Princes' genre. But Mirrors as such do not exist any more, with the exception (which proves the rule) of Stephen Baron's *Tractatulus de regimine principum ad serenissimum regem Anglie Henricum Octavum*, printed by Wynkyn de Worde in 1509.[31] Skelton's *Speculum Principis* runs to no more than 130 lines.[32] The precise date of George Ashby's work is far from clear, but the poem is definitely Lancastrian in tone and content.[33] That there is some interest in the traditional Mirrors is revealed by the making of *tabulae* by Thomas Abingdon,[34] John of Drayton,[35] Thomas Graunt[36] and John Whethamstede on works such as Vincent de Beauvais' *De Eruditione Filiorum Nobilium*, Roger of Waltham's *Compendium Morale*, John of Salisbury's *Policraticus*, and Giles of

---

[31] Stephen Baron (d. 1520), Provincial Prior of the observant Franciscans, dedicated to Henry VIII his *Tractatulus De Regimine Principum ad serenissimum regem Anglie Henricum Octavum*, printed by W. de Worde in 1509 (STC 1497).

[32] The short *Speculum Principis* of 1501 in MS. London B.L. Additional 26787 is printed in F.M. Salter, 'Skelton's Speculum Principis', *Speculum*, 9 (1934), 25–37 (see note 62 below on Skelton).

[33] George Ashby (d. 1475) was a clerk of the signet; his poems in MS. Cambridge UL Mm IV 42 are printed in M. Bateson, *George Ashby's Poems*, EETS, ES, 76 (1899). See *Dictionary of National Biography* and F. Holthausen, 'Ashby Studien', *Anglia*, 45 (1921), 77–104.

[34] On this and the following, see Ch. Briggs, 'Late Medieval Texts', see above note 13. Thomas Abingdon, OESA (d. ?1470), before embarking on a secular career, wrote a *Tabula in Aegidium De Regimine Principum*, two copies of which survive: MS. Oxford All Souls' College 92, ff. 159v–166r and MS. Oxford B.L. Auct. D 3 2, f.f 117r–124v; see *BRUO*, I, p. 3 and II, p. ix.

[35] Probably John Drayton, a Benedictine theology student at Oxford in 1445: his *Tabula super Aegidium de Regimine Principum* of 1436 is in Cambridge UL Ff 4 38, ff. 134–142; see *BRUO*, I, p. 593.

[36] Thomas Graunt (d. 1474) was an Oxford B.Th., who was a canon of St Paul's from 1452 onwards. He made tables for the *Sermones* of Robert Holcot, and for the *Compendium Morale* of Roger of Waltham. See *BRUO*, II, pp. 802–3.

Rome's *De Regimine Principum*.[37] But these *tabulae*, made by clerics and academics for their professional use, deserve to be reckoned among academic productions. In fact, the texts we find in this 'Mirrors' genre are texts which are very loosely connected to the tradition from a purely literary point of view, but which are nonetheless dedicated to kings and to members of the aristocracy and carry a moral objective. They include the usual flow of translations from the Latin and French literatures, from Robert Shottesbrook's translation of parts of Laurent de Premierfait's *Somme le Roi* (dated 1451)[38] to Brian Anstay's translation of Christine de Pisan's *Cité des Dames*.[39] Other texts are the completion of John Lydgate's translation of the pseudo-Aristotelian *Secree of Secrees* by Benedict Burgh;[40] the translation of Nicholas Upton's *De Studio Militari* by John Blount,[41] a fellow of All Souls'; Robert Parker's

---

[37] John Whethamstede (d. 1465), an Oxford D.Th., was Abbot of St Albans, 1420–40 and 1451–65. His *Super Polycraticum* is lost, if it ever existed; the *Tabula super Vincencium de Erudicione Puerorum Nobilium edita per Johannem de Sancto Albano abbatem* is in MS. London B.L. Arundel 11, ff. 164–171: see *BRUO*, III, pp. 2032–4. It is noteworthy that William Worcester (see below) also compiled a *Tabula Librorum Ethicae Aristotelis* (MS. London B.L. Cotton Julius F 7, f. 49) and made excerpts of Vincent of Beauvais' *De Puerorum Nobilium Eruditione* (ibid., ff. 139–141).

[38] Sir Robert Shottesbrook (d. 1471), a Berkeley retainer who took part in the conquest of Normandy and was several times MP, translated part of the French Somme le Roi: *Aventure and Grace*, dated 1451, in MS. Oxford B.L. e Musaeo 23: see R. Hannah, 'Sir Thomas Berkeley and his Patronage', *Speculum*, 64 (1989), 878–916 and E. Wilson, 'Sir Robert Shottesbrook (1400–1471) translator', *Notes and Queries*, 226 (1981), 303–5.

[39] Brian Anstay was in 1521 a yeoman of the wine cellar to Henry VIII. The *Boke of the Cyte of Ladyes* was printed by H. Pepwell in 1521. On this work, see D. Bornstein, *The Lady in the Tower. Medieval Courtesy Literature for Women* (Hamden, 1983), pp. 87–93, and J. Rooks, 'The Book of the Cyte of Ladyes and its Sixteenth-Century Readership', in G.K. McLeod, ed., *The Reception of Christine de Pizan from the Fifteenth through the Nineteenth Centuries* (New York, 1991), pp. 83–100.

[40] Benedict Burgh (d. 1483), an Oxford MA who became Archdeacon of Colchester in 1468, continued Lydgate's translation of a version of the pseudo-Aristotelian *Secreta Secretorum*; known as *Secrees of old philosoffres* or *The Book of the Governaunce of Kynges and Prynces*, this translation was quite successful and was printed by Pynson in 1511 (STC 17017) at the request of Lord Herbert (ed. R. Steele, EETS, ES 66, (1894)). On Burgh, see *BRUO*, I, p. 309.

[41] John Blount was a fellow of All Souls' College; his translation is printed by F.P. Barnard, ed., *The Essential Portions of Nicholas Upton's De Studio Militari translated by John Blount* (Oxford, 1931). See *BRUO*, IV, pp. 52–3.

translation of *Vegetius*;[42] Anthony Woodvile's translation of Christine's *Livre du Corps de Policie*;[43] and the many translations by William Caxton of Ramon Lull, Christine de Pisan, Jacques de Cessoles and Alain Chartier.[44] But here too, a new trend is clearly visible – the humanist one: the *Pro tyrannicida* of Lucian, translated by Thomas More for the collection of Lucien's dialogues, which he edited with Erasmus in 1506,[45] the translation of Isocrates' *Ad Nicoclem* by the Italian Giovanni Boerio for the then Prince Henry.[46] Dialogues in the new

[42] Robert Parker, a king's clerk who was rector of St Nicholas at Calais, translated Palladius (in M. Liddell, ed., *The Middle English Translation of Palladius De Re Rustica* (Berlin, 1896), and probably Vegecius: *Knighthode and Bataile*, dedicated to Viscount Beaumont, ed. R. Dyboski and Z.M. Arend, *Knyghthode and Bataile. A XVth. cent. verse paraphrase of Flavius Vegetius Renatus Treatise De Re Militari*, EETS, OS, 201, (1935): see H.N. McCracken, 'Vegetius in English', in *Kittredge Anniversary Essays* (Boston, 1913), pp. 389–404.

[43] Anthony Woodville, Earl Rivers (executed 1483), was Edward IV's brother-in-law. He translated from the French of Jean Miélot the *Cordiale quattuor novissimorum* attributed to Gerhard van Vliederhoven (*The Cordyal*, printed by Caxton in 1479, STC 5758), from the French of Guillaume de Tignonville the *Dicts and Sayings of the Philosophers*, printed four times by Caxton from 1477 to 1489 (STC 6826–30) and from Christine de Pisan *The morale proverbes of Cristyne* (printed by Caxton in 1478, STC 7273). *The Body whiche is called the body polycye*, in MS. Cambridge UL Kk 1 5 (it was published later, in 1521, by J. Skot, STC 7270) is printed by D. Bornstein, ed., *The Middle English Translation of Christine de Pisan's Livre du Corps de Policie*, Middle English Texts, VII (Heidelberg, 1977).

[44] See J.Ph. Genet, 'L'influence francaise sur la littérature politique anglaise au temps de la France Anglaise', in *Actes du 111e Congrès des Sociétés Savantes, Poitiers, 1986: La France Anglaise* (Paris, 1988), pp. 75–90. On William Caxton (d. 1491), see N.F. Blake, *Caxton: England's First Publisher* (1976). The French works with a political content which Caxton translated are *The game and play of the chess moralized* (STC 4920–1), a translation made from the two French versions of Jacques de Cessoles' *Ludus Scacchorum*, dedicated to George, Duke of Clarence; *The booke of the ordre of chivalry or knyghthode* (STC 3356.7), dedicated to King Richard III, a translation from a French version of Ramon Lull's *Le libre del Orde de Cavayleria*; *The Curial made by mayster Alain Charretier* (STC 5057–8), from Alain Chartier, and *The book of fayttes of armes and of chyvalrye* (STC 7269), from Christine de Pisan.

[45] Sir Thomas More (executed 1535) was educated at Oxford and Lincoln's Inn: see *BRUO*, II, pp. 1305–8. His translation of Lucien's dialogues, dedicated to Thomas Ruthal, including *Pro tyrannicida*, was printed in the 1506 Paris edition of *Luciani Dialogui* and frequently reprinted. To the original conclusion he added his own contrary conclusion. Unfortunately, there is only a bare outline of his 1529 opening speech to Parliament: *Lords Journal*, CLI. See R.W. Chambers, *Thomas More* (1938), 240–3.

[46] Giovanni Boerio, whose father was Henry VII's physician, dedicated his translation of Isocrates to Prince Henry in 1506.

style, such as John Mannyngham's *Contentio Alexandri, Hanibalis, Scipionis et Henrici Quinti de praesidentia coram Minoe judice*[47] and William Worcester's translation of Buanocorso de Montemagno's *De Vera Nobilitate* (The declamation of Noblesse),[48] fall into this category; the exhumation of Claudian's *De consulatu Stilichonis* is best understood in this context.[49]

What remains in this group is probably the most interesting. These are texts which were written for the king, but which, for one reason or another, their authors did not succeed in casting – or did not want to cast – in the 'Mirrors' style. These include Sir John Fortescue's tracts, such as *The Governance of England*[50] (even though some of these – especially the smaller ones – come very close to being purely

---

[47] This is apparently an edition of the work of the Italian Humanist, Aurispa, to which someone, probably Mannyngham, has added a supplementary discourse on Henry V. I have not seen the manuscript, Dublin Trinity College 438, and I wish to thank Dr David Rundle for information about this text.

[48] *The declamacyon which laboureth to shewe wherin honoure sholde reste* [The declamation of Noblesse], a translation of Buonacorso da Montemagno's *De vera nobilitate*, printed in Caxton's 1481 edition of William Worcester's translation of Cicero's *De senectute* (STC 5293), is in fact by William Worcester himself, not by John Tiptoft as usually said. It is edited in R.J. Mitchell, *John Tiptoft* (1938), pp. 215–41: see A. Sutton and L. Visser-Fuchs, 'Richard III's Books: XII. William Worcester's *Boke of Noblesse* and his Collection of Documents on the War in Normandy', *The Ricardian*, 9, 115 (Dec. 1991), 154–65, esp. 160–1. I thank Dr Visser-Fuchs for this reference and for giving me a copy of this paper.

[49] See J.L. Watts, 'De Consulatu Stilichonis: Texts and Politics in the Reign of Henry VI', *Journal of Medieval History*, 16 (1990), 251–66.

[50] The standard edition of the *Governance of England* is still Ch. Plummer, *The Governance of England . . . by Sir John Fortescue, Knight* (Oxford, 1885), which has been used for the computation. But see now the edition of the version in the oldest surviving manuscript, MS. London B.L. Additional 48031A: M.L. Kekewich, C. Richmond, A.F. Sutton, L. Visser-Fuchs and J.L. Watts, *The Politics of Fifteenth-Century England. John Vale's Book* (Stroud, 1995), pp. 226–50; the editors of this version suggest that the tract was never intended for Henry VI, but was written for Edward IV. See J.H. Burns, 'Fortescue and the Political Theory of Dominion', *Historical Journal*, 28 (1985), 777–97; Chrimes, *English Constitutional Ideas*; N. Doe, *Fundamental Authority in Late Medieval English Law* (Cambridge, 1990); J.Ph. Genet, 'Les idées sociales et politiques de Sir John Fortescue', *Economies et Sociétés Médiévales, Mélanges offerts à Edouard Perroy* (Paris, 1972), pp. 446–61, and J.G.A. Pocock, *The Machiavellian Moment: Florentine Political Thought and the Atlantic Republican Tradition* (Princeton, 1975), pp. 9–12 and 17–22; and J.L. Watts, *Henry VI and the Politics of Kingship* (Cambridge, 1996), esp. pp. 46–50.

'practical' texts),[51] William of Worcester's *Boke of Noblesse*,[52] John Rous' tracts (four of them are to be found in his *Historia Regum Anglie*, dedicated to Henry VII, one of them being apparently based upon one of his sermons)[53] and finally Edmund Dudley's *Tree of Commonwealth*, dedicated to Henry VIII.[54] They have not much in

[51] The smaller tracts of Fortescue include *De titulo Edwardi Comitis Marchie*, ed. in Lord Clermont, *The works of Sir John Fortescue . . .* (1869), pp. 63–74, a work of which two fragments survive, *Of the title of the house of York*, printed in Clermont, *Works*, pp. 497–502 and *A simple maid of the realm of England*, ed. in Plummer, *Governance*, pp. 355–6; *A defence of the title of the house of Lancaster or a replication to the claim of the Duke of York*, ed. in Plummer, *Governance*, pp. 353–4 and in Kekewich *et al.*, *John Vale's Book*, pp. 202–3; *Here folowen in articles certeyne advertisementes sente by my lorde prince to therle of Warrewic his fadir in lawe . . .*, ed. in Plummer, *Governance*, pp. 348–53, and in Kekewich *et al.*, *John Vale's Book*, pp. 223–5; *Example what Good Counsel helpith*, ed. in Plummer, *Governance*, pp. 347–8 and in Kekewich *et al.*, *John Vale's Book*, pp. 225–6 (according to Plummer, this is an alternative version of ch. 16 of the *Governance*, while for the editors of *Vale's Book*, it is an epilogue to the *Articles*); *Declaracioun upon certayn wrytinges sent oute of Scotteland ayenst the Kinges title to the Realme of England*, ed. in Clermont, *Works*, pp. 523–41. To the bibliography in the preceding footnote, add P.E. Gill, 'Politics and Propaganda in fifteenth century England: the polemical writings of Sir John Fortescue', *Speculum*, 46 (1971), 333–47, and V. Litzen, *A war of Roses and Lillies: The Theme of Succession in Sir John Fortescue's Works* (Suomalaisen Tiedeakatemian Toimituksia, Sarja B, nide 173) (Helsinki, 1971).

[52] *The Boke of Noblesse* is printed by J.G. Nichols, ed., *The Boke of Noblesse addressed to King Edward the Fourth on his Invasion of France in 1475* (Roxburghe Club, 1860; reprint New York, 1972). See C. Allmand, 'France-Angleterre à la fin du Moyen Age: le *Boke of Noblesse* de William Worcester', in *Actes du 111e Congrès des Sociétés Savantes* (Poitiers, 1986); *La 'France Anglaise' au Moyen Age* (Paris, 1988), pp. 103–11; and A.F. Sutton and L. Visser-Fuchs, 'Richard III's Books', see above, note 49.

[53] John Rous (d. 1491) was an Oxford MA who remained from 1445 Chaplain of Guy's Cliffe Chantry in Warwick. The *Historia* is printed in Th. Hearne, *Joannis Rossi Antiquarii Warwicensis Historia Regum Angliae . . . Accedit Joannis Lelandi Antiquarii Naenia in Mortem Henrici Duddelegi Equitis* (Oxford, 1716), pp. 1–219. The first tract (*De scientia et scienciae inventoribus*) is on pp. 28–44 (though some of the lengthy digressions which follow on the founding of a college in Rome by Inne, the founding of Paris University by four Englishmen, pupils of Bede – Rabanus, Alquinus, Claudius and Johannes Scotus – and of Oxford University by King Alfred may belong to it), the second (on the antiquity of English Law) on pp. 79–84, the third of the two long *exempla* borrowed from Césaire of Heisterbach one relates to King Philip-Augustus and the other to Landgraf Ludwig of Thuringia) on pp. 86–95, the fourth (the enclosure tract) on pp. 112–37. On Rous, see *BRUO*, III, pp. 1596–7 and A. Gransden, *Historical Writing in England c.1307 to the early Sixteenth Century* (1982), pp. 309–27.

[54] Edmund Dudley (d. 1510), educated at Oxford and Gray's Inn, wrote his *Tree of Commonwealth* in 1510 while in jail waiting for execution; the text is printed in D.M. Brodie, ed., *The Tree of Commonwealth* (Cambridge, 1949); see D.M. Brodie, 'Edmund Dudley, minister of Henry VII', *TRHS*, 4th ser., 15 (1932), 133–61, and *BRUO*, I, pp. 597–8.

common, and Rous' text is known to us only in Latin, a language also used by
Fortescue for his two longer texts, *De Laudibus Legum Angliae* and *De Natura Legis
Naturae*. Both the *Boke of Noblesse* and the *Historia Regum Anglie* may, on the whole, be
classified as history books, though they pretend to be political tracts relating
directly to burning issues of the day, such as war and peace between France and
England, or the spread of enclosures. One problem – also found in the 'speeches'
area – is the distinction between texts like these, which have theoretical pretensions,
and those texts which are simply 'practical' texts, written or spoken in the day-to-
day experience of political life, and sometimes non-authorial (though the words
'practical' and 'theoretical' may well be misleading). One distinctive feature
appears precisely in our period: the use of a factual and narrative framework for
expressing political ideas or principles. This was done only by poets in the
preceding period (for instance by Gower, Chaucer and Lydgate); now prose writers
did the same, using either historical facts (Fortescue, Rous, Worcester), or even
fiction: in the flattest manner, as Dudley with his *Tree of Commonwealth*, or in the
most brilliant and imaginative way, as Thomas More with his *Utopia*.

The last area, on the other hand, is in full expansion. An entirely new field of
literary expression, and one with obvious political connotations, is that of Tudor
court poetry. The absence of a court, as a cultural pole, is one of the most striking
phenomena of English history during the fifteenth century. In the late fourteenth
century, the court of Richard II may be overestimated as a cultural centre,
especially when compared with what Paris had to offer, but the Lancastrian kings
fell much below this modest level. If Hoccleve and Lydgate worked for the
Lancastrian kings, they cannot be described as court poets, and George Ashby,
for what little we know about him, is not a court poet either. On the other hand,
although Edward IV could have nurtured some new ideas after his stay at his
brother-in-law's magnificent court in the Low Countries, it is Henry VII who
gave employment at court to people who were expected to write for him, his
family and his policies.[55] Since there was no English tradition on which to build,

---

[55] On the beginnings of the Tudor court, see G. Kipling, *The Triumph of Honour: Burgundian Origins of
the Elizabethan Renaissance* (The Hague, 1977) and, on the literary aspects, A. Fox, *Politics and Literature
in the Reigns of Henry VII and Henry VIII* (Oxford, 1989).

and since such writings were most useful on the international stage, he used foreigners who could write either in Latin or in French. Bernard André de Toulouse,[56] a French Austin friar, who tutored the Princes Henry and Arthur, wrote in French *Les douze triomphes de Henry VII*. The most active poets, however, were the two Italians who became in turn Latin secretaries to Henry VII and Henry VIII. Petrus Carmelianus,[57] an Italian from Brescia, who became a canon of St Stephen's Chapel in Westminster wrote at least one poem on the birth of Prince Arthur and a *libellus* to herald the ceremonies designed to celebrate the negotiations for the marriage of Princess Mary with the future Emperor Charles V. Andrea Ammonio, Latin secretary to Henry VIII, came to London with the Bishop of Worcester, Silvestro de Gigli – whose relative Giovanni Gigli, also a Bishop of Worcester, had earlier written a Latin epithalamium for the marriage of Henry VII[58] – and resided

---

[56] Bernard André (d. 1521) was rector of Guisnes from 1500 till his death. *Les douze triomphes de Henri sept* is printed from MS. London B.L. Royal 16 E 17 in J. Gairdner, *Memorials of Henry VII*, Rolls Series, (1858), pp. 133–53. On André, see *BRUO*, I, p. 33 and C.W.T. Blackwell, 'Humanism and Politics in English Royal Biography: the use of Cicero, Plutarch and Sallust in the *Vita Henrici Quinti* (1438) by Titus-Livius de Frulovisi and the *Vita Henrici Septimi* (1500–1503)', in I.D. McFarlane, ed., *Acta Conventus Neo-Latini Sanctandriani: Proceedings of the Fifth International Congress of Neo-Latin Studies* (Binghamton, 1986), pp. 431–40.

[57] Pietro Faba di Valle Sabbia (d. 1527), known as Carmeliano, was Latin secretary to Henry VII from 1495 at least, but he had tried to enter royal service from 1481, presenting Edward IV with a copy of his edition of Cicero's *De Oratore*, printed at Venice in 1478: see A.F. Sutton and L. Visser-Fuchs, 'Richard III's books: Pietro Carmeliano's early publications: his Spring, the Letters of Phalaris, and his Life of St Katherine dedicated to Richard III', *The Ricardian*, 10, 132 (1996), 346–86. His edition of the Latin version by Francesco Griffolini of Arezzo of the *Letters of Phalaris* was presented either to Edward, Prince of Wales or to his uncle, Richard, though the only surviving manuscript belonged to a member of the Lee family. His *Suasorum Laeticiae ad Angliam pro sublatis bellis civilis et Arthuro principe nato epistola&*, written in 1486, is printed in D. Carlson, 'King Arthur and Court Poems for the birth of Arthur Tudor in 1486', *Humanistica Lovaniensia*, 36 (1987), 147–83, while what he wrote for the ceremonies accompanying the negotiations for the marriage of Princess Mary to the future Emperor Charles V was printed by Pynson in 1508 (STC 4659). See *BRUO*, I, pp. 358–9.

[58] Giovanni Gigli (d. 1498) was a papal collector from 1476 and Bishop of Worcester until his death: he dedicated his *Questiones de observantia quadragesimali* to Bishop Russell and dedicated his *Epithalamium* to Henry VII for his marriage with Elizabeth of York (both works in MS. London B.L. Harley 336); he also dedicated to John Morton a *Libellus de Canonisatione Sanctorum*: see *BRUO*, II, pp. 764–5, and R. Weiss, 'Lineamenti di una biografia di Giovanni Gigli, collettore papale in Inghilterra e vescovo di Worcester', *Rivista di Storia della Chiesa in Italia*, 1, 379–91.

there from 1504 onwards.[59] To those two names may perhaps be added that of Johannes Opicius, probably an Italian.[60] John Skelton and William Lyly – who wrote in 1506 a poem for the visit to England of Archduke Philip – also wrote some Latin poetry to honour the English kings and to glorify London and state pageantry alike.[61]

Now, for the English literary market, this was not very efficient. There was a need for poetry written in English, and since a brilliant court now existed, it was to be expected that the English poetry of the time would originate there rather than (or as well as) in the London social circles, as it had done to a certain extent in Richard II's time. Indeed, some English court poetry was now written and, though a disparaging view of the work of these early court poets has often been taken, its writers were pioneers. Skelton,[62] who was also tutor to the princes from at least 1490 to 1502, did

[59] Andrea Ammonio (d. 1517), a servant of Gigli, became a canon of Westminster. Several of his 'English' poems, which were printed in his *Lucensis Carmen Asclepiadeum* in 1511, are reprinted in C. Pizzi, *Andreae Ammonii Carmina Omnia* (Florence, 1958), pp. 16–23 and 35–40 (*Elegia de obitu regis Henrici VII et felici successione Henrici Octavi, Epithalamium in nuptiis regis Henrici Octavi et reginae, and Hymnus ad Regem Henricum VI*). He also wrote a *Panegyricus ad Henricum VIII* to celebrate the Peace of Thérouanne. On Ammonio, see C. Pizzi, *Un amico di Erasmo. L'umanista Andrea Ammonio* (Florence, 1956).

[60] Johannes Opicius (fl. 1497) has left Latin poems dedicated to Henry VII in MS. London B.L. Cotton Vespasian B 9. James Gairdner suggests he could be a member of the Opizi family: *Memorials of Henry VII*, Rolls Series (1861).

61 Lyly (d. 1522), the well-known High Master of St Paul's School wrote *Ad Philippum Archiducem Carmen* for the visit of Archduke Philip in England in 1506: MS. London B.L. Harley 540, f. 47ff. His 1522 verses were printed by Pynson (STC 15606.7); see C.R. Baskerville, 'William Lily's Verse for the Entry of Charles V into London', Huntington Library Bulletin, 9 (1936) and S. Anglo, *Spectacle Pageantry, and Early Tudor Policy* (Oxford, 1969), p. 187, who however thinks that he was not the mastermind behind the conception of the whole pageant.

[62] John Skelton (d. 1529), a Cambridge student, was tutor to the princes, before becoming rector of Diss in 1504: see J. Scattergood, ed., *John Skelton. The Complete English Poems* (New Haven and London, 1983), for the satires against Wolsey, *Here after foloweth Certayne Bokes of Speke Parott . . .*, pp. 230–46, *Here after foloweth a lytell boke called Collyn Clout*, pp. 246–78, *Here after foloweth a lytell boke, which hath to name, why come ye nat to courte?*, pp. 278–311, *A Couplet on Wolsey's Dissolution of the Convocation at Saint Paul's*, p. 358, and Ph. Henderson, *The Complete Poems of John Skelton, Laureate* (1931), pp. 434–8 for the Latin poems (*Henrici Septimi . . . Epitaphium, Elegia in serenissimae principis et domine, Domine Margarete* and *Eulogium pro suorum temporum conditione*). The often printed 'A lamentable of Kyng Edward the IIII' is not admitted in the canon (see R.S. Kinsman, 'Lamentable of Kyng Edward the IIII', *Huntington Library Quarterly*, 29 (1966), 95–108). *Magnyficence*, a morality of 1515–16 printed by Rastell in 1530

write poems which had both historical and political intentions, to celebrate the victories over the Scots, or to lament the death of the Earl of Northumberland. But, more interestingly, he created works of fiction and imagination which were neither sycophantic or laudatory in the crudest manner, but made for the poet a specific position which gave him some independence, allowed some sort of criticism: this is true of his morality play *Magnificence*, written *c.* 1515–16, of the poems he wrote later in his career, *c.* 1521–3, and of the group of poems criticizing Thomas Wolsey and his clique, *Speke Parott, Colin Clout and Why come ye nat to court?* Other English poets may be less remarkable: Stephen Hawes'[63] *Joyfull meditacyon to all England of the coronacyon of . . . Henry VIII* was published in 1509 and offers a good example of traditional panegyric, whereas his *Pastyme of Pleasure* is a more subtle approach to the challenge of politics. To these could have been added the first writings of William Cornish, had they not disappeared. Obviously this does not cover all the political poetry written at the time in England, but most of the remaining poems are anonymous, and have been published in R.H. Robbins' collection of historical poems.[64] On the whole, they are few and do not counterbalance the new kind of poetry which was written at court, often directly sponsored by the king and his courtiers.

A survey like this leads us to expect considerable differences among the various sorts of political languages, according to the subject, the time, the literary style and

---

(STC 22607), is printed in Scattergood, *op. cit.*, pp. 140–214. See *BRUO*, III, pp. 1705–6, and among recent publications, R. Holtei, '"Measure is treasure": John Skelton's Magnyfycence and Henry VIII', in U. Baumann, ed., *Henry VIII in History, Historiography and Literature* (Frankfurt, 1992), pp. 79–96, and B. Lusse, 'Panegyric Poetry on the Coronation of King Henry VIII', ibid., pp. 49–78.

[63] On Stephen Hawes (d. 1523), a groom of the chamber during the reign of Henry VII who seems to have left the court after the king's death, see *BRUO*, II, pp. 888–9, and the following: A.S.G. Edwards, *Stephen Hawes* (Boston, 1983), S. Lerer, 'The Rhetoric of Fame: Stephen Hawes's Aureate Diction', *Spenser Studies*, 5 (1985), 169–84; B. Lusse, 'Panegyric Poetry on the Coronation of King Henry VIII', in Baumann, ed., Henry VIII in History, pp. 49–78, and A. Fox, *Politics and Literature*, pp. 56–72. His works are printed in W.E. Mead, *The Pastimes of Pleasure*, EETS, OS, 173 (1928), and in F.W. Gluck and A.B. Morgan, *Stephen Hawes. The Minor Poems*, EETS, 271, (1974), pp. 85–92, with the exception of *An elegy on the death of Henry VII*, ed. in G.V. Scammell and H.L. Rogers, 'An elegy on Henry VII', *Review of English Studies*, n.s. 8 (1957), 167–170, the authorship of which is not certain.

[64] R.H. Robbins, *Historical Poems of the XIVth and XVth Centuries* (New York, 1959).

the audience for which the texts were intended. We can now make an attempt to build one or several 'significant *corpora*' (a 'significant *corpus*' is a *corpus* with enough homogeneity in one way or another for the distribution of vocabulary among its component texts to make sense), in order to apply the techniques of lexical statistics, the only set of methods capable of dealing with such an enormous body of material. However, we are immediately confronted by one of its major drawbacks, which arises when we try to use the varying frequency of these words in different texts as a means for determining significant difference in the use of words in general. The difficulty does not come from the differences in length of the texts: these can be taken into account. Instead, it lies in defining a norm of use, to which the observed frequencies can be compared, in order to decide if we have a deficit or a surplus of a given word in a given text. In fact, the 'normal use' is equated with the average use derived from each *corpus* itself (hence the importance of the notion of the 'significant *corpus*'). True, when working on modern texts, one can have recourse to dictionaries derived from the computerization of enormous sets of *corpora* and kept alive by the addition of new texts, such as the *Trésor de la Langue Française* for modern French: there we may find a norm of use which, at least for certain categories of texts (such as novels, for instance) comes very close to being a language norm, not a *corpus* norm. Obviously, however, this is not possible for the medieval period. We have to be content with norms produced by the *corpus*, and the only way of getting beyond this is to insert each text in several *corpora* of different composition, in order to test the specificities of its vocabulary in different surroundings. I shall use a very efficient and simple item of software, PISTES,[65] which will generate both an alphabetical dictionary and a hierarchical dictionary (i.e. a dictionary arranged in order of frequency), enabling us to visualize the different contexts of each word and indicating the frequency of each 'item' in each text (item, not word: an 'item' is defined as a succession of letters delimited by two spaces, or a space and a punctuation mark; the same item may be related to two different 'words', such as 'see', for example, in 'the see' and 'to see'). To these

---

[65] This software has been created by Pierre Muller and may be bought from the Institut National de la Recherche Pédagogique in Paris; see P. Muller and Ph. Dautrey, 'Un logiciel d'analyse lexicale, <<Pistes>>. Description et exemples d'utilisation', *Mémoire Vive*, 14 (1995).

results I shall apply a statistical method, factorial analysis, thanks to a piece of software devised by Philippe Cibois, TRIDEUX.[66]

Here I shall discuss results drawn from a *corpus* of Yorkist documents, or rather speeches, though some of the texts are not speeches properly speaking. In this *corpus* are the letters of Richard, Duke of York (YO1),[67] William Burley's speech in favour of Richard, Duke of York (BUR),[68] Richard's agreement to become Protector (YO2),[69] all dating from the 1455 crisis, and Richard's ill-fated claim for the crown in 1460 (YO3).[70] Then, we have George Neville's sermon for Edward IV (NEV)[71] and James Strangeways' speech as Speaker (STR)[72] in 1461, which resonates with another Speaker's speech in 1472, that of William Allington (ALI).[73] There are also two other parliamentary speeches, one attributed to Robert Stillington (STI)[74] in 1468, the other to Thomas Rotherham (ROT)[75] in 1474. The final three texts are the drafts of Bishop Russell's parliamentary sermon in 1483 (RU1, RU2, and RU3).[76]

A brief comparison with a second *corpus*, which might be described as a *corpus* of 'English tracts', will be made. It contains some of the items of the first *corpus*: the 1455 Yorkist texts (taken as one text) and the three drafts of Bishop John Russell's sermons (also taken as one text); to these have been added the Lancastrian *A Defence of the Proscription of the Yorkists* (DPY),[77] Sir John Fortescue's

---

[66] The software used here is Ph. Cibois's TRI-Deux, 2.2 (Sept. 1994).

[67] Letters to the Archbishop of Canterbury and to King Henry VI, in *RP*, V, 280–1.

[68] *RP*, V, 284–6.

[69] Ibid., V, 286–7.

[70] Ibid., V, p. 375: Richard's 'Writyng' and his 'Answer' to the Lords' objections.

[71] See above, n. 22.

[72] See above, n. 29.

[73] See above, n. 28.

[74] See above, n. 26.

[75] See above, n. 27.

[76] S.B. Chrimes, op. cit., pp. 168–78.

[77] *Somnium Vigilantis*, written 1459, is extant in a poor copy, MS. London B.L. Royal 17 D 15: printed in J.P. Gilson, 'A Defence of the Proscription of the Yorkists in 1459', *EHR*, 26 (1911), 512–25. On the text, see Watts, *Henry VI*, pp. 43–6. Some have suggested that Sir John Fortescue had a hand in its composition: but see the results of the factorial analysis at the end of the present paper, where the *Somnium* (DPY on the graph) appears on the first two factors opposed to Fortescue's known writings. This is not a proof, but *The Governance* and the smaller tracts are quite close on the graph.

The Governance of England (GOE), as well as Sir John Fortescue's smaller tracts (FOR),[78] *The Tree of Commonwealth* by Edmund Dudley (TOC) and *The Boke of Noblesse* by William Worcester (BON).

The first result we get is a frequency list, which can be used after sorting the items, leaving aside the purely grammatical words – they have usually a very high frequency, but they may be more interesting from a stylistic point of view than from a semantic one – and lemmatizing those words for which it appears to be necessary (that is, transforming the items into words spelt out as they are in a dictionary: i.e. 'come', 'comes', 'came' are all reduced to 'to come'). Lemmatizing is a rather tricky business in many cases: a word may have a different function, for instance, in the plural and in the singular, or it may be difficult to recognize particular words through the disguise of medieval orthography ('common' is an especially problematic example). We can start with a quick look at the lists of those words which have the highest frequency, and at that stage I shall introduce for the sake of comparison the results from a third *corpus*, made up of parliamentary speeches from the Lancastrian period (1399–1444), and discarding the words which are merely the architectural tools of Dudley's metaphor ('fruit', 'tree', 'root' and so on).

The first outstanding phenomenon we may observe is the general stability of the language: eleven words ('king', first in all three *corpora*, 'great', 'man', 'may', 'God', 'to make', 'time/s', 'well', 'people', 'realme', 'thing/s') are present in all three *corpora*; five words ('lord', 'lords', 'sovereign', 'person', 'estate/s') are common to the Yorkist and Lancastrian texts; six ('lands', 'prince', 'right', 'noble', 'to take', 'good') to the Yorkist texts and to the English tracts; only two ('to say', 'to come') are common to the Lancastrian texts and to the English tracts. Only fifteen words are specific to one of the three *corpora*: 'communes', 'child', 'Parliament', 'high', 'grace', 'true' and 'lordship' for the Lancastrian texts; 'body', 'same' and 'law/s' for the Yorkist texts; 'to keep', 'year/s', 'France', 'first',

---

[78] *The Governance of England* in Plummer's edition; the smaller tracts used here are *Here folowen in articles certeyne advertisementes sente by my lorde prince to therle of Warrewic his fadir in lawe* . . . (Plummer, *Governance*, pp. 348–53); *Of the title of the house of York* (Clermont, Works, pp. 497–502); *A simple maid of the realm of England* (Plummer, pp. 355–6); *A defence of the title of the house of Lancaster or a replication to the claim of the Duke of York* (Plummer, pp. 353–4).

'counsell' and 'subjects' for the English tracts. Some of the differences are to be explained by the fact that in both the Lancastrian and the Yorkist *corpora* there is a majority of parliamentary speeches: the specificity of 'Parliament' and 'communes' in the Lancastrian *corpus* is all the more telling, while the emergence of 'counsell' in the tracts *corpus* appears at first sight more appropriate for texts of moral advice.

TABLE 1: HIGHEST FREQUENCY WORDS IN THREE DIFFERENT *CORPORA*

(Words in **bold** are unique to the *corpus* in which they appear; words in *italics* appear in all three *corpora*)

	Lancastrian speeches		Yorkist speeches		English tracts	
1	*king*	68	*king*	123	*king*	713
2	lord	44	land/s	123	*great*	637
3	**communes**	34	*great*	102	*man*	431
4	lords	32	*may*	94	*may*	380
5	*well*	30	God	79	good	282
6	*man*	30	*time/s*	76	*to make*	263
7	estate/s	27	**body**	76	to say	262
8	*great*	26	*man*	71	*God*	247
9	*time/s*	24	lord	68	noble	247
10	*people*	23	lords	4	prince	243
11	**child**	21	*well*	61	*realme*	233
12	*God*	20	*people*	58	*time/s*	232
13	sovereign	20	*realme*	58	land/s	205
14	to say	19	*thing/s*	57	*people*	193
15	persone	18	prince	57	to take	186
16	**Parliament**	17	sovereign	56	right	181
17	*realme*	17	*right*	55	*well*	181
18	*may*	16	*to make*	54	**to keep**	155
19	to come	15	person	54	**year/s**	154
20	*to make*	15	noble	52	**France**	152
21	**high**	15	**same**	52	*thing/s*	141
22	**grace**	14	to take	44	to come	139
23	*thing/s*	13	good	42	**first**	137
24	**true**	13	estate/s	38	**counsell**	136
25	**lordship**	13	**law/s**	38	**subjectes**	133

If we want to go further, we have to take into account the differences between the texts themselves, to see what is happening in each of our two *corpora*, the Lancastrian speeches and the Yorkist ones. For this we must read the tables of frequencies and try to establish a hierarchy between all the differences which are spotted. This will take time, and it would be rash to put too much confidence in the observations, since frequencies are impossible to use at face value: the significance of the frequency of a given word in a text which is part of a *corpus* depends both upon its total frequency in the whole *corpus*, and upon the length of the text in which it occurs. It is therefore preferable to find a proper statistical method to explore this kind of information. The most useful, in my view, is factorial analysis.[79]

What is factorial analysis? Perhaps the best way to explain is to provide a brief introduction to the method. Let us start from an example, albeit a totally arbitrary one, concerning the frequencies of four words in three texts:

Texts	*1*	*2*	*3*	**Total**
king	10	2	18	**30**
council	32	3	5	**40**
commons	45	5	20	**70**
to say	43	10	7	**60**
Total	**130**	**20**	**50**	**200**

This matrix is the matrix T, the origin matrix; its sum is 200. However, it is difficult to point out the real information it may contain: given the relative length of each text, and the frequency of each word in the *corpus*, if each word had been used according to the mathematical mean we would in fact expect a very different matrix, which is easy to calculate by multiplying the margins and dividing the result by the sum of the matrix, in the following manner (for the first cell of the matrix): $30 \times 130 = 3900/200 = 19.5$. We repeat this simple calculation to get a new matrix: the independence matrix, styled T^0 (zero):

[79] On the method, the best introduction is Ph. Cibois, *L'analyse factorielle* (Paris, 1983). I have already given two examples of application of this method: J.Ph. Genet, 'Automatic text processing and factorial analysis: a method for determining the lexicographical horizon of expectation', in A. Gilmour-Bryson, ed., *Computer Applications to Medieval Studies* (Kalamazoo, 1984), pp. 147–75, and 'Un corpus de textes politiques: les textes parlementaires anglais 1376–1410', *Cahiers de la Méditerranée* (special issue: *Histoire et Informatique*, *Actes du IIe Congrès de l'Association Française pour l'histoire et l'informatique* (Nice, 1996), pp. 123–48).

$$T^0 = \quad 70 \quad x \quad \begin{array}{l} 30 \\ 40 \\ 130\ 20\ 50\ /\ 200 \\ 60 \end{array}$$

This, by the way, is a 'factorialization': a matrix may be replaced by a factorialization of its two margins – in fact the multiplication of two vectors – and this offers a useful summary of its content.

Texts	*1*	*2*	*3*	**Total**
king	19.5	3	7.5	**30**
council	26	4	10	**40**
commons	45.5	7	17.5	**70**
to say	39	6	15	**60**
Total	**130**	**20**	**50**	**200**

Now, this independence matrix T^0 is quite different from the origin matrix, maybe because each text has a different subject, maybe because each author has a highly personal style: we do not know yet, but at least if we can measure the differences between the two matrices, we shall be in a better position to look for an explanation. These differences will be made obvious if we calculate $T-T^0$, subtracting the independence matrix from the origin matrix:

Texts	*1*	*2*	*3*	**Total**
king	-9.5	-1	+10.5	**0**
council	+6	-1	-5	**0**
commons	-0.5	-2	+2.5	**0**
to say	+4	+4	-8	**0**
Total	**0**	**0**	**0**	**0**

Here we have in one matrix, R^1 all the 'difference' contained in the data. However, if we wanted to interpret this table, it would be necessary to measure the chi square, a statistical test (also called the Bravais–Pearson test) which would tell us if this 'difference' is statistically significant, given the size of the texts and the relative importance of each word. Factorial analysis is another statistical method, which, though it is close to the chi square, tries to find the best 'summary' of this matrix, that is to replace R^1 by a factorialization of two vectors, related to its margins (i.e. the texts and the words). Multiplied through the matrix, these two vectors/margins will produce a matrix T^1, but it will not be identical with R^1. The subtraction R^1-T^1 will give us a new matrix T^2, which, in turn, may be replaced by a set of two vectors. The values for each point corresponding to a row, and for each point corresponding to a column, which we find in each of these two sets of vectors, may be placed on two graduated axes which will represent each of the two factors. If we draw a first axis horizontally (corresponding to T^1 and the first set of vectors: this is factor 1) and a second axis vertically (corresponding to T^2 and the second set of vectors: this is factor 2), we can now place the points representing rows and columns in a two-dimensional space, according to the values which have been calculated. The distance between the points is significant: if they are close, these rows and/or columns are behaving in the same way; if they are far away, they are behaving differently.

This all sounds very complicated (and as a matter of fact it is even more complicated than this), but the general aim of the method is clear: to replace a complicated matrix by two vectors, on which are read values for each row and each column (which enable us to plot a representation of the distances between these rows and columns on the same graph) and to have for them a percentage of their contribution to each factor (which tells us which row and which column is responsible for shaping the factor). The number of factors to be extracted is equal to the smaller dimension of the matrix less one (i.e. two, in the above example) and, for each of them, the tables produced by the computer give us both a pair of coordinates, necessary to build the graph, and a CPF (contribution per factor). Negative and positive values are arbitrary, so it is therefore preferable to talk of the 'East' or 'West' of the graph, rather than of 'negative' or 'positive' sides. The best way to make use of the results is to get a general idea of what is happening from the graph of factors 1 and 2, and then turn to the table showing the contribution of each row and each column, in order to get a more exact picture.

A quick glance at the analysis done on the Yorkist speeches thus gives a general impression of a triangular opposition on the first two factors (amounting altogether to 39.6 per cent of the 'difference' – remember matrix R^1 – or, more exactly, the variance of the whole system of data): with the possible exception of Neville's sermon, the three Russell sermons are opposed to all other texts. A second opposition between YO3 (North) and BUR with YO2 (South) is also clearly visible. Some words are legible on the graph, but it will become easier to interpret the results if we supplement the graph with a table showing the contribution of the most signficant rows and the most significant columns for both sides (negative and positive) of factors 1 and 2.

TABLE 2

- (West)		Factor 1 + (East)		- (South) Rows		Factor 2 + (North)	
Body	165	said	106	Parliament	92	son	155
member	67	king	24	name	80	truth	61
way	42	son	16	auctoryte	54	duke	34
to say	42	truth	13	charges	39	just	26
man	30	highness	12	land	31	right	26
lost	27	lord	11	Commons	28	crown	21
thing	26	honour	11	present	26	God	19
to speak	25	duke	10	to ordain	23	man	14
well	23			counsel	19	realme	14
to fall	23			to take	18	law	12
to see	22			cause	15		
estate	21			highness	15		
part/s	18			entent	13		
public	16			lords	10		
city	14						
diverse	12						
number	11						
England	11						

				Columns			
RU3	32.4	YO1	7.3	YO2	35	YO3	40
RU2	29.5	YO3	6	BUR	17.4	STR	2.5
RU1	4.1	STR	5.8	ALI	1.3		
NEV	1.1	YO2	3.8				
		ROT	3.3				
		STI	3				
		BUR	2.8				

The first two words associated with Russell's sermons ('body' and 'member') come as no surprise: they express one of the main metaphors used by the bishop: 'That bodye ys hole and stronge whois stomake and bowels is ministered by the vtward membres that that suffiseth to be wele degested . . .'[80] This sentence, a comment on the Roman Senate, introduces a lengthy digression which leads to a quotation from St Paul, I Cor. xii, 26, *Si quid patitur unum membrum, compatiuntur etiam omnia membra.*[81] The second sermon starts where the first ends: from the concept of 'bodye politike', supported this time by a (supposed?) Roman Law quotation borrowed from Pomponius.[82] And the third one is built upon another Pauline text, *[Sicut enim in uno corpore] multa membra habemus, omnia autem membra non eundem actum habent . . .*[83] which, combined with I Cor. xii, enables Russell to use the saint's patronage for the assimilation of 'the mystik or the politike body of congregacione of peuple to the naturalle body of man'.[84] Some of the words associated with the first factor (West) may be linked with this strand of metaphors, such as 'man' (at least five times used in connection with 'body', as in 'body of man' or 'degested out of the best mannys foode and repast') and 'publike'. But these words are also used in other occasions: 'lords and noble men' (four times) and 'lords and wise men' (twice) are repeatedly used to evoke the Roman Senate and, through its example, the role of the English Parliament. 'Publike' is used chiefly in connection with 'body', but – albeit in the same sense – in a more precise context, mostly in the phrase 'this [the] (grete) public body of England'. However, two other words are connected with 'public': 'estates' and 'thing/s'. The word 'thing/s' is especially interesting: 'and by discord fulle grete thynges falle to ruine . . .' is a good example of Russell's large semantic field for this word, which includes the 'thynge public'. 'Estate' is more obviously political, but with Russell the meaning remains that of degree, as in the Three Estates, though he writes also of 'estate of peace', 'hye', 'prosperous' or 'grette' estate. Three words in the list have a life of their own, if I may say so: 'lost', 'number' and 'to fall', used in

---

[80] Chrimes, op. cit., p. 175.

[81] Ibid., p. 176.

[82] Ibid., p. 179; Russell, himself a civil lawyer of repute, purports to quote from *De Usucapionibus*.

[83] Rom. xii 4, and not I Cor. xii, 12 as supposed by S.B. Chrimes, op. cit., p. 185.

[84] Ibid.

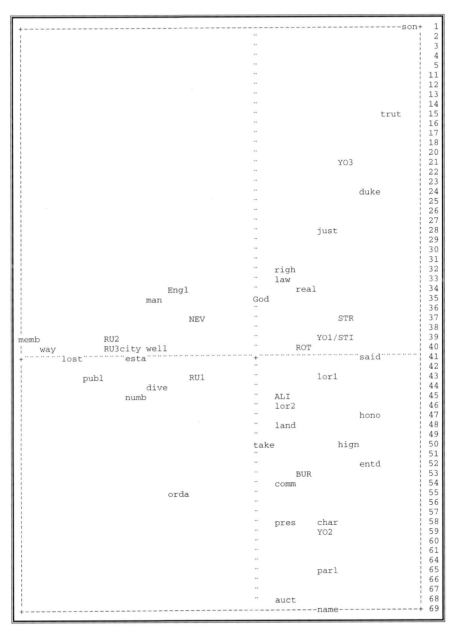

Factorial Graph 1: Axis 1 and 2 for 'Yorkist Speeches'

relation to a commentary on Luke's *Gospel*, xv, 8, which is to be found in the second and third sermons: the story of the woman who had ten 'besauntes or dragmes' and who, having lost one of them, has fallen from the perfection represented by the number ten and is therefore comparable to 'nostra res publica, whyche ys ferre fallen from her perfeccion . . .'[85] Other words are related to the personal style of Russell, such as 'way', or even 'city', often used as synonymous with 'borough' or with 'town', even with 'region' in a list, once with 'realme'. In fact this very word points to what lies at the centre of Russell's sermons, what gives his texts a striking originality which the factorial analysis reveals through this unexpected *catena* of words: the state, a word still unheard and unpronounced in its modern sense.

And what is opposed to Russell's discourse on the state? As a matter of fact, practically all the other texts, led by YO1, YO3 and STR. They tend to share a different group of words. Most striking is the use of 'said', especially prominent in the letters sent by Richard of York and totally absent from Neville's sermon, which probably explains why this last text sides with Russell's sermons: the word certainly betrays a pedestrian style, ill-suited to the high rhetorics of both bishops; it is reminiscent of the precision of the clerk or notary and suits the written document better than the delivered speech, which would account for its use in the rather technical speeches of the other two bishops. But there is more in it: if we take York's letter to the Archbishop of Canterbury which makes up most of YO1, 'said' is used thirty times and helps to reinforce the polarization of the discourse: fourteen times 'oure said' (nine times with 'Soveraine Lord', twice each with 'enemies' and 'commyng', once with 'entent') against eight times 'his saide' (three times with 'land and people', twice with 'reaume and people', and once with 'land', 'Highnesse' and 'most noble personne'), while it is used only five times with 'the' (three times with 'Lordes', and once with 'honoure and well', 'request', 'Jelosy') and twice with 'Faderhood' (for the archbishop to whom the letter is sent). The archbishop is called as witness to observe a political space the two poles of which are the king and the duke himself, with the lords moving between them. Such polarization can also be detected in Rotherham's use of 'the seid adversarie' in his 1474 bellicose speech.

[85] Ibid., p. 191.

The word 'king', though it has a high frequency everywhere – and this needs no explanation – is conspicuously absent from Russell's later sermons, and the reasons for this are so obvious that they need no explanation either, Russell using 'prince' when he needs to speak of kings in general in the first and the third of his sermons, while in sermon two, both these words have apparently dangerous connotations.[86] As for the other words in the East list for factor 1, if they have a low or very low frequency in RU1, they totally disappear from RU2 and RU3 (with the exception of 'lord' which has two occurrences in RU2), so increasing the opposition between Russell's sermons and the rest of the *corpus*. All the same, these words are far from being indifferently used in the other nine texts. 'Son' is there mainly because of its high frequency in Richard of York's claim to the throne in 1460, which contains, in the 'Writyng', a long genealogy. 'Trouth' is shared between Richard's letters (YO1) and his 1460 claim, but in opposite contexts: in 1455, Richard insists upon his keeping of his 'trouth and duetee unto his Highnesse', whereas in 1460, he is asking the Peers 'to helpe and assiste him in trouth and justice': that is, to accept his claim for the crown. In the Yorkist texts, 'Highnesse' and 'Lord' (used most of the time with 'Soveraine', which is also the case in Rotherham's speech in 1474) are substitutes for 'king'. Duke in BUR refers to the Duke of York; in YO3, it designates the English dukes in the genealogy delivered 'in Writyng' by Richard in 1460, while it means the dukes of Brittany and of Burgundy in Rotherham's speech in 1474. 'Honour' means in YO1 and YO3 the 'honour of our said Highness', while in ROT it is the 'honour' and fame won by war and conquest, and is linked more often with the 'land' than with the king.

For the sake of brevity, I shall give but a short analysis of the remaining factors (2–4). On the second factor, the main divide cuts across the Yorkist texts of the first period: on the Southern side (negative) of the graph are York's acceptance of the

---

[86] It may be necessary to remind the reader of the circumstances in which Russell's drafts were written: the first draft was written for a Parliament summoned in the name of Edward V, which never met; the second was written for a parliament of Richard III (but possibly not the one which actually met in 1484). The (very) brief summary in the Roll of Parliament seems to indicate that the speech as actually delivered was some sort of mixture between drafts two and three.

Protectorship (YO2) and Burley's advocacy of this promotion (BUR), while on the Northern side (positive) is York's claim for the crown in 1460 (YO3). The two *catenae* associated with those groups make clear the nature of the difference: with the Protectorship texts, Parliament is in the forefront. It is associated with specific words: 'present' (in 'this present Parliament'), 'matters' (we are dealing with 'matiers of Parliament'), 'the Communes of the land', while Richard's acceptance insists upon the Parliament's 'auctorite'. The king is not forgotten: it is because his 'Highness' is moved by certain 'causes . . . to ordain and name a Protectour and Defendour of this lande' that Richard has accepted to be 'called to the same name and charge', and to govern with the cooperation of the 'Lords Spiritual and Temporal' who will be members of the 'Counsel'. To sum up, this is a 'royal and political' vocabulary (to use Fortescue's phrase), and it is neatly opposed to the 'royal vocabulary' of the 1460 claim, which rests upon descent ('son'), for claiming the 'crown' and 'Realme' of England, according to 'truth', 'right' and the commandments of 'Godds lawe', which every 'man' is bound to observe. The second factor thus highlights the basic flaw in York's position: a constant hesitation between governing with the risk of dropping his claim to the crown, or seizing the crown with the risk of being unable to govern.

TABLE 3

- (West)		Factor 3 + (East)		- (South)		Factor 4 + (North)	
king	86	said	86	son	186	grace	45
war	81	truth	35	duke	73	noble	32
France	61	duty	33	Parliament	37	ennemy	26
adversary	41	God	29	matter	33	sovereign	25
outward	30	noble	27	law	32	realme	24
peace	23	son	23	truth	25	subgets	22
land	22	high	22	just	25	high	18
time	22	grace	16	commons	24	God	16
to consider	21	persone	14	name	23	to know	16
set	19	to ordain	11	auctoryte	21	adversary	14
world	17	body	11	crown	19	myght	14

- (West)		Factor 3 + (East)		- (South)		Factor 4 + (North)	
myght	16	right	10	present	17	honour	13
may	15			spiritual	15	lord	12
own	14			king	13	war	11
crown	12			may	13	to keep	11
grete	12			thought	10	duty	10
ROT	46.3	YO1	18.6	YO3	40.7	YO1	18.1
STI	11.5	YO2	7.9	BUR	14.2	STR	13.3
		STR	7.8	YO2	5.8	ROT	3.6
		YO3	3.9			ALI	2.2
		RU3	1.9				

The third factor exhibits a split between the two words with the highest frequency, 'said' and 'king', which were closely associated on factor 1. Rotherham's and Stillington's speeches have a much lower frequency for 'said' and a much higher frequency for 'king', whereas the 1455 texts and James Strangeways' speech have it the other way. It is quite clear that the two bishops' speeches are made at the king's command, and the importance of 'king' is further augmented by the fact that the chief adversary is the king of France. The two speeches deal with the 'outward' (outward peace, outward princes, outward enemies, outward war as opposed to 'inward' war), and the problem of making 'war' (or 'peace') with 'our adversary of France' in order to ensure the defence and prosperity of 'the King and his land' is the main theme of Rotherham's speech, following a general introduction on justice and on the laws which govern the 'world'. This kind of governmental discourse with its *Realpolitik* flavour is completely opposed to the moralistic vocabulary of dynastic claim, which is characteristic of the 1455 texts, and to the sycophantic excesses of dynastic love, which pervade Strangeways's speech, with the high frequencies of 'high', 'grace', 'noble', 'true', often used in periphrasis to mean the king: 'youre seid moost noble persone', 'your noble and benyngne grace' and the like. The fourth factor leads to the discovery of a fourth opposition, this time chiefly between YO3 (associated with BUR) and YO1 (associated with STR): where the 'constitutional' vocabulary' of YO3 sets it against BUR and YO2 on factor 2, it now unites all three against the 'sentimental' vocabulary of YO1 and STR.

This example shows the interest, but also the limitations of the method. Even so, these limitations are partly the result of imperfect and incomplete data. The selection of words has been made on the hundred words with the highest frequency in the whole *corpus*, but some words which are highly characteristic of only one text would not qualify, because if the text is not very long, the frequency would fall under the limit used here (=13). The possibility of working on the whole vocabulary of the *corpus* must not be discarded, though it has to be admitted that the preparation of the data will take a very long time. The counting of the words also remains insecure as long as a parallel text in lemmatized modern spelling has not been produced: it would be fine to have at least semi-automatic software to help us to achieve this, but none exists for Middle English, at least to my knowledge; if it did, the frequencies indicated here might be modified. But there is at least something which can be done to conclude this paper, and that is to reintroduce these same texts into another *corpus*, the *corpus* of 'English Tracts' which I have described above.

TABLE 4

Factor 1		Factor 2		Factor 3		Factor 4	
-	+	-	+	-	+	-	+
TOC 50.9	BON 43.2	BON 19.5	GOE 59.5	TOC 14	RUS 60.8	RUS 19.3	YOR 64.9
RUS 2.4	FOR 1.5	TOC 8.3	FOR 12.3	GOE 3.5	DPY 12.3	GOE 2.7	FOR 5.3

It is quite noticeable that, while in the Yorkist *corpus* there was a strong opposition between Russell's sermons (here RUS) and the Yorkist texts of the 1455–60 period (YO1–3, here YOR), in the new *corpus* both groups of texts are at the centre of the factorial graph, very close to one another, although the more stylistically elaborate Russell sermons appear more prominently on the first axis, standing more especially in opposition with the *Boke of Noblesse*. Is this a conclusive proof of the partisan tone of Russell's drafts? One must doubt it until the list of associated words has been examined in close detail. It is impossible to give here the detailed results of the analysis, but the main oppositions on the text are summarized in table 4, and this clearly proves that the opposition between RUS and YOR surfaces only on the fourth factor (only

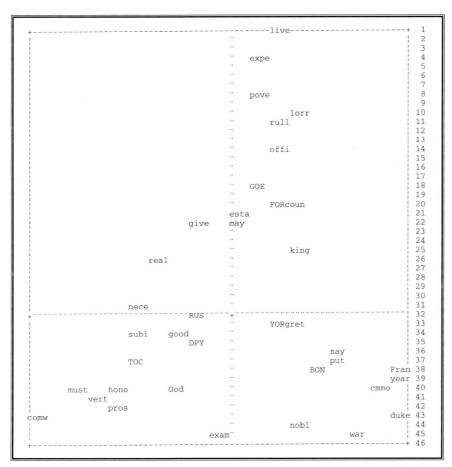

Factorial Graph 2: Axis 1 and 2, Seven English Political 'Tracts', 195 words

13.5 per cent of the variance of the system). The main opposition is that between the *Tree of Commonwealth*, on one side, and the *Boke of Noblesse*, on the other, which makes up most of the first factor (94.1 per cent), the first factor alone accounting for 28.2 per cent of the variance. The second factor expresses the opposition between Fortescue's writings on the positive side, and the two tracts by Dudley and William of Worcester (25.1 per cent) and the third is made up by an opposition between Russell and the *Somnium* on the positive side, and the *Tree of Commonwealth* on the negative one (15.9 per cent).

As one can see, the method offers a useful tool for exploring the distribution of the words between the different texts, and through such a statistical analysis it is possible to go beyond the surface of the words and to point out easily where the main changes occur, where the main tensions between those speaking are still audible. This is especially true if we manage to reach the next stage, of which I have here given only a few examples (for instance, with the contexts in which the word 'said' was used in York's letters): Russell may be using different words from those of Fortescue, of Sir Thomas More or of Edmund Dudley, but he is nonetheless discussing the same reality, that of an emergent modern state, even though that very word is not yet at his disposal. Before thinking about new politics, before connecting automatically Tudor times with modernity, much more work has to be done to explore the emergence of an English political language: for this, we need to build a dictionary of the political language of the later Middle Ages, taking into account both the chronology of texts and their nature (that is, literary genre, occasion of writing, stylistical choices). I have myself tried to arrange at least six of these *corpora*: one for religious–political texts (mainly Wycliffite); three for poetical texts (Langland and the alliterative tradition; Gower, Hoccleve and Lydgate; and R.H. Robbins' political poems), one for speeches; and one for political tracts (with a specific group for texts translated from the French). Each of these *corpora* makes it possible to see the emergence of new concepts and words, enriching the language with which the English communicate and discuss their political experience. The study of these *corpora* is an enormous task, especially if one applies the method outlined here, but England offers a comparatively more favourable field for this than most other European countries, since English was at the time in itself a relatively new language for political élites. In the first half of the fourteenth century, there is no doubt that much was still transacted in French. The *corpus* of political texts written in English is what it is: at least its limited length is an asset in such an undertaking.

APPENDIX

I. SPEECHES OF THE YORKIST PERIOD (1455–85): DATA

YO1: Letters of Richard, Duke of York, 1455.
BUR: William Burley speaks for Richard, Duke of York, 1455.
YO2: Richard, Duke of York, agrees to become Protector, 1455.
YO3: Richard, Duke of York, claims the crown, 1460.
NEV: George Neville, sermon for Edward IV, 1461
STR: James Strangeways, Speaker's Speech, 1461
STI: Robert Stillington, Speech, 1468.
ALI: William Allington, Speaker's Speech, 1472.
ROT: Thomas Rotherham(?), Speech, 1474.
RU1: Sermon of Bishop John Russell, draft 1, 1483.
RU2: Sermon of Bishop John Russell, draft 2, 1483.
RU3: Sermon of Bishop John Russell, draft 3, 1483.

	YO1	BUR	YO2	YO3	NEV	STR	STI	ALI	ROT	RU1	RU2	RU3	Total	
said	44	23	26	23		44	16	8	29	6	3	2	224	seid/e, said/e
king	7	11	3	15	1	5	28	6	48	20	2	1	147	king/s, kyng/e/s
land	11	19	10	1	1		13	5	32	14	5	5	116	lande/s, lond/e/s
gret	2	6	3	1	2	7	7	6	22	29	9	8	102	gret/e, grett/er/est
may	3	16	1	6	4	1	3	5	26	13	7	9	94	may/might
God	16		2	6	14	8	8	2	4	10	3	6	79	God
time	1	1		2	4	2	11	4	17	16	12	6	76	time/s
body	1			2	1		1	1		11	28	31	76	body/ies
man	2	2		7	7	2	1		8	14	15	13	71	man/men
lor1	14	1	7	3	1	4	2	6	18	10	2		68	lord/e
lor2	8	9	5	2	1	2	9	6	6	11	2	3	64	lords/es
well	3		1		4	2	3	1	11	14	11	11	61	well
peop	8	2	2		3	1	1	1	10	21	4	5	58	people
real	3			3	1	16	9	3	12	3	4	4	58	realme, reaume
prin	3			4	1	6	7	3	8	15		10	57	prince/s
thig	4		3	2	2	1	2	1	7	10	14	11	57	thing/s
souv	12		6			3	2	5	18	7	2	1	56	sovereign
righ	12	1		7	5	5	5	2	7	4	5	2	55	right
make	5	4	2	4	2	1	1	4	11	9	6	5	54	to make
pers	7	7	5	2		6	2	9	4	6	3	3	54	person/s
nobl	8			2	1	14	2	5	1	14	1	4	52	noble
same	5	1	1	4		5	6	4	11	7	4	3	51	same
take	2	4	7		2	3	3	4	4	8	4	3	44	to take
good	4	7	3	1	4	4	1	1	6	5	1	5	42	good
esta	1		2	1		1	3	5		7	10	8	38	estate/s
law		1	2	8	1		5	2	8	6	3	2	38	law/s
say				1		4			1	11	11	8	36	to say
hign	5	8	3			3	6	4	4	2			35	highness
call	3		2	5		7	1	1	4	8	2	2	35	to call

I. S PEECHES OF THE Y ORKIST P ERIOD (1455–85): D ATA (cont.)

												Total	
caus		7	3		1	1	2		6	8	2	4	34	cause/s
high	7	4				8	1	4		6	1	3	34	high
Engl	4			3		2	2		1	6	7	7	32	England
memb									1	6	7	16	30	member/s
parl		10	9			1	1	3	1	5			30	parlement
can	1	1	1		1	1			9	11	1	3	29	can
comm		11	1				5	3	1	7		1	29	Commons
subg	2				3		7	11	2			4	29	subget/tes
unde	4	1		3	1	2	1	3	3	8	3		29	understand
dive	1	1	2	2			3	4	3	6	6		28	diverse
ente	8	2		1		1	7	2	3	1	3		28	entent
fall	1			1		1		5	5	9	5		27	to fall
see								7	7	6	7		27	to see
come	1	6				3	3	3	5	3	2		26	to come
grac	8		1	7		1	1	5	2	1			26	grace
just	2	1		7		1	6	1	3	3	2		26	justice
matt	1	5	1	4			3	2	5	2	3		26	matter/s
adve						5	6	13		1			25	adversary/ies
own	3			1		3		10	2	3	3		25	own/e
Fran	1			2			9	12					24	Fraunce
char	1		10			2		7	3		1		24	charge/s
hono	9		5		1	1		7	1				24	honour/e/s
part	1		2	2	4	1	3	11					24	partie/s
peac			3			6	3	9	1	1	1		24	peace
mane	3			2		2	1	1	3	5	6		23	maner
war	1							20		1	1		23	war, werre/s
duke		3		9		1	1	6	2				22	duke
enne	5				4	3	2	5	1	1	1		22	enemie/s, ennemie/s
way			1			2		1		8	10		22	way/s
coun	3		6			2	1	1	7		1		21	counsel
day	2	3		1		2		5	3	3	2		21	day/s
defe		4			4	3		6	4				21	defense/ce
orda		3	5	1			2		4	5			20	to ordain
cour		4			1		5		5	1	3		19	court/s
mygh	2				3	5	1	8					19	mighty/iest
must		2	1	1		2		4	4	2	2		19	must
name		2	11		1		1	1	2		1		19	name
numb		2	1		1	1		1	4	5	4		19	number
show	7	1		1		1	3	1	3	1	1		19	to show
entd	5	5	2		1		2	3					18	to entend
know	5		1	3	1	1		4		1	2		18	to know
lost		2				1		1	1	6	7		18	lost
powe	1	2	3		1	3	2	1	2		3		18	power
true	2			2		3		5	2	1	2	1	18	true, trowe

												Σ	
city	1	1		2			1	1	1	2	4	5	17	city/ies
keep	3			1		1	4		4	1		3	17	to keep
long				1	2				3	6	3	2	17	long
outw					3				8	3	1	2	17	outward/s
set				1	4				6	2	2	2	17	to set
pres		4	4		3				1	4	1		17	present
son			14		2				1				17	son
spea									8	6	3		17	to speak
cons		1	1		3	1			7	3			16	to consider
plac			1			2			3	7	3		16	place/s
poli	1	4			1	1			2	3	4		16	politique
thou		4	1	1				5	3	1	1		16	thought/s
trut	7			8					1				16	trouth, trowth
pars									2	5	2	6	15	part/s
pros	4		2			1	1		4	2		1	15	prosperite
send	2	2			2	3	1		2	2		1	15	to send
auct		2	7						4	1			14	authority
duty	9	2	1			1						1	14	duty
labo	2	1			2	3			2	2		2	14	labour
publ	1		1						4	3	5		14	public
spir		3	2			6			1	1	1		14	spiritual
stan	1			1		1			4	5	2		14	to stand
sure	3		1		3	2			2	3			14	surety
crow			4			5			4				13	crown
reas	1		2	1		2			3	1		3	13	reason
roya	4			2	1	1	2			2		1	13	royal
worl					3				4	5	1		13	world

II. RESULTS OF THE FACTORIAL ANALYSIS

100 words, $f^2=1.108272$

Specific value	%	Specific value	%
Factor 1 0.291577	26.3	Factor 2 0.174513	15.7
Factor 3 0.143612	13.0	Factor 4 0.121899	11.0
Factor 5 0.090024	8.1		

1° Factorial Coordinates (F=) and Contributions Per Factor (CPF): Rows

	F=1	CPF	F=2	CPF	F=3	CPF	F=4	CPF	F=5	CPF
said	691	106	23	0	438	86	57	2	-3	0
king	409	24	194	9	-541	86	-190	13	10	0
land	250	7	-399	31	-306	22	-113	4	-46	1
gret	-152	2	-104	2	-245	12	48	1	-156	8
may	-23	0	-79	1	-283	15	-238	13	-272	22
God	73	0	380	19	429	29	296	16	184	9

1° Factorial Coordinates (F=) and Contributions Per Factor (CPF): Rows (cont)

	F=1	CPF	F=2	CPF	F=3	CPF	F=4	CPF	F=5	CPF
time	-300	7	136	2	-379	22	48	0	15	0
body	-1479	165	118	2	268	11	1	0	44	0
man	-658	30	350	14	111	2	-190	6	75	1
lor1	407	11	-76	1	69	1	268	12	233	12
lor2	250	4	-300	10	54	0	-106	2	-218	10
well	-622	23	68	0	-98	1	158	4	123	3
peop	-227	3	-94	1	-11	0	165	4	48	0
real	273	4	387	14	-37	0	416	24	-173	6
prin	-97	1	266	7	-57	0	63	1	-126	3
thig	-676	26	74	1	107	1	-8	0	225	9
souv	362	7	-177	3	-53	0	434	25	299	16
righ	219	3	530	26	293	10	151	3	98	2
make	-96	0	44	0	-10	0	-85	1	-47	0
pers	281	4	-305	8	353	14	55	0	-372	24
nobl	170	1	250	5	505	27	508	32	-407	28
same	165	1	239	5	-107	1	101	1	-52	0
take	-5	0	-498	18	178	3	-67	0	36	0
good	65	0	-245	4	190	3	-9	0	-166	4
esta	-743	21	-38	0	219	4	-46	0	-88	1
law	138	1	444	12	-204	3	-598	32	166	3
say	-1065	40	75	0	-42	0	-85	1	23	0
hign	597	12	-509	15	39	0	-20	0	-455	23
call	214	2	381	8	322	7	-44	0	-21	0
caus	-118	0	-518	15	-169	2	-323	8	-219	5
high	238	2	-57	0	567	22	478	18	-658	47
Engl	-578	11	393	8	316	6	-58	0	45	0
memb	-1497	67	67	0	203	2	-48	0	20	0
parl	487	7	-1359	92	309	6	-718	37	-259	6
can	-225	1	-117	1	-361	8	89	1	57	0
comm	250	2	-771	28	-203	2	-597	24	-996	92
subg	131	0	8	0	-284	5	563	22	-306	9
unde	-539	8	133	1	144	1	263	5	67	0
dive	-669	12	-176	1	103	1	61	0	76	1
ente	383	4	155	1	45	0	279	5	-66	0
fall	-933	23	123	1	-147	1	78	0	166	2
see	-904	22	55	0	-300	5	39	0	106	1
come	-99	0	-392	7	-202	2	-234	3	-667	37
grac	569	8	178	1	422	9	857	45	-5	0
just	422	5	778	26	-64	0	-642	25	8	0

	F=1	CPF	F=2	CPF	F=3	CPF	F=4	CPF	F=5	CPF
matt	8	0	51	0	13	0	-737	33	-261	6
adve	485	6	253	3	-901	41	478	14	128	1
own	-156	1	164	1	-531	14	327	6	324	8
Fran	567	8	397	6	-1120	61	-6	0	377	11
char	414	4	-998	39	-16	0	-275	4	1179	107
hono	672	11	-333	4	293	4	486	13	799	49
part	627	9	141	1	-346	6	261	4	123	1
peac	291	2	-266	3	-694	23	74	0	332	8
mane	-617	9	371	5	437	9	60	0	-37	0
war	259	2	136	1	-1326	81	452	11	496	18
duke	672	10	963	34	-108	1	-1188	73	-101	1
enne	399	3	208	2	39	0	703	26	-92	1
way	-1387	42	44	0	153	1	-76	0	252	4
coun	195	1	-730	19	339	5	-126	1	617	26
day	-119	0	-7	0	-272	3	-167	1	-137	1
defe	416	4	-171	1	-452	9	51	0	-515	18
orda	-513	5	-828	23	514	11	-400	8	197	2
cour	-229	1	-480	7	179	1	-126	1	-1065	69
mygh	603	7	220	2	-656	16	556	14	70	0
must	-180	1	-125	0	-337	4	-354	5	-10	0
name	412	3	-1597	80	586	13	-721	23	1237	93
numb	-759	11	-217	1	91	0	-194	2	-133	1
show	260	1	106	0	476	9	368	6	-210	3
entd	691	9	-648	12	349	4	86	0	-386	9
know	54	0	143	1	255	2	606	16	485	14
lost	-1220	27	-59	0	80	0	-195	2	-144	1
powe	428	3	-475	7	175	1	48	0	-15	0
true	202	1	340	3	375	5	292	4	-493	14
city	-884	14	34	0	161	1	75	0	-52	0
keep	-8	0	18	0	-26	0	529	11	-159	1
long	-574	6	104	0	-88	0	190	1	-60	0
outw	-106	0	88	0	-934	30	143	1	236	3
set	-238	1	146	1	-754	19	125	1	262	4
pres	251	1	-966	26	-42	0	-651	17	37	0
son	965	16	2346	155	828	23	-2152	186	132	1
spea	-1211	25	2	0	80	0	-141	1	-83	0
cons	348	2	44	0	-812	21	-68	0	265	4
plac	-369	2	85	0	-242	2	-123	1	-211	2
poli	-544	5	-581	9	464	7	-182	1	558	16
thou	95	0	-378	4	-366	4	-518	10	-278	4
trut	892	13	1524	61	1038	35	-805	25	346	6

1° Factorial Coordinates (F=) and Contributions Per Factor (CPF): Rows (cont)

	F=1	CPF	F=2	CPF	F=3	CPF	F=4	CPF	F=5	CPF
part	-1096	18	15	0	-61	0	-22	0	-2	0
pros	371	2	-177	1	106	0	413	6	498	12
send	343	2	-86	0	-86	0	221	2	-430	9
auct	227	1	-1534	54	570	9	-795	21	828	31
duty	673	6	82	0	1088	33	539	10	694	22
labo	159	0	69	0	-82	0	297	3	-171	1
publ	-1075	16	-131	0	347	3	-56	0	170	1
spir	285	1	-29	0	-84	0	-709	17	644	19
stan	-138	0	234	1	-411	5	-76	0	126	1
sure	485	3	31	0	189	1	525	9	88	0
crow	693	6	985	21	-684	12	-781	19	330	5
reas	-264	1	-61	0	610	10	-103	0	234	2
roya	326	1	631	9	529	7	101	0	151	1
worl	-69	0	30	0	-812	17	11	0	83	0
		1000		1000		1000		1000		1000

2° Factorial Coordinates (F=) and Contributions Per Factor (CPF): Columns

	F=1	CPF	F=2	CPF	F=3	CPF	F=4	CPF	F=5	CPF
YO1	477	73	142	11	534	186	486	181	141	21
BUR	359	28	-693	174	4	0	-523	142	-684	328
YO2	443	38	-1048	350	453	79	-357	58	744	342
YO3	581	60	1160	400	326	39	-978	407	98	6
NEV	-369	11	224	7	231	9	228	10	230	14
STR	508	58	255	25	412	78	495	133	-298	65
STI	320	30	100	5	-442	115	-54	2	51	2
ALI	218	8	-214	13	113	4	233	22	-521	148
ROT	236	33	51	3	-617	463	159	36	160	50
RU1	-282	41	-89	7	-57	3	-76	7	-107	19
RU2	-979	295	102	5	78	4	-41	1	67	4
RU3	-997	324	38	1	170	19	5	0	12	0
		1000		1000		1000		1000		1000

2

PATRONAGE AND POLEMIC

Colin Richmond

'My opinion is that one should always treat the utterances of old schoolmasters with
caution. They are forced by the circumstances of their job to amass a whole collection
of verbal patterns, and on these they come, in the long run, to depend, as on so many
secure nails, many of which are not wholly free from rust. . . . Very few of them keep
their minds supple enough to retain the power of criticising their own prejudices.'

Marc Bloch, *Strange Defeat* (English translation, Oxford, 1949), pp. 114–15.

The paper has three parts: Patronage, Ideas, Polemic, ideas having made an
appearance at a late stage.

Part one begins at Kirby Muxloe on 19 May 1957. That is the day on which
I first saw a fifteenth-century house and fell in love with it and the fifteenth
century. It was also the day on which I became involved with William, Lord
Hastings. Many files and nearly forty years later I still have not written about
William, even though he was my reason for going from Leicester to Oxford in
October 1959, and in spite of these words of William Huse Dunham Junior,
written to my Leicester tutor, Geoffrey Martin, on 23 March 1959:

I am delighted to learn that my study of Lord Hastings has encouraged
someone to go on to do a thorough job on a fascinating man with a most
remarkable career. . . . I have no intention . . . to pursue further research on
Hastings and so please tell Mr Richmond to go right ahead and make the
most of what I think an excellent opportunity to do a very useful and perhaps
even important bit of fifteenth-century history. . . . Thank you so much for
calling both Mr Richmond and his study to my attention. Do let me know how
he makes out and also what becomes of him in the next few years for the time
is coming for us to recruit a really outstanding young man [*sic*] in English
Constitutional History [*sic*].

As Michael Hicks has recently charged me with reducing the history of late medieval English society to 'meaningless anarchy', I do not quite think I have fulfilled Professor Dunham's hopes for English Constitutional History, or not at any rate in the manner he anticipated. Where late medieval English society and 'meaningless anarchy' are concerned there are two things to be said. First: thank you for the perceptive compliment, Michael – being an anarchist I am delighted that my history has been seen for what it is. Second: all life is 'meaningless anarchy'; it is only we historians who impose meaning and order upon it; thus, to be seen as a historian who has actually recreated the original in his work affords me double delight.[1] Possibly there is a third thing: did Michael mean to write 'meaningful anarchy'?

What I may have been able to do over the last forty years is to carry out Professor Dunham's specific wish that 'Maybe Mr Richmond can retrieve Hastings from the charge of "conspiracy" against Richard III made in that king's biography [Paul Murray Kendall's *Richard III*, published in 1955]. I certainly hope so'. The conspiracy that never was, rather than the study of William, Lord Hastings, that never was, brings us to the remarkable career of a Leicestershire gentleman. That career provokes two questions. First: was William a decent chap, that is a politically decent chap? His success as a politician and his dramatic failure in 1483 beg all the big questions. I shall return to so pivotal a theme in parts two and three, but I urge this particular question on you right away because 13 June 1483 is a date to concentrate the mind – above all, on the parameters within which the political class worked. Equally, Richard of Gloucester's behaviour, both as duke and as king – his callous treatment of elderly dowagers, including his mother-in-law, on the one hand, his not dowering his queen and the murder of his nephews, let alone the usurpation itself, a model of immoral management techniques, on the other – as well as the rhetoric of his proclamations, has to exercise us most fully in any discussion of constitutionality. Secondly: what is the significance of those famous fees William took from others – others than the Crown? It is a long list which has fascinated me for over thirty years, if only because I do not know what to do with it, where exactly to place it, what context into which to put it.

---

[1] For the 'meaningless anarchy' see the late and much-missed Roger Virgoe's review of two books by Michael Hicks, *EHR*, CX (1995), 171.

Here we come squarely face to face with patronage. In general I want to say nothing about the place of patronage in politics because I think Rosemary Horrox has said all that need be said, said with a sensitivity and an intelligence far beyond my own.[2] Yet, how does one assess those fees of William, Lord Hastings? Let me remind you of their number and variety. My latest count is twenty-three or twenty-four by 1483, if we exclude Charles the Rash and Louis XI, as I am not at all sure we should, for the fees they offered and which William gratefully received demonstrate the internationality of a senior English politician's position. The European nature, in other words, of English politics during the Wars of the Roses is something, despite Sandy Grant and Cliff Davies in particular, still not sufficiently stressed: if the battle of Waterloo was won on the playing fields of Eton, the battle of Dadlington was lost in the anterooms of Blois.[3]

There is, to my knowledge, no comparable list, save one of Sir John Howard's of about 1466, and that is not strictly comparable, because it dates from too early in the Suffolk gentleman's even more dramatic career than that of his Leicestershire friend (after all, Sir John was to achieve a dukedom before he too came crashing down) when Sir John was still four years away from becoming a

---

[2] 'Introduction: the roots of service', *Richard III: A Study of Service* (Cambridge, 1989), pp. 1–26; 'Service', in Rosemary Horrox, ed., *Fifteenth-Century Attitudes: Perceptions of society in late medieval England* (Cambridge, 1994), pp. 61–78; 'Personalities and Politics', in A.J. Pollard, ed., *The Wars of the Roses* (1995); 'Caterpillars of the Commonwealth? Courtiers in Late Medieval England', in Rowena E. Archer and Simon Walker, eds, *Rulers and Ruled in Late Medieval England: Essays presented to Gerald Harriss* (1995), pp. 1–15.

[3] C.S.L. Davies, 'The Wars of the Roses in European Context', in Pollard, ed., *Wars of the Roses*, pp. 162–85; 'Bishop John Morton, the Holy See and the Accession of Henry VII', *EHR*, CII (1987), 2–30; 'Richard III, Brittany and Henry Tudor', *NottMS*, XXXVII (1993), 110–26; 'The Alleged "Sack of Bristol": International Ramifications of Breton Privateering, 1484–5', *BIHR*, 67 (1994), 230–9; Alexander Grant, 'Foreign Affairs under Richard III', in J. Gillingham, ed. *Richard III: A Medieval Kingship* (1993), pp. 113–32. I ought also to notice A.V. Antonovics, 'Henry VII, King of England, "By Grace of Charles VIII of France"', in Ralph A. Griffiths and James Sherborne, eds, *Kings and Nobles in the Later Middle Ages. A Tribute to Charles Ross* (Gloucester, 1986), pp. 169–84. Is it not time for a thorough reassessment 'in European Context' of English politics 1469–71, or better 1467–71, or even 1464–75?

lord.[4] Still, the Howard list shows Sir John in receipt of about fifteen fees from a dozen persons, and although they were predominantly of a local and Mowbray kind, a comparison might be attempted; we would need to look at when William's fees were first proffered in order to make it, William having six fees in 1461–2, and twelve by May 1469. Here, however, is not the place to take a comparison further, any more than it is the place to construct chronologies of the rise and rise of William Hastings and John Howard. All that needs stressing in William's case is the range of fee-givers, from the queen, her father and mother, Richard, Earl of Warwick, George, Duke of Clarence, and Alice Chaucer, to Sir Walter Griffith, Thomas Chaworth esquire (both William's own retainers), Ramsey, Chester and St Albans abbeys, and the corporation of Derby.[5]

What is this list of over twenty fees about? Nothing to have been fascinated by for thirty years, you might be thinking. Were not the fees simply inducements to the Lord Chamberlain that he might look after the landed interests of his patrons (clients?) in the region where he and his quasi-royal affinity dominated, the Midlands, and more importantly that he might support the interests of those patrons (clients?) at the royal council and in the privy chamber? That, surely, is all that patronage-politics amounts to: public figures promoting private interests.

[4] The list is in *The Howard Household Books*, introduction by Anne Crawford (Gloucester, 1992), I, pp. 456–7. I say friends because it is unlikely they were enemies, if they ever were, until after 11 April 1483, when Howard dined with Hastings in London (ibid., II, p. 384). The dinner was two days after the death of Edward IV and over a week before his funeral. It is a pity that no informant of Dominic Mancini's was likely to have been there: for Mancini's informants, see A.J. Pollard, 'Dominic Mancini's Narrative of the Events of 1483', *NottMS*, XXXVIII (1994), 152–63. On the other hand, as John, Lord Howard appears as an agent of Richard, Duke of Gloucester, doing dirty work on his behalf at Christmas 1472, at the dinner on 11 April 1483 he might well have been making overtures to Hastings on Gloucester's behalf; it was Sir William Tyrell who remembered John, Lord Howard's 'great wordes of manasse' to Master Piers Baxter, confessor and feoffee of Elizabeth, Countess of Oxford: Michael Hicks, 'The Last Days of Elizabeth, Countess of Oxford', collected in his *Richard III and his Rivals* (1991), p. 310.

[5] My list has been composed from a number of sources, too many of them to be discussed here; the curious reader will also have to be patient: a paper on the list and its significance is one I do intend to write, as David Morgan is still declining to do so. Bodleian Library, Carte MS 78 is the most comprehensive list and was, if I recall correctly, compiled by William Dugdale; where it can be checked against the original it is, as one might anticipate, almost invariably accurate.

I suppose the only lively issue is the ethical one. This, I remember, was debated with some heat during the first of the Fifteenth-Century Colloquia at Cardiff in 1970, when Professor Roskell stoutly defended the immorality of Bastard Feudalism. I, on the other hand, being a Namierite, believe that patronage worked for good and bad depending upon the particular circumstances of persons, place, time and the matter involved. After all, and for example, a stewardship from Warwick the Kingmaker carrying a fee of £10 or £20 granted to William sometime in 1468–9 was not going to determine the Chamberlain's decision on whether it was to be war or peace with the Hanse, any more than a fee of 5 marks yearly from Welbeck Abbey in 1477 was going to upset anyone's applecart, unless it was those of the abbey's tenants. Big men ganging up on little ones is not the matter under discussion in part one; it will be in part three. Here I am suggesting that patronage gets certain things done, serves certain interests, but when the chips are down (the fat is in the fire), as in 1469–71, or 1475, or 1478, or especially in 1483 or 1485, the politics of patronage become subordinate to the politics of politics, which may comprise loyalties engendered by patronage but are determined by what we might choose to call political ideas, as it is those ideas which, at such moments, occupy to the exclusion of almost everything else the minds of the decision-makers.

This is not to say that the decisions made, the courses chosen, peace in the midst of war in 1475 for instance, are disinterested. 'What is right for me is right for England', has always been and always will be the order of priority of the English governing class: it would not be a governing class otherwise. The English political élite is, in an earlier political phrase, the community of the realm. If it regarded itself as anything less it would have vanished long ago. Such community of identity between governors, government and nation is *the* political idea in English history between the 1290s and the 1890s, the political idea of the governing class. That class's sole crisis of identity arrived in the mid-seventeenth century. It never achieved the dimensions of a trauma, as, say, in France in the 1790s: Oliver Cromwell, when all is said and done, knew he was as surely born to rule the realm at Westminster as he was the roost in Huntingdonshire.

What about that affinity of William, Lord Hastings, getting Edward IV his throne back in 1471, you ask? In other words, what about the military aspect of patronage, retaining and the affinity? Whatever else William's successful (and

oft-cited) call-up of his retinue to fight for Edward IV in March 1471 illustrates, it
has to be evidence of what a good chap William's retainers reckoned him to be, a
better chap than Richard, Earl of Warwick, and George, Duke of Clarence, a
better chap than Margaret of Anjou, and the best chap for them, for Edward IV,
and for England. The point is made in reverse by John Paston III not turning out
for John Howard, Duke of Norfolk, at Bosworth, and Sir William Stonor not
joining Francis, Viscount Lovell, to put down the Yorkist Uprising of October
1483: Richard III was not a king for whom they were willing to fight.[6]

I am, I have to confess, modifying what I wrote in 1965. It is not quite true
that I have never written up William, Lord Hastings. I did so for the Keele
University History Society, then called the Trevelyan Society, in a paper read to it
on 23 February 1965 and called 'William, Lord Hastings: The rise of a
gentleman'. Let me quote from that paper, which on the whole stands the test of
thirty years fairly well. Spot, however, the fatal flaws in the following:

> Just what was the power of which he [William] could dispose is the real subject
> of this paper, for in an age when politics was above all a matter of patronage,
> the greater a man's wealth and the higher his social standing the more political
> power lay ready for him to use. . . . His political influence sprang from two
> sources: his landed wealth and his close contact with the King. . . . [His fees]

---

[6] The retinue of William, Lord Hastings, joined him (and Edward IV) at Leicester, 'stiryd by his
messages sent unto them, and by his servaunts, frinds, and lovars, suche as were in the contrie', *Historie of
the Arrivall of Edward IV in England*, ed. John Bruce (Camden Society, 1838), pp. 8–9. Howard's summons
(or polite demand) to John Paston in August 1485 is in *Paston Letters and Papers of the Fifteenth Century*, ed.
Norman Davies (Oxford, 1976), II, no. 801; Lovell's to Sir William Stonor of 11 October 1483 (even
more courteous) is *The Stonor Letters and Papers 1290–1483*, ed. C.L. Kingsford (Camden Society, 3rd ser.,
1919), XXX, no. 333. Paston and Stonor presumably did not care for bullies, particularly no doubt royal
ones. For Lovell bullying Katherine, widow of William, Lord Hastings, see the indenture between them of
5 May 1485, BL Harleian MS 3881, f. 24, cf. John Nichols, *History and Antiquities of the County of Leicester*
(1804, republished Leicester, 1971), III, part II, p. 572, an instance of the dog taking a leaf out of the
hog's book. Those 'servants and lovers' of Richard, Duke of Gloucester, who 'were slayn in his service at
the batelles of Bernett, Tukysbery [and] at other feldes or jorneys' in 1469–71, and whom he gratefully
remembered by name in 1477, did not live to see the sort of man the youth turned into: Charles Ross,
'Some "Servants and Lovers" of Richard in his Youth', *The Ricardian*, 4, no. 55 (Dec. 1976), 2–4.

demonstrate the way in which society worked; it was a society where politics were as much a matter of intricate personal relationships and the give and take of patronage as they were in the eighteenth century.

Leaving everything else aside, social standing (and wealth) is no longer what counts for me; it began not to quite shortly after 1965. What I would stress, and began stressing soon after 1965, is what Thomas More stressed about William: his 'great authority with his prince'. Everything stems from that. When William lost his prince he lost his head. Nonetheless, you will have observed that in 1965 I was not as keen on political theory as I might or, some will think, ought to have been, and this despite the fact that my best marks in Finals in 1959 had been in the Political Ideas paper, said by the external examiner, none other than Professor Roskell, to be a paper of some merit, and despite having written a thesis entitled 'Royal Administration and The Keeping of the Seas, 1422–1485', a thesis which dealt with notions of naval defence and naval offence, notions which involved thinking and theory of some kind, though exactly how political we might wish to consider them I am less sure.

What more should be said about patronage? Having just mentioned one thesis let me cite another of ten years later, Christine Carpenter's Cambridge thesis of 1976, 'Political Society in Warwickshire 1401–1472':[7]

After 1446 'when the Warwick lands were farmed to John Beauchamp and [Lord] Sudeley on the death of Henry Beauchamp, patronage became blatantly partisan. The huge windfall of grants from the Warwick lands went exclusively to the [royal] Household. Edmund Mountford, who, through his father William, was closely involved with the ruling clique, was the only Warwickshire man to benefit. . . . Furthermore [we are now into the 1450s], the King and his friends, in supporting Somerset and Edmund Mountford against Warwick, ensured not only that Warwick would quarrel with Buckingham, but that this quarrel would push him into the Yorkist camp. This situation achieved, they then failed to give Buckingham the consistent

[7] I quote from pp. 152, 223, and 225–6.

support he needed. Buckingham probably lost Atherstone in 1453, and he and his men received virtually no patronage in the county until 1459–60, when their identification with the court meant that these grants only estranged them further from the rest of the Warwickshire gentry. . . . It may truly be said that the Yorkists won Warwickshire not because of any virtues of their own, but because the Lancastrians had made themselves unacceptable to the gentry.

Which reminds me of the comment of a Ugandan student in an application to the University of Keele in 1972: 'You see,' he wrote, 'I am such a man who likes patronage all the time, isn't bad is it?'

Let me end part one, and begin part two, by quoting from Tim Travers, *The Killing Ground: The British Army, the Western Front and the Emergence of Modern Warfare 1900–1918*.[8] I shall not discuss how General Sir Henry Wilson 'engineered his own appointment to command the Staff College in 1906', nor the hours of work at the War Office – arrival at 11 a.m., riding in Hyde Park every morning and often on arrival the command, 'don't bother to come back after lunch' – nor it being 'great personages, even great ladies, [who] exercised the higher patronage', but the author's summary of what he calls 'The System at Work':

> . . . one is struck by the presence of a highly personalized system in which the influence of friends and enemies made an enormous difference to a man's career. It is also noticeable that a confusing variety of influences made themselves felt. These ranged from personal, regimental and arm rivalries, to the question of whom one was or was not with at Staff College, and to the influence or otherwise of powerful individuals as protectors, besides the traditional army reliance on simple seniority. And there was not only the question of who got promoted and how, but also of who was passed over and why. Space forbids a detailed view of this aspect.

---

[8] Published in 1987. I am quoting from pp. 3–4, 6, 11–12, and 41–2.

Mr Travers' point is unprofessionalism. The British army in 1914 was led by amateurs. I incline to the belief that late medieval government, as well as politics, central and local, was unprofessional: much less bureaucratic and managerial than we think. Does that mean it was inefficient? In the end the British army won the war and the professionalized German army lost it. Moreover, General Haig won it. Was he a good chap despite the system or because of it? Did fifteenth-century English government work, did politics get things done, was the keeping of the seas a success? Historians do not use patronage to answer questions like these. Or do they?

Part two is called Ideas.

'These English', wrote the Milanese ambassador from Bruges on 2 June 1461, 'have not the slightest form of political order: *non han una minima forma de regimento*.'[9] What did he mean? Not what I would have liked him to, namely that the English have not got two political ideas to rub together. I have to own up: I still do not think they had. Surely, if the level of political thinking is pitched at the level – the height – of those political theorists I once studied at Leicester they did not. We never looked at an Englishman until Thomas More, and I am not certain we even looked at him, at any rate I cannot remember reading *Utopia*. Sir John Fortescue certainly did not delay us on the march towards Locke, Rousseau and John Stuart Mill. Were we right or wrong?

At the level of originality or profundity, surely not. I have read Edmund Dudley's *Tree of Commonwealth* at intervals over the last thirty years and have been able to make nothing of it in terms of relevance to the politics Edmund Dudley practised.[10] It might be said that the book has to be relevant, if only because Edmund wrote it. I take that point – one that we will arrive at in a moment. But does the *Tree of Commonwealth* illuminate the politics of even a few months before, when, as Steve Gunn has shown us, the death of Henry VII in April 1509 was kept from the nation over a long weekend so that (among other things) Dudley and Richard Empson might safely be arrested?[11]

---

[9] *Dispatches with Related Documents of Milanese Ambassadors in France and Burgundy 1450–1483*, ed. Paul Murray Kendall and Vincent Ilardi, vol. II, 1460–1 (Athens, Ohio, 1971), p. 382.

[10] *The Tree of Commonwealth: A Treatise Written by Edmund Dudley*, ed. D.M. Brodie (Cambridge, 1948).

[11] 'The Accession of Henry VIII', *HR*, 64 (1991), 278–88.

Just as I have always found it difficult (perhaps impossible) to relate the *Tree of Commonwealth* to the politics of the reign of Henry VII, so I have always found it difficult (if not quite so impossible) to relate other works of fifteenth-century political theory to fifteenth-century politics. Take, for example, my wrestlings as an undergraduate with *The Libelle of Englyshe Polycye*. These brought me to the conclusion that it was an anti-European diatribe which, if acted upon, would have brought disaster to one and all, English and Europeans alike, which is not to say that it does not reflect the chauvinism of a group within English politics of the mid-1430s; it does that only too well. It is the *Libelle*'s lack of realism, its lack of relevance to international politics as conducted, which I found hard to take, hard to take seriously as commentary on the realities of English commercial and therefore political policy, unless one concedes that English policy was entirely xenophobic.[12]

Equally formative where my education as a fifteenth-century historian is concerned was my D.Phil. thesis, 'Royal Administration and The Keeping of the Seas, 1422–85' (Oxford, 1963). Trying to find statements of policy, let alone statements which might be construed as theory, was indeed like looking for the proverbial needle. This did not mean there was not discussion, in and out of council and in and out of Parliament, on the best means of fighting a war at sea: there was plenty of evidence for such debate. Yet, while that was more than mere nuts and bolts stuff about how many ships, of what type, how many soldiers should be put in each, and about what could be afforded, and was important because naval offence and defence was important – although the work of the late James Sherborne is still largely ignored and the Hundred Years War is still apparently a war fought only on land – such debate was not reflective in the way political theory is reflective. It was about the use of naval power here and now – in 1436 at the siege of Calais, or in 1454 to patrol a Channel no longer English, and so on.[13]

---

[12] *The Libelle of Englyshe Polycye: A Poem on the Use of Sea-power 1436*, ed. Sir George Warner (Oxford, 1926). See also, G.A. Holmes, 'The "Libel of English Policy"', *EHR*, LXXVI (1961), 193–216, and now, Carol Meale, 'The Libelle of Englyshe Polycye and Mercantile Literary Culture in Late-Medieval London', in Julia Boffey and Pamela King, eds, *London and Europe in the Later Middle Ages*, Westfield Publications in Medieval Studies, 9 (1995), pp. 181–227.

[13] James Sherborne's important papers are now collected: James Sherborne, *War, Politics and Culture in Fourteenth-Century England*, ed. Anthony Tuck (1994). For the missing war at sea, try, for example, D. Seward, *The Hundred Years War, the English in France, 1337–1453* (1996).

Nor, frankly, have I ever found that the political manifestos of Yorkists, Lancastrians and Nevilles threw much light on politics.[14] With the exception of the manifestos of the rebels of 1450, these bland statements of the blindingly obvious told no one anything then and tell us nothing now, unless they tell us that propaganda is always propaganda, that a manifesto is always a manifesto. And if the response is, 'oh but we should study the blindingly obvious', I refuse to believe it, because we would not read party manifestos now to understand politics, even if we might choose to read them to understand the contempt politicians have for the intelligence of those they are, or appear to be, addressing.

I am afraid I have also to confess to similar difficulties with *The Governance of England*.[15] It may be that this has more to do with how, so to speak, I was brought up as a postgraduate than with anything else: it was *The Boke of Noblesse* which I was taught to consider more relevant to the politics of the fifteenth century than *The Governance*.[16] And I continue to prefer William Worcester to Sir John Fortescue as a political commentator. I am not suggesting that Fortescue is to be dismissed out of hand as an interpreter of his times, or that he did not make a number of pertinent and observant points about government in particular and

[14] I wrote over twenty-five years ago, 'The manifesto put out by Warwick and Clarence in July 1469 might consist of time-honoured catch-phrases, the usual recriminations and denunciations of opposition, but who can say that these did not express genuinely-held beliefs or touch such feelings in others?': 'Fauconberg's Kentish rising of May 1471', *EHR*, LXXXV (1970), p. 673. How naive it seems I was in those distant days, immediately after the 1960s; yet, recalling that the editor of *EHR* cut out from the paper most of my introductory remarks on the nature of fifteenth-century politics, J.M. Wallace-Hadrill might have made me out to be less sceptical than I (already) was.

[15] *The Governance of England by Sir John Fortescue*, ed. Charles Plummer (Oxford, 1885). For Fortescue, see most recently, Margaret Lucille Kekewich in *The Politics of Fifteenth-Century England: John Vale's Book*, ed. Margaret Lucille Kekewich, Colin Richmond, Anne F. Sutton, Livia Visser-Fuchs and John L. Watts (Stroud, 1995), pp. 53–66, and Anthony Gross, *Dissolution of the Lancastrian Kingship: Sir John Fortescue and the Crisis of Monarchy in Fifteenth-Century England* (Stamford, 1996).

[16] William Worcester, *The Book of Noblesse*, ed. J.G. Nichols (Roxburghe Club, 1860). As for the being taught, see K.B. McFarlane, 'William Worcester: A Preliminary Survey', collected in his *England in the Fifteenth Century* (1981), p. 217: 'It would be absurd to claim that the pamphleteering of either Fortescue or Worcester was of such an order as to appeal to the historian of ideas. But it is possible to think that the secretary was more perspicacious than the judge and had a better historical sense.' And, after all, having a 'better historical sense' is what matters, whether one is writing a political pamphlet, a political history, or a political novel.

society in general. All I have concluded is that he was not the acute reader of the English politics of his lifetime which some take him to be. We bother with him so much, I sometimes think, not because of what he has to say but because he is an English judge saying anything at all. Where a viable polity is concerned, is it the King's Council that is the central issue, or is it, as William Worcester maintained, the French War? What are English politics to consist of, and the choice is stark, foreign or civil war? Civil peace is not, as we all know, a medieval option. I do not need to go into why I do not think the composition of the royal Council a major political issue, any more than I do as to why the so-called problem of the so-called over-mighty subject is not a problem. These are no longer matters of substance. When they were in the fifteenth century it was only because the greater problem of an under-mighty king made them so, in the early years of Henry IV's reign and during the years of Henry VI's adulthood, which John Watts has examined so closely and illumined so greatly. Let me, however, come to such a matter: political culture – to use Ted Powell's phrase – and how we historians interpret that culture.[17] What is political culture?

William Caxton's *Game and Play of Chess*, published in 1474, was dedicated to George, Duke of Clarence.[18] The conjunction – although I do not think there ever was a conjunction in any real sense – of an early fourteenth-century book of advice to princes, written from what might be termed a mendicant point of view, and a wayward even whimsical royal politician of the late fifteenth century may be considered singular, and more importantly is a conjunction which, it may also be thought, has nothing whatsoever to do with politics. I have, however, the same difficulty in this case, albeit in an extreme form, as I do with Edmund Dudley, politician, and Edmund Dudley, political commentator. What (on earth) was Caxton thinking when he chose Clarence as the dedicatee of the *Game and Play of Chess*? Because even if he thought Clarence was royal, and being royal blots out

---

[17] Edward Powell, 'After "After McFarlane": the Poverty of Patronage and the Case for Constitutional History', in *Trade, Devotion and Governance: Papers in Later Medieval History*, ed. Dorothy J. Clayton, Richard G. Davies, and Peter McNiven (Gloucester, 1994), p. 13.

[18] Caxton's *Game and Playe of the Chesse, 1474. A Verbatim Reprint of the First Edition*, ed. William E.A. Axon (1883); my copy is a British Chess Magazine Reprint, no. 6, no date, but ex-Wandsworth Public Libraries.

character and career, both of which by 1474 had been shown to be as devious as they were undistinguished, he must have thought everyone else would think the same: I mean that book-buyers, like Sir John Paston, who owned the book, would not be deterred from purchasing it by its association with, to say the least, such a political no-hoper. In other words there seems little connection in fifteenth-century political culture between theory and practice. Is there any in twentieth-century political culture?

The question is strictly relevant. If the parameters of the political culture of the Pastons are much the same, resemble closely, are more or less synonymous with those of our political culture, what is the current flurry in fifteenth-century history about? What is there that has to be learnt? Not even the language, least of all the language. We might mean something slightly different when, for example, we use the word honourable, but our ideas of honour include enough of those comprising Sir John Paston's for us to grasp what he is saying when he uses the word, just as he would be able to grasp our meaning if he should overhear us using it. Do I make an obvious point? Forgive me if I do, or, indeed, forgive me also if I am missing a point. The point might be better demonstrated concretely. Whom, let us ask, did John Paston I, II and III admire and whom did they dislike among English fifteenth-century kings? And which of those kings do we, as knowledgeable about the fifteenth century, let us suppose, as were the three Pastons, admire and dislike?

At this halfway mark there ought to be a pause for us to discuss and come up with our best and worst English kings of the century. There might not be complete agreement, but there would surely be a consensus. In spite of the reservations expressed by Cliff Davies and Tony Pollard, strong in both cases, would not our choice be the Paston choice: Henry V as the best and Richard III as the worst? And for the same reasons: because Henry was a successful politician and Richard an unsuccessful one. Laying aside all sentiment and any clever-dickness, it is by their deeds that we judge them.

Or, it might be thought, it is I who am being the clever dick. If so, let me put the matter another way: McFarlane's Henry V was Kingsford's Henry V was Shakespeare's Henry V was Fastolf's Henry V was Cardinal Beaufort's Henry V was even (although Cliff Davies will say otherwise) Bardolph and Pistol's Henry V, I mean was the man-in-Cheapside's Henry V – not Fluellen's, not Sir John Oldcastle's, not Richard, Earl of Cambridge's, not in other words quite

everybody's, but certainly of every Englishman then who did not have a grudge
and of every English historian now who does not think killing people is wrong.
And at the lower end of this scale of perfection do we not find Rosemary
Horrox's Richard III, who was Thomas More's Richard III and every good
citizen of London, Market Bosworth and Dadlington's Richard III?

Not quite Thomas More's perhaps – we shall return to Thomas More and
Richard III in a moment. Meanwhile, two further points have to be raised. The first
is personalities – Henry V and Richard III were first and last personalities. The
point, and it is a principal and starting point of McFarlane's Raleigh Lecture of 1964,
is that we do not know the personalities of most fifteenth-century politicians. Unless,
that is, they are bishops. Richard Davies has recently given us marvellous cameos of
Thomas Bourgchier, George Neville, William Wainfleet and the 'peerless' John
Kemp.[19] I wish he had given us John Alcock – and perhaps he will, as he certainly
could – for if Alcock was the author of the 1472 speech to Parliament, the clearest
articulation of political principle of which I am aware, clearer and fuller than Bishop
John Russell's draft speech for the Parliament of June 1483, then John Alcock would
get my vote as Most Sophisticated Political Commentator of the Century.[20] That
award going to a bishop is unsurprising: bishops were the intellectuals in politics and
if theory was to come from anywhere it was going to be from one or more of them,
including, one should add, theory translated into action: Archbishop Thomas
Arundel in 1399, for example, and, as Gerald Harriss has told us, Cardinal Henry
Beaufort's Lancastrian Vision. Personalities are, therefore, important.[21] They are,
nevertheless, only important in the balance which Rosemary Horrox has reminded
us has to be struck between 'private obligations and concerns and the public good'.[22]

---

[19] In 'The Church and the Wars of the Roses', in Pollard, ed., *Wars of the Roses*, pp. 134–61.

[20] The speech of 1472 is in *Literae Cantuarienses*, III, ed. J. Brigstocke Sheppard (Rolls Series, 1889),
pp. 274–85; John Russell's drafts are in *Grants from the Crown during the Reign of Edward V*, ed. J.G.
Nichols (Camden Society, 1854), pp. xxxix–lxiii. For Alcock as the author of the 1472 speech, see
Gross, *Dissolution of Lancastrian Kingship*, p. 93, but cf. Genet, above, 'New Politics or New Language?',
n. 27.

[21] G.L. Harriss, *Cardinal Beaufort* (Oxford, 1988), and 'Henry Beaufort, "Cardinal of England"', in
Daniel Williams, ed., *England in the Fifteenth Century, Proceedings of the 1986 Harlaxton Symposium*
(Woodbridge, 1987), pp. 111–27.

[22] In Pollard, ed., *Wars of the Roses*, p. 98.

The second point, therefore, is that, whatever the almost limitless variety of personality and the need for a prefatory generalization that bishops in politics have to be seen as the least prone to 'private obligations and concerns', politicians were neither cynics nor sincerists, that is, about 'the public good'. Secular politicians of the fifteenth century, unlike twentieth-century ones, were almost all born to govern: the public good was their duty as well as their right. Were not those the parameters within which they operated, within which they did their best and worst for the commonwealth because that is what their position in society obliged them to be doing? All the nobility and all the greater, or county, gentry were political because that is what they were, either by the accident of birth or through the deliberate choice of service.

Richard III, like Henry V, like Richard Neville, Earl of Warwick, like Richard Beauchamp, Earl of Warwick, like William Paston I, like William Paston II, did not segregate political life into two compartments, the way Rosemary has and we all do, into private and public, self- and other-interest, what I can get out of politics versus what I may do for the commonwealth. Richard III, like all the others, believed he was doing what he ought to be doing and in doing what he ought to be doing was getting what he ought to be getting – in Richard's case the throne itself. None of them should be interpreted any other way. The good old standby 'greed' just will not do; it applies to every fifteenth-century nobleman and noblewoman, gentleman and gentlewoman who has ever been thoroughly studied, but the well-evidenced 'greed' of Thomas Chaucer esquire and Ralph, Lord Cromwell, did not prevent them performing their public service to the general good.[23] About Thomas More and Thomas Cromwell we might wish to

---

[23] For Chaucer, the case has yet to be fully made, and will be, I hope, by Rowena Archer; meanwhile, Colin Richmond, *The Paston Family in the Fifteenth Century: The first phase* (Cambridge, 1990), pp. 47–53 are suggestive. For Cromwell, the case is being made by Simon Payling, who will, I hope, continue making it; see, S.J. Payling, 'The Ampthill Dispute: A study in aristocratic lawlessness and the breakdown of Lancastrian government', *EHR*, CIV (1989), 881–907; 'Inheritance and Local Politics in the Later Middle Ages: The Case of Ralph, Lord Cromwell, and the Heriz Inheritance', *NottMS*, XXX (1986), 67–95; 'Arbitration, Perpetual Entails and Collateral Warranties in Late-Medieval England', *Journal of Legal History*, 13 (1992), 32–62; 'A Disputed Mortgage: Ralph, Lord Cromwell, Sir John Gra and the Manor of Multon Hall', in Archer and Walker, eds, *Rulers and Ruled in Late Medieval England*, pp. 117–36.

be more circumspect. And that was the way politics were until our century, when politicians choose politics and politics does not choose them. Even now Mr Blair believes he is doing what is right for the United Kingdom, although he is not, just as Richard III believed he was doing what was good for England, when he was not.

This all serves to make a reading of politics not black and white, but grey: even Henry V and Mr Blair are shades of grey. It is at this juncture that we re-encounter Thomas More and Richard III, or rather Thomas's unfinished drama-documentary, *The History of King Richard the Third*, as well as coming to deal with what Ted Powell has called 'the importance of political and constitutional principles as a subject for study in relation to political action'.[24] My difficulty discovering the importance of such principles was, I am convinced, Thomas More's difficulty when he came to study recent history – the history of the reign of Richard III. Did not Thomas want to write what we have been taught to call Humanist history, black and white history – in scarlet and black, one is tempted to say – a study in polarities, a Manichean book therefore, a book about Good and Evil, about tyranny and its opposite? And did he not discover that the more he learned of the recent past, the more oral testimony he took from old and ageing politicians who had lived through that apparently black and white period, that it was all much greyer, much murkier than he had expected? If Richard was black, and even he, Thomas's informants were no doubt indicating, was not as black as Thomas wanted to paint him, then who was white? Hardly Edward IV, not William, Lord Hastings, not the Woodvilles, not Margaret Beaufort, certainly not those bishops, clever and not so clever. No one at all who was adult and involved in the politics of 1483, whether they were victims, perpetrators, or bystanders. So Thomas stopped writing. He had realized that the writing of political history turns into a discussion of what Primo Levi called, in an entirely other context, the Grey Zone.[25] If he was to write in black and white, it would have to be something other than history which had to be written, certainly

---

[24] *Op. cit.*, p. 10. For *The History of King Richard the Third*, see *The Complete Works of Thomas More*, II, ed. Richard Sylvester (Yale University Press, 1963).

[25] Primo Levi, *The Drowned and the Saved* (1988), ch. 2, pp. 22–51.

something other than a drama-documentary. And what would that have to be? Why political theory, of course; so he wrote *Utopia*. In short, there was not a chivalry of politics and there is no Lady Politics as there is a Lady Poverty.

As a coda to part two I would make a plea for events rather than ideas. What significance did events have for political awareness? Take three happenings which continue to exercise me: the French sack of Sandwich in August 1457, called 'spectacular' by Ralph Griffiths, but which I seldom see adequately discussed in analyses of the demise of the Lancastrian dynasty;[26] secondly, the Love Day of March 1458, deemed 'an astonishing spectacle' by Ralph, called 'fatuous' by Richard Davies and 'famous' by John Watts, and which usually has been dismissed, it seems to me, without further reflection on what meaning the spectacle had for the participants;[27] thirdly, the naval achievements of Richard Neville, Earl of Warwick in the Channel in the second half of the 1450s, which no one has said anything about for many years.[28] Did they make him popular, as popular as Richard Beauchamp, Earl of Warwick, or, as Richard Marks told us in a recent inaugural lecture, as popular as Richard Beauchamp's executors were endeavouring to make him at that very time. Perhaps, indeed, they were trying to make him as popular as Richard Neville. It seems to me that as these things hardly get written up, let alone thought about, it is as if they had never happened. It is high time to take revenge on such Post-Modernism.

[26] Ralph Griffiths, *The Reign of King Henry VI* (1981), p. 815. Cora Scofield, as ever, gets nearest the mark, 'The looting of Sandwich was a national disgrace which Henry VI's subjects never forgot': C.L. Scofield, *The Life and Reign of Edward IV* (1923), I, p. 25.

[27] Griffiths, *Reign of King Henry VI*, p. 806; Richard Davies, in Pollard, ed., *Wars of the Roses*, p. 148; John Watts, in Kekewich *et al.*, eds, *The Politics of Fifteenth-century England*, p. 26, but note John's n. 97 on that page.

[28] There is a single paragraph in Ralph Griffiths, *Reign of King Henry VI*, p. 809. The inquisitive reader has to go back to G.L. Harriss, 'The Struggle for Calais: An Aspect of the Rivalry between Lancaster and York', *EHR*, LXXV (196), 30–53, or to my thesis, ch. 4, 'The Earl of Warwick, 1456–1461', pp. 256–89. In the near future I hope to deal again with the Earl of Warwick at Calais during the last years of Lancastrian government. Contemporary awareness of naval power is demonstrated not only by *The Libelle of Englyshe Polycye*; the poem 'Stere welle the good shype [of state]' is to be dated to 1458 or thereabouts: I have tried to use it in 'The nobility and the Wars of the Roses 1457–1459', *Journal of Historical Sociology*, 9 (1996), 395–409.

Part three is termed Polemic.

It will begin and end with documents. Historians may fetishize documents in the way archaeologists once made fetishes of artefacts, but whatever constructions fifteenth-century historians erect, their foundations have to be of paper. The following quotation is to remind us how shaky such foundations can be:[29]

> Just as I learned not to rely on spoken testimony without questioning it, I learned the same was true in interpreting documents. I was fortunate to be given three large collections of letters Beckett wrote over long periods of time to three different people with whom he enjoyed varying degrees of friendship. On one particular day, Beckett wrote a separate letter to each of his three friends. To the first, he wrote that he was happy living in Ireland in the mid-1930s, that he had made his peace with family and country, and envisioned himself staying there. In the second, to a friend in the United States, he said he was miserable because he could not decide what to do with his life, was angry that other Irish writers would not accept his friendship, but was otherwise content to be living in his family home again. To the third, Beckett wrote that he could find no work, was drinking heavily and feared he would commit violence against his mother; he thought that leaving Ireland permanently was his only course.

Which should make us cautious. However, I loathe caution, especially calculated caution, perhaps because like one of the Hasidic masters I believe the middle of the road is only for horses. Balanced views: who needs them? On the one hand this, on the other that type of history: who wants it? As for being judicious: leave that to judges.[30]

What, therefore, of me, a black and white historian, and the Grey Zone of political history? I am reminded of a photograph of Aneurin Bevan speaking at an election meeting in 1951; draped over a table beside him is a poster quoting Clement Davies, the then leader of the Liberal Party; it says:

---

[29] Deidre Bair, *Samuel Beckett* (Vintage Books, 1990), p. xv.
[30] The Hasidic master was Menahem-Mendl of Kotzk: Elie Wiesel, *Souls on Fire* (1972), p. 235.

I COULD NOT VOTE TORY.
IT IS WRONG.

Quite so. Unlike Thomas More I have not deserted history writing; so how do I get the black and white into fifteenth-century politics? By being polemical about them is the answer. Cliff Davies, himself no fence-sitter, as he has lately shown with regard to both Henry V and Henry VIII, describes Lawrence Stone in tutorials, 'he would . . . express his amazement at any suggestion that public life might be conducted on any but the lowest principles'; so too do I find it difficult to believe any good of public figures.[31] After the Watergate tapes what other possible belief is there?

For Richard Nixon read Richard of Gloucester. For William, Lord Hastings, read Harold Macmillan. Take Henry VII and his government of gamekeepers turned poachers. Take Gilbert Debenham, that 'Medieval Rascal in Real Life';[32] take 'Sir William Tailboys and Lord Cromwell: Crime and Politics in Lancastrian England';[33] take Richard, Earl of Warwick and 'Cardinal Beaufort's Almshouse of Noble Poverty at St Cross, Winchester' – it is Gervase Belfield who has summarized the sordid story:

To greed, the vice of dishonesty must also be attributed to him and his mother. Without a scrap of justification, they robbed St Cross of certainly four, and possibly five, of its manors, and by making false representations to the king and parliament in 1461, they attempted to justify their crime.

No mealy-mouthing about that. Like W.G. Hoskins in that wonderful preface to *The Age of Plunder*, Mr Belfield uses the language appropriate for the behaviour: vice, robbery, crime.[34] I am not so sure about Dom David Knowles. Here he is on our period:[35]

---

[31] *The First Modern Society. Essays in English History in Honour of Lawrence Stone*, ed. A.L. Beier *et al.* (Oxford, 1989), p. 10.

[32] W.I. Haward, 'Gilbert Debenham: A medieval rascal in real life', *History*, XIII (1928–9), 300–14.

[33] Roger Virgoe, 'William Tailboys and Lord Cromwell: Crime and Politics in Lancastrian England', *BJRL*, 55 (1973), 459–82.

[34] *Proceedings of the Hampshire Field Club and Archaeological Society*, 38 (1982), 110. For the great W.G. see, *The Age of Plunder: The England of Henry VIII 1500–1547* (1976), pp. xi–xiii.

[35] *The Religious Orders in England III: The Tudor Age* (Cambridge, 1961), pp. 5–6.

Pecuniary values and economic gains were very nearly exclusive of all others. Perhaps in no other epoch of English history have purely material interests had such a monopoly in all the records of the age. . . . Money and land are the only desirable things. For a brief space neither religious controversy, nor civil duties, nor the pursuit of adventure, nor the love of books or music, nor any theoretical or mental debate, had any appeal. The code of chivalry had gone; the code of loyalty and honour had yet to come. It is an earthy, selfish, grasping age.

Here we are beyond polemic and into rhetoric, absurdist rhetoric coming from a Benedictine, to whom every age of the world, one would think, would be earthy. And there is more, 'The term "gentleman" was indeed currently used, but the educated gentleman, one of a class, did not exist,' says Dom David, while in a footnote to that pronouncement he asked how many 'gentlemen' there were in the reigns of Henry VII and Henry VIII and came up with only two: Thomas More and Reginald Pole. This is the old question of 'when is a gentleman a gentleman?', a question to which Thomas More gave an uncompromising and resounding answer in *Utopia*, namely that those who claim to be never are and that their domination of English society is as grasping and as selfish as Dom David says it is.[36]

There is a good reason why we need to be reminded of *Utopia*: English society in the later Middle Ages is in danger of becoming too much approved. Nowadays it is often regarded as a stable society or one with a tendency towards stability, a self-regulating political society in which gentry drives for land and lineage are positive and positively constitutional because they are contained by institutional and institutionalized usages – of the law and of political life.[37] In the end it does

[36] The best discussions of *Utopia* from this angle are those of J.H. Hexter, 'The Radicalism of Utopia', pp. cv–cxxiv of the introduction to *Utopia*, ed. Edward Surtz and J.H. Hexter, *The Yale Edition of the Complete Works of St Thomas More*, IV (1965), and pp. 194–8 of his *The Vision of Politics on the Eve of the Reformation* (1973). I rather skirt the issue in 'Ruling Classes and Agents of the State: Formal and Informal Networks of Power', *Journal of Historical Sociology*, 10 (1997), 1–26.

[37] A revealing instance (and incident) has been published by Richard Hoyle, 'The Earl, the Archbishop and the Council: The Affray at Fulford, May 1504', in Archer and Walker, eds, *Rulers and Ruled in Late Medieval England*, pp. 239–56.

not seem to me to matter precisely how king, nobles and gentry did contain, as contain they must be said to have done, the violence that their land-seeking and their lineage promotion necessarily entailed. What J.B. Post has called 'the little alarms and diversions of everyday territorial aggrandizement and local politics',[38] and which in Elizabethan England Lawrence Stone likened to Chicago – 'Both in the brutality of their tactics and in their immunity from the law, the nearest parallels to the Earl of Oxford and Sir Thomas Knevett in the London of Queen Elizabeth are Al Capone and Dion O'Banion, Bugs Moran and Johnny Torrio in the Chicago of the 1920s'[39] – these had to be limited, not because 'anarchy' (meaningless or meaningful) was the alternative, but because ambitions to be achieved and not thereafter to be dismantled have to limit themselves. Self-regulating nihilism might be a better term for what the élite was up to, is always up to. It was Hubert Hall who over a hundred years ago published a paper with the title, 'An Episode of Mediaeval Nihilism', and nihilists, it seems to me, are what all these important people were.[40] Even nihilists, however, have to know how far they can go. Like the fifteenth-century piracy I studied when writing a thesis all those years ago, fifteenth-century nihilism had its limits. Those limits, those parameters to pride, are what is known as constitutional history.

I said I would end part three as I began it – with documents, one in this instance. British Library, Althorp Papers 8, file one, has in it a letter addressed to Edmund Dudley, 'being in the Tower of London be this delivered', and it looks as though it has been. The letter is from John Spencer, that is Sir John Spencer of Althorp and Wormleighton, who died in 1522. It concerns Edmund Dudley's shady dealings with Sir Simon Harcourt over the manor of Bosworth, that is Husbands Bosworth, Leicestershire, which dealings had put in jeopardy Spencer's purchase of the manor from Dudley: 'wherefore I have wrytte to you

---

[38] 'Crime in later medieval England: some historiographical limitations', *Continuity and Change*, 2 (1987), 218.

[39] *The Crisis of the Aristocracy 1558–1641* (Oxford, 1965), p. 234, and see the whole of the section, 'The Face of Violence', pp. 223–34.

[40] I owe my knowledge of this title to a footnote of Roger Virgoe's: 'William Tailboys and Lord Cromwell', p. 476, n. 1. Hubert Hall's paper appeared in *The Antiquary*, xii (1885); it concerned the same incident as that dealt with by Roger Virgoe.

the parcells preceding [a list of Harcourt lands and their values amounting to £116, which Sir Simon Harcourt said he had never had from Dudley in exchange for Husbands Bosworth] to the intent ye may certify to the King and Lords the truth and playnes of the premises with your own hand for my suyrte in my premisses etc.' I have not explored the outcome in detail, but the Spencers did not get Husbands Bosworth. Did Sir John Spencer get his money back, already paid, as he explained in the letter, to another of the Bray cartel, master [Edward] Belknap?[41] Whatever the outcome, it is the letter itself which is interesting; like Dudley's petition, like his arrest, like the reversal of his attainder in the Parliament following the one in which he was attainted, like keeping Henry VII's death hush-hush for two days, the letter is an aspect of the self-regulating of themselves that the élite went in for, aspects no less important than the constitutional checks and balances we once all learned about and no doubt should start teaching again: Parliament, council, common law and Chancery.

They were, of course, also devices to defraud the wider public. Most, perhaps all, of the men involved in the Husbands Bosworth affair were depopulators. Engrossing and enclosure are an excellent example of the shape-shifting that language can be made to undergo; what is actually the destruction of a traditional culture by the removal of people gets called agricultural improvement, and agricultural improvement, as everyone knows – although historians ought to know better – is for the public good. The Spencers and Belknaps, on the other hand, knew exactly what they were doing: making more money.[42] Yet, Bray, Empson and Dudley, we have been told, 'built up the King's wealth and authority – changing England into order'.[43] Depopulation, daylight robbery, destruction, nihilism – if it is practised by the ruling class it has to be called something else: progress, order, law, constitutional government. Constitutionalism therefore is like chivalry. It is a word to describe a sort of club, a club with rules, rules applied to keep royal, noble and gentle self-interest within bounds, but rules

---

[41] I can see nothing of the matter in C.J. Harrison, 'The Petition of Edmund Dudley', *EHR*, LXXXVII (1972).

[42] Now properly told 'like it was' by Edmund Fryde, *Peasants and Landlords in Later Medieval England* (Gloucester, 1996), ch. 16.

[43] J.C. Wedgwood, *History of Parliament 1439–1509. Biographies* (1936), pp. 285–6.

which applied only to members: non-members might be treated without reference to any rules.

I would have liked the conclusion to be from Proust – his marvellous passage on the old novelist and old artist, which will more than do for the old historian – but it is far too long. You will have to read it for yourselves.[44] In lieu here is Adorno:[45]

> Nothing is more unfitting than for an intellectual to wish, in discussion, to be right. The very wish to be right is an expression of that spirit of self-preservation which philosophy [history] is precisely concerned to break down. . . . When philosophers [historians], who are well known to have difficulty in keeping silent, engage in conversation, they should always try to lose the argument, but in such a way as to convict their opponent of untruth. The point should not be to have absolutely correct, irrefutable, watertight convictions . . . but insights.

---

[44] *Remembrance of Things Past*, trans. C.K. Scott Moncrieff, vol. 4, pp. 209–11.
[45] Cited in Derwent May, *Hannah Arendt* (1986), p. 31.

3

THE ENGLISH ECONOMY AND THE GOVERNMENT, 1450–1550

R.H. Britnell

The period 1450–1550 spans periods of economic and political history that historians usually hold apart. It begins in the middle of the great slump of the mid-fifteenth century,[1] and ends in the early decades of sixteenth-century inflation. Life would be simpler, no doubt, if there were an identifiable turning point to divide the period into two contrasting phases, but in reality there was no single time and single cause for a change of economic trend.[2] Much of the period cannot be bracketed with either fifteenth-century recession or sixteenth-century growth, since the available evidence does not clearly suggest change in any particular direction.[3] The following discussion will first evaluate the evidence for economic development, commenting in particular on the limited significance of overseas trade for growth throughout the economy. The second section will then consider the effects of government in furthering or retarding the growth of incomes. Finally, the third section will assess the problematic evidence relating to population growth.

I

One of the best-documented and most impressive aspects of England's economy between 1450 and 1550 was the rising volume of exports of woollen cloth, which

---

[1] J. Hatcher, 'The Great Slump of the Mid-Fifteenth Century', in *Progress and Problems in Medieval England: Essays in Honour of Edward Miller*, ed. R.H. Britnell and J. Hatcher (Cambridge University Press, 1996), pp. 237–72.

[2] J. Hatcher, *Plague, Population and the English Economy, 1348–1530* (Macmillan, 1977), pp. 63–7.

[3] This paper in part follows the final chapters of R.H. Britnell, *The Closing of the Middle Ages? England, 1471–1529* (Oxford, Blackwell, 1997), pp. 208–47. The two pieces were developed simultaneously and are intended to agree with each other.

increased from an annual average of 37,140 cloths in the years 1450–4 to
117,353 in the years 1540–4.[4] Though this growth was not smooth, it was
characteristic of much of the period, the 1470s, 1500s and 1530s all being
decades of exceptionally rapid increase. The figures cited represent an average
annual increase of 1.3 per cent between the early 1450s and the early 1540s, and
much, if not all, of this growth is likely to represent increased total national
output to meet expanding markets, rather than the diversion of cloth from the
home market to the Continent. There were rising centres of cloth production in
all corners of the kingdom, notably in southern Suffolk,[5] western Wiltshire,[6]
Somerset,[7] Devon,[8] central Gloucestershire,[9] and the West Riding of Yorkshire,[10]
though not all sustained growth equally well; Leland says that by the time of his
travels about the years 1535–43 some south-western clothing towns had seen
better days.[11]

Cloth exports created commercial opportunities for wool growers. The increase
between 1450–4 and 1540–4 would have required the equivalent of about 18,500
additional sacks of wool each year. Since the average annual export of raw wool

[4] E.M. Carus-Wilson and O. Coleman, *England's Export Trade, 1275–1547* (Oxford, Clarendon
Press, 1963), pp. 62–74; A.R. Bridbury, *Medieval English Clothmaking: An Economic Survey* (Heinemann,
1982), pp. 120–2.

[5] G. Unwin, *Studies in Economic History* (Macmillan, 1927), pp. 264, 266.

[6] E.M. Carus-Wilson, 'The Woollen Industry before 1550', *VCH Wiltshire*, vol. 4, ed. E. Crittall
(Oxford University Press, 1959), pp. 133, 138–40. John Leland, *The Itinerary*, ed. L. Toulmin Smith
(5 vols, G. Bell, 1907–10), vol. 1, p. 143 and vol. 5, pp. 82–4, mentions the importance of cloth-
making for Bath, Devizes, Steeple Ashton, Westbury and Bradford-on-Avon.

[7] Leland, *Itinerary*, vol. 5, pp. 97–8, 103; E.M. Carus-Wilson, *The Expansion of Exeter at the Close of the
Middle Ages* (Exeter, University of Exeter, 1963), pp. 17–22.

[8] Carus-Wilson, *Expansion of Exeter*, pp. 17–19; W.R. Childs, 'Devon's Overseas Trade in the Late
Middle Ages', in *The New Maritime History of Devon*, ed. M. Duffy, S. Fisher, B. Greenhill, D.J. Starkey
and J. Youings (2 vols, Exeter, Conway Maritime Press, 1992–), vol. 1, p. 79.

[9] Leland, *Itinerary*, vol. 5, pp. 96, 101; E.M. Carus-Wilson, 'Evidences of Industrial Growth on
some Fifteenth-Century Manors', *EcHR*, 2nd ser., XII (1959–60), 190–7.

[10] H. Heaton, *The Yorkshire Woollen and Worsted Industries from the Earliest Times up to the Industrial
Revolution*, 2nd edn (Oxford, Clarendon Press, 1965), pp. 73–8; D.M. Palliser, *Tudor York* (Oxford
University Press, 1979), pp. 208–9; R.B. Smith, *Land and Politics in the England of Henry VIII: The West
Riding of Yorkshire, 1530–46* (Oxford, Clarendon Press, 1970), pp. 23–8.

[11] Leland, *Itinerary*, vol. I, p. 143 (Bath), vol. 5, pp. 100–1 (Thornbury, Berkeley).

simultaneously declined by almost 4,000 sacks, not all the increased export of cloth represented a net gain to wool producers, but the net increase of 14,500 sacks going into exports would require about 3 million additional fleeces each year.[12] It is impossible to calculate how far this stimulus from exports was enhanced or offset by changes in the home market, but agrarian evidence suggests that, for many farmers, sheep were the one bright spot in an otherwise unpromising rural economy and that this induced many landlords to convert more land to pasture.[13] Price history alone cannot explain the expansion of sheep farming, since there was no great divergence between the movement of wool and cereals prices before the 1520s, when prices of grain (not wool) went ahead.[14] The continuing profitability of wool relative to cereals up to 1520 resulted in part from the high ratio of selling price to wage rates, which meant that farmers incurred lower recurrent costs in expanding their wool output than a comparable increase in grain sales would have required. The expansion of sheep farming was not a great source of new employment.

Though woollen cloth was the major success story, the customs accounts also indicate an increase in exports of minerals, and in this case estimates exist for output as well as exports. Ian Blanchard has suggested a national output of 80 tons of lead in 1464 and 715 tons in 1531, with rather lower figures thereafter. Exports were about equal to total output in both years; this did not starve domestic demand because of the large amount of old lead that came onto the market each year to be re-used.[15] Meanwhile the tin mined in Devon and Cornwall increased from 872,000 lb in the earlier 1450s to 1,690,000 lb in the

[12] This calculation assumes that a sack of wool made 4.33 cloths, that a sack weighed 364 lb avdp. and that each fleece weighed 1.75 lb: E. Carus-Wilson, *Medieval Merchant Venturers*, 2nd edn (Methuen, 1967), p. xxiv; A. Hanham, *The Celys and their World: An English Merchant Family of the Fifteenth Century* (Cambridge University Press, 1985), pp. 112, 115.

[13] P. Bowden, 'Agricultural Prices, Farm Profits and Rents', in *The Agrarian History of England and Wales, IV: 1500–1640*, ed. J. Thirsk (Cambridge University Press, 1967), pp. 636–8. For exceptions, see H.P.R. Finberg, *Tavistock Abbey: A Study in the Social and Economic History of Devon* (Cambridge University Press, 1951), pp. 148–9; C. Rawcliffe, *The Staffords, Earls of Stafford and Dukes of Buckingham, 1394–1521* (Cambridge University Press, 1978), p. 65.

[14] P. Bowden, 'Statistical Appendix', in *Agrarian History*, IV, ed. Thirsk, pp. 839–42, 846–8.

[15] I.S.W. Blanchard, *International Lead Production and Trade in the 'Age of the Saigerprozess', 1460–1560* (Stuttgart, Franz Steiner Verlag, 1995), p. 310.

later 1540s. The proportion of this exported at the beginning of the period is
uncertain – about a half, to judge from the available figures from the period
1485–99 – but it was about 64 per cent in the mid-1540s.[16] In both cases the
course of development was erratic. Increased employment in mining and
smelting these metals was just as scattered as that in the cloth industry. The
principal lead mines were in Derbyshire, but there were lesser centres in northern
England and in the Mendips. In some parts of Derbyshire, lead output grew from
the 1460s through to the 1530s, and in Weardale, too, there was some increase in
output over the period.[17] The mining and smelting of tin were concentrated in
the South-West in the stannary regions of Penwith, Kerrier, Tywarnhaile,
Blackmore and Foweymore in Cornwall, and around Chagford, Ashburton and
Tavistock in Devon.[18]

Though exports of textiles and metals were a stimulus to local economic
growth, and their regional effects on the structure of employment can often be
observed, their significance to the whole economy requires careful assessment.
Many textile workers and miners were unspecialized, and derived their
livelihoods from more than one source. To gauge the impact of these exports on
employment means considering not the total number of people who might
occasionally be employed in producing them but on their contribution to total
employment. This is best done by thinking in terms of man–year equivalents
(assuming a working year of 270 days).[19]

In Flanders ten broadcloths a year was as much as could be expected from a
single weaver, which implies that between the early 1450s and the early 1540s the
increased cloth production for export might have been accomplished by adding

[16] J. Hatcher, *English Tin Production and Trade before 1550* (Oxford, Clarendon Press, 1973),
pp. 158–9, 168, 176–93. The estimate for the mid-1540s is based on figures for 1543–4 and 1546–7.

[17] Leland, *Itinerary*, vol. 4, pp. 26, 32 and vol. 5, p. 129; I.S.W. Blanchard, 'Economic Change in
Derbyshire in the Late Middle Ages, 1272–1540' (unpublished Ph.D. thesis, University of London,
1967), pp. 273–5, 288.

[18] J. Hatcher, *Rural Economy and Society in the Duchy of Cornwall, 1300–1500* (Cambridge University
Press, 1970), pp. xiv, 172.

[19] For this assumption: D. Woodward, *Men at Work: Labourers and Building Craftsmen in the Towns of
Northern England, 1450–1750* (Cambridge University Press, 1995), pp. 131–2.

8,000 full-time weavers to the labour force. At least 8,000 man–years have to be added for wool-beating, carding, combing and spinning, and perhaps a further 4,000 man–years to account for the finishing crafts.[20] The increase in cloth exports may have created employment for at least 20,000 people. This was the chief source of employment in export-led growth. Meanwhile, though the additional 650,000 lb or so of tin exported annually from Devon and Cornwall may have required the addition of between 2,000 and 3,000 tinworkers to the mining workforce, the equivalent in man–years would be less than half this number because so much of the work was casual.[21] The increased output of the lead industry, which is unlikely to have exceeded 500 tons a year between 1450 and 1550, created perhaps 250 man–years of employment.[22] This modest assessment of the labour required in mining is in line with the understanding of the author of *A Discourse of the Common Weal*, who observed that 'as for oure woll, felles, tinne, lead, butter and chese, these be the commodities that the ground beares, requiring the industrie of a few persons' (meaning *only* a few persons).[23] On this calculation, the increased exports of woollen cloth, tin and lead between the early 1450s and the early 1540s created the equivalent of full-time employment for no more than 21,500 people. Yet this was only 1.3 per cent of the total population aged sixteen and over (it is necessary to consider this employment as a proportion of the total adult population because a large part of the employment in woollen textiles was female).[24] There are grounds

[20] J.H. Munro, 'Textile Technology in the Middle Ages', in J.H. Munro, *Textiles, Towns and Trade* (Aldershot, Variorum, 1994), item I, p. 17. The calculation in the text assumes that an English broadcloth needed the same amount of work as a Flemish one on the grounds that the weight of wool was the same; see above, n. 11.

[21] Hatcher, *English Tin Production*, pp. 158–9. The calculation in the text assumes that average output per capita was below 300 lb: cf. ibid., p. 85.

[22] This is calculated on the evidence of productivity levels on Mendip in 1536: I.S.W. Blanchard, 'Labour Productivity and Work Psychology in the English Mining Industry, 1400–1600', *EcHR*, 2nd ser., XXXI (1978), 24.

[23] *A Discourse of the Common Weal of this Realm of England*, ed. E. Lamond (Cambridge University Press, 1893), p. 92.

[24] Assuming that total English population was 2,774,000 in 1541 and that adults over the age of sixteen constituted 60 per cent of the total: E.A. Wrigley and R.S. Schofield, *The Population History of England, 1541–1871: A Reconstruction* (Cambridge University Press, 1981), p. 208; J.C.K. Cornwall, *Wealth and Society in Early Sixteenth-Century England* (Routledge and Kegan Paul, 1988), pp. 190, 213.

for increasing this figure above 1.3 per cent, since additional employment became available in the transport and handling of export goods. It would also be fanciful to suppose that all adults worked 270 days a year, since in some contexts there was considerable leisure preference. However, it would be difficult to argue up the proportion of added employment in these occupations by the 1540s to more than a small percentage of the total labour requirements of the English economy. Even if they were all net additions to national output, the capacity of export sectors to promote economic growth was slight over the period as a whole; the implied annual growth rate is no more than 0.1 per cent.

A similar conclusion is obtained by assessing the value of these exports at the end of the period under examination. This exercise is again beset by uncertainty, but it is of some interest to see what happens when the independent estimates of different historians are put together. Estimated roughly as before, between the 1450s and the 1540s cloth exports increased by about 80,000 cloths a year, tin exports by 300 tons and lead exports (excluding exports of used monastic lead) by 500 tons. The combined value of these at 1546 prices was about £335,000 a year.[25] This sum is equivalent to 4 per cent of English national income in 1546, as estimated by Nicholas Mayhew.[26] Even if all this increase in exports represented a net addition to national output, and not a diversion of goods from the home market, the significance for economic development over the century was low. The implied impact on the economy as a whole is again a growth rate of less than 0.1 per cent a year on average.

These calculations plainly have no claim to be a full assessment of the potential contribution of overseas trade to development, since there were other branches of

[25] This is based on prices of £4 per cloth, £44 per ton of tin, £4 per ton of lead. This cloth price is that of exported cloth in 1495–9, increased by 40 per cent to allow for the inflation of textile prices: J.H. Munro, 'Monetary Contraction and Industrial Change in the Late-Medieval Low Countries, 1335–1500', in *Coinage in the Low Countries (880–1500)*, ed. N.J. Mayhew (British Archaeological Reports, International Series, 54, Oxford, 1979), p. 155; H.P. Brown and S.V. Hopkins, *A Perspective of Wages and Prices* (Methuen, 1981), pp. 49–50. Prices of tin and lead are from Hatcher, *English Tin Production*, p. 121, and Blanchard, *International Lead Production*, pp. 319–22.

[26] N. Mayhew, 'Population, Money Supply and the Velocity of Circulation in England, 1300–1700', *EcHR*, XLVIII (1995), 244.

export trade that have not been allowed for and about whose performance little is known. However, argument along these lines serves to undermine the assumption that a high annual increase in the export of a few documented commodities implies bright prospects for the economy as a whole. Though that assumption is not one that any reasonably cautious historian would think of asserting, neither is it commonly denied, and it is one that might be readily derived from the high profile of rising cloth exports in general accounts of the period.[27]

Since the export industries were so scattered across the country, their growth had little power to create extensive regional poles of economic development. Undoubtedly wealth accumulated and population increased in some towns and villages, particularly in the south-western counties, but their number was not very great. The most obvious urban beneficiary of England's increasing export trade was London, which benefited from a unique combination of commercial and political stimuli. The population of the city centre, as Derek Keene's Cheapside survey has suggested, did not begin to grow till the very end of the period, but in Westminster numbers were increasing from about 1470. Martha Carlin's evidence from Southwark is even more decisive; it implies a rising population, and rising property values, from 1460 onwards, with a surge of expansion after 1500.[28] London's expansion was sufficiently strong to promote new agrarian, industrial and commercial development in parts of the lower Thames Valley and surrounding areas,[29] but the city's impact on the location and structure of industry was (selectively) more extensive. From around 50 per cent of total cloth exports in 1450, London's share rose to nearly 90 per cent by 1550.[30] A growing concentration of exports on the route from London to Antwerp enhanced the importance of mercantile networks of trade and credit that connected the provinces with London,

---

[27] For example, J.R. Lander, *Government and Community: England, 1450–1509* (Edward Arnold, 1980), pp. 24–31; P. Ramsey, *Tudor Economic Problems* (Victor Gollancz, 1963), pp. 47–68, 82–90.

[28] M. Carlin, *Medieval Southwark* (Hambledon Press, 1996), pp. 53, 58–60, 133–5, 143–4; D. Keene, *Cheapside before the Great Fire* (Economic and Social Research Council, 1985), pp. 19–20; G. Rosser, *Medieval Westminster, 1200–1540* (Oxford, Clarendon Press, 1989), pp. 174, 177.

[29] M.K. McIntosh, *Autonomy and Community: The Royal Manor of Havering, 1200–1500* (Cambridge University Press, 1986), pp. 223–35.

[30] A. Dyer, *Decline and Growth in English Towns, 1400–1640* (Macmillan, 1991), p. 26.

and benefited those entrepreneurs able to take advantage of them. John Greenway
of Tiverton, clothier (d. 1529), joined both the London Drapers' Company and the
London Merchant Venturers' Company and exported cloth to the Low
Countries.[31] Other commercial centres of production also became associated with
outstandingly successful merchants with London links, like James Terumber of
Bradford-on-Avon and Trowbridge (d. 1488),[32] and Thomas Spring III of
Lavenham (d. 1523).[33] Even smaller merchants like John Wyke of Trowbridge
(d. 1460), William Athelam of Westbury (flourished around 1460) and John Bailly
of Whaddon (flourished in the late fifteenth century) traded through Londoners.[34]
Thomas Paycocke, clothier of Coggeshall (d. 1518), left money in his will to
St Paul's, as well as to Henry Perpoint of London and his sister.[35] From as far away
as the West Riding of Yorkshire, clothiers sold their wares at the London fair of
St Bartholomew.[36] Corresponding observations may be made in the rare surviving
records of London merchants themselves. Thomas Howell of the London Drapers'
Company bought broadcloths and vesses from the Suffolk clothing towns between
1519 and 1527, and Thomas Kitson of London bought broadcloths from most of
the major centres of manufacture in west Wiltshire, Somerset and Gloucestershire
between 1529 and 1540.[37] Even in the North, the cloth industry of the West Riding
probably benefited from sales to London merchants who bought cloth there.[38] The

[31] E.M. Carus-Wilson, 'The Significance of the Secular Sculptures in the Lane Chapel,
Cullompton', *Medieval Archaeology*, I (1957), p. 115; A.E. Welsford, *John Greenway, 1460–1529, Merchant
of Tiverton and London: A Devon Worthy* (Tiverton, A.E. Welsford, 1984), pp. 4–5.

[32] Carus-Wilson, 'Woollen Industry', in *VCH Wilts.*, vol. 4, pp. 134–6.

[33] Spring was known as a merchant and clothier of Lavenham and London: *LP*, vol. 1(1), no. 438(3),
240. For links between Lavenham and London trade, see A. Betterton and D. Dymond, *Lavenham: Industrial
Town* (Lavenham, Terence Dalton, 1989), pp. 3, 26, 45–6; B. McClenaghan, *The Springs of Lavenham and the
Suffolk Cloth Trade in the XV and XVI Centuries* (Ipswich, W.E. Harrison, *c.* 1924), pp. 24, 33, 58.

[34] Carus-Wilson, 'Woollen Industry', in *VCH Wilts.*, vol. 4, pp. 134–5, 137.

[35] G.F. Beaumont, 'Paycocke's House, Coggeshall, with some Notes on the Families of Paycocke
and Buxton', *Transactions of Essex Archaeological Society*, new ser., IX (1906), 323.

[36] Heaton, *Yorkshire Woollen and Worsted Industries*, pp. 76, 146.

[37] Carus-Wilson, 'Woollen Industry', in *VCH Wilts.*, vol. 4, pp. 139–40; McClenaghan, *Springs of
Lavenham*, pp. 25–6.

[38] A.J. Pollard, *North-Eastern England during the Wars of the Roses* (Oxford, Clarendon Press, 1990), pp. 73–4.

growing number of prominent clothiers in provincial textile industries was a new development of the late fifteenth and early sixteenth centuries, and it was often seemingly a direct result of the growing importance of access to London capital and business connections.

This means that local economic development was often a consequence of the entrepreneurial restructuring of trade and industry, and the formation of new trading networks, rather than of net economic growth. Its benefits were restricted to a small number of places, and it was achieved partly at the cost of others elsewhere. London's growing overseas trade, for example, implied economic decay in numerous other port towns, especially those of the east coast where problems were often made worse by the silting up of harbours.[39] Even the best placed provincial ports were affected to some extent by London's competition, as at Exeter, where the decline of exports after the boom years 1497–1502 is attributed to the diversion of trade through London.[40] At the same time, the emergence of a network of entrepreneurs oriented to the London market also worked to the disadvantage of older cloth-making towns, notably Coventry and York.[41] Jenny Kermode has argued that merchants from northern towns, in particular, suffered for want of access to London networks of credit.[42] Smaller operators, or those impeded by institutional constraints, were put out of business. This means that any assessment of economic development relating to the cloth industry and cloth trade has to offset losses against gains. Only the evidence of the export figures allows us to say with confidence that the cloth industry as a whole was growing.

It is more difficult to find convincing evidence of stimuli in the home market to parallel those of the export trades. This is partly because there is no statistical

[39] C. Phythian-Adams, 'Urban Decay in Late Medieval England', in P. Abrams and E.A. Wrigley, eds, *Towns in Societies: Essays in Economic History and Historical Sociology* (Cambridge University Press, 1978), p. 168; S.H. Rigby, *Medieval Grimsby: Growth and Decline* (Hull University Press, 1993), pp. 133–5.

[40] Carus-Wilson, *Expansion of Exeter*, pp. 28–9.

[41] Palliser, *Tudor York*, pp. 208–11; C. Phythian-Adams, *Desolation of a City: Coventry and the Urban Crisis of the Late Middle Ages* (Cambridge University Press, 1979), pp. 48–9; Pollard, *North-Eastern England*, pp. 73–4.

[42] J. Kermode, 'Money and Credit in the Fifteenth Century: Some Lessons from Yorkshire', *Business History Review*, LXV (1991), 475–501.

source corresponding to the customs accounts to register changes in the volume of inland trade. However, the bulk of records relating to rural and urban activity should be great enough to identify industries expanding for domestic consumption, or of agricultural development in products other than export commodities. Coal-mining supplies one example of growth. The industry was most developed on the north-east coalfield, where the Bishop of Durham's revenues from coal leases and way leaves more than doubled between 1464 and 1496. Growth throughout the period was perhaps most marked at Whickham.[43] Coal exports from Newcastle increased from the 1490s, though growth was slow.[44] However, coal-mining was more scattered than either lead-mining or tin-mining, a feature of the industry well captured in Leland's account of his travels, and the inland location of many pits implies that the domestic market was the relevant one.[45] Growth of internal demand is suggested by development at inland sites such as some in Leicestershire.[46]

The iron industry, too, probably experienced some development for the home market. Towards the end of the period, Leland mentions the development of iron-making in the Mendips, where he records a recent discovery of ore deposits, and implies that new smelting operations had been undertaken as a result of it. There was perhaps increased activity of iron-using industries in Birmingham and Walsall, which he singles out for mention as centres of smithwork.[47] Iron-making

[43] D. Levine and K. Wrighton, *The Making of an Industrial Society: Whickham, 1560–1765* (Oxford, Clarendon Press, 1991), pp. 13–14; Pollard, *North-Eastern England*, p. 76.

[44] J.F. Wade, 'The Overseas Trade of Newcastle upon Tyne in the Late Middle Ages', *Northern History*, XXX (1994), 33, 39–40; J. Hatcher, *The History of the British Coal Industry, 1: Before 1700* (Oxford, Clarendon Press, 1993), pp. 77, 487.

[45] Leland, *Itinerary*, vol. 4, p. 123, and vol. 5, pp. 68, 126, 140 (Coquet Island, Morton in Glendale and Newcastle, Northumberland); vol. 4, p. 32, and vol. 5, pp. 129, 140 (Weardale and [Bishop] Auckland, Durham); vol. 1, p. 42 (around Wakefield, Yorks.); vol. 5, p. 43 (Bolton le Moors, Lancs.); vol. 2, p. 97, and vol. 5, p. 23 (Wednesbury and Walsall, Staffs.); vol. 5, pp. 18 (Wombridge, Salop, and the Clent Hills, Worcs.); vol. 3, pp. 59, 60, and vol. 4, p. 178 (Gwendraeth Fawr and Kidwelly, Carms.); vol. 3, pp. 69, 73 (the Alyn Valley and Hawarden, Flint); vol. 3, p. 117 (near Tenby, Pembs,); vol. 5, p. 105 (Mendip Hills, Som.); Hatcher, *History of the British Coal Industry*, pp. 112, 123–4, 131–2, 142, 149–52, 160–1, 165–6.

[46] Hatcher, *History of the British Coal Industry*, p. 166.

[47] Leland, *Itinerary*, vol. 1, p. 294; vol. 2, p. 97; vol. 5, p. 23.

for the home market also grew in the Sussex Weald, much of it for cast-iron cannons as a result of government initiative; blast furnace technology was introduced there from France in 1496.[48] All told, however, the increased employment and income generated by iron-making up to 1550 was very modest. To offset his examples of growth, Leland speaks of a decay of the iron industry in Bury and Horwich (Lancs.).[49] The contribution of new technology to growth was barely perceptible. As late as the 1520s there were only three blast furnaces operating in the Weald and most of the recorded expansion of output came only in the 1540s.[50] Slight development seems also to be characteristic of the salt industry, for although Leland spoke of the 'great advancement' of Droitwich, the evidence of the 1520s does not suggest that it was then generating much income.[51]

There are examples of growth in some urban manufacturing industries that can be attributed to domestic demand. Capmaking, an early branch of the knitting industry, grew in Gloucester, Coventry and York.[52] Evidence of such developments is hard to find, however, particularly before the 1530s and 1540s. Future research may be more productive in this area, but the scholarship of the past hundred years has not uncovered much to inspire optimism. In towns other than those engaged in export industries, contemporaries characteristically reported stagnation and decay rather than new development.[53] The small towns benefiting from rising exports were exceptionally fortunate. A recent study of the

[48] H.R. Schubert, *History of the British Iron and Steel Industry from c. 450 BC to AD 1775* (Routledge and Kegan Paul, 1957), pp. 147–8, 157–67.

[49] Leland, *Itinerary*, vol. 5, p. 43.

[50] Cornwall, *Wealth and Society*, pp. 81, 84; W.G. Hoskins, *The Age of Plunder: The England of Henry VIII, 1500–1547* (Longman, 1976), pp. 169–70; C.G.A. Clay, *Economic Expansion and Social Change: England, 1500–1700* (2 vols, Cambridge University Press, 1984), vol. 2, pp. 54–5. Blanchard estimates an increased output from 3,300 tons in 1500 to 9,620 tons in 1580: Blanchard, 'Labour Productivity', p. 24.

[51] Cornwall, *Wealth and Society*, pp. 79–80.

[52] N.M. Herbert, *Medieval Gloucester* (Gloucestershire Record Office, 1993), pp. 52–3; Phythian-Adams, *Desolation of a City*, p. 44; H. Swanson, *Medieval Artisans: An Urban Class in Late Medieval England* (Oxford, Blackwell, 1989), pp. 50–1.

[53] R.B. Dobson, 'Urban Decline in Late Medieval England', *TRHS*, 27 (1977), 1–22.

small market town of Northallerton in the North Riding, which had no export industry, shows little or no economic development between 1470 and 1540.[54] Though the evidence of tin output and exports is not wholly clear-cut, it suggests that the home market lagged behind the overseas market between 1485 and 1550, despite occasionally severe recessions in overseas markets.

Evidence of changes in agricultural production is poor in this period, but there is little sign of expansion in any branch other than wool. At Durham Priory's estate at Billingham on Teesside, exceptionally good evidence relating to tithe receipts shows stagnation of crop production between the 1460s and the 1510s.[55] Sluggishness in the domestic rural economy is also suggested by the history of rent movements. On some estates where extensive pasture farming could be practised, rents rose at times during the course of the period, reversing the downward trend that had characterized the third quarter of the fifteenth century. In many parts of England, however, there is no evidence of long-term increase in land values before the price rises of the 1520s and subsequently. Even after 1520, despite a chorus of complaint about rising rents, and the unrest that enclosing landlords caused in many villages, rising prices were imperfectly reflected in landlords' incomes on very many estates.[56]

It is likely, on the current balance of evidence, that exports were the most dynamic sector of the English economy and that the domestic market was growing more slowly. This in turn suggests that we should expect to find only a very gradual, hesitant and interrupted pattern of overall economic development. Nicholas Mayhew has recently put forward estimates that imply that English national income grew by 0.1 per cent a year between 1470 and 1526, and by 1.1 per cent a year between 1526 and 1546. Allowance must be made for wide margins of error in these figures, but they are likely to be correct in suggesting a

---

[54] C.M. Newman, 'Order and Community in the North: the Liberty of Allertonshire in the Later Fifteenth Century', in *The North of England in the Age of Richard III*, ed. A.J. Pollard (Stroud, Alan Sutton, 1996), pp. 50–1.

[55] R.A. Lomas, *North-East England in the Middle Ages* (Edinburgh, John Donald, 1992), pp. 111–12.

[56] *Discourse of the Common Weal*, pp. 38–9; I.S.W. Blanchard, 'Population Change, Enclosure and the Early Tudor Economy', *EcHR*, 2nd ser., XXIII (1970), 435; Britnell, *Closing of the Middle Ages?*, pp. 238–41.

very low rate of recovery from the mid-fifteenth-century slump. Both population and industrial history suggest that some modest acceleration should be located between the 1520s and 1540s, though there may have been a similar phase in the late fifteenth century. But the years 1450–1550 are likely to have contained long periods of stagnation and contraction, and it would not take much reassessment of the evidence to eliminate the plus sign altogether from some decades.

Even if there was economic growth in the second quarter of the sixteenth century, the basis for such development in the historical evidence is hard to detect. The movement of real wages suggests that increases in employment were insufficient to accommodate the population growth of these decades. Some increasing output was probably permitted by population growth that increased the availability of labour at traditional wage rates, and by rising prices that permitted higher profits and rents for a minority of the population. However, the course of development was strongly influenced during these decades by the effects of overseas war, and the possibilities for economic growth under Henry VIII were repeatedly curtailed by government action.

II

Medieval governments, like those of modern states, had some real influence on the course of economic development, not so much through deliberate economic policy as through decisions concerning war and peace, which had direct implications for levels of taxation and freedom to trade. The primary questions relating to government, for the purposes of this discussion, must therefore concern the impact of taxation and warfare upon the economy. Tax levels were extraordinarily low in the later fifteenth century, so the slow rate of development in the first half of the period in question can hardly be laid at the government's door. Thereafter levels of taxation rose, chiefly through the development of the assessed subsidy. Richard Hoyle's recent calculations imply that the burden of lay and clerical taxes averaged £91,561 between 1522 and 1527, and £128,440 between 1543 and 1549,[57] implying that government absorbed by this means

---

[57] R. Hoyle, 'War and Public Finance', in *The Reign of Henry VIII: Politics, Policy and Piety*, ed. D. MacCulloch (Macmillan, 1995), p. 93.

about 1.6 to 1.8 per cent of national income, assuming that Mayhew's estimates for 1526 and 1546 are somewhere near being right. It is interesting that changes in taxation levels followed a similar pattern to that proposed for economic development, with the most marked change occurring in the final decades of the period of study, and it is tempting to see these phenomena as directly related. Towards the very end of the period higher taxation was perhaps partly underpinned by economic development. However, this interpretation underrates the extent to which the rising level of taxation was a political rather than an economic phenomenon, and misrepresents the conditions in which higher taxes were levied in the 1520s, when they were largely at the expense of living standards and accumulations of private wealth.

Measures of the tax burden in relation to national income are misleading if they imply that taxes were easily borne or that their effects were insignificant. Taxation was erratic in its incidence, so that measures of annual averages give a false impression of the problems of years when taxes were heavy. Moreover, in terms of its impact upon the economy, the level of taxation is best considered not in relation to national income but in relation to money supply. This was a society in which many individuals had very modest cash holdings; the average money stock per head was probably less than £0.5 before the debasement of the late 1540s. Money in circulation was perhaps £1.4 million in 1526 and £1.45 million in 1546, which implies that about a fifteenth of the stock was diverted to government spending in the former year and about a sixth in the latter.[58] Since much government revenue was spent abroad, especially in wartime, its consequences were often deflationary. Henry VII diverted £138,000 to Philip of Castile in 1505, having committed himself to his interests in the Netherlands and Spain, and altogether the Habsburgs received £226,000 out of the king's chamber between 1505 and 1509.[59] From 1512 Henry VIII paid subsidies to the Emperor Maximilian to engage his interest against France; in 1515–16 perhaps

[58] Hoyle, 'War and Public Finance', p. 98; Mayhew, 'Population', p. 244.

[59] S.B. Chrimes, *Henry VII* (Methuen, 1972), p. 289; B.P. Wolffe, *The Royal Demesne in English History: The Crown Estate in the Governance of the Realm from the Conquest to 1509* (George Allen and Unwin, 1971), p. 224. See also F.C. Dietz, *English Government Finance, 1485–1558* (2nd edn, University of Illinois, 1964), p. 85, where Habsburg 'loans' are estimated at a minimum of £260,000.

£35,000 went abroad to finance the Emperor's siege of Milan and to keep some Swiss cantons in line with England against France. The defence of Tournai is estimated to have cost £40,000 a year between 1514 and 1518.[60] At the time of Suffolk's invasion of France in 1523 the English government was subsidizing the Duke of Bourbon's activities in southern France to the extent of £21,500, and the same sum was sent to him in 1524.[61]

The effect of government activities on economic development between the 1470s and the 1520s can be interpreted, in modern jargon, as equivalent to a random stop-go policy. Periods of warfare and preparation for warfare such as 1475, 1512–13, 1522–4, 1528, 1542–6, disrupted trade with the Continent and so reduced the profits of the export trades, which constituted the most dynamic sector of the economy. Simultaneously they took purchasing power away from the home market. These are points upon which contemporary comment is unambiguous. Skelton in 1522 compared the flourishing industry of the Burgundians, Spaniards and Flemings with that of England, attributing unemployment at home directly to taxation.[62] The same arguments, with elaborations, were used to justify determined resistance to the Amicable Grant of 1525, when shortage of coin was alleged to be the root of widespread poverty.[63] Early in 1528 hostilities with Charles V were held responsible both for disrupting grain supplies in a period of dearth, and with creating unemployment in the provincial woollen industry because of the poor sale of cloth at Blackwell Hall in London.[64] High taxes simultaneously checked inflationary pressures and depressed output and investment. Once the period of high taxation was over, and the economy left to recuperate, inflationary pressures

[60] P. Gwyn, *The King's Cardinal: The Rise and Fall of Thomas Wolsey* (Barrie and Jenkins, 1990), p. 64; Dietz, *English Government Finance*, p. 92.

[61] Dietz, *English Government Finance*, p. 94. The sum was defined on each occasion as 100,000 crowns, the crown at this time being valued at 4s 4d: *Tudor Royal Proclamations*, ed. P.L. Hughes and J.F. Larkin (3 vols, New Haven and London, Yale University Press, 1964–9), vol. 1, no. 95, p. 141.

[62] 'Why Come Ye Nat to Courte', lines 928–32, in John Skelton, *The Complete English Poems*, ed. J. Scattergood (Harmondsworth, Penguin Books, 1983), p. 302.

[63] G.W. Bernard, *War, Taxation and Rebellion in Tudor England: Henry VIII, Wolsey and the Amicable Grant of 1525* (Brighton, Harvester Press, 1986), pp. 110–30.

[64] E. Hall, *The Union of the Two Noble and Illustre Famelies of Lancastre and Yorke* (J. Johnson and others, 1809), pp. 736, 745–6.

resumed. This interpretation is supported by the way in which years of inflation alternated with periods of warfare between 1519 and 1529. The growth trends that our sources hint at from the later 1520s, together with the associated inflation, would presumably have been more pronounced at a rather earlier date if it had not been for Henry VIII's fits of bellicosity.[65]

The 1530s saw less warfare than the 1520s, and much of such military expenditure as there was was spent at home on fortifications. Taxation of the laity was light, though ecclesiastical incomes bore more of the brunt. These characteristics of the decade were more favourable to economic development than those of the 1520s. The 1540s, by contrast, saw the renewal of warfare on a reckless scale. There is no very reliable information about the extent to which Crown income was spent abroad during the French wars of 1544–6 and 1549–51 either in support of allies or to meet heavy expenditure on the defences of Boulogne (captured in September 1544), Calais and other French towns. The total cost of continental engagements in the years 1544–50 averaged about £200,000 a year, much of which leaked abroad for the payment of troops, construction costs and the prompt repayment of heavy loans contracted in Flanders.[66] Between 1542 and 1545 the export of hard currency was at least £45,250 a year on average, mostly paid in gold.[67]

The 1540s require to be analysed separately from the 1520s because of new elements of government policy. Taxation in the 1540s reached unprecedentedly high levels, but even lay and ecclesiastical taxes together funded only about a quarter of the cost of the war. A new source of income, which also to some extent took currency out of circulation, derived from the alienation of monastic estates. These two means of paying for war abroad were intrinsically deflationary. However, during the 1540s these effects of government expenditure were more than offset by debasement of the coinage, which may have funded half the costs of warfare.[68] It is possible, therefore, that the economic effects of warfare in the

---

[65] Hoyle, 'War and Public Finance', pp. 97–9.

[66] Dietz, *English Government Finance*, pp. 167–74; Hoyle, 'War and Public Finance', p. 90.

[67] C.E. Challis, *The Tudor Coinage* (Manchester University Press, 1978), p. 241.

[68] Hoyle, 'War and Public Finance', pp. 95–6.

1540s were less detrimental to some aspects of growth than those of the 1520s, since they raised commodity prices relative to rents and wages and perhaps stimulated some forms of investment. The doctor in *A Discourse of the Common Weal* is sure enough that the state of those on fixed incomes was damaged by inflation, but he is more sceptical about its adverse effects on artificers such as cappers, clothiers, shoemakers and farriers. Employers were hampered to the extent that they paid wages in kind, but not to the extent that they could pay wages in money, since money wages lagged behind prices.[69] In the absence of better information and analysis it would be unwise to place much stress on such opportunities; it is difficult to believe, during the years of high taxation, that they were sufficiently widespread to generate development in many sectors of the economy.

III

Somewhere between 1450 and 1550 are to be found the origins of sixteenth-century population growth, and this realization, not surprisingly, inspires directly or indirectly a good deal of questioning about the period. Both the timing of the turning point (or turning points) and its cause (or causes) remain debated issues. At times the search has involved finding the earliest vestiges of those economic trends known to have accompanied population growth in the mid-sixteenth century, but this reduces the enquiry to indirect evidence of a particularly precarious kind. At other times the search leads to real demographic evidence, but this is invariably restricted to such small groups that it cannot at present justify confident statements about the population of England as a whole. The following comments first explore the limitations of the indirect, economic evidence for population growth, and then the limitations of the direct demographic evidence, before coming to a modest but (inevitably) tentative conclusion.

One possible proxy for population growth is evidence of increasing vagrancy, a matter of common political concern in the early sixteenth century. Yet vagrancy is so poorly quantified, and had so many causes other than population growth,

[69] *Discourse of the Common Weal*, p. 33.

that any argument linking it to population growth must be of doubtful validity. In the normal state of affairs there was a good deal of migration and at least temporary vagrancy among the labourers of late medieval England. Some Essex statistics imply that the rate of spatial mobility in the years 1467–97 was, in fact, much the same as it was two centuries later.[70] Some unemployment and migration was occasionally created by the eviction of tenants to create sheep pastures.[71] More commonly, workers needed to migrate from regions of industrial decay to regions where employment was growing.[72] Other evidence of unemployment relates to the temporary effects of interruptions in overseas trade resulting from recurrent war.[73] None of these patterns of vagrancy and unemployment was a new phenomenon and none of them had anything to do with population growth. Contemporaries did not write about vagrancy as evidence of population growth – in fact they were more likely to believe that population was falling. Thomas Starkey's Lupset speaks of 'the grete multytude of beggarys here in our cuntrey in thys lake and skarsenes of pepul'.[74] Modern historians, too, even when they accept the reality of increasing vagrancy from the 1480s onwards, have generally attributed it to causes quite other than population growth.[75]

Increasing vagrancy need not, in fact, be taken for granted as an attested feature of the period. It is usually unclear whether contemporary observations relate to short-term or long-term changes, which makes them almost worthless for any assessment of the nature or seriousness of the problem. It is implausible to suppose that observers could reliably assess changes in the volume of vagrancy in

---

[70] Cornwall, *Wealth and Society*, pp. 216–30; L.R. Poos, *A Rural Society after the Black Death: Essex, 1350–1525* (Cambridge University Press, 1991), pp. 159–79, 181–2.

[71] Cornwall, *Wealth and Society*, pp. 236–8.

[72] Phythian-Adams, *Desolation of a City*, pp. 219, 260.

[73] Hall, *Union*, p.745.

[74] Starkey, *Dialogue*, p. 60.

[75] For example, M. Dobb, *Studies in the Development of Capitalism* (Routledge and Kegan Paul, 1946), p. 224, where increased vagrancy from 1485 is ascribed to 'the disbanding of feudal retainers, the dissolution of the monasteries, the enclosure of land for sheep-farming and changes in the methods of tillage'.

the absence of continuously recorded evidence, and much of what they say is too redolent of uninformed prejudice to be taken at face value. The most persistent official pronouncements about vagrancy arose from concern with political stability and the conservation of military resources, and are more easily explained as fashions in rhetoric than as a response to real changes in levels of unemployment. In particular, government measures against vagrants were used to back up government policy on law enforcement. Even when the activity of local courts suggests some significant number of vagrants, it is unrealistic to suppose that political and moral agendas played no part in the way they were perceived. A concern that was as great in regions of development as in regions of stagnation cannot be given any very obvious long-term dynamic significance.[76]

A second source feature of sixteenth-century population growth was price inflation and in some circumstances it is reasonable to think of the latter as evidence for the former. If prices of foodstuffs rise relative to less essential commodities over periods of years, and if average incomes can be shown not to have changed, then this might imply that the size of families was growing, so that more food was having to be purchased from family budgets. It is possible that this sort of inflationary pressure set in from around 1520, when a gradually rising price level became associated with a shift in relative prices as cereals prices suddenly rose more sharply than those of wool. However, causal relationships between inflation and changes in population in the decades before 1550 are very uncertain because inflation can be accounted for in other ways. Much of the price instability of the 1520s can be explained by temporary climatic conditions, coupled with some interruption of supplies of grain from abroad, as in 1527–8.[77] If these crises are allowed for, there was still an underlying inflationary trend, which continued through the 1530s and 1540s. Yet even this cannot be accepted as evidence for population growth in the absence of support from elsewhere. Movements of grain prices in England were sensitive to what was happening on

[76] M.K. McIntosh, 'Local Change and Community Control in England, 1465–1500', *Huntington Library Quarterly*, XLIX (1986), 227–33; Newman, 'Order and Community', in *North of England*, ed. Pollard, p. 65.

[77] D. Dymond, 'The Famine of 1527 in Essex', *Local Population Studies*, 26 (1981), p. 29; Gwyn, *King's Cardinal*, pp. 455–9.

the Continent, particularly in the Low Countries, since English produce was liable to be marketed overseas where transport costs allowed. The inflation of domestic prices may in part have non-domestic causes.[78] More significantly, there are monetary explanations for the inflation of this period. It is estimated that England's internal money supply increased from £0.9 million in 1470 to £1.45 million in March 1546 and perhaps £2.66 million in July 1551. In the 1540s this monetary inflation was fuelled by the government's debasement of the currency (in 1544–6 and 1549–51) as a device for financing warfare against Scotland and France.[79] Some further considerations would weigh against a demographic explanation of rising prices. It is far from clear what real investment in the home market could be generating steeply increasing demand for grain and creating pressures on normal supply.[80] Though there were some years of bad harvests when supplies were interrupted, contemporary comment does not support the idea that the long-term movement of prices was a consequence of deficiencies. Even at the end of the period, well-informed men could agree on this point. 'This is a mervelous dearthe', says the knight in *A Discourse of the Common Weal*, 'that in such plentie cometh, contrary to his kynd', and the acceptance of that proposition by the other participants in the discourse, the doctor, the husbandman and the capper, is the springboard for his following discussion.[81] It was just this confidence that high prices were not the result of supply problems that inspired contemporary monetary interpretations of inflation. Given the low level of population by past standards and the universal agreement among contemporaries that there was no shortage of resources for food production,[82] there can be no question of adopting a Malthusian argument to the effect that population growth was running up against scarcities of land.

[78] Hughes and Larkin, *Tudor Royal Proclamations*, vol. 1, nos. 26, 67, 239, 255, 262, 269, 280, 301, 315, 319, 365, pp. 27, 100, 340–1, 356–7, 362, 370–1, 386–7, 419–20, 435–6, 439, 499–503.

[79] Challis, *Tudor Coinage*, pp. 241–2.

[80] Any argument that links inflation and increasing destitution together as evidence for increasing population risks being self-contradictory, since rising numbers could not generate pressure on market demand if the increment to population was destitute.

[81] *Discourse of the Common Weal*, p. 37.

[82] For example, Thomas Starkey, *A Dialogue between Pole and Lupset*, ed. T.F. Mayer (Camden Fourth Series, XXXVII, London, 1989), pp. 58–9.

A third economic argument for rising population in the sixteenth century derives from evidence of real wages. Yet since money wage rates were virtually unchanged between 1450 and the final decades of the period, when they started to rise, any reduction of what wages would buy between 1450 and the 1550s was directly related to rising prices. This means that this argument for population growth can have no force until some time well into the sixteenth century. Builders' wages were stable at 4*d* a day for labourers from 1412 to 1545 and at 6*d* a day for craftsmen from 1412 to 1532, rising from 6*d* to 7*d* between 1532 and 1548.[83] Bowden's agricultural day wage-rate series from Oxford, Cambridge and Eton College is stable at 4*d* a day from 1450 to 1520, after which it rises to 4½*d* by 1550. This increase is not apparent at all in the Oxford series, and shows in the Cambridge series only during the 1540s.[84] Donald Woodward's recently published wage series from northern towns show stability in York between 1470 and 1550, with labourers getting 4*d* a day and craftsmen 6*d*. In Hull the labourer's wage increased from 4*d* to 5*d*, but only after 1540.[85] The failure of wage rates to rise with prices is surely significant for the state of the labour market, but it is only from the 1520s that this line of argument can lend any support to the idea that competition for work among employees was increasing.

The unreliability of these indirect types of evidence is unfortunate, since more direct evidence is hard to come by. Though estimates for the final decades of this period are more solidly founded than for any earlier period since 1377, they do not agree with each other sufficiently well to resolve the questions that concern us. The best estimate for 1522, based on the remaining muster rolls, suggests an English population of 1.84 million, while an independent estimate for 1541 suggests 2.77 million. These figures cannot both be right, since the rate of growth they imply over the intervening nineteen years is inconceivably high.[86] This greatly weakens their usefulness for modelling the history of population in the

[83] Brown and Hopkins, *Perspective of Wages and Prices*, p. 11.

[84] Bowden, 'Statistical Appendix', in *Agrarian History, IV*, ed. Thirsk, p. 864.

[85] Woodward, *Men at Work*, pp. 263, 274.

[86] B.M.S. Campbell, 'The Population of Early Tudor England: A Re-Evaluation of the 1522 Muster Returns and 1524 and 1525 Lay Subsidies', *Journal of Historical Geography*, VII (1981), 153; Wrigley and Schofield, *Population History*, pp. 208–9.

preceding period, and leaves open a wide range of conflicting interpretations of late medieval population history. However, they suggest that English population probably grew at some quite vigorous rate between 1522 and 1541, a conclusion that is supported by the decline of real wages from the 1520s.

Some of the best local evidence suggests that such sustained recovery of population was long delayed and that in many regions there were still no signs of it even in the 1520s. The tithingpenny figures discovered by Larry Poos for some Essex manors, where they run into the sixteenth century, show no upward swing before the 1530s.[87] Nor do the comparable figures from the Aquila honour in Sussex compiled by Mavis Mate.[88] There is very little evidence for any upswing in most of north-eastern England before the early sixteenth century, and in some parts of the region it was later than that. The population of the liberty of Northallerton, subject to repeated crises of mortality, rested at around 3,000 throughout the period between 1471 and 1548.[89] Population increase across the kingdom as a whole cannot be assumed to have been normal between 1450 and the 1520s.

Evidence for population growth between 1450 and 1550 turns up mostly in locations where industry and trade were expanding, such as parts of London, Westminster, and scattered centres of investment in textile manufacture and mining.[90] The population of Westminster and Southwark, as we have seen, were already recovering strongly by the 1470s. There is evidence of a growing population in smaller industrial and commercial centres such as Grasmere and Kendal.[91] Between 1381 and 1522 the recorded male population grew by 29 per cent in the Vale of Kennet near the textile centre of Newbury, and in the adjacent downland parishes.[92] However, at no point in the period can population growth

---

[87] Poos, *Rural Society*, pp. 96–103, 109.

[88] M. Mate, 'The Occupation of the Land: Kent and Sussex', in *The Agrarian History of England and Wales, III: 1348–1500*, ed. E. Miller (Cambridge University Press, 1991), p. 128.

[89] C.M. Newman, *Northallerton in the Later Middle Ages* (Stamford, Paul Watkins, forthcoming); Pollard, *North-Eastern England*, p. 48.

[90] Blanchard, 'Population Change', pp. 427–45.

[91] M.K. Jones and M.G. Underwood, *The King's Mother: Lady Margaret Beaufort, Countess of Richmond and Derby* (Cambridge University Press, 1992), pp. 123–4.

[92] M. Yates, 'Continuity and Change in Rural Society c. 1400–1600: West Hanney and Shaw (Berkshire) and their Region' (unpublished D. Phil. thesis, University of Oxford, 1997), pp. 61–2.

in these restricted contexts be assumed to represent aggregate population growth in the country as a whole since it was often the result of immigration from elsewhere, as at Havering between 1450 and 1480.[93] In the case of west Berkshire, it can be shown that growth around Newbury between 1381 and 1522 was offset by population decline in an adjacent region to the north, including the Vale of the White Horse, where the number of men declined by 18 per cent.[94] This example implies that recorded expansion in regions of commercial and industrial development might be the result of the spatial redistribution of families rather than of any net increase in their number. They may, in other words, illustrate no more than the willingness of fifteenth-century families to migrate in search of employment.[95] Comparisons between urban population histories suggest the same need for caution in the interpretation of local statistics. Numbers in London (excluding the suburbs) perhaps grew from 50,000 in 1500 to over 70,000 in 1550,[96] but at Coventry, the most dramatic example of industrial decay, the number of inhabitants fell from about 10,000 around 1440 to about 9,000 in 1500, 6,000 in 1523 and 5,000 or fewer in 1550.[97] There was also a decline in Shrewsbury's population in the last three decades under consideration.[98] These considerations discourage the use of local sources for identifying aggregate national trends, though there is a great deal of interesting research to be carried out in identifying the environmental circumstances that induced expansion and contraction.

Population growth between 1450 and 1550 is unlikely to have been continuous anywhere in the country. Evidence for repeated crises of mortality between 1450 and 1510 has improved over the years, and with it the likelihood that some of

---

[93] McIntosh, *Autonomy and Community*, pp. 221–3.

[94] M. Yates, 'Continuity and Change in Rural Society *c.* 1400–1600: West Hanney and Shaw (Berkshire) and their Region' (unpublished D. Phil. thesis, University of Oxford, 1997), pp. 61–2.

[95] A.F. Butcher, 'The Origins of Romney Freemen, 1433–1523', *Economic History Review*, 2nd ser., XXVII (1974), 20–7.

[96] S. Rappaport, *Worlds within Worlds: Structures of Life in Sixteenth-Century London* (Cambridge University Press, 1989), p. 61.

[97] Phythian-Adams, *Desolation of a City*, p. 281.

[98] W.A. Champion, 'The Shrewsbury Lay Subsidy of 1525', *Transactions of the Shropshire Archaeological Society*, LXIV (1985), 38–9.

them caused significant reductions in the population of the kingdom. The simultaneous decline in the expectation of life among the monks of Canterbury Cathedral Priory and Westminster Abbey between 1450 and 1480 may imply rising mortality outside the cloister walls.[99] Serious epidemics recurred right up to the end of the period, though less frequently towards the end of it. There were mortality crises in Westminster Abbey in 1457–8, 1463–4, 1478–9, 1490–1 and 1529–30.[100] The relationship between known crises and the changing level of population is nevertheless too uncertain for any consensus of opinion to have emerged about the changing impact of mortality rates. According to some, improved expectations of life after about 1500 were the foundation of sixteenth-century population growth.[101] Others see the last years of the fifteenth century and the early sixteenth century up to 1510–20 as a period of significant setback after an earlier transient recovery.[102]

It seems likely, given the evidence of static population in many places, the evidence that population growth in some parts was offset by contraction elsewhere and the evidence of recurrent mortality crises, that population in 1510 was little or no higher than in 1450, despite intermediate phases of aborted recovery. It also seems likely, to judge from the estimates for 1522 and 1547 and the concurrent decline in real wages, that numbers were increasing by the second quarter of the sixteenth century. On this understanding, however, the economic and demographic history of the 1520s has arrived at an interesting crux that calls for some focused research. On the one hand, any estimate of English population in 1522, when compared with the significantly higher figure for 1541, requires the 1520s to be a decade of sustained and probably accelerating population growth. On the other hand, recurrent episodes of dearth in 1521 and 1527, and

[99] B. Harvey, *Living and Dying in England, 1100–1540: The Monastic Experience* (Oxford, Clarendon Press, 1993), pp. 127–9; J. Hatcher, 'Mortality in the Fifteenth Century: Some New Evidence', *EcHR*, 2nd ser., XXXIX (1986), 28–31.

[100] Harvey, *Living and Dying*, p. 122.

[101] M. Bailey, 'Demographic Decline in Late Medieval England: Some Thoughts on Recent Research', *EcHR*, XLIX (1996), 1–19; Clay, *Economic Expansion*, vol. 1, pp. 14–15; D. Loschy and B.D. Childers, 'Early English Mortality', *Journal of Interdisciplinary History*, XXIV (1993), pp. 85–97.

[102] Blanchard, 'Population Change', pp. 434–5; T.H. Hollingsworth, *Historical Demography* (republished, Cambridge, 1976), p. 387.

repeated complaints of excessive taxation and consequent unemployment such as those of Skelton, do not encourage an economic explanation of population growth. Ian Blanchard, who favours a cyclical interpretation of economic performance between 1450 and 1550, identifies the early 1520s as the trough of a cyclical downturn that began early in the sixteenth century.[103] Current interpretations of the state of the economy in the 1520s are incompatible with either long-run or short-run cyclical models that assume exceptional opportunities for demographic recovery. In some sectors inflation between 1520 and 1550 was perhaps a source of renewed development through the agency of profit inflation, but there are numerous objections to using this as an explanation for rising population, not least that, as we have seen, inflation was associated with falling rather than rising real wages. These circumstances suggest that the population growth of the decade had powerful non-economic causes, and that it should be regarded as an independent rather than a derived variable in economic development.

IV

The distinction between medieval and modern times, entrenched in pedagogical tradition since the dawn of formal history teaching, has generated a powerful motive for identifying the period 1450–1550 as one of economic revival (at least) or economic modernization (at best). The latter interpretation is prominent in some of the classic texts of English economic history, and their influence has been the longer because of their high quality, their wide readership and the conformity of their ideas to traditional syllabus design. In Cunningham's history, for example, the late fifteenth century began a new age, characterized by 'discovery', 'growth of the mercantile system', 'accelerated rate of change', 'enclosing', 'the superseding of manorial economy' and 'changes in opinion'.[104] Tawney took his

---

[103] *Duchy of Lancaster Estates in Derbyshire, 1485–1540*, ed. I.S.W. Blanchard, Derby Archaeological Society Record Series, III (Derby, 1971), p. 13; Blanchard, 'Population Change', p. 434.

[104] W. Cunningham, *The Growth of English Industry and Commerce during the Early and Middle Ages* (5th edn, Cambridge University Press, 1910), pp. xxiii–xv, 473–566.

new rural economy back to the later fifteenth century, and wrote of 'the revolution in the technique of agriculture when sucked into the vortex of expanding commerce'.[105] Lipson's account of agriculture in this period is headed 'The Agrarian Revolution'.[106] Some later historians interested in the institutional changes of the period have continued to suggest a divide in the fifteenth century, as in John Martin's analysis of fifteenth-century enclosure, which compromises on a troublesome issue by identifying enclosures before 1450 as the result of feudal reaction and enclosures after 1450 as the result of a new form of landlord aggressiveness.[107] In some perceptions of the period, a new economy is an issue to be twinned with a 'new monarchy',[108] and historiographically these two formulations of change in the later fifteenth century are closely allied.[109] Cunningham saw Henry VII's reign as the time when mercantilism was consciously adopted as a new deal between trade and state-building, and this permitted him to divide 'modern times' into the age of the mercantile system (c. 1485–1770) and the age of *laissez faire* (c. 1770–1882).[110] Even Tawney was prepared to recognize Henry VII's accession as the start of 'a commercial age'.[111]

Classic interpretations of the period are more often concerned with describing structural changes in the occupation and management of land or the principles of government than with quantifying the rate of economic development, and to that extent they go beyond the subject matter of this paper. However, emphasis on the exceptional significance of these years for modernization of the economy has been

[105] R.H. Tawney, *The Agrarian Problem in the Sixteenth Century* (Longmans, Green and Co., 1912), pp. 196–7.

[106] E. Lipson, *The Economic History of England, I: The Middle Ages* (12th edn, Adam and Charles Black, 1959), ch. 4, pp. 133–84.

[107] J.E. Martin, *Feudalism to Capitalism: Peasant and Landlord in English Agrarian Development* (Macmillan, 1983), p. 123.

[108] For example, R. Lockyer, *Tudor and Stuart Britain, 1471–1714* (2nd edn, Longmans, 1985), pp. 1–15, 110–32, which is more sceptical of the new monarchy than of the new economy.

[109] For example, ch. 3 ('The Advent of the Middle Class') and ch. 4 ('The New Monarchy') in A.F. Pollard, *Factors in Modern History* (3rd edn, Constable, 1932), pp. 32–72.

[110] Cunningham, *Growth of English Industry and Commerce during the Early and Middle Ages*, pp. xxii, 471; W. Cunningham, *The Growth of English Industry and Commerce in Modern Times* (5th edn, 2 vols, Cambridge University Press, 1910–12).

[111] Tawney, *Agrarian Problem*, p. 185.

premised by the assumption that English society was commercializing more rapidly than during earlier centuries, and that this was why considerations of profit began to triumph in the management of landed property.[112] Such a dynamic interpretation of this period has long been questioned. It requires a strong prior commitment to academic convention to find any unprecedented development of commerce in the period 1450–1550, whose economic history rather suggests sluggish change in the core sector of the English economy (agriculture) and little dynamic development outside it except in the manufacture and export of woollen cloth. Such potential for growth as the early sixteenth-century economy may have possessed was thwarted, much of the time, by the belligerent ambitions of the monarchy, and this alone might be read, in accordance with another of Lipson's formulations of the contrast between medieval and modern, to attach the period 1450–1550 firmly to the period before 'the close of the Middle Ages'.[113]

Many aspects of the commercial exploitation of property that have been identified for the early sixteenth century had interesting equivalents two centuries earlier, at a time when the volume of commerce was probably greater.[114] The sort of transition towards monetized social relationships that was once thought to be characteristic of the early Tudor age can now be shown to have extended earlier over a much longer time period.[115] This reduces the desirability of making the sharp distinction between medieval and modern economy and society that came so easily to the earlier historians. The economic analysis of Cunningham, Tawney, Lipson, and the many writers they influenced, belonged to a deep-rooted perception of the European past, now challenged on many fronts, in which significant modernization of all sorts was telescoped into the period following the Italian Renaissance. Not even alternative academic orthodoxies

[112] For example, Tawney, *Agrarian Problem*, pp. 84–5, 185–6.

[113] According to this view, modernity dawned only when 'English sovereigns ceased to be preoccupied with sterile dreams of territorial aggrandisement on the Continent of Europe': E. Lipson, *The Growth of English Society: A Short Economic History* (4th edn, Adam and Charles Black, 1959), p. 72.

[114] See, in particular, E.A. Kosminsky, *Studies in the Agrarian History of England in the Thirteenth Century*, ed. R.H. Hilton, trans. R. Kisch (Oxford, Blackwell, 1956).

[115] This is argued more formally in R.H. Britnell, 'Commerce and Capitalism in Late Medieval England: Problems of Description and Theory', *Journal of Historical Sociology*, VI (1993), 359–76.

concerning 'the Industrial Revolution', and 'the origins of modern economic growth', which located the beginning of modern times in the mid-eighteenth century, succeeded in displacing the division between medieval and modern in economic and social history, despite the fact that many of the criteria that defined the later transition (including a transformation of the role of overseas trade, enclosure of peasant lands, the engrossment of land, the impoverishment of wage-earners, a harsher attitude towards vagrants, the triumph of mercantile interests and the origins of modern economic thinking) might be thought to have made the former an embarrassment. Now that historical scholarship has demonstrated the pervasiveness of economic development in the centuries before 1450, as well as the long continuation of earlier traditions into more recent centuries, the justification for locating some critical turning point in the period 1450–1550 has vanished, leaving only myth and illusion behind. Because such myth and illusion are communicated in influential texts, and are deeply embedded in periodizing constructs widely used by both historians and non-historians, they will long remain resistant to the impact of new research. It is nevertheless an irony of academic convention, and a testimony to the power of long-deceased authors over the historical imagination, that the hundred years of exceptionally gradual and unremarkable economic change in England between 1450 and 1550 should continue to be pinpointed as a period of pivotal importance for the kingdom's long-term economic development.

4

SIR THOMAS LOVELL (*c.* 1449–1524): A NEW MAN IN A NEW MONARCHY?

Steven Gunn

When did the Middle Ages end in Walsall? The historian of the town's metal industries might give us one answer, the historian of its parish church or of its grammar school another, but from the point of view of politics and government, 1504 looks as good a date as any. In 1504 the steward of Walsall died, and his successor was a man of very different stamp. The late steward was Sir Humphrey Stanley of Pipe, near Lichfield; his successor, Sir Thomas Lovell of Elsings in Enfield, Middlesex. Stanley's claim to the stewardship came at least as much from his Staffordshire landholdings and the power of his kin in the north-western counties as it did from his place in the king's household.[1] Lovell held no land at all in the county and sprang from a cadet branch of a minor Norfolk gentry family.[2] Stanley had a taste for the 'old Feudal amenities of Sackage, Carnage and Wreckage'. When he fell out with the Dean and Chapter of Lichfield in 1489, he cut off their water supply and had to be ordered in the Star Chamber to restore it; when he fell out with Thomas Brabyn in 1503, he led 120 followers into Derbyshire to drive him from his house; when he fell out with William Chetwynd in 1494, he had him ambushed

---

[1] Bodleian Library, MS dd Weld c1/5; C. Carpenter, *Locality and Polity: a Study of Warwickshire Landed Society, 1401–1499* (Cambridge, 1992), pp. 561–2, 572, 583. Fuller exposition of the general view of the development of early Tudor government adopted here, together with references to secondary sources, can be found in my *Early Tudor Government 1485–1558* (1995). I am grateful to the editor, Cliff Davies, Robert Peberdy, Gervase Rosser and Andrea Velich for their help with this chapter.

[2] G.L. Harrison, 'A few notes on the Lovells of East Harling', *Norfolk Archaeology*, 18 (1912), 46–7. I have estimated Lovell's date of birth from his admission at Lincoln's Inn: E.W. Ives, *The Common Lawyers of Pre-Reformation England. Thomas Kebell: a Case Study* (Cambridge, 1983), pp. 36, 47n.

and murdered on Tixall Heath.[3] Lovell, as we shall see, was not averse to violence, but his was more the impersonal violence of a monopolizing state. His preferred weapon was the pen. When possible he wrote suavely: 'And that I can reasonablie doo to your pleasure, I shalbe glad to my power. . . . By your lover, Thomas Lovelle.'[4] When necessary he wrote sharply: 'I mariveyll ye should be in any dowte ffor the matter ye wrytte to me ffor, ffor I shewyd you the kynges mynd in sertein.'[5]

Sir Humphrey Stanley took great interest in Walsall. He had been a burgess for twenty-four years when he became steward, joined the guild of St John the Baptist in 1485–6, and while in office twice oversaw the codification of the town's ordinances.[6] If anything he was still more involved in the affairs of Lichfield, where he served as master of the guild of St Mary for three years between 1478 and 1502, endowed it with two burgages in the city, helped make the guild's new ordinances for the regulation of civic affairs in 1486, and contributed to the foundation of an almshouse for poor women in Beacon Street.[7] He sat regularly at quarter sessions at Walsall, Lichfield and Stafford.[8]

Lovell might seem in contrast a distant placeman, but he was not. He ratified the new Walsall ordinances and signed the resulting entry on the burgess roll himself.[9] In 1514 he arbitrated a dispute between the mayor, burgesses and inhabitants of the town and John Lisle of Moxhull (Warwickshire) over the manor of Bascote in Long Itchington, awarding it to the townsmen on payment of £10 to Lisle.[10] In 1515 three men of Walsall parish included Lovell and his

[3] T. Harwood, *The History and Antiquities of the Church and City of Lichfield* (Gloucester, 1806), p. 297; Public Record Office, KB9/431/8; Carpenter, *Locality and Polity*, pp. 572–3.

[4] *Records of the Borough of Nottingham*, ed. W.H. Stevenson (9 vols, Nottingham, 1882–1936), vol. 3, p. 402.

[5] *Materials for a History of the Reign of Henry VII*, ed. W. Campbell, Rolls Series no. 60 (2 vols, 1873–7), vol. 1, p. 549.

[6] *VCH Staffordshire*, vol. 17 (1976), p. 213; Walsall Local History Centre, MS 276/67; MS 277/238, m. 3d, calendared in HMC, *Third Report* (1872), Appendix, p. 290.

[7] Harwood, *Lichfield*, pp. 303, 406–7, 410–11; *The Guild of St Mary, Lichfield*, ed. F.J. Furnivall, Early English Text Society, extra ser., no. 114 (Oxford, 1920), p. 11; *VCH Staffs.*, vol. 14 (1990), p. 234.

[8] PRO, KB9/379/5, 387/1, 391/49, 75, 410/38.

[9] HMC, *Third Report*, Appendix, p. 290.

[10] F.W. Willmore, *A History of Walsall and its Neighbourhood* (Walsall, 1887), p. 180.

late wife among the beneficiaries of the chantry they established in Bloxwich chapel.[11] All three founders had been among the forty-eight residents of Walsall and Bloxwich signed up as Lovell's retainers in 1508, in a fine cross-section of the local élite, including four past and three future mayors of Walsall, seven churchwardens of its parish church and the town's five richest inhabitants in the subsidy of 1525.[12]

These Walsalian great and good, the Bloxwich chantry founders and others in the retinue who held lesser parochial office were significant property-holders in the town and the surrounding fields. Sometimes they called themselves yeomen, sometimes loriners, spurriers or chapmen. Though their business interests spread into the surrounding counties, in Walsall they formed tight circles of feoffees and witnesses.[13] By 1508 Lovell's influence was almost as pervasive at Lichfield, where his retinue numbered forty-four. Of these, fourteen served in town office in the five years between 1494 and 1507 for which court rolls survive: four members of the Twelve (the bench of jurors at the borough court), eight tithingmen and two borough constables.[14] There was a place in all this for Sir Humphrey's son John Stanley, but it was not much of one. He collected the names of those in Walsall, Lichfield and Stone willing to serve Lovell, but at Walsall he was not even appointed deputy steward to the new

[11] *LP*, vol. 2, i, 201 (all *LP* references to document numbers except when specified otherwise).

[12] Willmore, *Walsall*, pp. 171, 202, 262; 'Church-wardens' accounts All Saints' Church Walsall 1462–1531', ed. G.P. Mander, *Collections for a History of Staffordshire*, 3rd ser. for 1928 (1930), pp. 178, 182, 230–40; PRO, E179/177/97, m. 4. All references to Lovell's retinue derive from Belvoir Castle, Additional MS 97, calendared in HMC, *Report 24: Manuscripts of His Grace the Duke of Rutland*, vol. 4 (1908), pp. 559–66; I am most grateful to His Grace the Duke of Rutland for permission to read and cite this manuscript, which is so far as I know the only extant list of a retinue licensed under the statute of 1504.

[13] 'Church-wardens' accounts', pp. 236–9, 246–7; Staffordshire Record Office, D260/M/T/1/1a/2, 3, 6, 8–19, 26–9; D260/M/T/1/11a; D260/M/T/7/3, 4; D593/A/2/20/1, 10, 17, 26, 31, 43, 44, 47; D593/A/2/22/19; D593/B/1/26/6/31/9; D593/B/1/26/6/39/13; *Calendar of the Deeds and Documents belonging to the Corporation of Walsall*, ed. R. Sims (Walsall, 1882), pp. 22–9; Keele University Library, SP10, unnumbered deed of 24 April 1495; PRO, C1/593/23–5; Lichfield Joint RO, Wills PR1, p. 90; Nottingham UL, Mi D 3878–80.

[14] Staffs. RO, D(W)1734/2/1/597, mm. 15–25; *VCH Staffs.*, vol. 14, p. 74. He may not even have been steward, for the office had been granted to the Earl of Shrewsbury in 1488: Lichfield JRO, B/A/1/12, f. 164r.

incumbent. That honour was reserved for William Hussey, son of Lovell's colleague on the King's Council Sir John Hussey and husband of Lovell's niece Ursula.[15]

How many of these burghers of Walsall and Lichfield had heard of Sir Thomas Lovell before 1504 we cannot guess. It is a good bet none of them had heard of him in 1485. The burgesses of Colchester could only identify him as 'a gentilman [of] Lyncolnes Inne' when he was chosen speaker of the Commons in that year, a middle-aged lawyer with an East Anglian practice and an insecure seat on the Norfolk commission of the peace who had joined the rebellion of 1483 and somehow won the confidence of Henry Tudor.[16] Lovell's grandfather and uncle were lords of Barton Bendish, but his father Ralph clawed his way to manorial lordship in Beachamwell only by marrying a widow and buying out the title of her daughter. John Paston III thought Lovell senior married the unfortunate heiress off 'to a knaue'; in a subsequent lawsuit her relations claimed worse, that he married the widow by force and exploited the daughter's weakness as 'a symple person & a very ideott frome tyme of her byrth tyll the tyme of her decease' to defraud her of her lands.[17]

Sir Thomas, then, was certainly a 'new man' socially, but was he so intellectually, a fitting agent of Renaissance monarchy? He was not trained in the classics, as later generations of Tudor statesmen were, and it was fair if somewhat graceless of the scholars of Oxford to acclaim the new steward of their university in 1524, Sir Thomas More, as more learned than his defunct predecessor, Sir Thomas Lovell.[18] Yet Lovell was well versed in the novelties that, as Francis

[15] Staffs. RO, D260/M/T/1/1a/8; D260/M/T/7/3; A.R. Maddison, *Lincolnshire Pedigrees*, Harleian Society, nos 50–2 (1902–4), vol. 2, pp. 527–8. The deputy may have been Sir John's younger brother rather than his son, but it was the son rather than the uncle who attended Lovell's funeral, and he was old enough to hold other offices by 1513 when these references occur: *LP*, vol. 4, i. 366; *History of Parliament: The Commons 1509–1558*, ed. S.T. Bindoff (3 vols, 1982), vol. 2, p. 427.

[16] *The Red Paper Book of Colchester*, ed. W.G. Benham (Colchester, 1902), p. 62; *CPR, 1476–85*, p. 566. This was presumably Lovell rather than his uncle of the same name, since three of these commissions were issued after the latter's death (Harrison, 'Lovells', p. 47). The two are hard to separate as feoffees, but the future Sir Thomas was involved in British Library, Additional Charter 27694 and CAD, vol. 1, A726 and vol. 5, A13127.

[17] Harrison, 'Lovells', pp. 46–7; *Paston Letters and Papers of the Fifteenth Century*, ed. N. Davis (2 vols, Oxford, 1971–6), vol. 1, pp. 558–9.

[18] *Epistolae Academicae 1508–1596*, ed. W.T. Mitchell, Oxford Historical Society, new ser. no. 26 (Oxford, 1980), p. 181.

Bacon noted, marked off the moderns from the ancients.[19] In 1492 he distributed the first set of printed ordinances of war ever produced for an English army, and at his death he owned forty-three printed books in French.[20] He was as familiar with gunpowder as with print, organizing the production or procurement of powder, shot, arquebuses, copper guns, falcons, serpentines, demi-culverins and a set of twelve guns 'called the xii sisters' in the wars of 1511–14.[21] In 1512 he refortified Calais to face siege-guns with new works including 'Lovel's Bulwark'.[22] As for the third innovation in Bacon's list, the compass which had made possible the discovery of the New World, Lovell's interest is attested by the arrangements he made late in life to meet Sebastian Cabot, Bristolian explorer and chief pilot of the Casa de Contratación of Seville.[23]

Not enough of Lovell's correspondence survives – five letters in all – to say much of his attitude to government, though two of the four suggest a concern with 'goode governaunce and rule' and with the 'condyng punysshment' of those who are minded 'of ther wilfulle disposicion to subuerte . . . good rule', a concern characteristic of the rhetoric of early Tudor kings and their councillors.[24] A less repressive facet of the same complex of ideas surfaces in the ordinances of the Nottingham free school Lovell helped to found in 1512, which maintained that 'by learninge the publicque weale commenlye ys gouerned'.[25] Like many of his colleagues in the service of Henry VII and Henry VIII, Lovell contributed to the glorification of the Tudors in words and in pictures. His chantry priests, like those of his colleagues in court and Council, Sir John Mordaunt, Sir John Cutt, Sir David Owen, Hugh Denis and Christopher Urswick, were to pray for the soul of the ruler Cutt called 'the most famous Kyng of most blessid memory',

---

[19] E.L. Eisenstein, *The Printing Revolution in Early Modern Europe* (Cambridge, 1983), p. 12.

[20] C. Richmond, *The Paston Family in the Fifteenth Century: The First Phase* (Cambridge, 1990), p. 202n; PRO, PROB2/199, mm. 4–5. These were in addition to the service books in his chapel; sections for English and Latin books may well be lost.

[21] *LP*, vol. 1, ii, 2604, p. 1515, Appendix 14.

[22] *The History of the King's Works*, vol. 3, ed. H.M. Colvin (1975), p. 342.

[23] *LP*, vol. 4, i, 366.

[24] PRO, SP1/8, f. 159v (*LP*, vol. 1, ii, 3087); *Records of the Borough of Nottingham*, vol. 3, pp. 342–3.

[25] *Records of the Borough of Nottingham*, vol. 3, p. 453.

Henry VII.[26] Lovell's will called Henry VIII 'my soueraigne lorde' and his probate inventory recorded only one painting in any of his houses, a portrait of Henry VII.[27] His own surviving portrait, in a bronze medallion attributed to Pietro Torrigiano, is surrounded by Tudor roses. These symbols of the dynasty's providential mission of political healing were displayed ubiquitously on the possessions of its agents, from the ceilings of Sir Edward Poynings' house at Westenhanger to Sir Henry Wyatt's charter of free warren in his manors in Kent.[28] At Enfield parish church, where Lovell installed the crowned royal arms in the stained glass, he doubtless used the closed imperial crown, symbol of the king's supreme temporal authority, as Poynings and Wyatt did.[29]

If we cannot directly recover much of Lovell's attitude to the development of the state, we can infer some from his education and more from his actions. At Lincoln's Inn, where he studied from 1464, he was reader in Autumn 1475 and Lent 1482. He shared in the debates which formed the inclinations of the common-lawyer lobby increasingly influential in royal counsels. He mixed not only with those who would be his legal colleagues on the Council of Henry VII, James Hobart and Robert Drury, but also with the Yorkist courtiers given special admission to the Inn in the 1470s, who would join them in Henry's service, Giles Daubeney, John Fortescue and John Sapcotes; and with Hobart and Fortescue at least he kept up contact outside the Inn.[30] The Inn taught him to organize revels

---

[26] PRO, PROB11/23/27; *Bedfordshire Wills proved in the Prerogative Court of Canterbury 1383–1548*, ed. M. McGregor, Bedfordshire Historical Record Society no. 58 (Bedford, 1979), p. 68; H.W. King, 'The descent of the manor of Horham, and of the family of Cutts', *Transactions of the Essex Archaeological Society*, 4 (1869), 34; W.H. StJ. Hope, *Cowdray and Easebourne Priory* (1919), p. 111; PRO, E211/291, f. 3v; Windsor, The Aerary, MS IV.B.1, f. 157v (I am most grateful to the Dean and Canons of Windsor for permission to cite their records).

[27] PRO, PROB2/199, m. 5.

[28] *Henry VIII: A European Court in England*, ed. D.R. Starkey (1991), p. 33; G. Clinch, 'Notes on the remains of Westenhanger house, Kent', *Archaeologia Cantiana*, 31 (1915), 80–1; PRO, E326/12541.

[29] HMC, *Rutland*, vol. 4, p. 265.

[30] *The Records of the Honourable Society of Lincoln's Inn: Admissions from AD 1420 to AD 1799* (1896), pp. 14–21; *The Records of the Honourable Society of Lincoln's Inn: The Black Books*, ed. W.P. Baildon, R. Roxburgh (5 vols, 1897–1968), i, pp. 58, 73; Ives, *Common Lawyers*, pp. 36–59; *Select Cases in the Council of Henry VII*, eds C.G. Bayne and W.H. Dunham, Selden Society no. 75 (1958), pp. xxxi, xxxv, 3–40; *Paston Letters and Papers*, vol. 1, p. 183; Norfolk RO, Bishop's Register 12, f. 23v.

as butler, to make up accounts as pensioner and to audit them as treasurer, and it retained his loyalty into his last years, when he gave at least £75 over four years towards the building of the new gatehouse bearing his arms, which still survives on Chancery Lane.[31]

What Lovell knew of the civil law, also influential among early Tudor statesmen, we cannot tell, though he worked closely with some of its aficionados, notably Richard Fox. With chivalry he was more familiar, knighted at Stoke and made banneret at Blackheath, an enthusiastic Knight of the Garter from his election in 1500 to the year before his death, honoured at his funeral with all the military pomp the heralds could muster.[32] He did not, as Poynings did at Westenhanger, place a carving of St George on horseback over the entrance to his houses at East Harling or Holywell, but inside them he had coverings and tapestries depicting St George and the Nine Worthies. How many of his French printed books were romances, histories or works of piety rather than law-French texts we shall never know, but his 'large boke wreten in parchment in frenche well bounde with bordes', worth £4, sounds more like Froissart than Fitzherbert.[33] He was well placed to blend lawyerly conceptions of obedience with knightly codes of loyalty in framing the obligations of the Tudors' subjects and the ambitions of their Crown.

In almost every sphere in which those ambitions manifested themselves, Lovell was active. As deputy lieutenant and then lieutenant of the Tower of London he was keeper of many of those who fell foul of tightening laws of treason and sedition amid an increasingly pervasive culture of informing: from February 1487, when one Plomer was committed to the Tower by Henry VII's Council '& Lovell commaunded to kepe hym under payne of 100 li', to 1521, when he interrogated

[31] *Black Books*, vol. 1, pp. 48, 50, 52, 55–7, 187, 191, 196, 199, 200; *An Inventory of the Historical Monuments in London*, vol. 2 (Royal Commission on Historical Monuments, 1925), pp. 45, 47.

[32] W.A. Shaw, *The Knights of England* (2 vols, 1906), vol. 2, pp. 24, 28; *The Register of the most Noble Order of the Garter*, ed. J. Anstis (2 vols, 1724), vol. 1, pp. 238–360; M.G.A. Vale, *War and Chivalry: Warfare and Aristocratic Culture in England, France and Burgundy at the end of the Middle Ages* (1981), p. 93.

[33] E. Hasted, *The History and Topographical Survey of the County of Kent* (12 vols, Wakefield, 1972 edn), vol. 8, p. 65; PRO, PROB2/199, mm. 6, 9; the last book may well have been the illuminated one rebound in 1522–3: HMC, *Rutland*, vol. 4, p. 264.

Edward Stafford, Duke of Buckingham about his designs on the throne.[34] As commissioner or juror he played his part in many of his charges' trials, and on occasion he travelled to take state prisoners into custody.[35] In 1502 he and Bishop Fox lured Sir James Tyrrell out of Guines Castle onto their ship and Lovell then threatened to throw him overboard if he did not order his son to surrender the castle and accompany his father to the Tower.[36] In 1506 Lovell went to Dover to collect Edmund de la Pole, shipped over from Calais by Henry Wyatt with an armed escort sixty strong.[37] Sir Thomas' supreme trustworthiness in the eyes of his Tudor masters was summed up by the identity of one of his two household falconers at the end of his life: a certain Lambert Simnel.[38]

Sir Thomas sought to stimulate loyalty as much as to punish disloyalty. He distributed Henry VIII's alms for the release of poor prisoners on the first anniversary of his accession, and advised the mayor and aldermen of Nottingham on how best to receive Henry VII on progress.[39] He contributed to displays of courtly magnificence large and small by his presence and his administrative talents, and invested time and money in architectural celebrations of Tudor rule, such as the ceiling of St George's Chapel, Windsor, the West-minster Almshouses and the Magnificat Window at Malvern Priory.[40] He shared in the distinctive court piety which trumpeted God's blessing on the Tudors, leaving to the Observant houses at Richmond and Greenwich double the

---

[34] Huntington Library, San Marino CA, MS El 2652, f. 10v; L.W.V. Harcourt, *His Grace the Steward and the Trial of Peers* (1907), pp. 465–6; *LP*, vol. 1, i, 1732 (41), vol. 3, i, 1284 (5).

[35] *Six Town Chronicles of England*, ed. R. Flenley (Oxford, 1911), pp. 164–6; *Third Report of the Deputy Keeper of the Public Records* (1842), Appendix 2, p. 226; *LP*, vol. 3, i, 1284.

[36] *Letters and Papers illustrative of the reigns of Richard III and Henry VII*, ed. J. Gairdner, Rolls Series no. 24 (2 vols, 1861–3), vol. 1, p. 181.

[37] *The Chronicle of Calais*, ed. J.G. Nichols, Camden Society no. 35 (1846), p. 6.

[38] Belvoir Castle, MS account no. 4, partially calendared in HMC, *Rutland*, vol. 4, pp. 260–5.

[39] *LP*, vol. 2, ii, 1445; *Records of the Borough of Nottingham*, vol. 3, p. 317.

[40] *Joannis Lelandi Collectanea*, ed. T. Hearne (6 vols, Oxford, 1774), vol. 4, pp. 207, 231, 243, 246, 253, 255, 260; *Letters and Papers . . . Richard III and Henry VII*, vol. 1, p. 403, vol. 2, pp. 88, 292; *LP*, vol. 1, i, 20, 82, vol. 3, i, 703; BL, Add. MS 45131, ff. 34v–35v; *History of the King's Works*, vol. 3, pp. 207, 312; G.McN. Rushforth, *Medieval Christian Imagery as illustrated by the painted windows of Great Malvern Priory Church, Worcestershire* (Oxford, 1936), pp. 369–75.

amount in his will that he left to other friaries.[41] He also played his part in the Tudors' massaging of recent history, arranging with Sir Reynold Bray the construction of Richard III's tomb with its condemnatory but not vilificatory epitaph.[42]

As the Tudor regime under Henry VII turned to an intensified fiscal exploitation of the church, Lovell was there, taking bonds for payment for mortmain licences, negotiating terms for the restitution of temporalities.[43] As Henry's councillors and judges tightened judicial supervision of the church, Lovell played his part, becoming lay steward of both universities.[44] As the regime turned under Wolsey to intensified intervention in social problems, Lovell was there again, investigating enclosures in Middlesex in 1517, sitting in Council to enforce food price regulations on the merchants of London in 1518, organizing searches for vagrants in the London wards nearest the Tower and his house at Holywell in 1519.[45] And since Parliament was the place where significant parts of this governmental enterprise were drawn together, Lovell was there too. As Speaker in 1485 he presumably steered the House through the periods of 'comonyng for the comen well of all the lond', such as the two-day discussion of false money, and steeled the king's friends through the choppy hours when the attainder of the Ricardians 'sore was questioned with'.[46] In all probability he went on to sit in every session until he died.[47]

[41] PRO, PROB11/23/27.

[42] PRO, C1/206/69; HL, MS El 1129.

[43] R. Halstead, *Succinct Genealogies of the Noble and Ancient Houses of Alno or De Alneto &c.* (1685), p. 211; BL, Add. MS 21480, f. 175r.

[44] In succession to his conciliar colleagues Bray at Oxford and Mordaunt and Empson (and perhaps also Bray) at Cambridge: Halstead, *Succinct Genealogies*, p. 513; R.L. Storey, 'University and government 1430–1500', in *The History of the University of Oxford volume 2: Late Medieval Oxford*, eds J.I. Catto and R. Evans (Oxford, 1992), pp. 743–5; *Epistolae Academicae*, pp. 12–13; C.H. Cooper, T. Cooper, *Athenae Cantabrigienses* (3 vols, Cambridge, 1858–1913), vol. 1, pp. 6–7, 9, 14, 32; *Grace Book B*, ed. M. Bateson, Cambridge Antiquarian Society Luard Memorial Series nos 2–3, (2 vols, Cambridge, 1903–5), vol. 1, pp. 119, 137–8, 153, 195, vol. 2, pp. 11, 34, 46, 118.

[45] *LP*, vol. 2, ii, 3297, vol. 3, i, 365, Addenda, i, 206.

[46] *Red Paper Book of Colchester*, pp. 63–4.

[47] *The Commons 1509–1558*, vol. 2, pp. 548–9.

One particular task he and other councillors faced in Parliament was the expansion of the Crown's financial resources through the development of the lay subsidy. In 1510 he led a deputation from the Commons to collect the subsidy bill at the bar of the Lords, but as several fifteenth-century kings had found, securing a subsidy act that promised to yield more than the traditional fifteenth and tenth by no means guaranteed the assessment and collection of large sums in taxation. Between 1504 and 1523 Lovell worked on outside Parliament as a subsidy commissioner for Middlesex, Buckinghamshire, Norfolk and the king's household.[48] It was such efforts that crowned the struggle for tax reform with success around the time of his death, as Henry VIII raised sums in direct taxation similar to those of Henry V and went on to raise far more. In this process unprecedentedly large non-parliamentary levies were combined with the subsidy, and again Lovell played his part. He led the commissioners for the benevolence of 1491 in Middlesex and chased up the takings of the levy around the country a dozen or more years afterwards, negotiating with the local collectors and sitting with Richard Fox, Edmund Dudley and Henry Wyatt to audit their accounts.[49]

The first Tudor looked to drive up income not only from occasional direct taxation but also from regular indirect taxation. Between 1500 and 1505 Lovell was in the forefront of the campaign against customs evasion, working with Sir Richard Guildford, Bray, Dudley, Wyatt and the king himself to follow up information about smuggling, interview suspect officials and negotiate fines on offenders.[50] Henry took fines for many offences other than smuggling, and Lovell knew it well. He acted as intermediary for those accused of seditious words, or otherwise confined in his custody in the Tower, conveying to the king their offers of cash for pardon.[51] He investigated the profits to be made from illicit hunters on the Isle of Wight and from a thief who had fled leaving behind £200 worth of plate.[52] He put forward

[48] Ibid.; *RP*, vol. 6, pp. 537, 540.

[49] *CPR 1485–94*, p. 354; *CPR 1494–1509*, p. 458; BL, Add. MS 21480, f. 155r; B.P. Wolffe, *The Royal Demesne in English History* (1971), p. 208.

[50] BL, Add. MS 21480, ff. 67v, 130v, 159v, 168v, 176r, 177r, 188v, 190r.

[51] Ibid., ff.175r, 187r.

[52] Ibid., ff. 170v, 175r, 190v

bids to purchase offices and to marry the king's widows.[53] With his colleagues he settled the details of impositions on leading subjects which were doubtless outlined by Henry himself.[54] For debts great and small, payable and suspended, reasonable and outrageous, Lovell took bond after bond on the king's behalf.[55]

Henry VII's ways were idiosyncratic, and we should not build all these expedients into a pattern for the overall development of government. Yet Lovell, Fox and others supervised the pursuit of Henry VII's debts through the courts in his son's early years, rather than abandon it, and Lovell did not stop taking bonds in 1509. A steady trickle in the early years of Henry VIII's reign grew stronger in the wake of the king's first wars, when it became necessary to call in the Crown's debts as Tudor governments were repeatedly to do at times of retrenchment or political uncertainty.[56] Thus the king's financial and political hold over many of his more significant subjects was perpetuated and tightened. And while some of Henry VII's methods were jettisoned, many of the sources of income he had sought to tap were not. Those with which Lovell became particularly concerned were the royal forests and wardship.

As warden and chief justice of the king's forests south of Trent from 1510, Lovell sold licences to cut timber within forest areas and granted out deer from the royal parks, but he does not seem to have done much to exploit the king's rights more intensively.[57] Indeed, in 1521 Henry VIII objected to Lovell's appointment to a commission to investigate the Earl of Arundel's conduct in his offices in the New Forest on the somewhat illogical grounds that Sir Thomas was

[53] Ibid., ff. 178r, 184r, 187v, 188v.

[54] *CClR, 1500–9*, nos 471, 480; *CPR 1494–1509*, p. 176; *Council of Henry VII*, p. xxxiv.

[55] *CClR 1485–1500*, nos 541, 1090, 1176, 1236; *CClR 1500–9*, nos 114, 132, 135, 208, 222, 403, 412, 434, 572, 591, 599, 602, 604, 610, 619, 634, 652, 659, 661, 665, 670, 679, 686, 739, 769, 820, 840, 848, 852, 870.

[56] PRO, C54/377, m. 3d, C54/383, mm. 1d, 5d, 10d, 12d, C54/384, m. 27d, C54/385, m. 2d, C54/386, mm. 3d, 3d, C54/388, mm. 4d, 27d; E210/10103; *LP*, vol. 1, i, 1493, vol. 2, i, 2739, ii, 2932, 3026, 4494, 4546, vol. 3, i, 102 (12), ii, 2074 (7); *CAD*, vol. 5, A13033, A13208, A13207.

[57] *LP*, vol. 1, i, 381 (19); BL, Add. Ch. 8404 (*LP*, vol. 1, i, 1673); *Descriptive Catalogue of the Charters and Muniments in the possession of the Rt Hon Lord Fitzhardinge at Berkeley Castle*, ed. I.H. Jeayes (Bristol, 1892), p. 203; HMC, *Seventh Report* (1879), Appendix, p. 600; W.C. Richardson, *Tudor Chamber Administration* (Baton Rouge LA, 1952), pp. 266–73.

unlikely to bother to attend the hearings and that his involvement might influence the result in Arundel's favour.[58] It may be that Bray's evident aggression over the king's forest rights did not seem to leave too much to do, or that following in the footsteps of Bray's doomed successor Dudley invited caution.[59]

Where wardship was concerned, Lovell seems to have been more effective. Early in Henry VIII's reign he joined other councillors in selling wardships, though Henry VII's appointee Sir John Hussey remained master of the king's wards.[60] Then, in June 1513, Sir Thomas was appointed in Hussey's place and set in sole charge of the process, with power to move the great seal by his own signed bills.[61] For the next seven years, latterly as joint master with Sir Richard Weston, he settled terms with grantees and made grants, with sufficient independence that Lord Dacre complained to the Council about one in 1514 and the Duke of Buckingham instructed his chancellor to obtain Lovell's approval before he sued to the king for one in 1520.[62] Such autonomy at the top of the wards organization was matched by clearer institutional definition throughout, as Lovell appointed feodaries to pursue the Crown's rights to wardships in every county and collect the resulting revenues.[63] Thus he laid the basis for the Court of Wards and Liveries which would raise at its peak, early in Elizabeth's reign, nearly £30,000 a year for the Crown.

The last great strand in the Crown's financial recovery was the expansion in its landed revenue, roughly quintupled between the 1430s and the 1500s. Lovell was involved in the legal formalities of that expansion, as a feoffee to Henry VII and Henry VIII on lands they took from their subjects permanently or temporarily.[64]

---

[58] *State Papers, King Henry the Eighth* (11 vols, 1830–52), vol. 1, pp. 19–20 (*LP*, vol. 3, ii, 1437); see also *LP*, vol. 3, ii, 1429, 2145 (26).

[59] Lincolnshire Archives Office, Bishop's Register 25, ff. 89r–91r; *VCH Buckinghamshire*, vol. 2 (1908), pp. 139–40; PRO, C1/467/37. I owe the second reference to the kindness of Richard Hoyle.

[60] *Tudor Chamber Administration*, pp. 169–75; *CAD*, vol. 5, A12575, A12855.

[61] *LP*, vol. 1, ii, 2055 (80, 104).

[62] *LP*, vol. 1, ii, 2913, vol. 2, i, 950, 1391, ii, 3793, 3897, 4199, 4225, 4263, 4539, 4622, 4634, vol. 3, i, 1070; William Salt Library, Stafford, D17 90/A/13/61.

[63] Richardson, *Tudor Chamber Administration*, pp. 284–8.

[64] *CPR 1494–1509*, pp. 54, 260, 353–4, 501, 583; *CClR 1500–9*, no. 765; *CAD*, vol. 3, D819, vol. 4, A7551; *Calendar of Inquisitions Post Mortem, Henry VII* (3 vols, 1898–1955), vol. 2, no. 861, vol. 3, no. 366; BL, Add. MS 21480, ff. 32r, 35r, 94r–v; PRO, C54/388, m. 27d. Many of these were temporary arrangements to ensure the payment of debts.

Sir Thomas also farmed lands from the Crown, as many councillors and courtiers did: in his case at Wratting in Suffolk, Walthamstow Fraunceys in Essex, Grimston and Castle Rising in Norfolk, Tolworth in Surrey, Enfield in Middlesex and London.[65] But his most important contributions to the system were as a local and central official. As joint steward of the Duchy of Lancaster in East Anglia with Hobart from 1489, he was named to a commission to improve the Duchy's revenue there, one of the Duchy's various contributions to the intensification in management of the Crown lands.[66] Early in the reign he was also a commissioner to let the king's mines and to demarcate the bounds between the king's lands and those of Waltham Abbey.[67] Lovell held local offices around the kingdom in various parts of the Crown estate and its temporary accretions: the honour of Wallingford in the Duchy of Cornwall, Enfield Chase in the Duchy of Lancaster, Wakefield and Hitchin in the Duchy of York, the liberty of Havering and the manor of Little Walsingham in the queen's jointure, the manors of Cheshunt and Ware in the forfeited estates of the Earldom of Warwick, and the Duke of Buckingham's estates in Norfolk and Suffolk during his minority.[68] But these were stewardships rather than accounting offices, their significance, as we shall see, more judicial and political than financial. He did hold one receivership, that of the forfeited lands of William de la Pole, brother to the Earl of Suffolk,[69] but his financial role was primarily in central administration, as the treasurer of the king's chamber to whom landed revenues began to be diverted from the Exchequer in July 1487 as Henry reinstated the Yorkist system of land revenue management.[70]

Record loss makes it impossible to reconstruct exactly Lovell's role in the coordination of Crown finances early in Henry's reign, but it seems to have

---

[65] *Calendar of the Fine Rolls preserved in the Public Record Office* (22 vols, 1911–62), *Henry VII*, nos 33, 311; BL, Add. MS 21480, ff. 193v, 195r; Harleian Roll Y28; *LP*, vol. 2, i, 2625, vol. 4, i, 546 (15).

[66] R. Somerville, *A History of the Duchy of Lancaster, vol. 1, 1265–1603* (1953), p. 267.

[67] *CPR 1485–94*, p. 69; *Council of Henry VII*, p. 3.

[68] BL, Harleian Roll Y28; *CPR 1485–94*, pp. 38, 205, 273; M.K. McIntosh, *Autonomy and Community: The Royal Manor of Havering, 1200–1500* (Cambridge, 1986), p. 271; PRO, C1/572/2; Somerville, *Duchy of Lancaster*, p. 612; *LP*, vol. 1, i, 132 (35), vol. 3, ii, 1451 (20).

[69] *LP*, vol. 4, i, 1298.

[70] Wolffe, *Royal Demesne*, p. 203.

been a large one, perhaps only less than that of Bray and Lord Treasurer Dynham. Though the sums passing through the chamber under Lovell were small compared to those managed in the last decade of the reign by his former clerk John Heron, who seems gradually to have taken over his work in the course of the 1490s, it was Lovell who firmly re-established the Yorkist pattern of making important payments at court on the king's command and drawing in taxation, land income and, if necessary, any other funds the Exchequer could find to do so.[71] Moreover, as Chancellor of the Exchequer from October 1485, he smoothed the relationship between the older revenue institutions and the newer by holding office in them both.[72] His one extant letter to an Exchequer teller, Thomas Pierson, though uncompromising in its demands, is casually friendly in tone, and a correspondent of the teller Thomas Stokes thought Lovell would be more likely to find him a job at Stokes's 'desire and prayer'.[73] Lovell used the privilege of the office to pursue his own suits and those of his relatives and servants through the Exchequer of Pleas.[74] He also used the powers of appointment it gave him to promote into the Exchequer men such as William Young and Thomas Sacheverell, who served as his deputies in various local offices and, as we shall see, helped to marshal his retinue in the localities.[75] At his funeral Lovell's Exchequer connection was made manifest. Thomas Pymme the foreign apposer and 2nd Baron Wotton, who had once been Lovell's deputy as Duchy of Lancaster steward at Fulmodeston in Norfolk

---

[71] Richardson, *Tudor Chamber Administration*, pp. 109–32; Wolffe, *Royal Demesne*, pp. 168–225; J.M. Currin, '"Pro expensis ambassatorum": Diplomacy and financial administration in the reign of Henry VII', *English Historical Review*, 108 (1993), 597–609.

[72] *CPR 1485–94*, p. 18; J.D. Alsop, 'The structure of early Tudor finance', in *Revolution Reassessed: Revisions in the History of Tudor Government and Administration*, eds C. Coleman and D.R. Starkey (Oxford, 1986), pp. 143–7.

[73] *Materials*, vol. 1, pp. 549–50; PRO, SC1/52/76.

[74] PRO, E13/178, rot. 35, E13/180, rot. 17d, E13/181, rot. 23d, E13/187, rot. 18d, E13/190, rot. 17d, E13/198, rot. 14. The chancellorship also made possible more significant interventions: G.R. Elton, *The Tudor Revolution in Government: Administrative Changes in the Reign of Henry VIII* (Cambridge, 1953), pp. 113–17.

[75] J.C. Sainty, *Officers of the Exchequer*, List and Index Society Special Series no. 18 (1983), pp. 96, 102; see below.

and a feoffee on Lovell's estates, joined the cortège alongside William Young and Robert Waleys, Lovell's gentleman-in-waiting whom he had appointed comptroller of the pipe.[76]

By 1503 Lovell had left the treasurership of the chamber for the more senior position of treasurer of the Household.[77] Most of the real work of the Household's financial management was done by the cofferer and comptroller, but that did not mean that Lovell was leaving financial administration behind.[78] At least three and probably seven or more times between 1497 and 1510, he travelled to Calais to collect the substantial pension Henry had secured from the kings of France by the treaty of Étaples.[79] One of these missions moved the Milanese ambassador to call him the king's chief financier.[80] In 1512 he was at Calais again, authorized to receive the war subvention due from Henry VIII's ally, the Emperor Maximilian.[81] Meanwhile he took part in the ad hoc auditing of accounts which substituted for the Exchequer's past and future monopoly of superior audit, combining at times with Sir Robert Southwell and Henry VII himself.[82] In 1504 he was one of the seven councillors to whom those who felt themselves wronged by the king in matters financial were invited by proclamation to complain.[83] His work continued into the next reign, as he, Fox and others tried to tidy up the disruption caused by Henry's death.[84] Whether in or out of formal office, Lovell exemplified the flexible efficiency in financial administration which was the aim of a regime bent on filling its coffers, first to fight almost inevitable

---

[76] *LP*, vol. 4, i, 366; Somerville, *Duchy of Lancaster*, p. 595; PRO, C142/41/62; HMC, *Rutland*, vol. 4, p. 261; Sainty, *Officers of the Exchequer*, pp. 75, 83.

[77] *CPR 1494–1509*, p. 326; Richardson, *Tudor Chamber Administration*, pp. 484–5; J.R. Hooker, 'Some cautionary notes on Henry VII's household and chamber "system"', *Speculum*, 33 (1958), 69–75.

[78] D.M. Loades, *The Tudor Court* (2nd edn, Bangor, 1992), pp. 74–5.

[79] PRO, E404/82/3/unnumbered warrant 3 Dec 1497, E404/85/1/85; HMC, *Ninth Report* (1883), Appendix 1, p. 146; Canterbury RO, FA2, f. 413v, FA9, ff. 42v, 137v.

[80] *Calendar of State Papers, Venetian*, eds R. Brown, C. Bentinck and H. Brown (9 vols, 1864–98), vol. 1, no. 799.

[81] *LP*, vol. 1, i, 1280.

[82] PRO, E40/14648; BL, Add. MS 21480, f. 183r; *LP*, vol. 1, i, 582.

[83] *CPR 1494–1509*, p. 380.

[84] *LP*, Addenda, i, 105.

civil insurrection and then to indulge in tempting overseas adventurism, without incurring unacceptable political costs. When called upon to enhance the flexibility of the fisc from his own resources, he was ready to do so, giving £400 to the king in the benevolence of 1491 and £500 in the forced loan of 1522–3.[85]

If good housekeeping was one criterion of good kingship by fifteenth-century standards, good justice was undoubtedly another. In the efforts of Henry VII and Wolsey to supply it, Lovell played his part above all in the Council courts, where business expanded dramatically in the decades around 1500. In Star Chamber, so far as the patchy surviving records allow us to judge, he was the second most active councillor of Henry VII's reign and the fifth most active of the years 1509–24.[86] He was there, for example, on 28 October 1519, when Sir William Bulmer was upbraided for his acceptance of the Duke of Buckingham's livery when already a servant of the king; he was there on 24 January 1520, when his friends and relations among the gentry of Norfolk and Suffolk were bound in £100 each not to depart from Westminster until they had accounted for their negligence in enquiring into murders and robberies done in their shires.[87] Lovell was equally prominent in the Council Attendant. He was one of the eight councillors required to be present throughout spring, summer and autumn 1494 when the attendance rota for that year's progress was planned, and in 1494–5 he sat regularly at Sheen, Canterbury, Woodstock and Langley with a core of colleagues including Fox, Bray, Daubeney and Guildford.[88] Under Henry VII he served on commissions of councillors appointed to examine parties in especially controversial cases, and under Wolsey he served on boards of arbitrators nominated by the Council to settle suits before it.[89]

---

[85] M.M. Condon, 'From caitiff and villain to pater patriae: Reynold Bray and the profits of office', in *Profit, Piety and the Professions in Later Medieval England*, ed. M.A. Hicks (Gloucester, 1990), p. 158; HMC, *Rutland*, vol. 4, p. 263.

[86] *Council of Henry VII*, p. xxxv; W.H. Dunham, 'The members of Henry VIII's whole council, 1509–1527', *EHR*, 59 (1944), 207–10.

[87] HL, MS El 2653, ff. 1r, 16v.

[88] PRO, REQ1/1, ff. 1r, 40r, 81r–110r.

[89] E.W. Ives, '"Agaynst taking awaye of women": the inception and operation of the Abduction Act of 1487', in *Wealth and Power in Tudor England*, eds E.W. Ives, R.J. Knecht and J.J. Scarisbrick (1978), p. 40; *Grace Book B*, vol. 2, p. 46; *Registrum Caroli Bothe, Episcopi Herefordensis*, ed. A.T. Bannister, Canterbury and York Society no. 28 (1921), p. 45.

This was but one of many ways in which Lovell was drawn into the arbitration of suits, a means both to seek peaceful resolution of disputes and to assert the influence of the king's closest councillors in local society. Often his local office-holding made him a suitable arbiter, as in a dispute about fair tolls in 1516 between the borough of Nottingham, where he was constable of the castle, and the Priory of Lenton, of which he was steward.[90] In 1503 he offered his arbitration in another of Nottingham's disputes.[91] In a less specific way, his local influence as a leading office-holder made him an appropriate choice for disputes involving lands in Nottinghamshire, such as those of the Strelley and Plumpton families.[92] In Norfolk, office-holding and land-holding combined with family relationships and old familiarity to draw him into disputes such as that between Sir John Paston and the husbands of William Paston's daughters, arbitrated by Lovell and Sir Henry Heydon with Bishop Alcock of Ely and Sir Reynold Bray. As the prior and convent of Norwich reminded him and Heydon in trying to secure the money William Paston left them in his will, of the four arbitrators, the monks were 'longest acqueyntyd with you' since 'ze be of our cuntre and', they added perhaps hopefully, 'speciall frendes to our monastery'.[93]

In arbitration as in the Council courts, Lovell worked again and again throughout the reign with his colleagues from the tight circle of councillors and household officers around the king. In five further arbitrations between 1487 and 1507 he acted in various combinations twice with Bray, Daubeney and Guildford and once with Morton, Dynham and Poynings.[94] This inner ring of the Council played key roles in the judicial system, not only in the provision of equitable remedies in the Council courts or by arbitration, but also on the commissions of the peace. Throughout Henry VII's reign and especially in the mid-1490s, they were injected into the commissions, apparently in an effort to enhance the

---

[90] *Records of the Borough of Nottingham*, vol. 3, pp. 345–8.

[91] Ibid., p. 402.

[92] *CAD*, vol. 3, no. C3436; *LP*, Addenda, ii, 1515; Nottingham University Library, Mi 2/72/40; *The Plumpton Correspondence*, ed. T. Stapleton, Camden Society, no. 4 (1839), pp. cxix–xxiii.

[93] *The Paston Letters 1422–1509*, ed. J. Gairdner (3 vols, 1872–5), vol. 3, 330–3, 392.

[94] *CClR, 1485–1500*, nos 198, 1096; *CClR, 1500–9*, no. 275; Essex RO, D/DFa F12; Windsor, The Aerary, MS IV.B.3, ff. 226v–130r; Keele UL, Paget Papers, General Correspondence, Box 1, no. 2.

control of central government over the county gentry who bore the brunt of the commissions' work.[95] Lovell was added to eighteen of the nineteen most heavily remodelled benches of 1492–5, but unlike some of his colleagues stayed on several of those he had joined.[96] This reflected the increasing spread of his interests in office and land: at the start of the reign he had been a JP only in Norfolk, but in 1491 he joined the bench in Middlesex where he took up residence at Elsings in Enfield.[97] In the mid-1490s he added Berkshire, Oxfordshire and Nottinghamshire, in each of which he had held prominent offices since 1489, together with Hertfordshire, where he may already have been steward of St Albans Abbey.[98] After his initial appointment he left the Staffordshire bench, but he rejoined it between 1504 and 1508, having entered office at Walsall.[99] Only in Surrey, where he joined the bench in 1505, was he not otherwise a leading figure; perhaps he was intruded there to maintain conciliar supervision following the deaths of Dynham and Bray.[100]

By 1514, Lovell was a member of the quorum of each of these commissions, and *custos rotulorum* in Middlesex, Nottinghamshire and Staffordshire.[101] He attended sessions occasionally in Norfolk, Middlesex and Hertfordshire and even in counties such as Sussex and Northamptonshire where his membership of the bench was merely temporary, but he was not dedicated to local justice in the fashion of some of his colleagues, above all the heroic Hobart.[102] Presumably kept busy enough by his duties about the king, he saved his effort for the more significant among the

[95] J.R. Lander, *English Justices of the Peace 1461–1509* (Gloucester, 1989), pp. 114–20, 124–9, 139–44.

[96] Ibid, pp. 114–15.

[97] *CPR 1485–94*, pp. 493–4; *CPR 1494–1509*, pp. 650–1; *LP*, vol. 1, ii, pp. 1540–1, vol. 2, i, 207, 427, ii, 4435, vol. 3, ii, 2993.

[98] *CPR 1494–1509*, pp. 630, 643, 653–4; *LP*, vol. 1, ii, pp. 1533, 1538, 1542; *LP*, vol. 2, i, 674, 1186 (13), 1379 (19), ii, 2074 (14).

[99] *CPR 1494–1509*, p. 659; *LP*, vol. 1, ii, 1543, vol. 3, i, 1081 (16).

[100] *CPR 1494–1509*, p. 661; *LP*, vol. 1, ii, 1544, vol. 2, i, 1220, vol. 3, i, 1081 (16); M.M. Condon, 'Ruling elites in the reign of Henry VII', in *Patronage, Pedigree and Power in Later Medieval England*, ed. C.D. Ross (Gloucester, 1979), p. 125.

[101] BL, Add. MS 36773, ff. 3r, 10r, 14r, 15r, 15v, 17r, 18r, 20v.

[102] Lander, *Justices of the Peace*, pp. 36–7, 72; PRO, KB9/378/9, 379/48, 382/38–49, 383/106–7, 400/54, 410/57, 68, 464/102.

innumerable special judicial commissions to which he was named.[103] Those he chose often involved treason or insurrection, but his attention extended beyond state security to notable disorder. In July 1502 he rode out to Caversfield in Buckinghamshire in the company of three peers and two other councillors to try an Oxfordshire gentleman for armed burglary and arson committed just six weeks earlier; in December 1514 he travelled to York to oversee the indictments of the feuding gentry responsible for rioting at the August sessions in the city and for a series of local murders.[104] The Tudor pacification of the English shires was a slow, partial and contingent business, but Lovell was playing his part in it.

While the clerics at the core of Henry's Council were more prominent in the work of the equity courts than were the laymen, especially once Chancery is included, their lay colleagues, and in particular the lawyers among them, held increasing concentrations of estate stewardships. Thus they controlled the manorial, franchisal or borough courts both on the Crown estate and on others. Lovell was steward to the abbeys of St Albans and Peterborough, the priories of Lenton, Wallingford and Sheen, St George's College, Windsor, and the dowager Duchess of York, and almost certainly to many other institutions and individuals.[105] For a busy councillor these offices might look like sinecures. It was indeed Lovell's deputies who actually held the courts, just as it was his deputies who kept the prisoners in the gaols for which his constableships of castles made him responsible. This delegation had certain advantages in shifting responsibility when things went wrong: it was not Lovell but his deputy at Wallingford Castle, Humphrey Wellesbourne, who was pursued and fined by the Council Learned in the Law in 1502–5 for the escape of prisoners in his custody.[106] Yet there was

[103] *CPR 1485–94*, pp. 73, 163, 180, 283, 348, 356, 442, 477; *CPR 1494–1509*, pp. 29–31, 33, 53, 86, 116, 231, 248, 287, 291, 293–4, 296, 326, 357, 404, 531, 546; *LP*, vol. 1, i, 731 (27–8), 1732 (2), ii, 2484 (27), 2684 (41), 3408 (37).

[104] PRO, KB9/373/3, 475/2, 478/8; KB9/442/110, 466/3. For similar instances, see KB9/395/32, 461/22.

[105] PRO, E315/272, f. 62r; E315/464, ff. 58v, 60v, 65v; SC2/210/35, mm. 3–4; *Select Cases before the King's Council in the Star Chamber*, vol. 2, Selden Society, no. 25 (1911), pp. 123–42; HMC, *Report 69: The Manuscripts of Lord Middleton, preserved at Wollaton Hall* (1911), pp. 124, 515; Windsor, The Aerary, MSS XV.49.6, XV. 49.13.

[106] PRO, DL5/2, ff. 38v, 48r–v, 50v, 52v, 57r; E404/85/100; KB9/415/5, 7; BL Add. MS 21480, f. 166r.

always the danger that deputies would take the initiative in ways which obstructed the wider workings of government, as when Roland Digby, Lovell's under-constable at Nottingham Castle, imprisoned the sheriff's bailiffs in irons in 1499 because they had arrested one of his servants on suspicion of felony.[107]

How closely Lovell supervised his deputies is hard to say. Some of them probably did not need much supervision: William Elys, deputy to Lovell and Hobart in the Duchy of Lancaster courts in Norfolk, was one of the most hard-working JPs of his generation.[108] As might be expected, challenges to decisions reached in the courts placed their emphasis on the wayward tyranny of the deputies, men such as Stephen Draper the understeward of the Duchy market-day court at Thetford, with his 'craftly handlyng' and 'pollytike counsaile'.[109] Yet the processes of investigation and redress in such circumstances brought Lovell at least nominally into play, and he clearly was involved in some of the courts' work, for instance signing copies of court roll from the Duchy's court at Aylsham.[110] Most of the time he was presumably a distant but meaningful presence, as at Peterborough in 1517, where his deputy tried to defuse a confrontation with the townsfolk in open court with the words 'Neyghbures and freandes I lett yow wytt thatt my syngular good master Sir Thomas Lovell ys hygh steward of thys lordshypp and all othur my lordes of Peturburgh and I am butt hys deputye and of yowr demeanour I wyll certyffye hym and when I know hys pleasure I wull demean me thereaftur.'[111]

Stewardships were highly desirable. Lovell paid Edmund Dudley £100 in cash for a royal grant of the stewardship of Wakefield.[112] Appointments in reversion to many of Lovell's Crown and monastic stewardships were sought and made in the years just before his death, and Sir Richard Weston sued the dean and canons of Windsor for breach of contract when they failed to appoint him on Lovell's demise, despite having promised him the succession, he claimed, seven years earlier.[113] The

---

[107] PRO, C1/192/24.

[108] Somerville, *Duchy of Lancaster*, pp. 595, 600; Lander, *Justices of the Peace*, p. 71.

[109] PRO, C1/530/26.

[110] PRO, DL5/2, ff. 133v–4v.

[111] *Select Cases . . . in the Star Chamber*, p. 141.

[112] BL, Lansdowne MS 127, f. 49r.

[113] *LP*, vol. 3, i, 1345, 1451 (20), vol. 4, i, 213 (17); Somerville, *Duchy of Lancaster*, p. 612; HMC, *Middleton*, pp. 124, 515; PRO, C1/594/5.

attraction did not lie primarily in the judicial function or even in the fee, though £16 a year from St Albans or £13 6*s* 8*d* from Windsor presumably left some change after paying the deputies.[114] Stewardships were prized rather for the influence they brought in local society and the military leadership of the tenants, what Sir Thomas Darcy called, in requesting a stewardship from the king, the 'strength to serve your grace'.[115] Thus Lovell's stewardships were one of the keys to his role in the redistribution of political power which accompanied and facilitated the other developments in government we have been considering.

Lovell's career served to make him a substantial landowner in his own right. Early in Henry VII's reign he was granted forfeited estates by the king in Oxfordshire and Cornwall, though the latter bore a large annuity to another courtier and were back in the king's hands by 1502–3.[116] He doubtless also owed to the king's influence his marriage to the twice-widowed Isabel, sister of Edmund Lord Roos, and an heiress to her mother Philippa, Lady Roos and thus to a share in the Tiptoft inheritance.[117] But he extended his lands well beyond these endowments by purchase, buying steadily throughout his career as Bray and other colleagues did, sometimes making small additions to consolidate his holdings or buying up lands in reversion, but often buying whole manors outright for large sums in cash.[118] Much of the money may have come from his official fees, which were certainly large enough: by 1515 he was drawing more than £400 a year from his six most lucrative offices alone.[119] Money could also be made by the exercise of

---

[114] PRO, E315/272, f. 62r; Windsor, The Aerary, MS XV.49.6.

[115] PRO, SC1/44/77; D. Luckett, 'Crown office and licensed retinues in the reign of Henry VII', in *Rulers and Ruled in Late Medieval England: Essays presented to Gerald Harriss*, eds R.E. Archer and S.K. Walker (1995), pp. 223–38.

[116] *CPR 1485–94*, pp. 25, 224; *CAD*, vol. 1, A545; BL, Add. MS 21480, f. 38v.

[117] *VCH Cambridgeshire*, vol. 6 (1978), p. 116, vol. 8 (1982), pp. 15, 182; *VCH Huntingdonshire*, vol. 3 (1936), p. 126; *VCH Hampshire*, vol. 4 (1911), pp. 130, 348, 526, 532; W.A. Copinger, *The Manors of Suffolk* (7 vols, 1905–11), vol. 3, p. 188; West Sussex RO, Chichester City Archives AY 133–8; *LP*, vol. 4, i, 367.

[118] Condon, 'Reynold Bray', pp. 140–58; PRO, E150/479/2; C142/45/56; C1/100/28; C54/383, m. 5d; *CClR 1485–1500*, no. 745; *CClR 1500–9*, no. 867; BL, Add. MS 12463, ff. 73v, 91v; *CIPM Henry VII*, vol. 2, no. 114; Bodl. MS ch. Kent 231; *VCH Rutland*, vol. 2 (1935), p. 270; *Feet of Fines for Cambridgeshire Henry VII to Elizabeth*, ed. W.M. Palmer (Norwich, 1909), p. 22; *A Calendar of the Feet of Fines relating to the County of Huntingdon*, ed. G.J. Turner, Cambridge Antiquarian Society, no. 37 (Cambridge, 1913), p. 115.

[119] *LP*, vol. 2, i, 2736, ii, p. 1468, Appendix 58 (10); PRO, SC6/Hen VII/1091.

influence, as Lovell discovered very early in his career in government, as Speaker of the Commons in 1485–6. On the day after Parliament returned from the Christmas recess, he was paid £3 6s 8d by the dean and canons of Windsor, who were lobbying hard to protect their interests under the new regime; at the end of the session they added a share in a further £6 13s 4d.[120] As we shall see, Lovell also received fees from a number of noblemen, though much of the tribute rendered to secure his friendship came not in cash but in kind, presents like the fish, wine and strawberries with which Canterbury entertained him whenever he passed through, or the assorted fish and fowl laid on at Dover.[121] One customer who did pay cash was the king of France, with a pension of some £44 a year from 1492.[122]

Lovell may also have used his influence to facilitate his land acquisition in more direct ways. Dudley showed it could be done, offering to pay off his victims' fines to the king, sometimes fines he had himself arranged, in return for the title to their lands; Bray struck similar if less blatant deals.[123] However Lovell made his money and found his sellers, his purchases were substantial. By 1522–3 he enjoyed a clear landed income of more than £450, very respectable for a knight or even for a baron; over half came from his purchased lands.[124] He augmented his holdings by extensive leasing, not only from the Crown but also from religious houses, university colleges and the nobility, driving up his profits by quibbling over the rent.[125] He did not pursue grants of Crown wardships with the same enthusiasm as many of his colleagues, though he allegedly made £2,289 11s 3d for an investment of £66 13s 4d in the wardship of his eight-year-old godson Thomas Elrington, whose lands lay mostly near Lovell's own in Middlesex.[126]

---

[120] Windsor, The Aerary, MS XV.48.50.

[121] HMC, *Ninth Report*, Appendix 1, pp. 146, 149; Canterbury RO, FA2, f. 413v; FA7, f. 137r; FA9, ff. 42v, 137v; BL, Egerton MS 2092, ff. 63r, 64v, 71r. Compare Condon, 'Reynold Bray', p. 158.

[122] C. Giry-Deloison, 'Money and early Tudor diplomacy. The English pensioners of the French kings (1475–1547)', *Medieval History*, 3 (1993), 140–1.

[123] Halstead, *Succinct Genealogies*, p. 69; Cheshire RO, DCH/B/43; Condon, 'Reynold Bray', pp. 144, 149–56.

[124] BL, Add. MS 12463 (*LP*, vol. 4, i, 367).

[125] *LP*, vol. 4, i, 366, 368; *Registrum Annalium Collegii Mertonensis 1483–1521*, ed. H.E. Salter, Oxford Historical Society, no. 76 (Oxford, 1923), p. 309; PRO, C1/632/50.

[126] PRO, C1/546/52; BL, Add. MS 21480, f. 93v.

The marriage bargain he struck for his niece Ursula, buying Sir John Hussey's son William for £666 13*s* 4*d*, temporarily increased the estates under his control; the match he made for her sister Elizabeth with his great-nephew Thomas Manners, future Lord Roos, decreased them.[127] Yet these landholdings could not by themselves make Lovell a major force in local politics anywhere: his estates were scattered too evenly through a dozen counties.

This returns us to the significance of the king's intervention in the establishment of Lovell's local influence. Of the 1,365 men in Sir Thomas's licensed retinue of 1508, scarcely any were drawn from his own estates or household, a dramatic contrast with the noble retinues of preceding centuries.[128] About one-third of the force was recruited through stewardships he held under the Crown and a further one-fifth through monastic and episcopal stewardships, doubtless granted to a man known to enjoy royal favour. A further fifth consisted of the personal followings of individual gentlemen and yeomen, but some of these were using their own offices on the Crown estate to recruit, as Robert Hasilrigge seems to have done at Castle Donnington in Leicestershire.[129] In a sense the one-sixth of the retinue provided by the tenantry of the Roos estates, predominantly in Yorkshire and Lincolnshire, was also owed to royal appointment. It was Lovell's marriage to Isabel Roos which made him an appropriate guardian for the estates of her deranged brother, but he surely owed the marriage to the king, as he certainly did the generous arrangement by which he held the estates from 1486, paying £466 13*s* 4*d* a year to Henry out of a total income valued in 1524 at £1,310 16*s* ¾*d*.[130]

The Roos tenantry gave Lovell's retinue the stereotypical footsloggers of the bottom of the bastard feudal pyramid: husbandmen from Thornton-in-Craven taxed on 20*s* or sometimes 40*s* in goods in the subsidies of the 1520s,

[127] *CClR 1500–9*, no. 338; PRO, PROB11/17/24.

[128] M. Hicks, *Bastard Feudalism* (1995), pp. 43–52.

[129] Somerville, *Duchy of Lancaster*, pp. 574, 773; for individuals named in the 1508 retinue, see Leicestershire RO, 1D50/XII/8; for slightly earlier and later tenants with the same surnames as those named in 1508, HL, MS HAM Box 8 (3,4).

[130] G.E. Cokayne, *The Complete Peerage*, ed. V. Gibbs *et al.* (13 vols, 1910–59) vol. 11, pp. 106–7; Statute 7 Henry VII c. 20; PRO, C54/392, mm. 30d–31d; SC6/Hen VII/1242; E404/54/3/unnumbered warrant 12 November 1503.

parishioners from Chilham in Kent where the Roos arms shone down from
the stained glass to remind them of their duty.[131] The Roos connection also lay
behind some of Lovell's recruitment of monastic tenants, as at Rievaulx and
Warter, founded by Lord Roos's ancestors, though Lovell made an effort to
cultivate such links, presenting the abbot of Rievaulx to a rectory in 1505.[132]
But it is not the Roos sections of the retinue that look strongest by our usual
criteria for assessing the political weight of affinities. Gentlemen-bailiffs such
as James Carr of Thornton-in-Craven, Ralph Elwick of Seaton Ross or
Thomas Heven of Wragby, able to equip themselves as demilances and worth
around £40 in goods or £25 in lands, were wealthy and influential by
the standards of their villages but insignificant in the world of county
government.[133]

By this test Lovell's following in Nottinghamshire, where his influence rested
on royal and monastic office backed by a handful of Roos manors, looks much
more impressive. Three Nottinghamshire JPs, two of them very active at quarter
sessions, signed up to serve Lovell in person at the head of their tenants, as did
two more who would join the bench within three years; these five furnished two
sheriffs and two escheators between 1491 and 1519.[134] Several of them also
served as Lovell's subordinates in his offices in the county.[135] These men were
from the second rank of county families rather than the knightly élite who

---

[131] *Early Tudor Craven: Subsidies and Assessments 1510–1547*, ed. R.W. Hoyle, Yorkshire Archaeological
Society Record Series no. 145 (Leeds, 1987), pp. 4, 50, 61; C.R. Councer, 'The medieval painted
glass of Chilham', *Archaeologia Cantiana*, 58 (1945), 9, 11.

[132] W. Dugdale, *Monasticon Anglicanum*, eds J. Caley, H. Ellis and B. Bandinel (6 vols in 8, 1817–30),
vol. 5, p. 277, vol 6 (i), p. 297; Borthwick Institute, Register 25, f. 66v.

[133] *Early Tudor Craven*, pp. 4, 50, 61; PRO, E179/203/183, m. 15d; Lincolnshire AO, LCC wills
1535–7, f. 42r–v.

[134] *CPR 1494–1509*, pp. 653–4; *LP*, vol. 1, ii, p. 1542; PRO, KB9/413/34, 417/41, 425/6,
428/22, 436/45, 437/17, 438/15, 438/85, 440/22, 441/18, 442/13, 442/106, 443/46, 446/18,
449/2, 464/60, 470/41, 477/6, 28, 496/52; *List of Sheriffs for England and Wales*, PRO Lists and
Indexes no. 9 (1898), p. 104; *List of Escheators for England and Wales*, List and Index Society
no. 72 (1971), p. 113.

[135] Nottingham UL, Mi 6/175/13 (Humphrey Hercy); Nottinghamshire AO, DDP 17/2, f. 22v;
Birmingham Central Library, Wingfield Digby A690 (Simon Digby); Notts. AO, DD 2P 27/9
(Thomas Leek, Hugh Annesley).

famously ran Nottinghamshire, but even the greater gentry did not hold themselves apart from Lovell entirely.[136] Sir John Markham served as his lieutenant in Sherwood Forest and attended his funeral, and Sir Gervase Clifton named him supervisor of his will.[137] In 1509 Lovell nominated Sir Henry Willoughby for election to the Garter.[138]

Where gentlemen with their own links to the court and their own retinues to raise were thinner on the ground, stewardships gave a freer hand in recruiting the local élite. From the sprawling, booming, clothmaking parish of Halifax, where the Saviles were in minority and the Tempests were his deputies, Lovell drew 142 men.[139] Sixty-nine of them can be tentatively identified in the 123 lay wills surviving for Halifax between 1494 and 1532. These, together with the subsidy of 1524, show the place many of them occupied among the circle of yeoman clothier families who dominated local life.[140] They were tied up with one another as feoffees, executors and witnesses; their younger brothers were the clergy serving the local chapels; some of them, like Brian Otes, who supervised four wills between 1494 and 1509, were leaders even among the leaders.[141] At Wakefield nine of Lovell's sixty retainers had £10 or more in lands or goods in 1524, and another four had £3 or more in lands.[142]

The story was similar in the towns further south where Lovell was steward, from Walsall and Lichfield to Hitchin, Henley and Thame, and presumably at

[136] S.J. Payling, *Political Society in Lancastrian England: The Greater Gentry of Nottinghamshire* (Oxford, 1991); A. Cameron, 'Sir Henry Willoughby of Wollaton', *Transactions of the Thoroton Society*, 74 (1970), 10–21.

[137] HMC, *Rutland*, iv, p. 264; *LP*, vol. 4, i, 366; *Testamenta Eboracensia*, vol. 4, ed. J. Raine, Surtees Society no. 53 (1868), pp. 276–7.

[138] Anstis, *Garter*, vol. 1, p. 271.

[139] R.B. Smith, *Land and Politics in the England of Henry VIII: The West Riding of Yorkshire 1530–1546* (Oxford, 1970), pp. 8, 24–5, 147–8; *Testamenta Eboracensia*, vol. 4, p. 251.

[140] *Halifax Wills*, eds J.W. Clay and E.W. Crossley (Halifax, 1904), pp. 27–84, 184–6; 'A subsidy roll for the wapentake of Agbrigg and Morley of the 15th Henry VIII', ed. J.J. Cartwright, *Yorkshire Archaeological Journal*, 2 (1873), 57–60.

[141] *Halifax Wills*, pp. 27, 31–2, 35, 37 and *passim*.

[142] 'Subsidy roll for Agbrigg and Morley', pp. 52–3.

Nottingham and Derby too.[143] Only at Newark did the borough élite, for reasons which are not apparent, seem to hold themselves back from Lovell's service.[144] At Hitchin Lovell recruited seven of the nine richest men in the 1524 subsidy.[145] In the Bishop of Lincoln's borough of Thame, seven of Lovell's nineteen named retainers served as churchwardens, two bore lesser parochial office and another was a tithingman.[146] They included innholders, butchers, fishmongers, brewers, chandlers and tailors and some were of substantial means: in the course of a busy career John Goodwin managed to be churchwarden, guildwarden, constable, chandler, whitebread baker, fishmonger and innkeeper, while amassing the £60 worth of goods on which he was taxed in 1524.[147] Geoffrey Dormer, the biggest farmer in the fields around the town, was richer still.[148] At Henley ten of the twenty-four named retainers were part of the thirty-strong circle of burgesses, most from its richer, office-holding section. John Wyllys, warden of the town in 1508 as he had been for seven of the past twelve years, did not serve in person, but did provide the service of two, presumably younger men.[149] Some of those retained were little better off than the Roos tenantry in 1524, but some were distinctly rich, taxed on £40 or £80 in goods.[150]

[143] For Walsall and Lichfield see above; for Hitchin see Huntingdonshire RO, Archdeaconry Wills 5, f. 119r–v, 6, f. 16r–v, 8, ff. 147r–148r, 199r–200r, 10, ff. 82v–83v, 11, f. 306r–v. At Nottingham the names of the retainers are not given; at Derby I have not yet found other records from which to identify those named, though the damaged subsidy list of 1524 yields only one match and names many substantial men who were not part of the retinue in 1508: PRO, E179/91/106.

[144] C. Brown, *A History of Newark-on-Trent* (2 vols., Newark, 1904–7), vol. 1, *passim*.

[145] PRO, E179/120/110.

[146] F.G. Lee, *The History, Description and Antiquities of the Prebendal Church of the Blessed Virgin Mary of Thame* (1883), *passim*; Bodl. MS dd Bertie c16/20.

[147] Ibid.; MS dd Bertie c16/22–4; PRO, E179/161/198.

[148] Ibid.; *VCH Oxfordshire*, vol. 7 (1962), p. 190.

[149] R. Peberdy, 'The economy, society and government of a small town in late medieval England: a study of Henley-on-Thames from *c*. 1300 to *c*. 1540', University of Leicester Ph.D. thesis 1994, pp. 198–249; *Henley Borough Records: Assembly Books i–iv, 1395–1543*, ed. P.M. Briers, Oxfordshire Record Society no. 41 (Oxford, 1960). I am most grateful to Robert Peberdy not only for permission to cite his thesis but also for much other assistance with south Oxfordshire records.

[150] PRO, E179/161/195.

These Oxfordshire town contingents, as we shall see, interlocked with Lovell's wider retaining in the county. But they also represented another important aspect of early Tudor policy, a mutually beneficial rapprochement between the Crown and its ministers and urban oligarchies. At York and Lincoln, Lovell agreed to take only a fraction of the fee-farms he could have claimed in the name of Lord Roos in order to ease the cities' financial problems.[151] At Nottingham and Walsall he was both patron and overseer, rather as his conciliar colleagues were elsewhere: Hobart at Great Yarmouth, John Lord Cheyne at Salisbury, Poynings at Canterbury and among the Cinque Ports.[152] Lovell's reaction to popular agitation for a widening of the franchise in Nottingham leaves no doubt about the equation in his mind between order and oligarchy. In 1512 the recorder Thomas Babington reminded the mayor and aldermen of 'the saying of Mr Tresorer, of the inconveniences that hath ensued opon the callyng of the commons to geder in the Citie of London, and in oder Cites and Borowes'.[153] At Walsall the only ordinance he saw added to the set approved by Sir Humphrey Stanley concerned the punishment of anyone who 'mys ordeynyth hym self in wordes or deedes' against the town's rulers.[154] The government's relationship with the London élite was the most important of all, and here too Lovell played his part, cultivating links with the city's leaders as Cromwell or Cecil would do. Mayor Shaa named Lovell one of his executors, Mayor Ward bequeathed him a cup and three of the mayors of the early 1520s attended his funeral.[155] Ward was five times master of the Grocers' Company, of which Lovell was a brother and for which he rebuilt the Weighhouse in Cornhill.[156] Lovell

---

[151] *LP*, Addenda, i. 268; *CCIR 1500–9*, no. 952; HMC, *Report 37: The Manuscripts of Lincoln, Bury St Edmunds, and Great Grimsby Corporations* (1895), p. 31; Lincolnshire AO, L1/1/1/1, f. 186r; PRO, C1/860/8.

[152] HMC, *Ninth Report*, Appendix 1, p. 307; HMC, *Report 55: Manuscripts in Various Collections*, vol. 4 (Dublin, 1907), p. 211. I hope to discuss Poynings, together with Lovell, Wyatt and others, in a future book.

[153] *Records of the Borough of Nottingham*, vol. 3, p. 342.

[154] Walsall LHC, MS 277/238, m. 4d.

[155] J.C. Wedgwood, *History of Parliament: Biographies of the Members of the Commons House, 1439–1509* (1936), pp. 758–9, 921; *LP*, vol. 4, i, 366; J. Stow, *A Survey of London*, ed. C.L. Kingsford (2nd edn, 2 vols, Oxford, 1971), vol. 2, p. 181.

[156] Stow, *Survey*, vol. 1, p. 192; *Calendar of Wills proved and enrolled in the Court of Husting, London, AD 1258–AD 1688*, ed. R.R. Sharpe (2 vols, 1889–90), vol. 2, pp. 635–6.

appeared regularly in the lobbying accounts of various livery companies.[157] Though first Bray and later Dudley tended to head council delegations to discuss with the governors of London, Lovell's presence must also have been a help.[158]

In Oxfordshire special factors extended Lovell's relationships with the towns into the construction of an affinity stretching across the southern part of the shire. Here he held a series of intermeshing stewardships from the Duchy of Cornwall, the Bishop of Lincoln and St George's College, Windsor. The links these provided with yeomen and husbandmen were reinforced and further extended by the private interests and other offices of the administrative gentry who served as Lovell's deputies. Thirteen gentlemen with nineteen followers of their own, fifty-three yeomen serving in person, and fourteen substitutes provided by richer (or frailer?) yeomen were signed up in 1508 by William Young of Little Wittenham, Lovell's deputy in all three stewardships.[159] Sixteen more were gathered by Henry Reynolds, receiver and surveyor of the forfeited De la Pole estates in Oxfordshire and Berkshire and of the honour of Wallingford estates of which Lovell was steward.[160] Other groups were drawn together by Hugh Shirley of Henley, farmer of the De la Pole manor of Nuneham Courtenay, and John Daunce of Thame, the Exchequer teller, men whose interests stretched well beyond the towns where they lived.[161]

The yeomen and lesser gentlemen they recruited were often the dominant figures in their communities. There were bailiffs and demesne farmers from each set of estates: Thomas Skydmore from Watlington in the honour of Wallingford, William Bigger from Hook Norton and Thomas Calcote from Aston-Tirrold among the De la Pole lands, Thomas Boldrey from Great Haseley and Edmund Gadbury from Pyrton among the St George's estates.[162] There were a number who were the richest or second richest taxpayers in their vills in 1524, some very prosperous like Thomas

---

[157] I owe this information to Dr Andrea Velich.

[158] *The Great Chronicle of London*, eds A.H. Thomas and I.D. Thornley (1938), pp. 263, 274–5, 310, 333.

[159] PRO, SC6/Hen VII/1091, mm. 2r–4r; Bodl. MS dd Bertie c24/1; Windsor, The Aerary, MS XV.49.11.

[160] *LP*, vol. 1, i, 190 (28); *CPR 1494–1509*, p. 312.

[161] *CPR 1494–1509*, p. 619; PRO, SC6/Hen VIII/5978; *LP*, vol. 1, i, 438 (3 m. 7).

[162] PRO, SC6/Hen VII/1091; KB9/440/14; C54/388, m. 7; Windsor, The Aerary, MSS XV.48.58, XV.49.10, XV.49.15;

Boldrey with his £133 6s 8d in goods or Humphrey Elmes of Bolney with his £40 in lands, others more modest but still *coqs de village* like Richard Grymsby and John Petty of Tetsworth, William Tanner of Bix Gibben, Richard Dawbery of Bensington or Edmund Whitehill of Buckland, each taxed on between £16 and £40 in goods.[163]

The local influence exercised by such men was evident in many ways. Some served the Crown in minor but responsible posts, eleven as subsidy collectors in 1523–4.[164] Others held manorial offices: Richard Blackhall of Nettlebed was woodward at the St George's manor of Pyrton.[165] Some were named umpires or arbitrators in disputes: the university chancellor's court delegated one settlement to Thomas Skydmore and another to John Trayford and William Shoesmith, the warden of the Oxford barbers' guild, who went on to serve as town bailiff.[166] Some made their mark through philanthropy: Richard Beauforest, the richest man in Dorchester in 1524, bought the abbey church for the townsfolk in 1536, while Christopher Swan, draper, grazier, clothmaker and yeoman of Abingdon, left his house to St Nicholas' church in 1514.[167] Some made their impression in a more aggressive way, as enclosers and large-scale sheep farmers, following the example of such gentlemen of the retinue as Henry Reynolds, Edmund Bury and William Cottesmore.[168] Leading yeomen and gentry alike were bound into local circles of feoffees, witnesses and executors, which must have given the retinue internal cohesion.[169]

---

[163] PRO, E179/161/195, 198; E315/464, f. 73r.

[164] PRO, E179/161/198.

[165] Bodl. MS Top Oxon c207, ff. 44r, 46r, 47r.

[166] *Registrum Cancellarii 1498–1506*, ed. W.T. Mitchell, Oxford Historical Society no. 27 (Oxford, 1980), pp. 118, 183, 186, 188; *Selections from the Records of the City of Oxford*, ed. W.H. Turner (Oxford, 1880), p. 11.

[167] *VCH Oxon.*, vol. 7, pp. 47, 59; A.E. Preston, *The Church and Parish of St Nicholas Abingdon*, Oxford Historical Society no. 99 (Oxford, 1935), pp. 80–1.

[168] *The Domesday of Inclosures*, ed. I.S. Leadam (2 vols, 1897), vol. 1, p. 145; *VCH Oxfordshire*, vol. 5 (1957), pp. 103, 243, vol. 6 (1959), p. 164, vol. 7, pp. 13, 47, 190, vol. 8 (1964), pp. 28, 268–9; *Some Oxfordshire Wills proved in the Prerogative Court of Canterbury, 1393–1510*, eds J.R.H. Weaver and A. Beardwood, Oxfordshire Record Society no. 39 (Oxford, 1958), p. 88; Oxfordshire RO, MS Wills Oxon. 178, ff. 96r–7v, 135v–6v; PRO, C1/142/39, 317/23.

[169] For examples see Bodl. MSS dd Barrett a2 (i18), (i20), (k2), (k6), (m12), (o1); MS ch. Oxon. 274; Brasenose College, Oxford, Muniments Faringdon 34, Wheatley 12; Merton College, Oxford, MCR 887, 3342; Oxon. RO, DD Par Great Haseley c4/2; MS Wills Oxon. 178, f. 45v; *Oxfordshire Wills*, pp. 88, 91–3.

What did this retinue mean to Sir Thomas Lovell and the king he served? It certainly had a military value. Wills, town records and the military survey of 1522 testify to the ownership of arms and armour by a number of the members.[170] As to their aptitude for war we can only speculate. We might picture them alongside Hugh Latimer of Thurcaston (Leics.), like many of them a comfortable yeoman on the fringe of the bastard feudal nexus, in receipt of a 40*s* annuity from Thomas Cotton, Esq. of Hamstall Ridware (Staffs.). Hugh was not unfamiliar with violence, private or public. He was tried and acquitted for murder in 1512; his son Hugh, the future Bishop of Worcester, learned from him how to draw his bow and buckled on his father's armour as he went off to fight at Blackheath.[171] No doubt many of the 493 men Lovell led in the campaign of 1497 or those in the companies he raised in 1512–14 were among those listed in 1508.[172] Yet Henry VII and his councillors had an agenda beyond mere military survival, and here too Lovell's retinue had its uses.

In Oxfordshire as elsewhere, Lovell could not draw the leading county gentry into his service; nor, probably, could any but the very greatest peers. His relations with the knightly élite were distant but not uncooperative: his retainer William Cottesmore was son and heir to Sir John Cottesmore, and Sir John Longford, sheriff in 1508–9, seems to have recruited four yeomen for Lovell though he did not serve himself.[173] For those less entrenched in the county élite and seeking to rise by their talent, however, those who had often been the most dynamic force in the noble retinues of the past, Lovell's service and the Crown's paid dividends, dividends for which they paid in hard work and loyalty. William Belson of Brill claimed he had ridden more than 800 miles a year holding courts as Lovell's last deputy in the stewardship of the honour of Wallingford; Lovell's executors did not dispute this, but

---

[170] *Oxfordshire Wills*, p. 81; *Henley Borough Records*, pp. 118, 167; PRO, E315/464, f. 72v; PROB11/16/35; *Halifax Wills*, pp. 72–3; Lichfield JRO, will of John Slanye 9 May 1541.

[171] Leicestershire RO, DG41 box 45/L30; PRO, KB9/466/82; *Sermons by Hugh Latimer*, ed. G.E. Corrie (Cambridge, Parker Society, 1844), pp. 101, 197.

[172] I. Arthurson, 'The king's voyage into Scotland: the war that never was', in *England in the Fifteenth Century: Proceedings of the 1986 Harlaxton Symposium*, ed. D.T. Williams (Woodbridge, 1987), p. 19; *LP*, vol. 1, i, 1176, 1661 (3); *Chronicle of Calais*, p. 15.

[173] *Oxfordshire Wills*, pp. 100–1; *List of Sheriffs*, p. 109.

refused his claim to a share of Lovell's fee on the grounds that the understewardship was 'greatly advaylable and profitable to the occupyer and mynyster therof'.[174] Belson's predecessor, William Young, drew more direct reward from Lovell: patronage within Lincoln's Inn, an Exchequer office and the feodaryship of wards for Oxfordshire and Berkshire.[175] Such men were key figures in realizing the fiscal, judicial and political ambitions of early Tudor government. Young himself was escheator of Oxfordshire and Berkshire continuously from 1505 to 1510 and again in 1513–14. Three other members of the retinue served as escheators in these counties between 1492 and 1515, and a fourth as sheriff.[176] William Young, Edmund Bury, Henry Reynolds and Hugh Shirley were regularly named to the commissions of Henry VII's last years to search out concealed lands, wardships, mortmains, enclosures, illegal retainers and so on.[177] Edmund Bury became an active JP in Oxfordshire soon after his nomination in 1504, and others joined the bench there or in Berkshire in the next ten years while continuing to collect local offices such as Bury's recordership of Oxford or John Daunce's stewardship of Donnington.[178]

Lovell's retinue in 1508 contained similar figures in other counties. John Monson, captain of the Caister contingent, John a Lee, bailiff of three Leicestershire manors and Humphrey Hercy of Nottinghamshire would all be chosen his feodaries in the wards office, and Monson had already served as escheator of Lincolnshire from 1505 to 1510.[179] What made the Oxfordshire retinue unusual was the breadth of its penetration into the élites of small towns and villages. When these gentlemen sat as commissioners or justices, they faced juries on which their fellow retainers were heavily represented. Eight inquisition *post mortem* juries gathered by William Young at Dorchester, Oxford, Crowmarsh

---

[174] PRO, C1/383/4–5.

[175] *Black Books*, vol. 1, p. 167; Sainty, *Officers of the Exchequer*, p. 96; *LP*, vol. 1, ii, 2222 (12).

[176] *List of Escheators*, p. 125; *List of Sheriffs*, p. 108; D. Luckett, 'Henry VII and the south-western escheators', in *The Reign of Henry VII: Proceedings of the 1993 Harlaxton Symposium*, ed. B. Thompson (Stamford, 1995), pp. 60–1.

[177] *CPR 1494–1509*, pp. 421, 437, 458, 491, 507, 582, 593, 608.

[178] PRO, KB9/440/44, 442/38, 466/73; *CPR 1494–1509*, p. 655; *LP*, vol. 1, i, 132 (120), ii, pp. 1533–4, 1542; *Records of the City of Oxford*, p. 5.

[179] *LP*, vol. 1, ii, 2222 (12), vol. 3, i, 206 (16); *List of Escheators*, p. 82.

and Henley in 1505–7 featured nineteen or twenty of Lovell's retainers, seven of whom also sat at quarter sessions in 1504–6.[180] Altogether some fifty-four of the retinue sat at quarter sessions, inquisitions *post mortem*, coroner's inquests or before commissioners of sewers in Oxfordshire in the years 1499–1525, and at least four more sat on Berkshire juries in the same period. Some were very regular jurors: John Richardson appeared at least thirteen times between 1502 and 1508. And some panels were as packed as any in Henry VII's dreams: at one hearing into concealed lands at Henley, Edmund Bury, Henry Reynolds and two other commissioners questioned a jury of twelve, only three of whom were not Lovell's men.[181]

Though less comprehensively than in Oxfordshire, Lovell was recruiting men of similar standing elsewhere: between 1503 and 1521 at least forty-six of his retainers sat on juries before justices, escheators or coroners in Yorkshire, Staffordshire, Nottinghamshire and Hertfordshire.[182] Here perhaps was a regime starting to reach into local society beyond the county gentry, just as fourteenth-century regimes had reached beyond the peerage to the gentry.[183] What kind of loyalties were fostered is hard to say. Quarter sessions presentments suggest that those retained by Lovell were not transformed overnight into law-abiding Tudor subjects: Nicholas Woodleff did business in clipped groats at Henley and three of the retinue infringed in various ways on Sir George Foster's land at Rotherfield Greys, though there may well be more to the latter case than meets the eye, since Foster was shortly afterwards indicted by an Abingdon jury including another of

---

[180] PRO, C142/19/40; C142/20/35, 122, 150; C142/22/38; C142/23/266; E150/783/11, 13; KB9/436/72; KB9/439/32; KB9/440/14, 44, 46; KB9/442/38.

[181] PRO, C142/16/28; C142/20/42; C142/24/16; C142/28/36; C142/29/41, 64, 121; C142/30/92; KB9/422/23; KB9/426/12; KB9/427/1; KB9/434/26; KB9/435/38; KB9/446/51; KB9/447/22, 24; KB9/453/69; KB9/459/51; KB9/461/17; KB9/464/95; KB9/466/24; KB9/467/4; KB9/468/2; KB9/473/32; KB9/475/46; KB9/479/27–8; KB9/480/42; KB9/482/27; KB9/489/44; KB9/491/10; KB9/495/59; KB9/497/51, 90.

[182] PRO, C142/16/90, 18/66, 25/114, 119, 30/103; KB9/429/11, 457/47, 461/31–2, 462/25, 467/24, 473/55, 475/35, 476/9, 488/41–2; *Calendar of Nottinghamshire Coroners' Inquests 1485–1558*, ed. R.F. Hunnisett, Thoroton Society Record Series no. 25 (Nottingham, 1966), pp. 12, 20.

[183] C. Given-Wilson, 'The king and the gentry in fourteenth-century England', *TRHS*, 5th ser. 37 (1987), 87–102.

Lovell's retainers for the arsenic poisoning of a young gentleman thirteen years previously. On the other hand, in several cases members of the retinue were prepared to return indictments against other members.[184] That some deeper loyalty to the king's purposes may have been planted by Lovell's service is hinted at by events in Thame three decades later. Thomas Striblehill, one of Lovell's retainers in 1508, challenged the vicar when, in 1537, he held a solemn feast on the banned festival of St Thomas Becket. 'I think thou art of the Northern sect,' he told him, 'thou wouldst rule the King's Highness and not to be ruled.' John Benet, his fellow from 1508, backed him; Sir John Daunce, organizer of Lovell's Thame contingent, was one of the two justices to whom they reported the confrontation.[185]

Lovell's retinue, though constructed on the basis of office-holding and royal favour rather than personal landed wealth and dynastic tradition, was as large and well-entrenched as those of all but the greatest fifteenth-century noblemen. Being recruited with a royal licence under the terms of the statute of 1504, it was also legal at a time when more traditional retinues faced the threat of prosecution.[186] This change in the balance of retaining, like many other developments we have been considering, threatened to unsettle if not to subvert the accustomed power of the peerage. Some noblemen blamed those around the king: Lovell was second only to Wolsey on Buckingham's list of those he would execute when he came to the throne.[187] The prosperity born of Lovell's power – in 1524 he was taxed on £2,000 in goods, more than all but the greatest peers – was painfully evident to Buckingham and Northumberland, who both had to borrow money from him.[188] Others sought to buy influence within the new regime, such that, as it was said of Dudley, 'the Chyeff lordys of England were gladd to be in his ffavour'.[189] Lovell was granted fees by the earls of Derby,

---

[184] PRO, KB9/439/17, 32; KB9/440/14, 43.

[185] *LP*, vol. 12, ii, 357.

[186] A. Cameron, 'The giving of livery and retaining in Henry VII's reign', *Renaissance and Modern Studies*, 18 (1974), 25–35.

[187] *LP*, vol. 3, i, 1284.

[188] PRO, E179/141/109; *LP*, vol. 3, i, 1285 (5), vol. 4, ii, 3380 (5).

[189] *Great Chronicle*, p. 348.

Huntingdon and Northumberland, Viscount Beaumont and Lord Willoughby d'Eresby.[190] The Earl of Arundel and Lord Delawarr gave advowsons to him and to various associates, and Northumberland and George Lord Bergavenny sent him deer from their parks, though Bergavenny's was so scrawny that Lovell's cook thought it an insult.[191]

Sir Thomas' relationships with those firmly within Henry VII's charmed circle, whether peers, bishops or knights, were far more relaxed. He seems to have been especially close to Oxford, Daubeney and Fox, and to have cooperated with Fox in the promotion of Wolsey.[192] One of his surviving letters to the two bishops in 1514 ends banteringly, 'If I have doon yll ye muste repute in me but ffolye', and when the Abbot of Waltham sent him a buck on 19 July 1523 he ate it with Fox, perhaps talking over their four decades in power.[193] He was executor or supervisor to Sir Thomas Brandon, Sir John Cutt and Sir Robert Sheffield.[194] Councillors such as Lord Dynham and Sir Charles Somerset corresponded with Lovell when they were away from court.[195] Lesser ties bound him to many more: Guildford and Risley, Litton and Windsor, Wyatt and Southwell, Ormond and Willoughby de Broke.[196]

Their cooperation was reflected and enhanced by the links some of Lovell's followers maintained with his fellow councillors. Of his retinue of 1508, Simon Digby was an executor to Bray, Thomas English to Daubeney, and John Norton

---

[190] *LP*, vol. 3, ii, 2822, vol. 4, i, 976, 1857; Suffolk RO, Bury St Edmunds, Ac 449/E3/15.53/2.8; PRO, SC6/Hen VIII/345, m. 51v.

[191] *LP*, Addenda, i. 745; Lincs. AO, Register 23, f. 99r–v; Norfolk RO, Register 12, f. 183r; HMC, Rutland, vol. 4, p. 265.

[192] S.J. Gunn, 'The structures of politics in early Tudor England', *TRHS*, 6th ser. 5 (1995), 80; *Plumpton Correspondence*, p. cxiii; *CPR 1494–1509*, p. 266; *The Life and Death of Cardinal Wolsey by George Cavendish*, ed. R.S. Sylvester, Early English Text Society no. 243 (Oxford, 1959), pp. 7, 9–10.

[193] PRO, SP1/8, f. 126v (*LP*, vol. 1, ii, 2974); Belvoir Castle, MS a/c no. 4.

[194] King, 'Family of Cutts', p. 33; *Testamenta Vetusta*, ed. N.H. Nicolas (2 vols, 1826), vol. 2, pp. 496–7, 556–7.

[195] PRO, E404/81/3; Canterbury RO, FA2, f. 358v.

[196] Norfolk RO, Register 12, f. 182r; PRO, C142/41/62; Guildhall Library, MS 9531/8, f. 73v; *CClR 1485–1500*, nos 898, 1201; *CClR 1500–9*, no. 755; P. Morant, *The History and Antiquities of the County of Essex* (2 vols, Wakefield, 1978 edn), vol. 2, p. 152.

was a Kentish associate of Poynings.[197] An even clearer case was that of Lovell's brother Sir Robert, one of the powerful circle of knights around the Earl of Oxford.[198] Lovell's continuing contacts with him, as with his many other East Anglian relatives and associates, lent him a role in regional affairs complementary to that of Oxford, even when he could spare little time to visit East Harling.[199] Thus Sir Thomas's Norfolk retainers John Cusshyn of Hingham and Richard Gousall of Fordham were more closely linked to Sir Robert than to Sir Thomas himself.[200]

It was such fluidity of roles and connections that made the governing cliques of early Tudor England flexible and effective. Lovell's personal versatility – lawyer, financier, soldier, diplomat, courtier – made him more than a stereotypical departmental bureaucrat, just as the centrality of his relationship with the king to the construction and maintenance of his power made him less than an independent civil servant.[201] In some ways his lifestyle looked forward to that of a Cromwell or a Cecil. Various contemporaries, most admittedly out to flatter, stressed his devotion to business and sheer hard work; perhaps petitioners explained of him, as the Archdeacon of Wells did of Fox, 'Ye wolde wondre what causes he hathe to do, and therfore we muste abyde hys leysere'.[202] He seems to have dressed more soberly

---

[197] *CPR 1494–1509*, p. 338, 366; PRO, PROB11/16/16; C54/379, m. 3d; *Chronicle of Calais*, p. 8; Lichfield JRO, B/A/1/14i, f. 8r.

[198] 'The last testament and inventory of John de Veer, thirteenth earl of Oxford', ed. W.H. St J. Hope, *Archaeologia*, 66 (1914–15), 318; W.G. Benham, 'Shakespearean characters connected with Essex', *Essex Review*, 14 (1905), 100–1; Essex RO, D/DWd 1; BL, Add. Ch. 41711; Add. MS 21480, f. 66v; PRO, E36/215, f. 324v; *CClR 1485–1500*, no. 777; *CClR 1500–9*, no. 364; *Testamenta Vetusta*, vol. 2, p. 484; *CPR 1485–94*, pp. 271–2, 357, 360, 393, 438, 494; *CPR 1494–1509*, pp. 265, 322, 361, 379, 408, 424, 474, 550, 560, 651; *List of Sheriffs*, p. 88; Longleat House, Misc. vol. 11, f. 2r (I am grateful for permission to read and cite material from Longleat).

[199] PRO, DL5/4, f. 125r; *LP*, vol. 3, ii, 1648, vol. 4, i. 366; *Testamenta Eboracensia*, vol. 4, pp. 151–4; CIPM Henry VII, vol. 2, nos 892, 946, vol. 3, no. 435.

[200] PRO, C142/39/54; C1/499/57.

[201] S.J. Gunn, 'The courtiers of Henry VII', *EHR*, 108 (1993), 27–8; on diplomacy see T. Rymer, *Foedera, Conventiones, Literae et cujuscunque generis Acta Publica* (20 vols, 1704–35), vol. 12, pp. 285–93, 397–405, 451–2; *Calendar of State Papers, Spanish, vol. 1*, ed. G. Bergenroth (1862), no. 204; *LP*, vol. 1, ii, 3268.

[202] *Epistolae Academicae*, pp. 12–13, 25–6; *LP*, vol. 3, i, 1121; PRO, C1/632/50; HMC, *Report 12: Manuscripts of the Dean and Chapter of Wells, vol. 2* (1914), p. 192.

than many of his colleagues at court, and his great palace at Elsings was deliberately built, like an Elizabethan prodigy house, to accommodate the king and queen on progress.[203] In other ways his habits were those of the noblemen he had displaced. He feasted on swans from his Norfolk estates, dressed his eighty-five servants in light tawny orange livery and built himself a burial chapel at Holywell Nunnery with windows poetically inscribed, 'All the nunnes in Holywel / Pray for the soul of Sir Thomas Lovel'.[204]

Lovell's career was not without precedent: the knights and esquires of the king's Household active in the royal councils of Richard II or Henry IV prefigured him in some ways, William Lord Hastings or William Catesby in others, just as they had preceded him in some of his stewardships.[205] Earlier or parallel phases of governmental intensification called other new men to the fore. One might, for instance, compare Lovell to the Angevins' 'men raised from the dust' or to his Flemish contemporary Lieven van Pottelsberghe.[206] Equally, Lovell's new monarchy was not the only new monarchy England ever had, and perhaps none of them was as new as we once thought: the more we understand of the continuities between Anglo-Saxon and Anglo-Norman government, the less we can credit McFarlane's view that 'The only New Monarchy that England

---

[203] PRO, PROB2/187, 199; PROB11/17/18; PROB11/16/29; E154/2/5, 10, 17; 'Last testament of John de Veer', pp. 342–3; A.F. Sutton, 'Order and fashion in clothes: the king, his household, and the City of London at the end of the fifteenth century', *Textile History*, 22 (1991), 258–9; D. Pam, *A Parish Near London* (Enfield, 1990), pp. 51–4; S. Thurley, 'The domestic building works of Cardinal Wolsey', in *Cardinal Wolsey: Church, State and Art*, eds S.J. Gunn and P.G. Lindley (Cambridge, 1991), p. 90.

[204] Belvoir Castle MS a/c no. 4; BL, Add. MS 12463, ff. 66v–7r; Dugdale, *Monasticon*, vol. 4, p. 391.

[205] *History of Parliament: The House of Commons 1386–1421*, eds J.S. Roskell, L. Clark and C. Rawcliffe (4 vols, Stroud, 1992), vol. 2, pp. 99–103, 449–54, vol. 3, pp. 225–8, 843–6, vol. 4, pp. 39–44, 306–10, 620–8; *Registra Johannis Whethamstede, Willelmi Albon, et Willelmi Walingforde, Abbatum Monasterii Sancti Albani*, ed. H.T. Riley, Rolls Series no. 28f, vol 2 (1873), pp. 199–200, 255–7, 265–7; HL MS HAP oversize box 5 (11, 18); R. Horrox, *Richard III: A Study of Service* (Cambridge, 1989), pp. 222, 259–60.

[206] R.V. Turner, *Men Raised from the Dust: Administrative Service and Upward Mobility in Angevin England* (Philadelphia, 1988); P.P.J.L. Van Peteghem, *De Raad van Vlaanderen en Staatsvorming onder Karel V (1515–1555)* (Nijmegen, 1990), pp. 266–74.

ever had came in with William the Conqueror'.[207] Yet neither a man nor a monarchy need be completely or uniquely new to be significantly new: a man newly socially mobile and politically powerful for his position, a monarchy newly ambitious, assertive and effective not least through the efforts of such new men. No one in Walsall ever consciously bade farewell to the Middle Ages, but perhaps they did realize that in Sir Thomas Lovell they had met a new man in a new monarchy.

[207] K.B. McFarlane, *The Nobility of Later Medieval England* (Oxford, 1973), p. 283.

5

BARONIAL CONTEXTS?
CONTINUITY AND CHANGE IN THE
NOBLE AFFINITY, 1400–1600*

Simon Adams

The title 'continuity and change' has been employed so regularly that it has almost become a confession of failure to find a better one. However, there is a justification for its use here. The purpose of this exercise is a straightforward one: to compare a late sixteenth-century noble affinity, that of Robert Dudley, Earl of Leicester, with its predecessors. The reason for doing so is no less obvious. The affinity is understood to be one of the pillars (if not the central pillar) of aristocratic power in the late medieval period; changes in the affinity should therefore reflect any changes in the overall structure of politics. The areas of comparison – composition, structure and function – present no difficulties. The wider context, on the other hand, particularly the role and effectiveness of the sixteenth-century affinity, raises some complex questions.

Until relatively recently, these questions were not even considered worth posing. Following the publication of Lawrence Stone's monumental work, it was regarded almost as axiomatic that there was an absolute decline in noble power between

*Reference to the Longleat House, Berkeley Castle and Bedford Estate MSS is made with the kind permission of the Marquess of Bath, the Berkeley Trustees and the Marquess of Tavistock and the Trustees of the Bedford Estate. The majority of my essays cited here will be reprinted in *Leicester and the Court: Essays on Elizabethan History 1974–1995* (Manchester University Press, forthcoming), but for ease of reference the original version is employed. I am extremely grateful to the editor for his forbearance and his stimulating comments on earlier versions of this essay; he of course bears no responsibility for the views expressed here.

the fifteenth and the seventeenth centuries.[1] In the late 1970s this attitude began
to change, as Barry Coward noted in his study of the Stanleys: 'Only recently have
a few historians begun to question whether Stone's concept of a crisis in the
peerage's power, prestige and self-confidence might be equally unfounded as his
economic crisis hypothesis.' He referred in particular to Conrad Russell, Kevin
Sharpe and Clive Holmes.[2] The immediate stimulus for this revived interest was
the attempt by Russell and Sir Geoffrey Elton to reshape the parliamentary
history of the period by 'restoring' the House of Lords to its primacy over the
Commons. In the 1980s, however, a different group of early-modernists began to
re-examine the wider role of the sixteenth-century peerage: David Starkey, Steven
Gunn, George Bernard and the contributors to Bernard's 1992 collection, *The
Tudor Nobility*.[3] Most dramatically, and controversially, at the beginning of the
present decade, John Adamson advanced a new interpretation of Civil War
politics, which saw the peerage as the pivotal force on the parliamentary side, with
its power apparently undiminished.[4] Adamson's approach owes much to the
Elton–Russell re-emphasis on the House of Lords, but (like Starkey) he sees the
politics of the Lords as derived from a tradition of aristocratic constitutionalism.

[1] Lawrence Stone, *The Crisis of the Aristocracy 1558–1641* (Oxford, rev. edn, 1979). M.E. James
adopted a more nuanced approach, see *Society, Politics and Culture: Studies in Early Modern England*
(Cambridge, 1986), esp. 'The concept of order and the Northern Rebellion', 'English politics and the
concept of honour, 1485–1642', and 'At a crossroads of the political culture: the Essex revolt, 1601'.
The combined influence of Stone and James can be found in Felicity Heal and Clive Holmes, *The
Gentry in England and Wales 1500–1700* (Basingstoke, 1994).

[2] Barry Coward, *The Stanleys, Lords Stanley and Earls of Derby 1385–1672. The Origins, Wealth and Power
of a Landowning Family* (Cheetham Society, xxx, 1983), p. xiii. He also notes the origins of the crisis of
the aristocracy in the rise of the gentry debate.

[3] (Manchester, 1992). The contributors include the author, Steven Gunn and Richard Hoyle.
Starkey is best known for his influence on the study of the court, but his views on the importance of
the peerage can be found in the introduction to Starkey, ed., *Rivals in Power: Lives and Letters of the Great
Tudor Dynasties* (1990), pp. 8–25. The contributors to this volume include Steven Gunn and the
author. Helen Miller's valuable *Henry VIII and the English Nobility* (Oxford, 1986) should not be
overlooked, although it does not deal directly with these issues.

[4] 'The Baronial Context of the English Civil War', *TRHS*, 5th ser., xl (1990), 93–120, and
'Parliamentary Management, Men-of-Business and the House of Lords, 1640–49', in Clive Jones, ed.,
A Pillar of the Constitution: The House of Lords in British Politics, 1640–1784 (1989), pp. 21–50.

The last two decades have also witnessed an intense debate over the power and political role of the late medieval nobility. Christine Carpenter has recently drawn attention to what appear to be 'different agendas' in the two periods, quoting with approval Steven Gunn's reference to a 'fault-line of mutual incomprehension'.[5] On one level there is something to this. Much work has been undertaken on the noble affinity in the fourteenth and fifteenth centuries.[6] By contrast, my own research into the Earl of Leicester and his affinity has been carried out almost *in vacuo*, there being no comparable studies of other Elizabethan peers when I began.[7] Coward's book on the Stanleys certainly addresses many of the issues, but in a very general and thematic way.[8] Of the historians of the early sixteenth century only Gunn has studied affinities in any detail.[9] Even more important is the fact that there is practically no work at all on this aspect of the early seventeenth-century peerage, which creates serious difficulties for the overall Adamson thesis.[10] The 'fault-line' is

[5] Christine Carpenter, 'Who Ruled the Midlands in the Later Middle Ages?', *Midland History*, xix (1994), 1–2.

[6] To select only a few of the major titles out of many, Carole Rawcliffe, *The Staffords, Earls of Stafford and Dukes of Buckingham, 1394–1521* (Cambridge, 1978); C. Carpenter, 'The Beauchamp Affinity: a study of bastard feudalism at work', *EHR*, xcv (1980), 514–32, and *Locality and Polity: A Study of Warwickshire Landed Society, 1401–1499* (Cambridge, 1992); Simon Walker, *The Lancastrian Affinity 1361–1399* (Oxford, 1990). The extensive periodical literature is surveyed in Michael Hicks, *Bastard Feudalism* (1995).

[7] This is changing now, see, for example, Paul E.J. Hammer 'Patronage at Court, faction and the earl of Essex', in John Guy, ed., *The Reign of Elizabeth I: Court and Culture in the Last Decade* (Cambridge, 1995), pp. 65–86; Hammer, 'The Uses of Scholarship: the Secretariat of Robert Devereux, Second Earl of Essex', *EHR*, cix (1994), 26–51; and G.R. Morrison, 'The Land, Family and Domestic Following of William Cecil, Lord Burghley, *c.* 1550–1598' (unpublished D.Phil. thesis, University of Oxford, 1990).

[8] See his chapters 7–10. The loss of most of the Stanley archive in the destruction of Knowsley during the Civil War (see p. xii) makes a detailed study of the sixteenth-century earls of Derby difficult. Claire Cross, *The Puritan Earl: The Life of Henry Hastings, Third Earl of Huntingdon* (1966), an otherwise valuable work, concentrates on Huntingdon's public career and religious patronage.

[9] Specifically in *Charles Brandon, Duke of Suffolk 1484–1545* (Oxford, 1988), 'Henry Bourchier, Earl of Essex (1472–1540)', in Bernard, *Tudor Nobility*, pp. 158–66, and his contribution to this volume. 'Bourchier' and my essay, 'The Dudley Clientele 1553–1563', are in fact the only studies of affinities in *Tudor Nobility*. The discussion of the Talbot affinity in Bernard, *The Power of the Early Tudor Nobility: A Study of the Fourth and Fifth Earls of Shrewsbury* (Brighton, 1985) is limited to pp. 158–66.

[10] An example is Roger Lockyer's otherwise excellent biography, *Buckingham: The Life and Political Career of George Villiers, First Duke of Buckingham* (1981). See my review, *EHR*, xcviii (1983), 625–8.

also reflected in the terminology. My approach to Leicester was very much shaped by the fascination of early modern historians in the 1970s and 1980s with factional politics. Searching for a more neutral term than faction to describe Leicester's following, I adopted clientele.[11] By contrast late medieval scholarship has employed the term affinity almost exclusively. To simplify matters, affinity will be employed here as well, as the basic characteristics are the same, and any wider significance of the term clientele can be left for a future occasion.[12]

On another level, however, Carpenter may have drawn the contrast too sharply, for the thrust of her argument is that the basic issues are common to both periods. She makes little reference to recent sixteenth-century work, and it could be argued that her comparison of the late medieval debate with the 1970s debate over the 'county communities' and the Civil War is an extreme one.[13] The wider intellectual influences may be more pervasive than she allows for; I know for a fact that I am not the only early-modernist who would admit to being inspired by Namier, Syme and McFarlane.[14] Recent sixteenth-century scholarship is fully aware of fifteenth-century work, not least her own.[15] The basic issues are

---

[11] Initially I employed the French form but variant house styles led to abandoning of the accent in some essays, and it will be abandoned here as well. This is not the place to discuss the issues raised by the debate on factional politics or its relationship to the politics of patronage. My own views can be found in 'Favourites and Factions at the Elizabethan Court', reprinted in Guy, ed., *The Tudor Monarchy* (1997), pp. 253–74, 'The Patronage of the Crown in Elizabethan Politics: The 1590s in perspective' in Guy, *Reign of Elizabeth I*, pp. 20–45, and 'The Eltonian Legacy: Politics', *TRHS*, 6th ser., vii (1997), 247–65. See also the survey of the debate in Gunn, 'The Structures of Politics in Early Tudor England', *TRHS*, 6th ser., v (1995), 59–90.

[12] French usage of the term *clientèle* has a heavy bureaucratic emphasis, see the contributions to Charles Giry-Deloison and Roger Mettam, eds, *Patronages et Clientèlismes 1550–1750 (France, Angleterre, Espagne, Italie)* (Lille, 1995).

[13] With the exception of David Starkey's collection, *The English Court from the Wars of the Roses to the Civil War* (1987), her sources are entirely local studies, chiefly of the seventeenth century, see notes 3, 5 and 8. On the other hand, this is an essay on the Midlands and there has not been much work on the sixteenth-century Midlands with which to make comparisons.

[14] See the stimulating discussion of their influence in Edward Powell, 'After "After McFarlane": The Poverty of Patronage and the Case for Constitutional History' in D.J. Clayton *et al.*, eds, *Trade, Devotion and Government: Papers in Late Medieval History* (Stroud, 1994), pp. 1–16. This and Carpenter's own, 'Before and After McFarlane', R.H. Britnell and A.J. Pollard, eds, *The McFarlane Legacy: Studies in Later Medieval Politics and Society* (Stroud, 1995), pp. 175–206, are essays of major historiographical importance.

[15] See, for example, Guy's general introduction to *Tudor Monarchy*, pp. 1–8

straightforward enough. No one denies that some form of transformation of noble power took place between the fifteenth and the seventeenth centuries, with the gentry republics of late Elizabethan and seventeenth-century politics as the apparent result. What are debated are the chronology and causes of this transformation. For Carpenter lordship was the 'norm' of early fifteenth-century politics, the change coming at the end of the century with the rise of 'court-centred politics'. She is outspokenly dismissive of the existence of a county community or 'county identity' in Warwickshire or 'any midland county created artificially out of Mercia' in the fifteenth century.[16] Nigel Saul and Simon Payling, on the other hand, have argued that counties dominated by the baronage were the exceptions even then; the early fifteenth century (to use Saul's words) 'saw the emergence of the social order that characterised England in the age of the Tudors'.[17] Felicity Heal and Clive Holmes, approaching the subject from a third perspective, claim that 'a traditional political community, a fraternity or caste defined by lineage, military virtue and, personal honour' still existed, though under threat, at the end of the sixteenth century.[18]

The mechanisms of change are no more straightforward. Since the late nineteenth century the symbol of the decline of noble power was the Crown's apparently successful attack on indentured retaining. However, the picture is now a good deal more nuanced.[19] Formal retaining was of decreasing importance throughout the fifteenth century and it declined naturally rather

[16] 'Who ruled the Midlands', 6, 13. See also *Locality and Polity*, pp. 33, 290–1, 318 and conclusions.

[17] Nigel Saul, *Knights and Esquires: The Gloucestershire Gentry in the Fourteenth Century* (Oxford, 1981), p. 29. Simon Payling, *Political Society in Lancastrian England: The Greater Gentry of Nottinghamshire* (Oxford, 1991), p. 88. See also the survey of this debate in John Watts, *Henry VI and the Politics of Kingship* (Cambridge, 1996), pp. 91–101, and his reference to the 'normal form of local rule', p. 91.

[18] *The Gentry*, p. 194. Their discussion of relations between the peerage and the gentry (pp. 190–214) verges on the anecdotal. It is not entirely clear if they regard the Marquess of Newcastle's well-known description of the 7th Earl of Shrewsbury and his affinity at the beginning of the seventeenth century (quoted on pp. 190–1) solely as 'romantic nostalgia'.

[19] The best discussion can be found in the introduction to Michael Jones and Simon Walker, eds, 'Private Indentures for Life Service in Peace and War 1278–1476', *Camden Miscellany XXXII* (Camden Society, 5th ser., iii, 1994), pp. 1–190.

than as a result of the Crown's campaign. Retaining disappeared into the less formal but more complex affinity.[20] The relationship between the nobility and the Crown is equally debated. Much of the evidence for the early Tudor monarchy's hostility to the nobility is drawn from the Tudors' curious, persistent, yet still unexplained suspicion of the Percies.[21] Other noble families, the Stanleys or the Talbots, for example, were left with their local power undiminished.[22] Related to this is the question of the creation of a 'new nobility' by the Tudors. The distinction between old and new takes its origin in a contemporary political debate, but its modern usage begins with Tawney.[23] The most recent attempt to discuss Tudor politics in such terms can be found in David Loades's biography of the Duke of Northumberland, in which he argues that Northumberland was an example of a Tudor 'service nobility', epitomized by Thomas Cromwell. This nobility was distinguished from the 'traditional nobleman' by the absence of an established local affinity.[24] The distinction may rest on a romanticized view of the Stanleys (who were hardly old in fifteenth-century terms) and the Percies, the more so as neither of these affinities has been studied closely.[25]

It could be argued that K.B. McFarlane's major achievement was to revise the ingrained belief that the nobility was a uniquely destructive force and to see it as but a part of a society that as a whole was competitive and belligerent.[26]

---

[20] Carpenter, 'Beauchamp Affinity', 515–7. Watts, *Henry VI*, p. 93, n. 66.

[21] See, for example, Heal and Holmes, *The Gentry*, pp. 195–7. However, they also see the attack on the nobility as more widespread and ideological, see pp. 197–201.

[22] See Bernard's introduction to *Tudor Nobility*.

[23] For the contemporary debate see below, p. 179.

[24] *John Dudley, Duke of Northumberland 1504–1553* (Oxford, 1996), esp. pp. ix, 97, 285–6. Cf. my review in *Parliamentary History*, xvi (1997), 361–3. Hicks draws a similar distinction between a courtier following, which he terms an affinity, and a local territorial connection, *Bastard Feudalism*, pp. 104–8, 222–3.

[25] For the difficulties posed by the Stanleys, see above, n. 8. James, 'Concept of Order' is the best introduction to the Percies.

[26] See the comments of Powell, 'After "After McFarlane"', pp. 9–10, Carpenter, 'Before and After McFarlane', pp. 192–3, and G.L. Harriss, 'The Dimensions of Politics', in Britnell and Pollard, p. 3. That 'disputes were endemic in this landed society' (p. 393) is one of the axioms of Carpenter, *Locality and Polity*.

Carpenter describes Warwickshire politics in almost military terms.[27] The 'gentry' were not possessors of superior civic virtue; the gentry republics of Elizabeth's reign were not uniformly successful systems of local government.[28] What distinguished the nobility was its superior power, as manifested in its affinities. The lord ruled his country almost as the king ruled the kingdom.[29] Carpenter argues that security of property was the motivating force for, and the cement of, the affinity.[30] The affinity was the main stabilizing force in local politics because it provided the means for the mediation and peaceful resolution of disputes. The incidence of violence and cases reaching the courts becomes almost an index of the affinity's effectiveness.[31] However, there is also a certain tension in this definition of the affinity. On the one hand it was unstable, dependent very much on the personal effectiveness of the lord.[32] On the other it was to some extent natural, held together by local social connections rather than financial reward, access to royal patronage or a commitment to military service.[33]

At this point we should turn to the Earl of Leicester's affinity. What makes it particularly interesting in this context is that it was both late and the creation of a supposedly 'new' nobleman. As mentioned at the outset, it will be examined under the broad headings of composition, structure and function. Before doing so, some comments on the sources are necessary, for they are obviously much richer than those for fifteenth-century peers. In Leicester's case there is a

---

[27] For example, ' In the vacuum left by the Duchy of Lancaster, he [the Earl of Warwick] could not afford a struggle for control that would have unleashed the well-known fury of Edmund Ferrers against the inexperienced and untried Sutton of Dudley and Buckingham', *Locality and Polity*, p. 375.

[28] The two best-known Elizabethan gentry republics emerged in Norfolk and Suffolk, but after the spectacular collapse of the Howards in 1572, see A. Hassell Smith, *County and Court: Government and Politics in Norfolk 1558–1603* (Oxford, 1974), and Diarmaid MacCulloch, *Suffolk and the Tudors* (Oxford, 1986). However, while Norfolk became faction-ridden, Suffolk saw the creation of an effective county administration.

[29] See Watts, *Henry VI*, pp. 65–7, on the analogies.

[30] 'Beauchamp Affinity', 520–1. *Locality and Polity*, p. 284.

[31] An observation made by Harriss, 'Dimensions of Politics', p. 4.

[32] See also J.M.W. Bean, *From Lord to Patron: Lordship in late medieval England* (Manchester, 1989), pp. 185–8.

[33] Carpenter, 'Beauchamp Affinity', 519–20, 523–4.

voluminous, if widely scattered, range of surviving papers, including an extensive correspondence and a number of accounts, household lists and muniments of title.[34] His papers are not, of course, complete. Missing are his central household records for the 1570s, the bulk of Kenilworth estate records and all but a few fragments of the papers of his brother, Ambrose, Earl of Warwick.[35] Of very real value, therefore, are the surviving collections of the correspondence of gentry families in the affinity: the Ferrers of Tamworth papers,[36] the Wynn of Gwydir papers[37] and the More of Loseley papers[38] being of particular importance.

For the reconstruction of the composition of Leicester's affinity there is a unique source: the membership of the 1,000-strong cavalry contingent of the Netherlands expedition of 1585. The circumstances under which it was raised

[34] For his papers in general, see Adams, 'The Papers of Robert Dudley, Earl of Leicester I–IV', *Archives*, xx (1992–3), 63–85, 131–44, xxii (1996), 1–26, forthcoming. The surviving household accounts and household lists are printed in Adams, ed., *Household Accounts and Disbursement Books of Robert Dudley, Earl of Leicester 1558–1561, 1584–1586* (Camden Society, 5th ser., vi, 1995).

[35] The importance of Warwick's papers lies in the evidence of the considerable overlap of personnel that to some extent created a joint affinity, see below, p. 171. It is possible that a number of men not identified in the list in the Appendix were Warwick's.

[36] In '"Because I am of that Countrye and & mynde to plant myself there", Robert Dudley, Earl of Leicester and the West Midlands', *Midland History*, xx (1995), 24, n. 2, I discussed the dispersal of the Ferrers papers. At the time I was not aware of the large Ferrers collection currently being catalogued in the Folger Shakespeare Library, Washington DC. See N.W. Alcock, 'The Ferrers of Tamworth Collection: sorting and listing', *Archives*, xix (1991), 358–63. I am most grateful to Dr Alcock for bringing his work to my attention and to Mrs Laetitia Yeandle, manuscripts librarian at the Folger, for supplying me with a microfilm of some of the correspondence. As will be seen in the references below, most of the FSL collection are drafts of Humphrey Ferrers' letters to Leicester and the dates are not always clear. In 1580 Ferrers claimed to have been in Leicester's service for twenty-one years, see FSL, MS Le 634.

[37] For convenience, reference to the Wynn Papers will be made to the article numbers in the *Calendar of Wynn of Gwydir Papers 1515–1690* (Aberystwyth, 1926) rather than the actual catalogue references to the various sections of this collection in the National Library of Wales. For (Sir) John Wynn's membership of Leicester's household, see below, p. 166.

[38] Sir William More of Loseley was the keeper of several of the walks of Windsor Forest, and his correspondence (Surrey RO, Guildford, and FSL) is a valuable source for Leicester's administration as constable of Windsor Castle. His son (Sir) George was a gentleman of Leicester's household in the 1570s.

have been discussed in *Household Accounts*.[39] The process began with a series of some 200 circular letters from Leicester in late September 1585. The horse were mustered first at Tothill Fields, Westminster, in late October or early November, and then a second time at The Hague on 10 January 1586. On both occasions they were mustered by retinue, and after The Hague muster they were formed into companies or cornets. Some 400 horsemen were mustered at Westminster and 750 at The Hague. This, of course, amounted to only three-quarters of the contracted total and the remainder was raised by other means during 1586.

Two lists of these retinues have been in print for some time. One was an enclosure in a despatch to Madrid from the Spanish ambassador in Paris. It is a Spanish translation of an English original, and it assigns the men and horses to specific ships.[40] The second is a list of the retinues mustered at The Hague in January 1586, but it is a copy made at least a year later, for it includes under the knights men who were knighted by Leicester during the course of 1586.[41] The first reconstruction of 'Leicester's train' was undertaken by Sir Roy Strong and Professor J.A. van Dorsten in the 1960s.[42] On the basis of this I concluded in the early 1970s that the lists would be central to a study of Leicester's affinity and they have served that purpose ever since.[43] At Bangor in 1973 I discovered in the Wynn of Gwydir papers the first of two copies of Leicester's circular letters to

---

[39] Pt I, Appendix ii, pp. 388–92.

[40] *Calendar of Letters and State Papers . . . preserved in the Archives of Simancas*, iii (1580–86) (1896), pp. 554–6. The editing is not perfect, and the original, Archivo General de Simancas, Estado K 1564, fo. 4, should be consulted.

[41] The original is PRO, SP84/6/79ff, which is printed in E.M. Tenison, *Elizabethan England* (14 vols, Leamington Spa, 1933–61), vi, pp. 45–7. The copy was probably made during a later settlement of pay and would include all the horse 'in pay' from 10 January 1586.

[42] *Leicester's Triumph* (Leiden and Oxford, 1968). Jan van Dorsten told me in the 1970s that the inspiration for this book came from his discovery of a billeting list for Leicester and his men in Leiden in January 1586. In compiling their general list of the train (Appendix III) they drew on some documents that are not strictly relevant, see *Household Accounts*, pp. 22–3.

[43] 'The Protestant Cause: Religious Alliance with the West European Calvinist Communities as Political issue in England, 1585–1629' (unpublished D.Phil. thesis, University of Oxford, 1973), pp. 62–73. This is a very primitive initial sketch.

survive.[44] Several years later, two further lists of the retinues in collections in the Bodleian Library came to my attention, one in the Rawlinson MSS,[45] and the other in what had once been a section of the Gurney MSS.[46] Although they are not exactly identical, there are sufficient similarities between them and the 'Spanish list' to suggest that all three have a common origin.

The lists have been used previously in studies of the Welsh contingent of the expeditionary force and its overall religious orientation, and to identify the MPs of the 1584 Parliament and the members of the West Midlands affinity who took part.[47] However, this essay provides a suitable occasion for an examination of the whole, and a complete list is supplied in the Appendix. The four lists are all ordered by rank, led by three peers, the 2nd Earl of Essex, the 2nd Lord North and the 11th Lord Audley, but thereafter there are some interesting differences.[48] The Hague list is the largest, with 199 retinues and the names listed in a completely different way from the others. The two Bodleian lists are almost identical in number (the Rawlinson 167 retinues, the Gurney 160), with the Spanish less at 122.[49] The smaller total in the Spanish list was reached by excluding men found mainly at the end of the Bodleian lists, so that

[44] This discovery led to my article, 'The Gentry of North Wales and the Earl of Leicester's Expedition to the Netherlands, 1585–1586', *Welsh History Review*, vii (1974), 129–47. The letter, addressed to John Wynn, is printed there as an appendix. More recently another copy, addressed to one of the Warwickshire Burdetts, has appeared in several manuscript dealers' catalogues, see *Household Accounts*, p. 388, n. 18.

[45] MS Rawlinson B. 146, f. 235–v.

[46] MS Eng. Hist. C. 272, pp. 82–7.

[47] 'North Wales', though this was written before the discovery of the two Bodleian lists; 'A Puritan Crusade? The Composition of the Earl of Leicester's Expedition to the Netherlands', Paul Hofthijzer, ed., *The Dutch in Crisis 1585–1588* (Leiden, 1988), pp. 7–34; 'The Dudley Clientele and the House of Commons, 1559–1586', *Parl. Hist.*, viii (1989), 228–30; and 'West Midlands', 73–4.

[48] As the peers pose no difficulties they have been omitted from the Appendix.

[49] The differences between them can be explained as follows. The two Bodleian lists were derived more or less directly from a list of the Tothill Fields muster. The Spanish list (given its references to ships) was a copy of an embarkation list. Since the horse were shipped over to the Netherlands in two contingents, one in November 1585 and the other with Leicester himself in December, it may therefore have been a list of only one of them (see *Household Accounts*, p. 393). The men who appear only in The Hague muster list probably arrived after Leicester did, or possibly even after 10 January, as the purpose of the list was to establish who was in pay from then. The later arrivals do not represent a separate section of the affinity, the range of connections is similar to that found in the main body.

its earlier sections are identical to them with two significant exceptions. All three divide the men into categories, but not identically, and the Gurney list uniquely includes one of retainers, a category missing entirely from the other two, although the same names are present and in the same order. Both the Spanish list and the Rawlinson move one large group of names to a different position in an identical manner, which suggests that there is some direct connection between them.[50]

The Gurney list is reproduced in part A of the Appendix, with the names found only in the other lists gathered in part B. Identities, where known, have been supplied, together with attendance at Leicester's funeral, the one other occasion when one might expect the affinity to have been present *en masse*.[51] The degree of overlap between the Netherlands expedition and the funeral is considerable but not overwhelming, and for this several reasons may be advanced. Members of both the household (of all ranks) and the West Midlands affinity were heavily represented at the funeral, while some of those in the 1585 lists were dead by 1588 and others were still serving in the Netherlands.[52] Although the 1585 lists themselves provide no guide to the connection with Leicester, they confirm what is known from other sources.[53] Overall, despite the absence of a number of household officers who remained in England (as did both the recipients of Leicester's surviving letters), they give a remarkably complete snapshot of the affinity as it existed in 1585.[54] A list of Leicester's own of the men to whom the 200 letters were sent would obviously be of considerable assistance in explaining why these particular men were chosen. In its absence we are dependent on a comment he made at the time that they were 'most of them gentlemen of good likings and callings in their countries, though my servants', and the terms of his summons. The relevant clause of the letter to Wynn reads:

[50] See the notes to the Appendix.

[51] The 'funeral lists' are printed in *Household Accounts*, pt II, arts i and j.

[52] It is probable that a number of those still unidentified, especially the men who also attended Leicester's funeral, were members of the Midlands affinity who cannot be identified owing to the disappearance of the Kenilworth records. Others may have had a connection to Warwick.

[53] The principal exceptions are those men who can only be identified as officers of the infantry contingent, who may not have been directly connected to Leicester.

[54] In Wynn's case the reason may have been genuine ill health. In a later note to his doctor (*Wynn Cal.*, art. 102), he recorded that 'the last year vid. 1585 in Autumne taken with a sharpe choleric flux in so much that I had within 24 hours 40 stoles'.

I am to make choice of such my good friends and servants, as I may make an
assured accompte of, amongst which number yourself are one. And therefore
I do not doubt, but that according to the shew of your good will always toward
me, and my good opinion of you, you will now manifest & perform the same
. . . to serve your sovereign under me. . . .[55]

As revealed here, the composition of the affinity was conventional, with the usual
overlapping groups of family, household and estate officers at the core. There is a
strong contingent of members of the household, both past and present. Leicester
appears to have employed some form of rotation of young gentlemen in his
household (as he did with his chaplains), and a considerable number of the men
in the lists had been gentlemen of the household at an earlier date.[56] John Wynn
himself falls into this category, for a close reading of the surviving Wynn
correspondence reveals that he was a gentleman of Leicester's household in
1577–80 and in attendance during Leicester's visit to Buxton in June 1578.[57] The
other contingents are largely defined by the geographical pattern of his estates
and offices.[58] The two largest, the Welsh and the West Midlands, have already
been mentioned. The Welsh was based on the lordships of Denbigh and Chirk
(granted in 1563) and Arwystli and Cyfeiliog (1572). The West Midlands came
from Kenilworth (1563) and its surrounding manors, and others in
Worcestershire, Gloucestershire and Shropshire.[59] The East Anglians belong to
the old Robsart connection; those from Essex were associated with the Wanstead
estate (1578); the Lancashire and Cheshire connection was formed by his

---

[55] 'North Wales', 147, and, for the comment, 138. I have only been able to examine a photograph
of the Burdett letter in a dealer's catalogue, but I can detect no significant difference in the text.

[56] For the 1570s we are dependent on anecdotal evidence for identities, so those noted here are
probably an underestimate. For the chaplains, see Adams, 'A Godly Peer? Leicester and the Puritans',
History Today, xl (Jan. 1990), 18.

[57] See *Wynn Cal.*, arts 76, 79, 85, 89. Wynn was also engaged on Leicester's business in Wales in
1581 and 1587, see arts 97 and 104.

[58] An overall survey of Leicester's offices and estates can be found in Adams, 'Dudley Clientele and
the House of Commons', 220–1. The occasional geographical grouping of names in the lists may
reflect an earlier ordering by county.

[59] A map of Leicester's West Midlands estates can be found in 'West Midlands', 23.

chamberlaincy of the county palatine of Chester (1565); the Berkshire, Buckinghamshire and Surrey from the constableship of Windsor Castle (1562); and the Northamptonshire from the stewardship of Grafton (1571).

As well as a few Dudley relatives, there is also a group of men for whom the connection was supplied by the countess and her family.[60] Three other aspects are worth noting. First, despite a long-established legend, there are very few 'courtiers' to be found here. There are only two sons of senior officers of the court or Household (Richard Ward and Francis Fortescue), while Francis Castilion was the son of Elizabeth's Italian tutor and Groom of the Privy Chamber, Giovanni Baptista Castiglione.[61] On the other hand, two of the gentlemen of Leicester's household (George Brooke and Edmund Carey) were the younger sons of important peers, both usually considered enemies of his. The second aspect is the presence of a considerable number of sons or brothers of an earlier generation of the affinity: John Glasier, Christopher Blount, Ralph Huband, Thomas Price, Edward Jobson and Clement Fisher all fall into this category. The last aspect is a group of men who held no formal estate or household office (as far as can be ascertained), but who were clearly among Leicester's intimates. In lieu of a better description (though cronies would not be unjustified) they have been identified as 'entourage'.[62]

One further aspect should also be addressed at this stage: the retainers. In August 1565 Leicester received a licence to retain 100 men, one of a series of licences granted to privy councillors and other leading officers of the Crown during the first twelve years of the reign.[63] The precise reasons why they were granted and the use

---

[60] This group is not as large as it appears from other sources, *Household Accounts* especially, but it would include the Earl of Essex himself, as well as George Digby, one of Leicester's intimates, who had previously been a ward of Sir Francis Knollys. Another connection, the Cumbrian, is represented here only by John Lamplaugh. This was created through a cadet branch of the Dudleys, the Dudleys of Yanwath, Cumb., two of whose members were among Leicester's longest-serving household officers.

[61] Castilion may also have served in Leicester's household. He witnessed a deed together with several household officers on 10 June 1583, Berkeley Castle, General Series Charter 5397.

[62] Lord North, although excluded for reasons mentioned above, would also fit into this category.

[63] BL, Lansdowne MS 14, f. 1v, gives a list. See also the discussion in *Household Accounts*, p. 22.

made of them are unknown. Elizabeth's hostility to retaining was open and consistent, but she sought to regulate it by proclamation rather than by fresh legislation. Two proclamations on the subject were published, one in January 1572 and the second in April 1583.[64] Both claimed that unlawful retaining was on the increase and ordered the justices of assize to see that the statutes on the subject were enforced. As well as referring to the existing statutes in general, both also mentioned specifically the Statute of Liveries of 1487 (3 Hen. VII, c.12) and the 1583 proclamation the Statute of Liveries of 1468 (8 Edw. IV, c.1).[65] Precisely why the proclamations were felt to be necessary is not clear, although the reference in the 1572 proclamation to retaining leading to unlawful assemblies suggests that it may have been a response to the agitation over the trial of the Duke of Norfolk.[66] Both proclamations barred retainers from serving on juries, and on several other occasions Elizabeth ordered that retainers also be barred from serving on the commissions of the peace. In 1595 the Earl of Essex stated that the latter prohibition prevented him from retaining gentlemen.[67] In some respects it is tempting to conclude that formal retaining more or less disappeared during Elizabeth's reign, except for the odd survival. However, there is evidence of continued retaining in 1583 in the form of a letter from Viscount Montague dismissing a retainer after the proclamation (which at least suggests that it was obeyed) and a list of the Earl of Hertford's retainers.[68]

[64] Paul L. Hughes and James F. Larkin, eds., *Tudor Royal Proclamations* (3 vols., New Haven, 1969), ii, items 582 and 664. See also J.P. Cooper, 'Retainers in Tudor England' in *Land, Men and Beliefs: Studies in Early-Modern England*, eds, G.E. Aylmer and J.S. Morrill (1983), pp. 89–90.

[65] My statement in *Household Accounts*, p. 22, that the proclamations rehearsed the 'Great Statute' of 1504 is wrong as that statute expired in 1509. I am grateful to Dr Gunn for bringing this error to my attention. I was misled by a footnote in Hughes and Larkin (p. 105) to the pardoning of illicit retaining in the coronation pardon proclamation of 1559, which included the 1504 statute among the relevant legislation.

[66] Why this proclamation also drew attention to the clause in the 1487 statute barring retaining of officers of the Crown is not clear either.

[67] Penry Williams, *The Council in the Marches of Wales under Elizabeth I* (Cardiff, 1958), p. 286, and James, 'Crossroads', p. 424. Stone, *Crisis*, p. 207, n. 1, suggests that an attempt in 1561 to exclude retainers from commissions of the peace had remained a dead letter.

[68] Montague's letter (16 May 1583) is Henry E. Huntington Library, San Marino, CA., Battle Abbey MS 56, f. 6. The list of Hertford's retainers (2 May 1583), undoubtedly related to the proclamation, can be found in Historical Manuscripts Commission, *Report on the Manuscripts of the Marquess of Bath IV: Seymour Papers 1532–1686* (1967), pp. 198–9.

Leicester himself complained of 'patriotic' retaining interfering with the militia system when commanding the army at Tilbury in 1588.[69]

No indentures of retainer by Leicester have been discovered, but since the last known indentures date from the 1480s, this may not be particularly significant.[70] Only two direct references to his retainers have been encountered. One is the category of gentlemen retainers in the Gurney list. The other is found in another document from the expedition, a list of his guard compiled by Henry Goodere, the captain, on 12 January 1586.[71] This divides the guard into three categories: 'ordinary servants in your house' (thirteen men), 'old retainers' (twelve), and twenty-four men preferred to the guard by third parties. However, we also have lists of his servants given badges and liveries in 1559–60 and 1567–8.[72] The later lists are dramatically larger than the earlier, but this should be seen as a consequence of the expansion of his household in the interval.[73] Gentlemen are found in both sets of lists, but no knights, and the later lists also include a number of tradesmen. The 'retainers' in the Gurney list are gentlemen of some stature and among them are a number of Leicester's officers (though not all) as well as past and present members of his household. They are certainly the sort of men one might expect to have been retainers in a fifteenth-century affinity, but a Gentleman Pensioner (and possibly a second) and an officer of the Stables, whom, as servants of the Crown, it was illegal to retain, are also found among them. Seven of the twelve 'old retainers' in the guard can be identified. Three, and possibly a fourth, attended Leicester's funeral.[74] One of them, William Blackwell, was the keeper of the park at Drayton Basset and the only one of the twelve also included in the list of

---

[69] PRO, SP12/213/40, to Walsingham, 24 July 1588. This is presumably the complaint to which Hicks refers in *Bastard Feudalism*, p. 132.

[70] See Jones and Walker, 'Private Indentures', pp. 30–1.

[71] BL, Cotton MS Galba C VIII, ff. 96v–7. See also *Household Accounts*, pp. xiv and 24.

[72] Printed in *Household Accounts*, pt II, arts b–e. As will be seen there these lists are, strictly speaking, bills, but fortunately they supply the names of those supplied with liveries.

[73] The significance of the numbers in these lists depends to some extent on whether they were inclusive (i.e. the award of livery or a badge to all entitled to one) or supplementary to earlier awards. I would regard the 1567–8 lists as inclusive, see *Household Accounts*, p. 21.

[74] 'Possibly' (here and below) because the relevant lists give only a surname.

retinues.[75] Another, Toby Mathew, was a household servant of some prominence, who undertook a survey of the lordship of Denbigh.[76] Of the remainder, one may have been a steward of Balsall, and one, and possibly a second, was given livery in 1567.

It is not easy to reach a firm conclusion on this evidence. If we assume that those granted livery in 1567–8 included retainers, then the retainers were undoubtedly yeomen. The presence of the tradesmen in the lists may be significant, for a number of the Earl of Hertford's retainers in 1583 were also tradesmen. But were these the licensed retainers? Given the absence of any other reference to retainers we must assume that they were, and this in turn would suggest that Leicester was obeying at least the spirit of Elizabeth's opposition to retained gentry. Yet if this was the case, why was the licence, which allowed him to retain men who were not his officers or household servants despite the statutes, necessary? One would expect the licence to have been used to retain gentlemen similar to those found in the Gurney list, but many of these men had household connections, while servants of the Crown were specifically excluded from the licence. Similar difficulties exist over a related issue, that of obligations of military service on his tenants.[77] Military service clauses in his leases can be found, but, so far as I have been able to ascertain, they appear to be limited to his Welsh lordships, where military service was still a customary tenurial obligation.[78] In 1566 Leicester's surveyors drew attention to the military potential of the lordship

---

[75] The probable reason for his appearing among the horse is given in a note to the list of the guard that he had been licensed to serve as guidon-bearer to Thomas Fairfax's cornet. Blackwell was already a servant when appointed keeper by Leicester in July 1580, see Index of Servants in *Household Accounts*. The letter to Humphrey Ferrers appointing him is now in a private collection and I am grateful to the owner for sending me a photocopy.

[76] See *Household Accounts*, Index of Servants.

[77] Cooper, 'Retainers', tends to conflate retainers and military tenants. Military service clauses in Elizabethan leases are also discussed in Stone, *Crisis*, p. 216.

[78] See Adams, 'Military obligations of leasehold tenants in Leicesterian Denbigh', *Transactions of the Denbighshire Historical Society*, xxiv (1975), 205–8, and 'North Wales', 137. Of particular interest is the quite specific obligation in the lease of a park in Denbigh to his household officer Robert Hutton, cited there from NLW, Ruthin Lordship MS 71. Unfortunately other leases granted to household servants do not survive.

of Chirk: 'There be in Chirkland at the least fyve hundred tall men that hold of your Lordship both able and readie to serve.'[79] This potential was realized in 1585, when Leicester raised two companies of 200 foot each from his Welsh tenants (and was prepared to raise more), though not apparently from any of his other estates.[80]

Turning to the overall structure of the affinity, the central household is discussed in *Household Accounts*. It numbered between 30 and 50 at the beginning of Elizabeth's reign and rose to between 100 and 150 in 1585, roughly average for a peer of his rank and prominence.[81] The structure of his estate administration is more difficult to describe with precision because few of his patents of office survive, and therefore the terms of office, remuneration and function are unclear.[82] The Welsh lordships, given their more developed administration, provide the most detailed evidence of their officers, and court rolls, where they survive, supply the stewards of individual manors.[83] Several features stand out. Firstly there was a central pool of leading officers, whose responsibilities and range of employment were extremely wide; manorial stewards were drawn either from this pool or from local gentlemen.[84] Secondly, most of the initial generation of officers were inherited from the Duke of Northumberland, and many of them (and their successors) served Warwick as well. There is a distinctly Dudley, as against Leicester, aspect to this branch of the affinity.[85] By background, the officers were a mixture of gentlemen and

[79] Longleat, Dudley Papers XVII, f. 186.

[80] 'North Wales', 133–6. The captains, William Thomas of Caernarvon and Evan Lloyd of Bodidris (the steward of the lordship of Chirk), were key members of his Welsh administration.

[81] *Household Accounts*, pp. 24–30.

[82] The patent of Sir John Hubaud (see below) has disappeared, but it was seen in the seventeenth century by Sir William Dugdale, see 'West Midlands', 41, n. 172. A surviving example is Longleat MS 4109, Edward Blount's patent as steward of Cleobury Mortimer (Salop.) in 1587.

[83] Tables of the relevant officers and stewards can be found in 'West Midlands', 71–3, and Adams, 'Officeholders of the Borough of Denbigh and the Lordships of Denbighshire in the reign of Elizabeth I', *Trans. Denbs. Hist. Soc.*, xxv (1976), 98–9.

[84] A list of the 'central pool' can be found in 'West Midlands', 71.

[85] The continuity of the Dudley affinity is one of the themes of 'Dudley Clientele 1553–1563'. It has been challenged by Loades (*Northumberland*, pp. 274–86), but his arguments and evidence are not convincing. For shared officers with Warwick, see 'West Midlands', 40ff., and 'Denbigh Office-holders', 95–100.

professionals, either practising lawyers or men of legal training seeking a career in administration.

There were three pre-eminent officers: Thomas Blount of Kidderminster until his death in 1568, Sir John Hubaud of Ipsley (Warks.) from *c.* 1572 until his death in 1583, and (probably) Edward Boughton of Cawston (Warks.) from 1584 until 1588.[86] All were of established gentle rank (Blount was a cousin) and all served Warwick as well. All headed the Kenilworth administration, but also ranged more widely; Hubaud's role in Wales is well known.[87] All obtained prominence in local government and served as Members of Parliament, though not before they entered Leicester's service. Hubaud appears to have occupied a position similar to that of Sir Richard Shireburn in the administrations of the 3rd and 4th earls of Derby, or Sir John Chichester with the 2nd Earl of Bedford.[88] Boughton does not appear to have possessed the same degree of intimacy, though his importance was certainly growing after 1584. He was the most formally employed of a group of Warwickshire gentlemen close to Leicester in the 1580s, which included George Digby, Henry Goodere, Clement Fisher and, at a further remove, Sir Thomas Lucy and Sir John Harington.

With regard to rewards and remuneration, we have only one surviving wages book, and that for the central household in 1559–61.[89] As might be expected, it includes wages for yeomen servants and expenses only for the gentlemen. Leicester appears to have made relatively little use of annuities and rent-charges. In his earlier accounts the annuitants were mainly former servants of his mother, the Duchess of Northumberland, and their annuities were clearly the honouring of bequests in her will. Two of his officers received annuities, but one was undoubtedly also a bequest from the duchess.[90] In his later accounts a few annuities can be found, but in the main they appear to have been used to buy out the claims of interested parties in land settlements and (occasionally) to retain

---

[86] For a more detailed discussion and references, see 'West Midlands', 41–3.

[87] See the extensive references to him in the *Wynn Cal.*, esp. arts 47, 58, 68–9, 79–80, 83, 85, 89.

[88] For Shireburn, see Coward, *Stanleys*, pp. 85–6.

[89] Printed in *Household Accounts*, pt II, art. a.

[90] Ibid., pp. 69–70, 101–2, 128.

lawyers.[91] In the absence of patents of office there is not sufficient evidence to draw any conclusions about the value of salaries or fees attached to the offices on his estates. Rewards to his officers tended to take the form either of leases of his own lands or shares in grants from the Crown.[92]

Less formal rewards are by their very nature difficult to pin down. The accounts of towns doing business with Leicester include the occasional reward to his servants, but it is not clear whether these were demanded, expected or simply proffered.[93] Even more difficult is the question of a 'cut' in more dubious transactions.[94] Similar problems are encountered over Leicester's exploitation of his access to royal patronage to reward his own men. There are a number of clear examples of promotions into the Crown's service: at least two of his men became officers of the Stables (which is not surprising) and others included the keeper of the gardens at Hampton Court and a groom of the Privy Chamber.[95] However, it is difficult to quantify them overall or (in the present state of our knowledge) draw meaningful comparisons with his peers. The same can be said for his influence over appointments to offices in local government. It was clearly at work in the appointments of sheriffs and JPs in the West Midlands and in North Wales, especially in the late 1570s and early 1580s, but it cannot be assumed that it was absolute.[96]

[91] Examples of the first type can be seen in the annuities paid out of the rents of the manor of Long Itchington (Warks.), listed in Longleat, Dudley Papers XX [The Complete View of the Evidences], f. 34v., 36v. An example of the second type can be found in the rent charge of £5 p.a. from Kenilworth granted to Edmund Plowden for legal counsel on 7 December 1565, see HMC, *Tenth Report*, pt IV (1885), p. 409.

[92] For examples, see 'West Midlands', 35, n. 124, and 43.

[93] Examples include the 30s Bristol gave his secretary Arthur Atye in 1577 ('Leic. Pap. II', 133) and the substantial £50 the Vintners' Company gave to his household officer Richard Ellis in 1567 (*Household Accounts*, Index of Servants, sub Ellis).

[94] Hubaud, for example, left £1,300 owing to him from the complex settlement of the Chester Dean and Chapter lands to a variety of Warwickshire civic charities, see his will, PRO, PROB 11/66/232. Leicester's role in this affair was controversial.

[95] See *Household Accounts*, Index of Servants, sub Thomas Eaton, William Grice, William Huggins, and Ferdinando Richardson. A number of others entered the Crown's service after his death.

[96] See 'West Midlands', 44. For the related subject of his influence on parliamentary elections, see Adams, 'The Dudley Clientele in the House of Commons'. The conclusions reached there are, if anything, an underestimate.

His household accounts reveal that he was generous in reward, and there was some competition to enter his service.[97] Yet the overall conclusion (if a tentative one) is that Leicester's affinity was not 'patronage-driven'; his men worked for their rewards. What this involved brings us to the subject of function.

A discussion of Leicester as a territorial lord cannot avoid addressing certain mysteries surrounding the circumstances of his creation, for it was the first major grant of lands to him (July 1563) that established the broad outline of his estate, particularly the West Midlands–North Wales axis.[98] Lands obtained later, either by grant from the Crown or by private purchase, merely fleshed out this skeleton. There was only one major exception, the estate he built up round Wanstead House in western Essex after he purchased it in 1578. There is no doubt that Leicester was the recipient of Elizabeth's generosity to an unrivalled degree. In the overall history of Elizabeth's treatment of the peerage, the cases of Leicester and Warwick were unique; no one else was raised directly to an earldom.[99] But Leicester's creation can be viewed from several angles. There is the obvious one of the queen's indulgence of a favourite. On the other hand, it can also be seen as her establishment of a senior officer of the Household and a loyal supporter, whose estate at the beginning of the reign was minimal, complicated by the fact that those lands to which he had any claim were granted to his elder brother after he was 'restored' to the earldom of Warwick in 1561. Lastly it can be seen as part of a wider Edwardian restoration.

What is particularly mysterious about the first grant is that it preceded his creation by a year, yet the lands and titles were directly related (Kenilworth and the earldom of Leicester and Denbigh and his barony). The precise circumstances surrounding the choice of both lands and titles are unclear. Kenilworth was the only part of the old earldom of Leicester granted to him, and the only other

---

[97] Evidence of the scale of casual rewards can be found throughout *Household Accounts*. The one complaint of meanness by Leicester that I know of was made by Jean Hotman, who was to some extent a special case. See G.H.M. Posthumus Meyjes, *Jean Hotman's English Connection* (Medelingen van de Afdeling Letterkunde, Koninklijke Nederlandse Academie, nieuw reeks, liii, 1990), pp. 25–6. For an example of the competition to enter Leicester's service, see Longleat, Dudley Papers II, f. 224, Alexander Neville to Leicester, 23 July 1582.

[98] For what follows, see 'West Midlands', 24–32.

[99] See 'Patronage of the Crown', pp. 28–30, for a further discussion.

connection between the various estates is that some had once been part of the earldom of March. Leicester himself had a considerable knowledge of, and fascination with, the Dudley claim of descent from the Beauchamp earls of Warwick, but no other real territorial ambitions.[100] Indeed it is possible that the terms of the grants made to both brothers at this time may have reflected an assumption that Leicester would succeed his brother as Earl of Warwick in the immediate future, particularly given Warwick's weakened health following his command at Le Havre in 1562–3. If this was the case then the grant to him in 1563 was to some extent a provisional one, and not intended to form a permanent endowment. On the other hand, the fact that both Leicester and Warwick were ultimately to be ephemeral peerages is not in itself significant. If Leicester may have been expected to succeed Warwick in 1563, it is doubtful that anyone in 1565 would have predicted that Warwick's marriage in that year to the young Anne Russell would have been childless. Elizabeth may have wished Leicester himself to have remained unmarried, but he, on the other hand, was deeply concerned to perpetuate the house of Dudley and came close to doing so. His own estate policy reveals a clear intention of creating a permanent estate of inheritance.[101]

These considerations must be borne in mind if any purpose in creating a lordship for Leicester in these particular counties is to be discovered, other than the cobbling together of a selection of lands to provide a certain level of income.[102] In the case of the West Midlands, and Warwickshire in particular,

[100] As noted in 'West Midlands', 30, Leicester's obtaining of various lands in the East Riding of Yorkshire in 1559–61 may have been related to a possible creation as Lord of Holderness, as it was claimed that the Sutton Dudleys descended from an Anglo-Saxon Lord of Holderness. It is no less revealing that these lands were sold off immediately after his creation as Earl of Leicester.

[101] The fairly rapid sale of outlying lands in later grants from the Crown is evidence of a self-conscious policy in the expansion of his estate.

[102] It might be noted that our general knowledge of the way in which Crown lands were granted in Elizabeth's reign is still limited, though a start has been made in R.W. Hoyle, ed., *The Estates of the English Crown, 1558–1640* (Cambridge, 1992). The grantee certainly petitioned in many cases (there are examples in Leicester's later grants), but this does not appear to have been one of them. Elizabeth was not without her own strong views on specific grants; she resisted a request by the Earl of Bedford for the keepership of a royal forest on the grounds that he 'had not loved game or cared much for the preservation of them' (Bedford Estate Office, 2nd Earl's Papers, no. 5, Leicester to Bedford, 4 August [1583]).

Leicester's lands would reinforce his brother's (or, given their respective political importance, it should probably be the other way round), and moreover this was a region to which they had a strong sentimental attachment. Yet there is no evidence of any obvious need for the Crown to create a powerful lordship there, only perhaps an appreciation that since there was no resident major peer the Dudley intrusion would not cause any great disturbance. Wales, however, was a different case, because the Crown's immediate possession of the majority of the marcher lordships since the beginning of the century had been seen as a cause of the perceived lawlessness of the region and had inspired both the creation of the Council in the Marches and the extension of the shire system.[103] Yet the planting of Leicester in North Wales cannot be considered part of any broader policy of restoring lordship to Wales, for apart from the grants to him and the lordship of Ruthin to Warwick, Elizabeth appears to have made no other major grants of marcher lordships. If there was a 'policy' at work, it may have been a purely financial one, for there is evidence both of a perception on the Lord Treasurer's part that the rents of the marcher lordships were now grossly out of date and of the possible beginnings of a campaign to revive them. Since Leicester initiated just such a revival after taking possession of the lordships of Denbigh and Chirk, it is possible that it was expected that he would do so.[104] In this respect the grants represent a form of delegation in which the increased income he would derive from his Welsh lordships would (hopefully) make further grants from the Crown unnecessary and save the Crown the expense of revising the rents itself. The attractive aspect of this argument is that it explains why the Crown later granted him the Montgomeryshire lordships of Arwystli and Cyfeiliog and then the keepership of Snowdon Forest (1574), with the celebrated encroachment commission to follow.

---

[103] Williams, *Council in the Marches of Wales*, p. 6.

[104] In 1561 a general commission to survey all the Crown lands in Wales was issued, under which surveys of the lordships of Denbigh and Bromfield and Yale were undertaken in that year, and possibly Arwystli and Cyfeiliog in 1564. See Adams, 'The Composition of 1564 and the Earl of Leicester's Tenurial Reformation in the Lordship of Denbigh', *Bulletin of the Board of Celtic Studies*, xxvi (1976), 490–1. Leicester's survey of Denbigh in 1563 followed the Exchequer survey closely.

Leicester's three other major territorial offices under the Crown, the constableship of Windsor Castle, the chamberlaincy of Chester and the stewardship of Grafton, were all in counties where he possessed no land of any consequence. Windsor Castle and Grafton (which was, it might be noted, in easy distance of Kenilworth) basically involved the administration of extensive royal forests, an established form of patronage to courtiers. They certainly added to his affinity (as can be seen in the Netherlands expedition) but any power, other than patronage, that they conferred is not immediately obvious. Chester is more ambiguous. It could be seen as a bolstering of his position in North Wales, but it had also become an established perquisite of the earls of Derby. However, there is no evidence of Elizabeth's (or Leicester's) hostility to the 3rd Earl of Derby, and once again the precise motive for the appointment is unclear. By planting the Dudley brothers in Warwickshire, Elizabeth made possible the revival of the affinity formed by Northumberland and to some extent maintained by his sons during Mary's reign. The displacement they caused appears to have been minimal. Wales was, once again, a different matter, for here there were few existing Dudley followers. The appointment of their brother-in-law Sir Henry Sidney as President of the Council in the Marches in 1560 certainly eased the process. The Council became closely associated with Leicester's business; many of his officers sat on it (most prominently Hubaud, who nearly became vice-president) and he employed members of it in his estate management. However, it is doubtful that Sidney's appointment was made in anticipation of the planting of Leicester in North Wales. Similarly the fact that Leicester's legal agent, the Chester lawyer William Glasier, was appointed vice-chamberlain of the county palatine in 1559 cannot be seen as an anticipation of Leicester's appointment as chamberlain either.

Leicester took some time to establish a personal physical presence in Warwickshire. An initial visit in early 1566 proved abortive, and the first occasion was during the progress later in the year. There was a second visit during the progress of 1568, but from 1570 he visited regularly until 1585, the sole exception being 1583.[105] The outlying estates were a different matter, though his trips to the spa at Buxton in 1577 and 1578 certainly provided opportunities to meet the

---

[105] See 'West Midlands', 34. Details of the visit in 1585 can be found in *Household Accounts*, pp. 285–301.

Denbighshire gentry.[106] The year 1584 saw his most extensive tour, which took him to Denbigh for the only time, via Shrewsbury and, on return, Chester. His purpose is not clear, though the visits to Shrewsbury and Chester may have involved an attempt to mediate the dispute between them.[107] On the other hand the employment of young gentlemen from the counties in his household provided a major point of contact for the affinity, and his officers, Hubaud in particular, travelled extensively. It may not be irrelevant to note that Leicester possessed a map of Denbighshire with instructions on how to read Welsh.[108] However, non-residence was not without some importance. A comparison of Leicester's involvement in the affairs of King's Lynn and Great Yarmouth with the Duke of Norfolk's reveals how much more regularly Norfolk was consulted about local business.[109]

Our present knowledge of Warwickshire politics in the sixteenth century is so limited that it is difficult to be precise about the effects of the Dudley planting.[110] Some displacement did occur, notably the semi-retirement of Sir Robert Throckmorton of Coughton, though here religion undoubtedly played a major role. The Protestant wing of the extensive Throckmorton clan certainly became more prominent, as did such other Protestant gentlemen like Sir Thomas Lucy and Sir John Harington. Yet Leicester's affinity was far from being a Protestant, let alone Puritan, monopoly; there were semi-Catholic elements in it (notably Christopher Blount) and even Hubaud's leanings were ambiguous. In Wales the situation was dramatically different, for Leicester's appearance on the scene

---

[106] *Wynn Cal.*, art., 85, Wynn to Arthur Atye [autumn 1578], refers to Katherine of Berain going to see Leicester at Buxton in the summer.

[107] The dispute involved the Welsh wool trade. It will be discussed in 'The Earl of Leicester as a patron of boroughs', a previously unpublished paper to be included in *Leicester and the Court*.

[108] General Household Inventory 1582 (Leicester House), n.f. Formerly Christ Church, Evelyn MS 264, now being catalogued at the British Library.

[109] Leicester succeeded Norfolk as high steward of Great Yarmouth in 1572 and became King's Lynn's first high steward in the same year. The general conclusion is based on the entries in the King's Lynn Hall Books for 1544–69 and 1569–91 (Norfolk RO, KL/C7/6–7) and the Great Yarmouth Assembly Books for 1560–70, 1570–79, and 1579–98 (Norfolk RO, Y/C/19/2–4). A full discussion will be found in 'Leicester as a patron of boroughs'.

[110] See 'West Midlands', 38–44.

soon challenged the dominance Sir Thomas Salusbury of Lleweni had possessed over Denbighshire for several decades.[111] This led to a major reshaping of county politics, in which Leicester attracted the lesser gentry hostile to the Salusburies, and they soon formed his local affinity. The result was the participation of Salusbury's grandson and heir in the Babington Plot of 1585–6, and then a major power struggle after Leicester's death in which the plotter's brother Sir John regained the family's control of the county from the former Leicesterians. Members of Leicester's local affinity joined his officers in the Forest of Snowdon encroachment commission, but the extent to which the opposition to the commission was related to the struggle with the Salusburies is still unclear.

The realities of Leicester's local power have been distorted by a powerful historiographical tradition originating in the celebrated Catholic tract, *Leicester's Commonwealth*. This was an example, and possibly the most powerful, of a strand of Catholic polemic that portrayed the Reformation as the displacement of the ancient nobility by new men.[112] It compared him to the fourteenth-century favourites, but not so much as the beneficiary of an over-indulgent monarch than as a faction leader who ruled all and kept the queen a near captive.[113] There may have been a polemical purpose in doing so, yet it created an internally contradictory image. On the one hand Leicester was hated by all except the queen, on the other his faction was everywhere. Not surprisingly, Leicester's own rapacity was the main cause of dissension and discord. Evidence is supplied by a number of well-known episodes of the 1570s: the revival of the 'Great Berkeley Law-Suit' in 1572–3, the Snowdon Forest commission of 1574, and the Drayton Basset riot of 1578. *Leicester's Commonwealth* also had a major influence on the county histories written during the subsequent century, in particular Samson Erdeswick's *Survey of Staffordshire*, John Smyth of Nibley's 'Lives of the Berkeleys' and Sir William Dugdale's *The Antiquities of Warwickshire*. Both Smyth and

---

[111] This is based on an article on Leicester and the politics of North Wales in preparation for many years; a brief initial account can be found in 'Officeholders', 101–11.

[112] See 'Favourites and Factions', pp. 255–60.

[113] Ibid., pp. 257–8. The comparison is found in Dwight C. Peck, ed., *Leicester's Commonwealth: The Copy of a Letter written by a Master of Art of Cambridge (1584)* (Athens, Ohio, 1985), pp. 188–9.

Dugdale refer to it directly.[114] They also had political or personal reasons for finding its portrait of Leicester sympathetic: Erdeswick was a semi-recusant, Smyth a servant of Lord Berkeley's, proud of his role in the restoration of the Berkeley fortunes, and Dugdale a committed royalist. Moreover, Dugdale's patron, who subsidized the lavish illustration of the *Antiquities*, was Lady Katherine Leveson, one of the daughters of Leicester's illegitimate son, Sir Robert Dudley, who could claim to have been cheated of her rightful inheritance by her grandfather's infidelity to Douglas Sheffield. Moreover, the emphasis in these histories on the antiquity of the established county families further shaped their view of the favourite's local impact.[115] Leicester's men were portrayed as upstarts as well, Dugdale's snide comments on Hubaud's family being a case in point.[116]

The reality behind the various embellishments of the legends of these incidents is thus difficult to disentangle, and this is not the place to discuss any of them in detail, but some general points can be made. A central feature of both the Snowdon Forest commission and the revival of the Berkeley Law-Suit is that they took place under the authority of the Crown. The Snowdon Forest commission was in the queen's name and it was the Crown that raised the suit against Berkeley.[117] There was certainly a degree of collusion. Leicester was forester of Snowdon Forest, his officers (led by Hubaud) headed the commission and he was to receive the immediate profits. Likewise, after regaining the Berkeley lands the queen granted them to Leicester and Warwick by letters patent and in the interval appointed their officers as stewards for the Crown.[118] Leicester may have

---

[114] See 'West Midlands', 24–6, 47–8, for references.

[115] I owe this point to Dr Richard Cust. See also the discussion of the gentry concern with lineage in Heal and Holmes, *The Gentry*, pp. 34–42.

[116] See 'West Midlands', 42, n. 185.

[117] For a brief account of the Berkeley Law-Suit, written before I was able to consult the Berkeley Castle muniments, see 'West Midlands', 47–8. The Crown's formal role in the Berkeley Law-Suit arose from the terms of the repeal of Leicester and Warwick's attainder in 1558, which included the renunciation of any claim of right to their father's lands or offices, see ibid., 30.

[118] See *Wynn Cal.*, art. 58, Hubaud and John Nuthall to the gentry of Caernarvonshire, 6 December 1574, and Berkeley Castle, General Series Charter 5119, commission from the Crown to Nuthall and John Goodman, 30 May 1573.

had his own reasons for wishing to revive the Berkeley Law-Suit, but he could not have done so without Elizabeth's connivance, and therefore the real question is why she turned against the Berkeleys, something John Smyth could never resolve.[119] Likewise, the origin of the Snowdon Forest commission is also unknown; if Leicester were the immediate beneficiary the Crown would gain in the long term. In both of these episodes Leicester's initial desire was to reach some form of compromise. It was the absolute resistance of the gentlemen of Llyn that caused the Snowdon affair to blow up.[120] Similarly the effect of Berkeley's (or possibly more accurately Lady Berkeley's) rejection of the offer of the marriage of Philip and Robert Sidney to his daughters on the revival of the lawsuit is unclear. Lastly, both episodes saw Leicester's affinity fully deployed. Another of Smyth's difficulties was explaining why, if Berkeley was so established in his country, so many Gloucestershire gentlemen assisted Leicester. In Wales the situation was more nuanced. Maurice Wynn of Gwydir, whose surviving correspondence is one of the main sources for the Snowdon Forest affair, was unhappy at being caught between Leicester and his 'country'.[121] John Wynn was later warned by one of Leicester's officers that he was seen as too protective of his countrymen.[122]

The Drayton Basset riot of September 1578 was a different affair altogether.[123] Here the Crown was not directly involved. On the surface this was a dispute over a foreclosed mortgage between the mortgagee (the London merchant Richard Paramour) and the well-connected mortgagor (Thomas Robinson), which had been through the courts for some years. When Paramour's attempt to take possession in June 1578 was resisted by Robinson's friends, the sheriff of Staffordshire (Richard Bagot) proved ineffectual and various mediation efforts failed, Humphrey Ferrers of

---

[119] See 'West Midlands', 47–8.

[120] See *Wynn Cal.*, arts 58 and 62.

[121] On the other hand, the antagonism between the Wynns and the gentlemen of Llyn, which continued into the 1620s, may also have played its role in the affair. For references to this see J.G. Jones, *Law, Order and Government in Caernarfonshire 1558–1640* (Cardiff, 1996), pp. 84–7.

[122] *Wynn Cal.*, art. 104.

[123] See 'West Midlands', 47–8, for a brief account, written before the FSL Ferrers Papers were brought to my attention. The extensive sources for this affair make possible a detailed study, which I hope to have the time to undertake.

Tamworth was ordered to gain possession for him.[124] This he did in August with the assistance of George Digby. However, on 2 September, when he and Digby were away hunting, Robinson's allies seized the manor house by surprise. Ferrers' attempt to regain the house led to the death of one of his men and he withdrew, reporting the incident to Leicester and the Privy Council. The Council ordered a massive intervention, but in the meantime the rioters dispersed and the upshot was a long-drawn-out investigation by Star Chamber and a separate trial for murder in 1580.

There are a number of fascinating aspects to this affair, not the least of them the extensive local support for the rioters both at the time and during their subsequent flight. The affair may also be connected to several other incidents in local politics.[125] However, Leicester's involvement is particularly curious. Six months after the riot (April 1579) he bought out Paramour, whose willingness to be rid of the property is quite understandable. The controversial aspect was Leicester's concern to keep his role concealed, which raises the question of whether he had been Paramour's sleeping partner all along.[126] His involvement in September is clear enough, but the June to September period is more obscure. Ferrers and Digby were unmistakably his men, but under whose authority was Ferrers acting? This remains unclear. Ferrers referred at the time to 'the trust I had to keppe the grounds not only by a lettre of attorney from Paramour but most chefely from your lordship for whom I entered'.[127] Two years later he complained, 'The burden hath layn on my back when your lordship would not

---

[124] Ferrers was undoubtedly the man on the spot as the manor house at Drayton Basset would have been visible from Tamworth Castle. Ferrers later blamed the whole affair on Bagot's weakness or collusion, see FSL, Le 544 and 549, to Leicester, 22 September and 24 October 1578.

[125] One was Ferrers' clash with the Earl of Essex over the stewardship of Tamworth earlier in the year, see 'West Midlands', 48. Another was the Warwickshire by-election in 1579–80, see below, n. 131.

[126] Ferrers, who became acting steward of Drayton Basset after Leicester's purchase, complained about the difficulties the concealment caused him. See FSL, Le 548 and 634, Ferrers to Leicester [13 April 1579] and [post 22 July 1580], quoted below. Paramour was known to Leicester for some time, he was in fact the supplier of the livery cloth in 1567–8.

[127] FSL, Le 633, Ferrers to Leicester [between 3 and 6 September 1578]. On 15 September Paramour wrote to Ferrers as though Leicester was simply helping him to regain possession, see 'West Midlands', 49.

have it known you mynded further to deale in it. Then your lordship well knows I dealt not for the merchant [Paramour] and what I dyd att the fyrst was uppon the Lord Chancellor's letters that now is [Sir Thomas Bromley] to frend hym which I did or els he had never devysed the possession unto your lordship's use.'[128] The ambiguity of Leicester's position was later claimed to have been one of the causes of the riot.[129] It certainly did not see his affinity deployed in strength. In early September 1578 Hubaud was in Beaumaris dealing with the Snowdon Forest enclosures; he returned to Kenilworth ill in early October and took to his bed for the rest of the month.[130] More importantly, while Ferrers was supported by some of Leicester's men, notably Digby and William Horton, at least two members of affinity, Henry Goodere and William Harman, were accused of aiding the rioters.[131]

The wider significance of this incident is found in two further aspects. Leicester informed Ferrers of the Council's reaction to the 2 September riot in the following terms: 'My lords having since more delyberately considered of the matter & finding hit so rare & straunge a cause as hath not happened in the tyme of her majesty's [reign?] as well for the notorius royatt as for the murder [of one?] of her subiects.' The Council had ordered the 'lords Dudley and Stafford to be your better assistants in such a cause as this ys, being the principal noblemen of that shire' and he was confident that 'Thomas Trentam & Rafe Aderley, with others such as you know to be my frends will help with ther best'.[132] No less interesting were the efforts to restore good relations after the affair was over.

---

[128] FSL, Le 634. The acerbity of Ferrers' comments on Paramour was the product of a falling out between them in the meantime.

[129] Walter Harcourt offered to surrender possession to Leicester if he made his interest clear, but Ferrers thought this a trick, see FSL, Le 544, to Leicester, 22 September 1578.

[130] For Hubaud at Beaumaris (8 September), see *Wynn Cal.*, art. 88, and for his return to Kenilworth, Longleat, Dudley Papers II, f. 193, Henry Besbeech to Leicester, 23 October 1578.

[131] Goodere's house at Polesworth was also just outside Tamworth. In the winter of 1579–80 Digby and Goodere contested a by-election to replace a deceased knight of the shire for Warwickshire, see 'Dudley Clientele and the House of Commons', 218. This is an obscure episode, but the coincidence is curious; it would suggest a serious division within the affinity.

[132] Pierpont Morgan Library, New York, Rulers of England Box III, Elizabeth I, pt 2, no. 29.5, Leicester to Ferrers, 13 September [1578]. The letter is damaged.

Leicester himself spent a considerable sum in buying out the other claims on the estate.[133] Ferrers interceded with Paramour for two of the rioters for 'I am not to forgett ther old frendshipp and good neighbourhood'.[134] Later, after Leicester preferred William Blackwell as keeper of Drayton Park to one of his own men, Ferrers complained that he hoped that Leicester 'would not have my country see much into my discredit to have hym displaced that bothe deserved well and was of my placing before your lordship had shewen me your pleasure'.[135] Not least significant is the fact that practically all the principal figures in the affinity involved, except Ferrers, later took part in the Netherlands expedition.

Leicester's comments on the novelty of the riot, give or take a certain hyperbole, are possibly the most important comment on the affair. For all that is said about violence in Elizabethan society, this was clearly not business as usual. Neither the Berkeley Law-Suit nor the Snowdon Forest enclosures resulted in violence. Nor did the simultaneous dispute between the Earl of Shrewsbury and his Glossopdale tenants, though the coincidence of the Council's major intervention in this affair in the spring of 1579 is interesting.[136] Tudor historians have assumed a lower level of violence than fifteenth-century historians, as is revealed by Geoffrey Elton's mischievous introduction to a collection on crime and society:

> The exercise seems the more desirable because such conclusions as do get established tend to be somewhat unsurprising. Dr. Cockburn tells us that homicide was rare and most murderous violence occurred within families. Though it is satisfactory to have the more lurid notions of a people forever battering one another disproved, this remains what one would have expected. Similarly Dr. Curtis finds that violence was usually casual and unpremeditated: were we to think that the realm was full of professional hitmen?[137]

---

[133] 'West Midlands', 36.

[134] FSL, Le 548, Ferrers to Paramour [13 April 1579].

[135] FSL, Le 634.

[136] On this episode, see Steven Kershaw, 'Power and Duty in the Elizabethan Aristocracy: George, Earl of Shrewsbury, the Glossopdale dispute and the Council', Bernard, *Tudor Nobility*, pp. 266–95. Was the Council's intervention motivated by fear it might lead to another Drayton Basset?

[137] J.S. Cockburn, ed., *Crime in England 1550–1800* (1977), p. 9.

Having said this, on another level, that of enforcement, there are strong similarities. The Council was still dependent on the leading noblemen and Leicester's affinity. If this affair ended as a Star Chamber case, did this make any difference? Should we not simply see Star Chamber as replacing a feature of fifteenth-century government, the issuing of noblemen with commissions of oyer and terminer?[138] There is some instructive evidence relating to the involvement of Leicester's affinity with Star Chamber. In 1579, during one of the interminable disputes surrounding his deputy in Chester, William Glasier, Glasier's own deputy (and Leicester's officer) John Yerwerth wrote: 'we have no other means but to complain before the lords of her majesty's Star Chamber, which were a thing not meet to be dealt withal in that place, growing among your lordship's people and where you are our chief officer.'[139] Resort to Star Chamber clearly represented a failure of internal resolution within the affinity. This gives an added interest to the two Star Chamber cases in which members of Leicester's affinity were directly concerned. One was the dispute in 1582–3 between Edward Boughton, then a rising figure in Leicester's administration, and the Bishop of Coventry (Richard Overton, a former chaplain of Leicester's) over the mastership of Rugby School.[140] The issue at stake was the right of appointment, with Boughton standing for local choice, and Overton for episcopal authority. There was a clear element of personal animus involved, with Overton accusing Boughton of being simultaneously a Puritan, a papist and a keeper of harlots, and Boughton attacking a tyrannical bishop. There are similarities here to the bishop-baiting going on in East Anglia at the same time, and Overton claimed that Boughton was being sustained by the favour of a great man (clearly Leicester). Just what his role was is unclear. The other case was a dispute in the same period (1582–4) between Humphrey Ferrers and a neighbour, John Breton. What makes this particularly interesting is that

---

[138] For examples of the latter, see the comments on the Duke of Norfolk's commission in Watts, *Henry VI*, pp. 64–5, and the references in Payling, 'Law and Arbitration in Nottinghamshire 1399–1461', Joel Rosenthal and Colin Richmond, eds., *People, Politics and Community in the later Middle Ages* (Gloucester, 1987), p. 141.

[139] Longleat, Dudley Papers II, f. 206, Yerwerth to Leicester, 8 October 1579. For Yerwerth, see *Household Accounts*, List of Servants.

[140] For references, see 'West Midlands', 46, n. 220.

Breton was Warwick's man, and the two earls tried to mediate it between them. It was their failure that led to the case ultimately being heard in Star Chamber.[141]

In this respect Carpenter's argument that the resort to law represented the failure of noble mediation is still valid for the sixteenth century. The affinity was still alive and well. So too was its military function, if the Netherlands expedition is anything to go by. To raise over 700 horse, of whom at least 100 were members of the gentry, was no mean feat, as some immediate comparisons reveal. In 1475, the Dukes of Clarence and Gloucester provided retinues of 120 each, the 3rd Duke of Buckingham a mixed retinue of 500 horse and foot in 1513, and the Duke of Suffolk mixed retinues of 1,800 in 1513 and 1,700 in 1523, although only 100–50 horse in 1544.[142] In the St Quentin expedition of 1557 none of the retinues of horse was larger than 200.[143] On the other hand, there were special circumstances at work in 1585. Only three other peers were directly involved (so there was less competition), and Leicester was a senior member of the government acting directly as the queen's deputy. If there was some scepticism about her commitment, his was unquestioned, and he certainly pulled out all the stops.

However, there are two novel aspects to the affinity detectable; one that strengthened it and one that weakened it. The first was the role of religion. Here there is an element of ambiguity, given the semi-Catholicism of some of Leicester's family connections, and the absence of any clear evidence of a religious test on entry, although conformity to the queen's proceedings was clearly the base. However, there is a gravitation to Leicester among the more 'puritan-minded', who might not

[141] For the mediation efforts, see FSL, Le 550, 632 and 471, Leicester to [Edward Boughton], 27 February 1583, Ferrers to Leicester 22 August [1582/3?], and Boughton to Ferrers, 21 January 1584. I have not yet been able to see the Star Chamber case papers, but the case is mentioned in P.M. Hasler, ed., *The History of Parliament: The House of Commons 1558–1603* (1981), sub Breton. One of Leicester's sanctions was to refuse to take Breton's son Nicholas into his service until the dispute was settled.

[142] For Clarence and Gloucester, see Michael Hicks, *False, Fleeting, Perjur'd Clarence: George, Duke of Clarence 1449–1478* (Bangor, 1992), p. 169, and for Buckingham, Miller, *Henry VIII and the Nobility*, p. 140. For Suffolk's retinues, Gunn, 'The Regime of Charles, Duke of Suffolk in North Wales and the reform of Welsh Government, 1509–1525', *WHR*, xii (1985), 463–4, and 'The Duke of Suffolk's March on Paris in 1523', *EHR*, ci (1986), 598.

[143] HMC, *Fifteenth Report, Pt. V: The Manuscripts of F.J. Savile Foljambe* (1897), pp. 5–6.

otherwise have entered his orbit, and which to some extent may have affected participation in the Netherlands expedition.[144] By the same token, the contrary may have been true, that Leicester's power may have frightened Catholics into conformity. This is certainly the implication of *Leicester's Commonwealth*, and it is found in other Catholic accounts, although they had a polemical purpose in making this case.[145]

The second aspect is the clear tension between loyalty to the affinity and loyalty to the county community. This can be seen in both Wynn's and Ferrers' attempts to balance their service to Leicester with their allegiances and standing within their counties. Not unrelated to this is a detectable unwillingness by several of his followers in later years to admit that they had ever been in his service. Some certainly did; an early seventeenth-century poem on Sir Hugh Cholmondley's widow referred proudly to Cholmondley's service as treasurer of Leicester's household in the Netherlands.[146] On the other hand, John Wynn's history of his family and memoirs of his friends and contemporaries makes no mention at all of his having been in Leicester's household. Particularly curious in this respect is his memoir of William Thomas of Caernarvon, the commander of one of the companies of Leicester's tenants, who was killed at Zutphen: 'a brave, courageous and wise gentleman as any in this country produced in his time.' Thomas was clearly a personal friend, but what is omitted is that he and Wynn had been closely associated in Leicester's service.[147] The late seventeenth-century life of Sir Richard Bulkeley of Beaumaris makes great play of his defence of his country against the tyrannical favourite in the Snowdon Forest affair, but does not mention that he too had once been in Leicester's household.[148] After Sir Thomas Bodley died, John Chamberlain sardonically observed that he had left a memoir:

---

[144] Sir Robert Jermyn, who had been removed from the Suffolk bench for his participation in the attacks on the Bishop of Norwich in 1582–3, and Sir Robert Stapleton, notorious for his involvement in the conspiracy against the Archbishop of York, are cases in point.

[145] An example can be found in the account of the Welsh Catholic martyr Richard Gwyn, see D. Aneurin Thomas, ed., *The Welsh Elizabethan Catholic Martyrs* (Cardiff, 1971), pp. 229, 251.

[146] Cheshire RO, DBC 2309/1/11 [Thomas Lytler, Life of Lady Cholmondley], p. 69. I owe this reference too to Dr Cust.

[147] *The History of the Gwydir Family, written by Sir John Wynne*, ed. Askew Roberts (Oswestry, 1878), see pp. 98–9 for Thomas. Wynn makes only one or two distant references to Leicester but he does record the generosity of Northumberland, 'so good a master', to one of his relatives. For his relations with Thomas, see *Wynn Cal.*, art. 97, Thomas to Wynn, 11 December 1581.

[148] See 'North Wales', 145, n. 99. I suspect that Bulkeley was the Mr Bulkley in the 1567 livery list.

written by himself on seven sheets of paper with vanitie enough, wherein omitting not the least *minutezze* that might turne to his glorie, he doth not so much as make mention of . . . Mr Secretarie Walsingham, nor the Earl of Leicester; who were his maine raisers, whereby may be seen, what mind he caried to his best benefactors.[149]

Wynn's *History* was inspired by the often-quoted sentiment: 'Yet a great temporall blessing it is and a greate hearts ease to a man to find that he is well descended.'[150] The increased gentry concern with their own lineage and stature has long been seen as one of the reasons for the decline of the traditional affinity.[151] Yet there was no immediate reason why it should have done. Leicester's fascination with his own descent was no different, and in that sense there was a definite community of self-regard. Indeed the very point about having gentlemen servants was precisely the honour of being served by men well descended.[152] However, an aspect of gentle pride was being an established member of a county community. Leicester himself saw no conflict in theory between being a member of his affinity and being of local standing, as his description of the men he summoned to the Netherlands makes clear. Indeed he recommended his household servant Richard Browne to the electors of Maldon in 1584 as their countryman and one who would serve their interests.[153] Yet in practice the two may not have been so compatible and the heightened sensitivity to membership of the community made it no longer so easy to give precedence to the demands of the lord.

The fact that it is in seventeenth-century memoirs that this reticence about service is found may also be significant. There is a case to be made that the late medieval peerage effectively came to an end in 1603, for the Stuart expansion of

---

[149] N.E. McClure, ed., *The Letters of John Chamberlain* (Memoirs of the American Philosophical Society, xii, 1939), i, pp. 430–2, to Dudley Carleton, 25 February 1613.

[150] p. 57.

[151] Jones and Walker, 'Private Indentures', p. 32.

[152] This was the point of Newcastle's description of Shrewsbury's affinity, quoted in Heal and Holmes, *Gentry*, pp. 190–2.

[153] Essex RO, D/B/3/3/422, art. 9. Maldon had, in fact, already made its decision.

the peerage – which raised it from the consistent 40–60 after 1399 to 126 in 1628 – transformed it entirely. However, if this has been noted, its effects have yet to be explored.[154] It does, however, raise question marks about the continuity of noble power that underpins the Adamson thesis. The most dramatic aspect of this thesis is the evidence for the interesting experiments in aristocratic constitutionalism in the 1640s. More controversial, and to some extent contradictory, are two further arguments, one for a revival of aristocratic self-consciousness in the 1630s, the other for a continuous tradition of aristocratic constitutionalism. The latter is based on some inaccurate Elizabethan examples.[155] This is not to deny that there was a rise in aristocratic constitutionalism in the seventeenth century, which would turn to medieval precedents; nor that some elements can be found in Elizabeth's reign, notably in the various regency schemes. Foreign examples, particularly Scotland or the Netherlands, may have played a role, and Essex may have dabbled with it. But it is difficult to see a self-conscious tradition at work.

Underlying this thesis is an assumption of a continuity of aristocratic power. But before this can be accepted, much more work on the situation before and after 1603 needs to be done. Indeed it could be argued that the expansion of the peerage reduced many peers to the rank of greater gentlemen and if there is a greater self-consciousness among the peerage in the 1630s this was the result of a need to bolster their weakened status. Membership of a noble affinity was no longer reputable and therefore the possibilities for a great affinity similar to Leicester's would disappear. A question mark hangs over Buckingham, but there is reason to doubt whether he attempted to form such an affinity rather than a

---

[154] Described in Stone, *Crisis*, pp. 97–119, and noted in Hicks, *Bastard Feudalism*, p. 7, but neither draws any wider conclusions. See also my comments in 'Patronage of the Crown', pp. 26–7.

[155] Adamson states that Leicester had claimed the Lord High Stewardship ('Baronial Contexts', 96–7). An antiquarian treatise on Leicester's descent by Robert Bowyer (now Huntington Library MS HM 160) does refer to the historic association between the earldom of Leicester and the stewardship of England, but Leicester does not appear to have shown any interest in the claims of his earldom, unlike his fascination with the Beauchamp descent. There is no evidence that his appointment as Lord Steward of the Household in 1587 was the result of pressure on his part. Further on in the same essay (p. 105, n. 56) Adamson refers to Leicester being 'Captain-General' in the 1580s. This can only be explained as a conflation of his commission as captain-general in the Netherlands with his temporary commission as lieutenant-general in the South Parts in July 1588.

series of court alliances. In this respect Leicester (or possibly Essex) does mark the
end of an era. It is not so much that his affinity itself was changing, for it still
shared the main characteristics of the late medieval affinity, but the wider context
in which it operated was, and in consequence its effectiveness was threatened. In
the following century these wider changes would accelerate.

APPENDIX. THE NETHERLANDS RETINUES*

A. *The Gurney List*

Knights[1]

Sir William Russell	[*c.* 1553–1611, 4th son, 3rd Earl of Bedford, MP]
Sir Robert Jermyn	[*c.* 1540–1614, of Rushbrooke, Suff., MP]
Sir Arthur Bassett	[1541–86, of Umberleigh, Devon, MP, relative]
Sir Thomas Shirley	[*c.* 1542–1612, of Wiston, Suss., MP]
Sir Henry Berkeley	[*c.* 1547–1601 of Bruton, Som., MP]
Sir John Harington*	[*c.* 1540–1612, of Combe Abbey, Warks., MP, entourage]
Sir Robert Stapleton	[*c.* 1547–1606 of Wighill, Yorks., MP]
Sir Richard Dyer	[cousin of Sir Edward Dyer]
Sir John Conway	[of Arrow, Warks., Governor of Ostend 1587–90]
Richard Huddleston[2]	[d. 1589, Treasurer Netherlands 1585–7]
William Knollys[1]*	[*c.* 1545–1632, MP, brother-in-law]
William Bassett	[1551–1601 of Blore, Staffs., MP, poss. household]
George Digby[1]	[1550–87, of Coleshill, Warks, MP, entourage]
Richard Ward	[of Hurst, Berks., son of Richard Ward, Cofferer of the Household]
John Peyton[1]	[1544–1630, of Beaupré Hall, Norf., MP]
John Watts*	[of Blakesley, Northants.]
George Farmer[1]	[d. 1612, of Easton Neston, Northants., entourage]
Michael Harcourt*	[d. 1597, of Leckhampstead, Bucks., MP, tenant]
Thomas Arundel	[poss. son of Sir Matthew Arundel]
Philip Butler[1]*	[d. 1592, of Watton Woodhall, Herts., m. Catherine Knollys]
Robert Sidney[1]*	[1563–1626, MP, nephew and godson]
Captain William Selby	[d. 1612, MP, officer of the Berwick garrison]

The Earl's Gentlemen, Retainers[3]

William Harman*   [of Hampton, Warks., estate officer]

John Fullwood   [of Warks., poss. tenant]

William Pearson

Roger Brereton*   [household]

Edward Bourchier

Ralph Hubaud*   [d. 1605, of Ipsley, Warks., brother of Sir John Hubaud]

Clement Fisher*   [c. 1539–1619, of Great Packington, Warks., MP, entourage]

Thomas Denys   [1559–1613, of Holcombe Burnel, Devon, MP, household]

Henry Jones   [household, tenant in Denbigh]

Ambrose Butler

Richard Weston   [1564–1613, of Sutton Place, Surr., MP]

George Tuberville*   [of Wars., tenant/estate officer]

William Skipwith   [1564–1610, of Cotes, Leics., MP]

Walter Tooke   [poss. son of Northumberland's servant George
                         Tookey of Worcs.]

Richard Acton*   [of Elmsley Lovett, Worcs.?, household]

David Holland   [d. 1616, of Vaerdrey, Denbs., son of estate officer]

Edward Avelin*   [household]

John Glasier*   [son of William Glasier of Lea, Ches., MP, officer]

Charles Acton*   [of Worcs., ward of Thomas Blount, father of John
                         Acton, MP]

Edward Barrow   [of Hants., Captain, Netherlands, 1586]

John Breton   [c. 1530–87, of Tamworth, Staffs., MP, tenant, servant
                         of Warwick]

Nicholas Breton   [d. 1624, son of John]

William Green   [household, gentleman usher 1580s]

William Tatton*   [of Cheshire]

George Booth*   [of Cheshire?]

George Leycester*   [c. 1566–1612, of Toft, Ches., MP]

Edmund Trafford*   [c. 1560–1620, of Trafford, Lancs., MP]

William Gorge*   [household officer 1567–88]

Richard Browne*   [1538–1604, MP, household officer 1566–88]

John Wake*   [d. 1621, of Salcey Forest, Northants., keeper of Grafton]

Edward Watson	[c. 1549–1621, of Rockingham, Northants., MP]
John Wotton*	[Gentleman Pensioner, Captain, Netherlands 1586]
George Brooke*	[1558/9–1604, son of Lord Cobham, household 1580s]
John Hynde*	[household, gentleman of horse]
Thomas Parker[2]	
Michael Dormer[2]	[of Oxon.?, servant of Warwick]
Edward Jobson[2]*	[household 1560s, relative]
Henry Barrington[2]	[poss. MP, Gentleman Pensioner, of Essex, d. c. 1590]
Arthur Berners	[Captain, Netherlands 1586]
Edward Pinchon	[poss. son of John Pinchon, of Writtle, Essex, MP]
John Fisher	[of Wars., poss. brother of Clement Fisher]
Thomas Harrison	[poss. officer of the Stables]
Henry Goodere[1]*	[1534–95, of Polesworth, Warks., MP, entourage]
John Poyntz*	[c. 1560–1633, of Iron Acton, Glos., MP, tenant]
Mr Chester	[poss. William, of Almondsbury, Glos., former page]
Mr Smith	

The Earl's Gentlemen, Servants

Arthur Atye[4]*	[d. 1604, MP, chief secretary 1574–88]
Hugh Cholmondley*	[1552–1601, of Cholmondley, Ches., MP, household officer]
Richard Bold*	[c. 1541–1602, of Bold, Lancs., MP, household 1570s]
Walter Leveson*	[1551–1602, of Trentham, Staffs., MP, officer]
George Fearne*	
Thomas Stafferton*	[officer of Grafton]
Walter Parsons	
William Clarke	[d. 1604, of Watford, Northants.]
Thomas Catesby	[poss. MP, of Whiston, Northants. d. 1592]
William Walsh	[c. 1561–1622, of Abberley, Worcs., MP]
Thomas Chaloner	[c. 1564–1615, of Steeple Claydon, Bucks., MP]
Francis Bromley	[c. 1556–91, of Hodnet, Salop., MP, m. Thomas Leighton's sister]
Thomas Leighton	[c. 1554–1600, of Wattlesborough, Salop, MP]
Francis Clare*	[d. 1608, of Caldwell, Worcs., entourage]

William Helmes   [Captain, Netherlands 1586]

Robert Dymoke*

Edward Cave   [household]

Christopher Goldingham   [brother? of Henry Goldingham, entourage]

Francis Fortescue   [c. 1563–1624, of Salden, Bucks., MP, son of Sir John Fortescue]

Thomas Price   [c. 1564–1634, of Plas Iolyn, Denbs., son of Ellis Price, MP]

Humphrey Stafford

George Turfield   [Captain, Netherlands 1586]

Sebastian Osbaston   [of Long Compton, Warks., tenant of Warwick]

Mr Zouch   [poss. household, poss. Richard Zouch, MP]

Thomas Cottington

William Sprint*

George Ashby   [poss. of Quenby, Leics.]

Philip Babington   [household 1570s]

Robert Hill*   [of Shilton, Devon, household 1570s]

Edmund York*   [household, son of Sir John York]

Stephen Thornhurst*

George Bingham*

Nicholas Poyntz*   [of Alderley, Glos., tenant, poss. household]

William Waight*   [of Warks, household]

John Hughes   [poss. tenant of Kenilworth]

William Goodere*   [brother of Henry]

William Heydon*   [household, gentleman usher 1580s]

Bernard Whetston*   [household]

Edward Barker   [of Little Ilford, Essex, household, tenant of Wanstead]

George Noel*   [brother of Henry Noel, MP]

Christopher Wright*   [JP, Warks.]

George Kevitt*   [poss. related to Thomas Kevitt, tenant of Balsall, Warks.]

William Sneyd   [of Keele, Staffs.?]

Francis Trentham*   [son of Thomas Trentham of Rocester, Staffs, MP, entourage]

Rowland Selby   [connection to Captain William Selby unclear]

Mr. Fardshel

Anthony Flowerdew   [son of William Flowerdew of Hethersett, Norf.,
                           estate officer]

Anthony Nott

John More*

Walter Clopton   [of Clopton, Warks.?]

Richard Lloyd*   [1545–?, secretary, poss. MP]

Thomas Chatterton   [Captain, Netherlands 1586]

John Leventhrop   [of Herts., former ward]

Hampden Paulet   [1550–?, of Nether Wallop, Hants., MP]

John Knight   [poss. MP]

Edmund Carey[1]   [1558–1637, 6th son of Lord Hunsdon, MP, officer of
                           Grafton]

James Hobson*   [poss. son of James Hobson, MP, of Suss.]

Henry Parker

Edward Lomner

William Butler   [poss. tenant of Kenilworth]

Isaac Wincoll

Rowland Mills

Thomas Smith   [Captain, Netherlands, 1586]

William Highgate

John Carrell

Alexander Morgan*

Henry Unton[2]   [c. 1558–96, of Bruern Abbey, Oxon., MP]

Richard Holney   [household]

William Goslett*

John Leigh*   [Captain Netherlands, 1586]

Robert Hutton*   [household officer]

Thomas Fairfax   [1560–1640, of Denton, Yorks., MP, household
                           1580s]

Thomas Bickley

William Rogers

Jenkin Lloyd   [c. 1560–1628, of Berthlwyd, Monts., tenant]

Cadwaladr Price   [1561–?, of Rhiwlas, Merion., MP]

William Penrhyn*	[of Rhysnant, Monts., recorder, lordship of Chirk]
John Wynne Edwardes	[of Cefn y Wern, Chirk, tenant]
Thomas Morrell	
Richard Morris	[of Rhiwsaeson, Monts., tenant]
Robert Spring	
Edward Boughton*	[c. 1545–89, of Cawston, Warks., MP, officer]
Sylvanus Scory*	[d. 1617, MP, son of the Bishop of Hereford, household 1570s]
Thomas Salusbury	[of Denbigh Castle, tenant]
John Marvin	[of Wilts., poss. MP]
William Hopton*	[household]
Mr Gwin	[poss. reference to men sent by John Wynne of Gwydir]
Captain William Reade	[d. 1604, MP, officer of Berwick garrison]
Christopher Blount	[d. 1601, MP, master of horse, son of Thomas Blount]

B. Retinues found in the other lists

Henry Appleyard	[of Bracon Ash, Norf., nephew of Amy Robsart, poss. household]
William Blackwell*	[keeper of Drayton Basset, 'old retainer']
Edward Blount*	[d. 1630, estate officer, brother of Christopher]
Peter Boiles	
William Boughton	[of Long Lawford, Wars., cousin of Edward]
John Brock	
Francis Castilion*	[1561–1638, MP, poss. household, son of G.B. Castiglione]
Thomas Chetwynd	
William Clavell	[poss. brother of John Clavell, MP, of Dorset]
William Cowper	
Henry Day*	[poss. household]
Jasper Dering	
William Downhall*	[secretary and gentleman of the horse]
Lawrence Fenwick	
John Flackett	
Richard Flowerdew	[relationship to Anthony unclear]

Thomas Fowler	[poss. household servant of that name]
Robert Fulford*	[household, of Devon?]
Gilbert Gerard*	[prob. MP Chester 1593, son of Sir William]
Bernard Grenville	[1567–1636, MP, son of Sir Richard]
Edward Grey	[of Buildwas, Salop., household and relative]
Nicholas Hardlow	
William Hartop	[servant, tenant]
George Harvey*	[household, steward in Netherlands]
Richard Hodges	
Piers Holland	[d. 1596, of Dinmael, Denbs., brother of David]
Reginald Hollingworth*	[lieut. of Leicester's guard 1586]
Richard Holte	[of Aston, Warks.?]
John Hornedge	
William Horton	[relative of William, MP, of Catton, Derbs. and Caloughdon, Warks.]
Henry Isley*	[of Kent, household, relative]
William Jermyn	[of Suff., brother of Sir Robert]
John Lamplaugh	[of Cumberland?]
Philip Lappe	
Arthur Longfield*	
Jerome Markham*	
Thomas Peniston	[prob. son of Thomas, MP, of Oxon., d. 1601]
Christopher Pescott	
Thomas Powlewhele	[household]
William Poyntz*	[household, brother of Nicholas]
Anthony Puleston	[of Denbs.?]
Ambrose Rogers	
William Rowse	[poss. household]
Christopher Saunders	
Edmund Stafford	[household]
Thomas Storey	[rider of the Stables, household Netherlands]
George Tipping	[of Oxon.?]
Giles Tracy	[household, brother of John]
John Tracy*	[c. 1561–1648, of Toddington, Glos., MP, household]

Thomas Turner

Henry Vaughan   [either of Hergest, Herefs., or Cors y Gedol, Merion.]

Hugh Vere*

Charles Walcot   [c. 1542–96, of Walcot, Salop., MP, poss. tenant]

William Walker*

Robert Williams

William Wood   [household]

* List A is derived from the Gurney list and follows its order and structure, omitting only the numbers of men and horses. List B comprises those men omitted from the Gurney list, the great majority found only in the January 1586 muster list, and is arranged alphabetically. There are, of course, numerous variations of spelling between the lists (particularly in the Spanish list, where the clerk had some difficulty with English names) and this has been standardized. (*) indicates attendance at Leicester's funeral. The identities supplied are as brief as possible, emphasizing any known connection to Leicester. For those identified as servants or members of the household, see the Index of Servants in *Household Accounts*. As was my practice in *Household Accounts*, membership of the House of Commons has been indicated; biographical information will be found in *The House of Commons 1559–1603*, though only occasionally the connection to Leicester. Further information on the Midlands and Welsh contingents can be found in my articles. Many of these men also appear casually in *Household Accounts*.

[1] The Spanish list omits Dyer and Conway. The Rawlinson adds Sir Thomas Cecil and Sir Philip Sidney. The Hague muster includes all except Conway, but in a different order and Sir Robert Stapleton twice. It also includes those knighted during 1586, indicated ([1]). Many others were to be knighted after 1586.

[2] The Spanish list identifies this group as Esquires and adds the five names numbered ([2]). The Rawlinson list runs this group on from the knights with no gap or identification, omits Hurleston and adds the section Thomas Parker to Thomas Smith as well as Jasper Dering.

[3] A similar gap exists in the Spanish list, but the rest of the names are simply identified as the Earl's Gentlemen. The Rawlinson has here a group of four 'Officers': Hurleston, George Harvey, Captain Read and William Gorge, and heads the remainder 'My Lords Servants'.

[4] Both the Spanish and the Rawlinson lists vary the order of names of this section in the same way. Both begin with Atye, but between Francis Clare and William Helmes insert the section William Harman to John Hynde. The Spanish list ends with John Leigh, but the Rawlinson continues as the Gurney.

6

VITALITY AND VULNERABILITY IN THE LATE MEDIEVAL CHURCH: PILGRIMAGE ON THE EVE OF THE BREAK WITH ROME

G. W. Bernard

John Maddicott recently referred to 'two sorts of historian whose reading, one imagines, rarely overlaps: those concerned with popular religion and those interested in aristocratic affinities'.[1] I hope that this attempt by someone who began as a student of the Tudor nobility to explore some characteristics of religious life on the eve of the break with Rome, and so risk merely discovering for myself what specialists have long known, does not reinforce the case for such intellectual apartheid. It was when church-crawling, Pevsner in hand, in time off as a graduate student pursuing the Talbot earls of Shrewsbury, that the then dominant orthodoxy on the supposedly decadent condition of the late medieval English Church and the inevitability and popularity of the English Reformation first struck me as inadequate. How could one reconcile alleged clerical neglect, lay ignorance and hostility with the evident glories of countless parish churches remodelled in the Perpendicular style in the century and a half before the 1530s? As Lander wrote in the catalogue to the exhibition marking the quincentenary of St George's Chapel, Windsor, in 1975, 'if profuse expenditure on ecclesiastical building amongst all levels of the population be accepted as an index of religious devotion and enthusiasm the advent of the reformation in England is a surprising fact indeed'.[2] Some of those churches were of course the fruit of the patronage of individuals – kings,

[1] *EHR*, cix (1994), 699.

[2] J.R. Lander, 'The historical background to St George's chapel in the fifteenth century' in M. Bond, ed., *The Saint George's Chapel Quincentenary Handbook* (Windsor, 1975), p. 9.

merchants, nobles. But many if not most were the result of the contributions of a large number of donors, as at Bodmin or Louth. The subject of churchbuilding before and after the break with Rome is one on which I have long been collecting references and hope one day to develop substantially. But already as a graduate student my sense of the significance of parish church rebuilding led me to question that orthodox view of the late medieval Church, and consequently made me look on largely approvingly as a series of scholars created what has become a new orthodoxy, with late medieval bishops revealed as effective administrators of their dioceses, parish clergy devoted pastors to their flocks, laymen and laywomen deeply attached to the rituals of their Church.

And yet, and yet, and especially on reading Eamon Duffy's *Stripping of the Altars*, I have found myself unable fully to follow the Haigh–Scarisbrick–Harper-Bill–Duffy line.[3] What it does is to make the English Reformation inexplicable: if the late medieval Church was so successful, so well integrated into the fabric of society, then how can one account for the relative ease with which so much of late medieval religion was dismantled? My case in this paper is that the answer lies in the combination of qualities that I see in the late medieval Church. It was full of vitality – even more so in such matters as churchbuilding and pilgrimage than has been recognized – but its strengths were in many ways also potential weaknesses, since practices such as pilgrimage were intrinsically vulnerable to criticism. Of course, that is not to say that there was anything inevitable about the course the Reformation took: late medieval piety could simply have ridden out the sceptics and reformers, as it had the criticisms of the Lollards, and continued much the same, as perhaps it still does to this day in say the churches of Naples. And again, perhaps all human institutions are vulnerable in the ways that I shall suggest the late medieval Church was vulnerable. No doubt I am in

[3] E. Duffy, *The Stripping of the Altars* (1992); J.J. Scarisbrick, *The Reformation and the English People* (Oxford, 1994); C. Haigh, 'The recent historiography of the English Reformation', *HJ*, xxv (1982), 995–1007 (first published in W.J. Mommsen, ed., *Stadtburgertum und Adel in der Reformation* (Stuttgart, 1979), and 'Anticlericalism and the English Reformation', *History*, lxviii (1983), pp. 391–407, reprinted in C. Haigh, ed., *The English Reformation Revised* (Cambridge, 1987), pp. 19–34, 56–74; C. Haigh, *The English Reformations* (Oxford, 1993); C. Harper-Bill, *The Pre-Reformation Church in England 1400–1530* (1989), and 'Dean Colet's convocation sermon and the pre-reformation church in England', *History*, lxxiii (1988), 191–210.

danger of having it both ways. But it does seem to me that only an approach that emphasizes both its vitality and vulnerability can do justice to the condition of the late medieval Church.

My hope is in due course to complete a comprehensive survey of the Church as a whole. But in preparing this paper I thought it would be more fruitful and less compressedly schematic to take a single feature as an illustration of my twin themes – and the example I have chosen is that of pilgrimage: devotional journeys to a sacred object or place. Pilgrimage was still a vital part of English religious life in the early sixteenth century, as the vigour with which it was attacked by Protestant reformers shows. It is striking that the leaders of the largest movement of protest against religious change in the reign of Henry VIII called it a Pilgrimage of Grace. A great many shrines attracted pilgrims. A few Englishmen even went to Jerusalem, notably Sir Richard Guildford, who died there in 1506, Richard Torkington, a protégé of Sir Thomas Boleyn, who went in 1516–17, and Roger Wood, a Norfolk gentleman, who went in 1520. Anne Boleyn's fool had been to Jerusalem, presumably on pilgrimage. Obviously such examples are rare, but they testify to a continuing strand of devotion.[4] Some Englishmen went on pilgrimage to Rome. The hospital of the English college at Rome welcomed 82 visitors between November 1504 and May 1505, 202 between May 1505 and May 1506, 205 between May 1506 and May 1507: presumably these were mostly pilgrims.[5] Santiago de Compostela attracted the steward of Tattershall College in 1479, John Bewde of Woolpit, Suffolk, in 1501, Robert Langton, Canon of York, in 1510 and Sir Thomas Boleyn in 1523; Anne Boleyn's father had vowed to go on pilgrimage to Santiago de Compostela during a violent storm while crossing to Spain in 1523: he had just begun his journey there when Henry VIII recalled him for diplomatic duties.[6]

---

[4] *LP*, VI, 585; C.Tyerman, *England and the Crusades 1095–1588* (Chicago, 1988), pp. 309–11.

[5] J.A.F. Thomson, *The Early Tudor Church and Society 1485–152*9 (1993), p. 29.

[6] D.M. Owen, *Church and Society in Medieval Lincolnshire: History of Lincolnshire, v* (Lincoln, 1971), p. 126, Duffy, *Stripping of the Altars*, p. 167; D. Lepine, *A Brotherhood of Canons serving God: English secular cathedrals in the later Middle Ages* (Woodbridge, 1995), p. 143; *LP*, III, ii, 2908, 2617, 2591; R.B. Tate, 'Robert Langton, Pilgrim (1470–1524)', *NottMS*, xxix (1995), 182–90.

Within England Walsingham was among the most popular of pilgrimage centres. Richard Pynson printed a ballad history in 1496. Henry VII visited it in 1487, 1489, 1498 and 1506.[7] Wolsey went there in September 1517.[8] Sir Robert Wingfield vowed to go there in 1517;[9] Sir Richard Wingfield was keen to accompany Wolsey in 1520.[10] The Duke of Buckingham made an offering there in March 1519;[11] the Marquess of Exeter in November 1525;[12] the Duke of Norfolk in 1528.[13] The Bishop of Ely was riding there before Michaelmas 1523.[14] Queen Catherine of Aragon asked in her will for someone to go there on pilgrimage for her.[15] Lord Lisle, in 'mervelous danger and hope gone' on board ship, called upon Our Lady of Walsingham for help and comfort and vowed that if it pleased God and her to deliver him from that peril, he would eat neither flesh nor fish till he had seen her.[16] A poor widow, Elizabeth Newhouse, who had just been to Walsingham, sent her son in London a Walsingham brooch as a token.[17] According to the *Valor Ecclesiasticus* £260 12s 4d was donated to the chapel, the highest recorded amount by far for any shrine in the country; and £6 13s 4d was given in a week a little later.[18]

Canterbury remained an important shrine. In his will, Henry VII wished a life-sized kneeling silver-gilt image of himself to be 'set as nigh to the shrine [of Becket] as may well be'.[19] Foreign visitors marvelled at its gold and

---

[7] J.C. Dickinson, *The Shrine of Our Lady of Walsingham* (1956), pp. 41–2.

[8] *LP*, II, ii, 3675, 3655, 3701, Appendix 41; IV, iii, 5750, p. 2560.

[9] *LP*, II, ii, 3199.

[10] *LP*, III, i, 894, 905.

[11] *LP*, III, i, 1285 p. 499.

[12] *LP*, IV, i, 1792.

[13] *LP*, IV, ii, 4012.

[14] *LP*, III, ii, 3476.

[15] *LP*, X, 40.

[16] *LP*, I, i, 1786; cf. B. Spencer, *Salisbury Museum Medieval Catalogue: part 2 Pilgrim Souvenirs and Secular Badges* (Salisbury, 1990), p. 31 from M. St C. Byrne, ed., *Lisle Letters* (6 vols, 1982), i, 158.

[17] *LP*, Addenda, i, 29.

[18] R. Finucane, *Miracles and Pilgrims: Popular beliefs in medieval England* (1977, 2nd edn, Basingstoke, 1995) p. 205; Dickinson, *Walsingham*, p. 60; A. Savine, 'English monasteries on the eve of the dissolution', in P. Vinogradoff, ed., *Oxford Studies in Social and Legal History*, i (1909), p. 103; *LP*, XI, 165.

[19] B. Dobson, 'The monks of Canterbury in the Later Middle Ages, 1220–1540', in P. Collinson, N. Ramsay and M. Sparks, eds, *A History of Canterbury Cathedral* (Oxford, 1995), p. 137.

jewels.[20] Cardinal Campeggio went in procession to the high altar in 1518. Charles V visited it in 1520. In 1520 the jubilee celebrated every fifty years on the canonization of Becket was expected to be attended by a large confluence of people; though it seems that it did not in fact take place because Pope Leo X refused to grant a plenary indulgence unless half went to St Peter's rebuilding costs.[21] 'It might well be surmised', Barrie Dobson suggests, 'although it cannot be proved, that there were few late medieval Englishmen (and even Englishwomen) who did not harbour at some time or other of their lives the desire to go on pilgrimage to Canterbury.'[22] The vehemence of the attacks on Becket in the late 1530s reflects the continuing potency of his cult.[23] Comments made after the dismantling of the shrine in 1538 testify to the continuing influx of pilgrims right to the end. John Hales asked for Cromwell's favour towards the city and mayor to grant the watermill and lands belonging to St Augustine's: a great part of their yearly charge used to be paid, he said, by the victuallers and innholders of the city 'havyng then grette gayne by pylgrymes and others whiche heretofor cam to the seyd citye of Caunterbury and noue not so contynewyng'.[24]

The town of Thetford would later claim that it had 'ever ben gretly mayntayned relevyd and preservyd by the resort and trade of pylgremys ther passing thorowe . . . but now the pilgrims are abhorryd exesepulsyd and sette apart for ever, wherby a grett nombyr of peopyll be idylld and lyke to be brought ynto extreme beggarye'. Pilgrims had come to the parish church, where St Audrey's smock was kept 'as a great jewell and precious relique'.[25] Ellis Price, commissary-general of the diocese of St Asaph, described how people came in daily pilgrimage with kine, oxen, horses or money to the image of Derfel Gadarn ('Darvell the Mighty', whose body was on Bardsey) at Llandderfel, near Bala. Some 500 to 600 pilgrims, he said, had offered there on 5 April 1538, believing, he claimed, that the image had the power to fetch

---

[20] *LP*, I, i, 395; XIII, ii, 257.

[21] Dobson, 'The monks of Canterbury', p. 149; *LP*, III, i, 695, 791.

[22] Dobson, 'The monks of Canterbury', p. 140.

[23] Cf. C. Brooke, 'Reflections on late medieval cults and devotions', in R.G. Benson and E.W. Naylor, eds, *Essays in Honor of Edward B. King* (Sewanee, Tennessee, 1991), p. 42.

[24] PRO, SP1/140/f. 185 (*LP*, XIII, ii, 1142).

[25] J.S. Craig, 'The "godly" and the "froward": protestant polemics in the town of Thetford', *Norfolk Archaeology*, xli (1990–2), 290 n. 10.

persons that be damned out of hell. A little later the parson and parishioners would offer £40 that the image should not be conveyed to London.[26] Latimer had highlighted people coming by flocks from the West Country to the blood of Christ at Hailes,[27] and described the image of our lady at Worcester as the great sibyll who had been the devil's instrument to bring many to eternal fire.[28] The image at Cardigan was 'used for a great pilgremage to this present daye', the prior testified in 1538, so worshipped and kissed by pilgrims that it yielded 20 nobles annually as a pension to the abbot of Chertsey.[29] The prior of the Cambridge Blackfriars said that there had been much pilgrimage to an image of Our Lady in that house, especially at Stowbridge fair.[30] The Council in the North noted that many pilgrims went to St Saviour's chapel, Newburgh Priory.[31] John London recorded that there was great pilgrimage to Caversham.[32] Even when he was there pulling down the image and defacing the chapel, 'nott so few as a dosyn with imagies of wexe' came in.[33] Foxe frequently testifies to the popularity of pilgrimage. At Dovercourt, 10 miles from Dedham, there was a rood 'said to have done many miracles' – shown by the fact that no man was strong enough to shut the door of the church – 'whereunto was much and great resort of people'.[34] Leland's *Itinerary* is peppered by references to shrines and pilgrimage, often 'great' or 'much' pilgrimage.[35] The Rood of Grace at Boxley, near Maidstone, Kent, was much sought after from all

[26] *LP*, XIII, i, 694; SP1/131 f. 182 = XIII, i, 863; W.D. Hamilton, ed., *Wriothesley's Chronicle*, Camden Society, 2nd ser., xi (1875), i, 80; R. Finucane, *Miracles and Pilgrims*, p. 205.

[27] *LP*, VI, 247: J. Foxe, *Acts and Monuments*, ed. J. Pratt, (8 vols, 1877), vii, pp. 475–6.

[28] *LP*, XIII, i, 1177: G.E. Corrie, ed., *Latimer's Sermons and Remains*, Parker Society, 2 vols, (Cambridge, 1844–5), ii, 395.

[29] T. Wright, ed., *Letters relating to the Suppression of the Monasteries*, Camden Society, 1st ser., xxvi (1843), pp. 186–7 (*LP*, XIII, i, 634 (2)); Finucane, *Miracles and Pilgrims*, p. 205.

[30] *LP*, XIII, ii, 224.

[31] *LP*, XII, ii, 1231.

[32] *LP*, XIII, ii, 346, 367: Wright, *Suppression*, p. 221; Finucane, *Miracles and Pilgrims*, pp. 205–6.

[33] *LP*, XIII, ii, 368: Wright, *Suppression*, p. 224.

[34] Foxe, *Acts and Monuments*, iv, pp. 706–7.

[35] J. Leland, *Itinerary*, ed. L.T. Smith (11 parts in 5 vols, 1906–10): Howden, i, 52; Sonning, Berkshire, i, 109; St Anne, Bristol, i, 134; Dunster, cliff chapel, i, 165; Bodmin, Devon, i, 180; Scilly Isles, i, 190; Our Lady in the Park, Liskeard, i, 208; Netley, Hampshire, i, 280; Southwick, Hampshire, i, 284; Penrice, Glamorgan, iii, 16; St Barrok, Barry Island, iii, 24; Yale, Bromfield, iii, 70; Wirral, Hilbre point, iii, 92; Wakefield, bridge chapel, v, 38; Appleby, Brougham (Westmorland), i, 47.

parts of the realm, Archbishop Warham noted in 1524: 'so holy a place where so many miracles be shewed'.[36] When it was dismantled in 1538 it was recorded that 'thinhabitauntes of Kent hadde in tyme past a greate devocion to the same and to use contynuall pilgramage thether';[37] a London chronicler, recording Bishop Hilsey's sermon, described the Rood of Grace 'that had byn many yeris in the Abbey of Boxley in Kent, and was gretely sought with pilgryms'.[38] Many wills of course record bequests for candles to be lit at particular shrines. When pilgrimages were attacked, there was often trouble. When Latimer spoke against pilgrimages in Bristol in the early 1530s, the people were not a little offended.[39] It is interesting that William Herbert was ordered to take down the image of Our Lady at Pen-rhys as secretly as might be.[40] When three commissioners came to make an end of the shrine of St Swithun at Winchester, they did so at about three in the morning.[41] Henry, Lord Stafford, ordered to remove the idol that ignorant persons called St Erasmus, sent for it next morning, early.[42] What this catalogue cannot well convey, for lack of appropriate evidence, is the felt experience of many thousands of ordinary pilgrims – not least for women, if Margery Kempe can be seen as in any way representative – and the place of pilgrimage in their often hard lives.

What I hope I have shown, however, is that pilgrimage was prevalent and popular in the late fifteenth and early sixteenth centuries. I must dissent from Keith Thomas's remark that 'in the fifteenth century pilgrimages and hagiography were on the decline',[43] and from Colin Richmond's questioning of Geoffrey Dickens's assertion of a 'crazed enthusiasm for pilgrimages around 1500'.[44] Of

---

[36] PRO, SP1/131 f. 10 (*LP*, IV, i, 299).

[37] PRO, SP1/129 f. 210 (*LP*, XIII, i, 231); Finucane, *Miracles and Pilgrims*, p. 209, reads those words as evidence of decline and notes the absence of references to offerings in the commissioners' reports.

[38] *Camden Miscellany iv*, Camden Society, lxxiii (1859), p. 11.

[39] *LP*, VI, iii, 433; VII, 32.

[40] *LP*, XIII, ii, 345; Finucane, *Miracles and Pilgrims*, p. 206.

[41] *State Papers of Henry VIII* (8 vols, 1830–52), i, pp. 621–2, no. cxxii (*LP*, XIII, ii, 401).

[42] *LP*, XIII, ii, 516.

[43] K.V. Thomas, *Religion and the Decline of Magic* (paperback edn, 1973), p. 85.

[44] A.G. Dickens, 'The Last Medieval Englishman', in A.G. Dickens, ed., *Reformation Studies* (1982), p. 281; C. Richmond, 'Religion', in R. Horrox, ed., *Fifteenth-Century Attitudes: Perceptions of society in late medieval England* (Cambridge, 1994), p. 195.

course, most of the cults mentioned so far were long established. But two new cults, in many ways very different, strikingly illustrate the continuing vitality of pilgrimage and call into question the claim that 'the impetus behind the worship of the saints seems to have slackened considerably during the fifteenth century'.[45]

My first example, familiar but open to more forceful emphasis, is the development of the cult of Henry VI in the later fifteenth century. In many ways it was a popular cult. Offerings to an image of the king in York Minster were recorded by 1475.[46] In 1480 the London Mercers' Company advised its members that pilgrimages to Henry VI had been forbidden.[47] A year later, in August 1481, the inhabitants of Westwell, Kent, looked to Henry to release and bring back to life the body of a small boy who was trapped below the waterwheel of the mill.[48] The social setting of the 174 miracles attributed to Henry VI in the collection compiled in Henry VII's reign as part of the campaign for his canonization presents the cult as very much a popular phenomenon, with its emphasis on healing.[49] Fifty involved a sick or afflicted adult, thirty an adult injured in an accident, twenty-seven an injured child and fifteen a sick child.[50] A man crippled for ten years after falling from a horse made the pilgrimage and was cured.[51] A four-year-old boy drowned in a mill stream: at the invocation of Henry VI he was rescued and revived.[52] A girl suffering from swelling of the tibia, could not move

---

[45] Thomas, *Religion and the Decline of Magic*, p. 31.

[46] S. Walker, 'Political saints in later medieval England', in R.H. Britnell and A.J. Pollard, eds, *The McFarlane Legacy: Studies in late medieval politics and society* (Stroud, 1995), p. 85.

[47] L. Lyell and F.D. Watney, eds, *Acts of the Court of the Mercers' Company 1453–1527* (Cambridge, 1936), p. 139.

[48] B. Spencer, 'King Henry of Windsor and the London Pilgrim', in J. Bird, H. Clapman and J. Clark, eds, *Collectanea Londoniensia, Studies in London Archaeology and History presented to Ralph Merrifield, London and Middlesex archaeological Society, Special Papers*, ii (1978), pp. 240–1.

[49] Cf. R.G. Davies, 'The Church and the Wars of the Roses', in A.J. Pollard, ed., *The Wars of the Roses* (Basingstoke, 1995), p. 145. The miracles are edited by P. Grosjean, ed., *Henrici VI Angliae Regis Miracula Posthuma, Societe des Bolandistes, Subsidia Hagiographica*, xxii (Brussels, 1935), and more accessibly by R. Knox and S. Leslie, eds, *The Miracles of Henry VI* (Cambridge, 1923), to which references will be given.

[50] My counts from ibid.

[51] Leslie and Knox, *Miracles of Henry VI*, pp. 118–19.

[52] Ibid., pp. 34–8.

or bear to be touched for fifteen weeks. As many as twenty skilled doctors, physicians and surgeons, were called by her parents in a single week, but it was her parents' invocation of Henry VI that cured her, and once restored to health she made a pilgrimage with her parents to Henry's tomb, leaving her crutches there.[53] This was very obviously a popular cult, meeting the most fundamental human yearnings for recovery from illness and injury. Pilgrim badges confirm that impression. Pilgrims usually brought back badges from the shrines they visited, attached by pins to clothing and to hats, usually decorated on one side. Erasmus' character Ogygius arrives covered with scallop shells, stuck all over with leaden and tin figures.[54] Such badges are interesting evidence of the popularity of pilgrimages. By 1978 some 90 pilgrim badges from the shrine of Henry VI had been found in various places, including Ludlow, Oxford, Salisbury and Bristol. This compares with some 300 that survive from Canterbury, but these were produced over a much longer period of three and a half centuries.[55] As late as the mid-1530s Robert Testwood saw pilgrims, especially from Devon and Cornwall, coming to Windsor with candles and images of wax in their hands, to offer to Henry VI.[56] (One of the miracles attributed to Henry VI is especially interesting in showing the fluctuating attitudes to different saints. A nine-month-old boy swallowed a silver badge of Becket and choked upon it: significantly it was when his parents invoked Henry VI that the boy drew breath and spat out the badge.)[57]

Clearly the cult of Henry VI had political dimensions too. Was it the safest way in the 1470s and early 1480s to express Lancastrian sympathies and implicitly to question the legitimacy of Edward IV's crown?[58] It was certainly important

[53] Ibid., pp. 105–9.

[54] J.G. Nichols, ed., *Erasmus' Pilgrimages to Saint Mary of Walsingham and Saint Thomas of Canterbury* (1875), pp. 1–2.

[55] Spencer, 'Henry of Windsor', pp. 238–9; Spencer, *Medieval Catalogue*, pp. 52–3 ('an abundance of pilgrim signs found in Salisbury and elsewhere confirm that for perhaps two or three decades Windsor became perhaps the primary national pilgrim resort').

[56] Spencer, 'Henry of Windsor', p. 244, citing Foxe, *Acts and Monuments*, v, p. 467.

[57] Knox and Leslie, *Miracles of Henry VI*, pp. 166–7.

[58] Cf. J.W. McKenna, 'Piety and propaganda: The cult of Henry VI', in B. Rowland, ed., *Chaucer and Middle English Studies* (1974), pp. 72–88.

enough for kings to challenge or to foster. The translation of the shrine of John Schorn, late parish priest of North Marston, Buckinghamshire, to Windsor in 1478 has been seen as an effort to create a counter-weight to the attraction of Henry VI.[59]

More significantly still, in 1484 Richard III had the body of Henry VI moved from Chertsey to Windsor. His motives have been variously interpreted. Was it, as Charles Ross suggested, 'a generous move' by Richard?[60] 'He may', Jonathan Hughes has written, 'have wanted to be associated with a king with a posthumous reputation for sanctity.'[61] Or was this perhaps an attempt 'to effect the recreation of concord in a disordered body politic by the reintegration of the defeated and marginalised', the power of a saint being 'not the least' of later medieval England's 'resources of compromise and conciliation'? In taking this line, Simon Walker notes, 'there is always a danger of mistaking rhetoric for reality': 'the proclamation of harmony could become the assertion of a still-disputed hegemony, which only served to remove the conflict from one arena to another'. But the ideal of reconcilation and harmony nonetheless remained, Walker argues, and the cult could contain the political struggle.[62] Just how much of Henry VI's holy innocence and reputation as peacemaker would have rubbed off onto the reputation of Richard III had time allowed must remain problematic. Possibly, in the long run, a royal saint such as Henry VI might have contributed to an 'enhancement of the spiritual status and claims of the English monarchy', reinforcing 'the growing conviction that kings stood in an especially close relationship to God', but, apart from the somewhat questionable assumption about the earlier spiritual status of kings, this would seem more a long-term consequence than in any specific sense a plausible cause of protection and encouragement of the cult.[63] Walker's interpretation seems to treat with excessive intellectual sophistication what was more likely an instinctive political reaction. Was not the body of Henry VI

---

[59] Spencer, 'Henry of Windsor', p. 240; cf. Lander, 'St George's Chapel', pp. 9–10.

[60] C. Ross, *Richard III* (1981), p. 226.

[61] J. Hughes, '"True ornaments to know a holy man": religious life and the piety of Richard III', in A.J. Pollard, ed., *The North of England in the Age of Richard III* (Stroud, 1996), p. 184.

[62] Walker, 'Political saints', pp. 94–8.

[63] Ibid., pp. 86–7, for this 'admittedly speculative' hypothesis.

transferred to keep closer watch over the cult, and to neutralize its political implications by locating it close to the body of Edward IV?[64]

Whatever Richard III's motives, sincere or hypocritical, his action vividly illustrates the continuing power of such cults. Under Henry VII the cult of Henry VI developed still further. 'The monarchy of Henry VII, however oppressive, was perhaps more difficult to strike at because of such associations.'[65] Henry VII began to reconstruct the Lady Chapel at Windsor, intending a shrine for the remains of his uncle, and to be buried there himself. He asked for a papal commission to inquire into Henry VI's miracles, a request granted in 1494. Then in 1498 the King's Council debated where Henry VI should lie: should he be reburied in Westminster Abbey, as the abbot and convent claimed, or Chertsey (as claimed by the abbot), or remain at Windsor (as claimed by the dean and chapter). Witnesses claimed that Henry VI had often visited Westminster Abbey and had chosen the exact spot where he wished to lie, immediately north of St Edward's shrine: Henry VII appears to have been convinced and announced his intention of reburying Henry VI in a new Lady Chapel at Westminster Abbey, where he would also be buried himself. Chamber accounts show £14,856 paid between 1502 and 1509; an indenture dated 13 April 1509, eight days before the king's death, entrusted the abbot and convent with a further £5,000; Henry's will instructed his executors to see the chapel perfectly finished. If, after Henry VII's death in 1509, the momentum disappeared and Henry VI remained at Windsor while the chapel intended for him at Westminster was turned into one for Henry VII, the development of the cult nonetheless vividly illustrates the continuing vitality and potency of the tradition of 'political saints' in the later Middle Ages.[66] Perhaps 'the heyday' of political saints in England is indeed to be found in the thirteenth and fourteenth centuries, yet the cult of Henry VI admirably fits into the world of 'political canonization and political symbolism' that has been seen as most characteristic of earlier periods.[67]

---

[64] Davies, 'The Church and the Wars of the Roses', p. 145; Spencer, 'Henry of Windsor', p. 241.

[65] A. Goodman, 'Henry VII and christian renewal', *Studies in Church History*, xvii (1981), 123.

[66] S. Anglo, *Images of Tudor Kingship* (1992), pp. 61–74.

[67] J.M. Theilmann, 'Political canonisation and political symbolism', *Journal of British Studies*, xxix (1990), 241–66, at 242, 265–6. Cf. also J.R. Bray, 'Concepts of sainthood in fourteenth-century England', *BJRL*, lxvi (1984), 40–77, esp. pp. 51–68; Walker, 'Political saints', pp. 77–106.

My second example of a new cult comes from the 1520s and is in some ways more remarkable. A display of mass piety surrounded Elizabeth Barton, the nun of Kent. We only know about this from the later sermon denouncing her political predictions against Henry VIII's marriage to Anne Boleyn and from the summary of a non-extant book by Edward Thwaites in William Lambard's *Perambulation of Kent*.[68] But the scenes described by Dr Capon, then Bishop-elect of Bangor, in November 1533, and by Lambard had occurred well before Henry sought an annulment of his marriage to Catherine of Aragon.[69] Barton was a servant of one of the Archbishop of Canterbury's tenants at Aldington, Kent. She correctly predicted the death of her master's desperately sick child, 'the first matter that moued her hearers to admiration'. She was able to tell them of things that happened in places where she was not present: for example, what meat the hermit of the chapel of Our Lady at Court of Street had for his supper.

Falling sick, she had gone to the local shrine of Our Lady at Court of Street, and implored her to cure her sickness. Our Lady had responded by ordering her to make an offering to the taper in her honour there, and to declare boldly to all Christian people that it was Our Lady at Court of Street that had revived her from the point of death, and that it should be rung for a miracle. The parish priest reported to Archbishop Warham how she spoke 'of high and notable matters in her sickness, to the great marvel of the hearers'. Warham declared that such words were the words of God and that they should be recorded.

In one of her trances she announced that she would go to the chapel of Our Lady at Court of Street and be restored to health by a miracle. Many priests and monks were present, we are told, as were many ladies and gentlemen of the best degree, together with some 2–3,000 people, who went on procession, singing the litany and saying divers psalms and orations on the way. In the chapel, as mass began, Barton was in a trance. According to Cranmer, she was brought and laid before the image of Our Lady:

---

[68] L.E. Whatmore, 'The Sermon against the Holy Maid of Kent and her adherents, delivered at Paul's Cross, November the 23rd, 1533, and at Canterbury, December the 7th', *EHR*, lviii (1943), 463–75; W. Lambard, *Perambulation* (1596 edn (RSTC 15176)), pp. 187–94.

[69] Most probably 1526 (cf. Lambard, *Perambulation*, p. 189), but possibly a year or two earlier.

her face was wonderfully disfigured, her tongue hanging out, and her eyes being in a manner plucked out and laid upon her cheeks, and so greatly disordered. Then was heard a voice speaking within her belly, as it had been in a tun; her lips not greatly moving; she all that while continuing by the space of three hours and more in a trance; the which voice, when it told anything of the joys of heaven, it spake so sweetly and so heavenly that every man was ravished with the hearing thereof; and contrary, when it told any thing of hell, it spake so horribly and terribly, that it put the hearers in a great fear. It spake also many things for the confirmation of pilgrimages and trentals, hearing of masses, and confession, and many such other things.[70]

After the mass was over she knelt before the image of Our Lady at Court of Street and declared that she was perfectly whole. The miracle of healing was reported to the archbishop by Dr Edward Bocking, doctor of divinity and cellarer of Christ Church, Canterbury. In a vision she was then commanded to become a nun at St Sepulchre, Canterbury. As was customary, she was assigned a spiritual adviser. Edward Bocking was chosen since in one of her trances a voice had stated that that would be God's pleasure. She continued to have visions and revelations weekly or fortnightly. As a result, and also because of the 'great perfectness' that was thought to be in her, many came to see her, both great men of the realm and mean men, many learned men and especially many religious men, hoping that through her they might know the will of God.[71] One Ellyn, a maid living at Tottenham, who had been troubled by trances and revelations, had been to see her: Barton told her that the revelations were but illusions of the devil and that she should cast them out of her mind. Ever since she had been less troubled by them.[72] Barton continued to go often to Court of Street, performing miracles such as lighting candles without fire, moistening women's breasts that were dry, curing the sick and even, we are told, 'reducing the dead to life

[70] Lambard, *Perambulation*, pp. 189–92; J.E. Cox, ed., *The Writings and Letters of Thomas Cranmer* (Parker Society, 1846), pp. 273–4; *LP*, VI, 1546.

[71] Cranmer, *Writings and Letters*, pp. 272–3: *LP*, VI, 1546.

[72] *LP*, VII, 287.

againe'.[73] A book was written of the whole story and put into print, according to Cranmer, 'which ever since that time hath been commonly sold and gone abroad amongst all people'. Moreover by reason of the miracle of her cure, 'there is stablished a great pilgrimage, and ever since many devout people hath sought to that devout . . . lady of Courte of Strett'. The hermit of Our Lady at Court of Street was enriched by the daily offerings made there,[74] further evidence of the popularity of the pilgrimage.

Of course, all this might easily be condemned as imposture, as it was in Capon's sermon, where he claimed that she had completely recovered before the day of her alleged miraculous healing.[75] It is quite plausible to read these events as stimulated by the clergy, Richard Master, the parson of Aldington, in the first instance (though the chapel of Court of Street was not within his parish), and the Canterbury Charterhouse monk Edward Bocking later (though he does not seem to have been involved until attending the miracle of healing). Master was alleged to have spread reports of Barton's trances and speeches 'by cause he wolde have incressed the devocion of the people in commyng on pilgremage to a chapell sett in Courte at Strete . . . within hys seid parisshe . . . for hys own lucre and advauntage': in her trance on the day that she proclaimed her miraculous recovery, Barton urged that the chapel of Our Lady should be better maintained and staffed by a priest who would sing mass daily.[76] Master and Bocking between them allegedly devised the miraculous healing.[77] It was Dr Bocking who first prepared a great book of the wonderful work done at Our Lady at Court of Street, a study evidently taken further by Thomas Master, Edward Thwaites and Thomas Lawrence of Canterbury (the Archdeacon of Canterbury's registrar). Dr Bocking had 500 copies of the Nun's book and the printer 200.[78] John Dering, another Canterbury monk, compiled a tract in defence of the nun's revelation.[79]

---

[73] Lambard, *Perambulation*, pp. 192–3.

[74] Ibid., p. 193.

[75] Whatmore, 'Sermon against the Holy Maid of Kent', pp. 464–6, 469, 471.

[76] *Statutes of the Realm*, iii, 447 (25 Henry VIII, c. 12).

[77] Lambard, *Perambulation*, p. 192.

[78] *LP*, VI, 1194, 1589.

[79] *LP*, VII, 17, 72.

Edward Thwaytes's book – 'a little pamphlet, conteining foure and twenty leaves' – called *A marveilous worke of late done at Court of Streete in Kent*, was printed by Robert Redman, but survives only in Lambard's *Perambulation*. Bocking then allegedly got Barton to have revelations about the king's marriage, which brought her to those troubles which left the sources on which my account is based. Still, and especially if Barton's revelations were invented by a priest and a monk, it is a striking testimony to popular beliefs that critics of the king's divorce should have thought that revelations given to and prophecies uttered by a nun would have the greatest effect in spreading their opposition.

Above all, the display of lay piety revealed by the mass procession is perhaps more significant than the truth of, or the persons behind, Barton's political revelations, and it vividly shows the continuing strength, on the eve of the break with Rome, of popular belief in the healing power of an image visited in pilgrimage. The question addressed by this volume is 'the end of the Middle Ages?', and to that question the evidence of the emergence of the cult of Elizabeth Barton in the 1520s must surely give a firmly negative answer. This is a story that, if one did not know its occurrence in the early sixteenth century, one might think dated from the high Middle Ages, the twelfth and thirteenth centuries of Jonathan Sumption's *Pilgrimage* or Ronald Finucane's *Miracles*, or the early Middle Ages of Patricia Morison's French tenth- and eleventh-century hagiographies.[80] Here in Kent in the 1520s something very similar is *still* happening: we are *still* in the Middle Ages. As related here, the orderly story reveals no mass hysteria, but something more emotional does not seem far away. This is not a comfortable, measured, moderate, lukewarm Barchester-style religion, free from extremism and enthusiasm.[81] And it is worth emphasizing that, but for the nun's involvement in the king's divorce, we should know next to nothing about her.[82] How many more local, popular, cults were there, unrecorded for posterity?

[80] J. Sumption, *Pilgrimage: An image of medieval religion* (1975); Finucane, *Miracles and Pilgrims*; P. Morison, 'The miraculous and French society, *c.* 950–1100', unpublished D.Phil. thesis, University of Oxford, 1983.

[81] *Pace* Richmond, 'Religion', p. 195.

[82] In October 1528 Archbishop Warham wrote to Wolsey that Elizabeth, a nun at St Sepulchre's, Canterbury, 'which hadd all the visions at Our Lady of Courtostreet' and was a virtuous woman, wished to speak to Wolsey, and had asked Warham to inform him (*LP*, IV, ii, 4806).

Many parish churches contained relics or images to which pilgrimage was made. Often our knowledge rests on a single, passing, reference, in Foxe's *Acts and Monuments*, or a brief mention at the Dissolution. For example in Buckinghamshire, apart from the well-known shrines of John Schorn at Marston and the holy blood at Ashridge, there were relics of St Rumwold in the parish church at Buckingham, a rood at Wendover, images of Our Lady at Missenden, an image of Our Lady at Bradwell to which offerings were made, and a chapel and image of the virgin at High Wycombe.[83] Robert Whiting, who has studied Devon and Cornwall intensively, found several local cults in parish churches and local chapels, including at Looe an image to which 100 pilgrims came one feast day just on the eve of the 1530s.[84] At the Greyfriars just outside Coventry offerings were made to an image of Our Lady and to a rood.[85] Chapels in churchyards have been described as 'an area of growth in late medieval religion': some became important pilgrimage centres, for example, Buxton in Derbyshire and Muswell in Middlesex.[86] Local cults could develop rapidly. The newly appointed parish priest of Morebath, Exeter, gave the parish a statue of St Sidwell: soon the altar was surrounded by candles and received bequests.[87] A study of the late medieval church in Rouergue, south-west France, found that in 1524–5 one in ten parishes included a pilgrimage site.[88] Were there as many in England? According to Bishop Barlow of St David's, in his diocese 'ydolotrous abused ymages' did 'horribly . . . abounde'.[89] There must have been many images such as that at Ashford, a rood in a chapel in the north aisle, before which stood a box to receive offerings: people made daily reverence to it, it was claimed.[90] At Leintwardine, Herefordshire, the Abbot of Wigmore used to preach on the Nativity of the Virgin, where the people had been wont to offer to an image.[91]

---

[83] Foxe, *Acts and Monuments*, iv, 580, 225; *LP*, IV, i, 2217 (2); *VCH, Buckinghamshire*, i, p. 303.

[84] R. Whiting, *The Blind Devotion of the People* (Cambridge, 1988), pp. 54–5.

[85] *LP*, XIII, ii, 674.

[86] N. Orme, *Unity and Variety: A history of the church in Devon and Cornwall* (Exeter, 1991), p. 64.

[87] Duffy, *Stripping of the Altars*, pp. 168–9.

[88] N. Lemaitre, *Le Rouergue Flamboyant* (Paris, 1988), p. 384.

[89] *LP*, XIII, ii, 111: Wright, *Suppression*, p. 206.

[90] *LP*, XIV, i, 1053.

[91] *LP*, XII, i, 742.

On Midsummer day pilgrims came to a chapel of St John at Broghton, where the curate said mass.[92] Pilgrimages were made to hermits' chapels, such as St Augustine, Brampton Ash, Northamptonshire, or at Colnbrook, near Windsor.[93]

It would be tempting to put forward a social explanation of the development of pilgrimage along the same lines as Southern's influential exposition of the development of the doctrine of purgatory in the eleventh and twelfth centuries. Just as purgatory offered a system of religious discipline and hope for the afterlife to a much larger number of the laity than had been effectively catered for by the more cultic Church of the Dark Ages, so the practice of pilgrimage, the veneration of saints and their relics, offered to the whole population a religious challenge and balm. As with purgatory, pilgrimage was the fruit of a society enjoying a greater degree of economic prosperity and internal peace and a more elaborate system of Church discipline.[94]

Pilgrimages, then, attracted the poor and the uneducated, but also the rich, the powerful and the educated. Rulers sought the assistance of the saints in the destruction of their enemies. In 1487 Henry VII prayed devoutly before the image of the Virgin at Walsingham that he should be delivered from the wiles of his foes. After his victory at the battle of Stoke, he sent Christopher Urswick to Walsingham with the military standard used in battle to offer thanks.[95] Erasmus vowed to make a pilgrimage to Walsingham in 1512 for the success of the Church against the schismatic Louis XII of France.[96] Catherine of Aragon was intending to go on pilgrimage to Walsingham on hearing of the victory against the Scots at Flodden, to see Our Lady 'that I promised so long ago to see'.[97] This was connected to a continuing belief in the power of saints to bring victory. Saints served as protectors in war. Thomas Ruthal, later Bishop of Durham, testified to the power of St Cuthbert in his account of the battle of Flodden in 1513. Thomas, Lord Howard had led the van, followed by St Cuthbert's banner.

---

[92] *LP*, XII, ii, 610.

[93] R.M. Clay, *The Hermits and Anchorites of England* (1914), p. 187.

[94] R.W. Southern, *Times Literary Supplement*, 18 June 1982, pp. 651–2. Or is this dangerously marxist? See E. Hobsbawm, *On History* (1997), p. x.

[95] Dickinson, *Walsingham*, pp. 41–2.

[96] *LP*, I, i, 1188.

[97] *LP*, I, ii, 2268.

The banner men won great honour and gained the king of Scots' banner which now stood beside St Cuthbert's shrine. In his own hand, Ruthal added that all believe it (the victory) has been wrought by the intercession of St Cuthbert, who never suffered injury to be done to his Church unrequited.[98] When in 1522 Thomas Lord Dacre informed the Bishop of Durham about the condition of Norham Castle, he reported that the inner wall was finished and of that strength that with the help of God and the prayer of St Cuthbert it was impregnable.[99] In autumn 1523 the king ordered Surrey not to go further than St Cuthbert's banner could go with him.[100] All this seems too definite, too particular and too committed for it to be dismissed as insincere and manipulative, or as conventional and unthinking. How can the frequency of the 3rd Duke of Buckingham's visits to shrines be explained, except in terms of his religious sensibility? His accounts show that in 1508 he was a pilgrim at St Augustine's, Bristol, Glastonbury, St Anne in the Wood, Keynsham, Our Lady of Pew at Westminster, Our Lady of Barking and the Holy Rood at Greenwich, all between April and July. In the months before his arrest for treason in 1521 he visited Our Lady of Kingswood, St Aldelm, Malmesbury, Our Lady of Belhouse, Bristol, the relics at Hailes, the child of grace at Reading and Our Lady of Eton at Windsor.[101] In the autumn of 1520 Buckingham had vowed not to shave until such time as he had gone on pilgrimage to Jerusalem.[102] One senses an emotionally troubled man seeking spiritual solace.

However, what principally underpinned the practice of pilgrimage was the hope of relief from sickness and disability. Healing was a central feature in the miracles attributed to Henry VI and in Elizabeth Barton's activities, as we have seen. That the belief in saints as healers was universal is suggested by Hugh Latimer's admission that 'I have thought in times past that divers images of saints could have holpen me, and done me much good, and delivered me of my diseases'.[103] The ballad printed by Pynson stressed the miracles of healing that had occurred at

[98] *LP*, I, ii, 2283.

[99] *LP*, III, ii, 2031.

[100] *LP*, III, ii, 3841.

[101] *LP*, III, i, 1285 (1).

[102] *LP*, III, i, 1284 (4).

[103] *LP*, V, 607: Foxe, *Acts and Monuments*, vii, p. 489.

Walsingham: the sick cured, the dead revived, the lame straight, the blind able to see.[104] It was during a period of widespread sickness that Wolsey went to Walsingham in 1517.[105] Saints were specialists in healing, each with different expertise. The shrine of St Guthlac and his bell at Repton were thought to alleviate toothache.[106] The old chapel at the east end of Sonning church, Berkshire, attracted many pilgrims 'for the disease of madness'.[107] St Audrey's smock at Thetford was specially useful 'in putting away the tooth ach and swelling of the throte'.[108] The hat of Thomas, Earl of Lancaster, venerated at Pontefract, was thought to be good for headaches.[109] So was an image called Maiden Cutbroghe, at Tellisford, Warwickshire. Under the feet of the image was a trough of wood descending under the altar. Those in search of a cure put a peck of oats into the trough.[110] The image of John Schorn at Marston, Buckinghamshire, standing blessing a boot, into which he conveyed the devil, was much sought after for the ague.[111]

Pilgrimage saints were also much invoked to mitigate the pains of childbirth. The image of St Anne of Buxton and St Modwyn of Burton upon Trent with her red cow and staff, which women labouring of child in these parts were very desirous to have with them to leap upon and walk with it,[112] 'dyd alure and intyse the ignorantt pepull to the seyd offeryng', referring to 'the opynion of the pepull and the fonde trust that they dyd putt in those ymages'.[113] Commissioners in the 1530s found the girdle of St Mary, Haltemprice; the girdle and part of the tunic of St Francis, Grace Dieu; part of the shirt ofSt Thomas, at St Mary's Derby; the girdle of St Bernard, Melsa, Holderness; the girdle of St Saviour, Newburgh; the girdle of St Ailred, Rievalux; the finger of St Stephen, at Keldholm; the necklace called *agnus dei* at Holme Cultram; the girdle of St Mary at Calder; the girdle of St Mary at Conishead; the girdle of

---

[104] Dickinson, *Walsingham*, pp. 124–8.

[105] *LP*, II, ii, 3655, 3675, 3701; Appendix 38, 41.

[106] *LP*, X, 364.

[107] Leland, *Itinerary*, i, p. 109.

[108] Craig, 'Thetford', p. 290 n. 10.

[109] *LP*, X, 364.

[110] *LP*, XIII, ii, 719.

[111] *LP*, XIII, ii, 235.

[112] *LP*, XIII, ii, 256.

[113] *LP*, XIII, ii, 244: Wright, *Suppression*, p. 143.

St Werburgh, Chester; the belt of Thomas, Earl of Lancaster, Pontefract; the belt of blessed Mary at Kirkham; the girdle of St Bernard at Kirkstall; the girdle and book of St Robert at Newminster. Were these girdles and tunics borrowed temporarily, implying that someone went to or from the shrine to collect them?[114]

Vows of pilgrimage were often made by those who were ill. It was when he was sick that the 4th Earl of Shrewsbury evidently resolved to go on pilgrimage to Doncaster;[115] it was when he was sick that Thomas Alen, the 4th Earl of Shrewsbury's chaplain, vowed to ride to Canterbury in pilgrimage.[116] It was during the sweating sickness of 1528 that Bishop Longland of Lincoln promised a pilgrimage to Walsingham.[117] In a series of events similar to those involving Elizabeth Barton, Sir Roger Wentworth took his twelve-year-old daughter, who suffered from violent fits, on a famous pilgrimage to the shrine of Gracechurch, Ipswich, after a vision of the Virgin looking as she did in the picture and statue of Our Lady of Ipswich effected a cure. A thousand people escorted her; the Abbot of Bury travelled 30 miles on foot 'of pilgrimage'. But a relapse occurred after a promised repeat pilgrimage was delayed. Four thousand then attended a renewed pilgrimage, at which others were also cured. The girl then became a nun. Wolsey and Catherine of Aragon visited the shrine in 1517 and Wolsey's statutes for his college at Ipswich drew upon Gracechurch, which obtained a fresh papal indulgence in 1526.[118]

---

[114] *LP*, X, 364.

[115] *LP*, II, i, 1959.

[116] *LP*, I, i, 1870.

[117] *LP*, IV, ii, 4418.

[118] Haigh, *English Reformations*, p. 69; D. MacCulloch, *Suffolk and the Tudors* (Oxford, 1986), pp. 143–5, who dismisses it as 'a classic case of child hysteria and manipulation' (p. 145). Cf. T.M.C. Lawler, G. Marc'hadour and R.C. Marius, eds, *The Complete Works of St Thomas More*, vi (i), pp. 93–4. Another contemporary occurrence of miraculous survival was recorded at Doncaster. More than 300 people came to the image of Our Lady at the Whitefriars of Doncaster on the feast of St Mary Magdalen (22 July) when a miracle was rung and sung. William Nicholson and Robert Leche and his wife and children had been crossing the River Don at a ford, only to be overwhelmed by the current. They implored God and Our Lady of Doncaster, as, kneeling, did 'all the peple beyng on the land seyng this pituous and hevy sithte', praying to God and Our Lady, 'if ever she shewed any merakill', to save Robert Leche's wife: safe, she then spoke to the people, saying that God and Our Blessed Lady in Doncaster had preserved her. Those who had escaped drowning declared the miracle on oath before the prior and convent, supported by witnesses (HMC, *Kenyon MSS*, xxxv (1894), p. 1).

So vibrant a faith might seem firm against criticism. Yet there were potential weaknesses within the system of belief and practice represented by pilgrimages. In general terms, the distinction between what was true religion and what was superstition or magic was not always easy to maintain.[119] The official line of the Church was to stress that pilgrimages and prayers to saints were intercessions and aids to piety, inculcating obedience, humility, reverence, forbearance, charity; that contemplation of saints' lives and relics inspired men and women to emulate their conduct.[120] But the Church could not deny the occurrence of miracles – from the Creation itself to the daily miracle of the mass. And miracles had been essential instruments of conversion in the Dark Ages. The Church of the high Middle Ages was more sceptical of miracles, making miracle an explanation of last resort, and the canonization of saints an increasingly lengthy and difficult process. In practice, however, people might have rather stronger hopes than the Church would have preferred to allow that their specific requests in prayer would be granted, and there were obvious temptations for those clergy or monks involved in a pilgrimage site to make claims on behalf of their saint and relics, treating miracles as a 'primary advertisement for the shrine or saint'. The whole procedure could take on a mechanical quality, not very different from magic, as significant numbers of miracles were reported as having taken place at saints' shrines, as saints were seen as having almost divine powers of intervention in this world.[121] Elizabeth Barton claimed to have seen souls in purgatory, and in particular to have watched the disputation of the devils for the soul of Cardinal Wolsey after his death: by her penance he was brought to heaven.[122]

Such mechanical and magical approaches to salvation were readily attacked by reformers. William Barlow denounced those who saw saints such as St David as having the power not just on earth but also in heaven 'to geve it whom he wold, to discharge hell, to emptie purgatory, to pardon synne, to release payne, yee to

---

[119] M.H. Keen, *English Society in the Later Middle Ages* (1990), pp. 278–9.

[120] G. Williams, *The Welsh Church from Conquest to Reformation* (Cardiff, 2nd edn, 1978), p. 488; Morison, thesis cit., p. 10.

[121] B. Ward, *Miracles and the Medieval Mind* (Oxford, 1982), pp. 3–8, 10–11, 34; Williams, *Welsh Church*, pp. 488–9, 504; Sumption, *Pilgrimage*.

[122] Wright, *Suppression*, p. 16.

save his beneficiall frendes, to curse and kyll his unfavorable adversaries': such power, Barlow insisted, was rather God's alone.[123] It is always tricky to generalize on trends in such matters, but had there perhaps been a drift towards a more magical conception of sainthood in the fifteenth and early sixteenth centuries? Was the late medieval Church more tolerant of such things, less prepared to prohibit and to excommunicate, less forward in explaining the distinction between magic and faithful intercessory prayer, less prepared to prune the luxuriant growth of abuses?[124] Were there fewer bishops willing as Bishop Grandisson of Exeter (1327–69) had been to prohibit the offering of public veneration to those who had not been canonized, to expose a supposed miraculous recovery of sight as a financial fraud and or to complain at a developing but unauthorized pilgrimage to a chapel with an image at Erithelstock, Torrington?[125] However that may be, late medieval pilgrimages increasingly involved images made by men – statues, paintings, crucifixes and crosses – rather than to the relics of saints: such manmade images were perhaps more vulnerable to be turned into a form of worship approaching idolatry.[126] Can we believe Robert Testwood of Windsor's description, recorded by Foxe, of pilgrims at St George's Chapel 'licking and kissing a white lady made of alabaster' in a wall behind the high altar, wiping their hands on it and then stroking their eyes and faces?[127]

It would be easy to claim that the worship of saints had taken the place of that devotion due to Christ, to assert as Erasmus' Menedemus did, that he had never read a commandment that he should entrust the care of his daughters, maids and wife to the saints.[128] But that is not wholly fair, since one of the most fashionable late medieval devotions was that to the stricken Christ on the cross.

---

[123] *LP*, XIII, ii, 111.

[124] Williams, *Welsh Church*, pp. 488, 504.

[125] N. Orme, 'Bishop Grandisson (1327–69) and popular religion', *Transactions of the Devonshire Association*, cxxiv (1992), 107–18.

[126] R. Swanson, *Church and Society in Late Medieval England* (Oxford, 1989), p. 289; Owen, *Medieval Lincolnshire*, pp. 126–7; Orme, *Unity and Variety*, p. 64; Duffy, *Stripping of the Altars*, p. 167; M. Aston, *England's Iconoclasts: vol.1: Laws against Images* (Oxford, 1988), p. 21.

[127] Foxe, *Acts and Monuments*, v, p. 467.

[128] Nichols, *Erasmus*, p. 67.

Many roods were claimed to have worked miracles, for example, those at Chester, Brecon and Tremeirchion.[129] Perhaps, however, 'the power of the individual rood itself, rather than the merits of the great sacrifice of which it was the symbol, . . . [was] assuming the largest place in the worship of its devotees'.[130] Certainly the popularity in the later Middle Ages of the iconography of instruments of passion, and the five wounds of Christ, is striking.

More directly vulnerable to criticism was the heightened devotion to the Virgin Mary in the late Middle Ages, another very fashionable practice. The rosary, especially, lent itself to mechanical observance.[131] The specialization of late medieval saints – each with his or her own areas of responsibility – reinforced that approach and lent itself to ridicule.[132] For example, a list of relics compiled by the commissioners in 1535 (no place is mentioned) includes the wimple of St Etheldreda, through which they draw knotted strings on silken threads, which women think good for sore throats, the wimple of St Audrey for sore breasts, the comb of St Audrey for headaches, the rod of Aaron for children troubled by worms, the ring of St Ethelred for lying-in women to put onto their fingers.[133] Monasteries which accumulated a miscellaneous collection of relics – such as Bury St Edmund's, which had the shirt of St Edmund, blood of Christ, some parts of the holy cross, the stone with which St Stephen was stoned, the coals with which St Laurence was roasted, the parings of the nails and hair of St Edmund in a pix, some skulls, including that of St Petronilla, which the feverish put on their heads, the boots of St Thomas of Canterbury, the sword of St Edmund, the bones of St Botolph carried in procession during droughts – invited satire and incredulity.[134] At Reading Abbey Dr London made an inventory of the relics: two pieces of the holy cross, St James' hand, St Philip's stole, the bones of Mary Magadalene, St David, St Edward the martyr,

[129] G. Williams, 'Poets and pilgrims in fifteenth- and sixteenth-century Wales', *Transactions of the Honourable Society of Cymmrodorion* (1991), pp. 69–98 at pp. 77–8.

[130] Williams, *Welsh Church*, p. 480.

[131] Ibid., p. 486; Williams, 'Poets and pilgrims', pp. 78–9.

[132] Duffy, *Stripping of the Altars*, p. 179; Morison, thesis cit., p. 2.

[133] *LP*, X, 364 (3).

[134] *LP*, X, 364.

St Jerome, St Stephen, St Blase, St Osmond, St Margaret, St Anne and many more obscure saints.[135] At the priory of Coventry Cathedral Dr London listed part of the holy cross, a relic of St Thomas of Canterbury, a piece of Our Lady's tomb, St Cecilia's foot, a cross with a relic of St James, an image of St George with a bone in his shield, a relic of St Andrew, a rib of St Lawrence, an image of one of the children of Israel, a small shrine of the Apostles, a relic of St Katherine, Our Lady's milk in silver and gilt and a piece of the most holy jaw bone of the ass that killed Abel.[136] The churchwardens of Wisboroughe Green, Kent, surrendered a crucifix with a crystal containing a little quantity of Our Lady's milk, relics of tombs and vestments of St Thomas of Canterbury, a hairshirt and bones of St James, a cloak in which St Thomas the martyr was killed and his blood, St Peter's beard and hair, stones with which Stephen was stoned, St James's comb. . . . Sage men of the parish said that these 'have been used and offered time out of mind'.[137] At Caversham, as well as an image of Our Lady, there was the holy dagger which killed Henry VI, the holy knife that killed St Edward and an angel with one wing that brought to Caversham the spearhead that pierced Jesus's side upon the cross.[138] At Bangor Richard, Bishop of Dover, found the servant's ear that Peter struck off.[139] More of the holy cross had been found than three carts could carry.[140]

As presented by the commissioners, all this is intended to provoke incredulity when it does not simply shock. But it would be wrong to suppose that these relics were the neglected leftovers from a distant past. On the contrary, the possession of relics continued to matter and demand the attention of rulers of Church and State within this period. The dispute over the location of the body of Henry VI, determined by Henry VII's Council, shows that well. Another quarrel illustrates it clearly. The early sixteenth-century dispute between the abbey of Glastonbury and Archbishop Warham over the relics of St Dunstan might have come from a saint's

---

[135] *LP*, XIII, ii, 377: Wright, *Suppression*, p. 227.

[136] *LP*, XIV, i, 69 (2).

[137] *LP*, III, ii, 101.

[138] *LP*, XIII, ii, 367, 368, 377: Wright, *Suppression*, pp. 222, 224, 225.

[139] *LP*, XIII, ii, 200.

[140] *LP*, XIV, i, 402.

life from the twelfth century. Archbishop Warham had directed a search at
Canterbury in 1508 which found the coffin and bones of Dunstan. Glastonbury,
however, maintained that the saint's relics had been brought there from
Canterbury and that tradition held that the larger bones were now at Glastonbury,
the smaller remaining at Canterbury. Moreover, Glastonbury suggested that the
relics at Canterbury should be concealed till the truth was established. In
response, Warham questioned the authenticity of the relics at Glastonbury and
claimed that it would be impertinent for him to conceal the relics at Canterbury,
which he had himself seen. He ordered instead that Glastonbury's relics should be
brought before him.[141] This shows how much such practices were still part of a
living tradition: no doubt, it might have continued indefinitely. But it does seem to
me to be desperately vulnerable to any kind of searching scepticism. As even Jack
Scarisbrick was provoked to ask (when reviewing Eamon Duffy's book), 'had
veneration of relics come close to mere magic?'[142]

The more or less automatic sale and distribution of indulgences at pilgrimage
sites reinforced such mechanistic attitudes. Bishops had long offered indulgences
– often specifying the number of days remitted from penance in purgatory – to
those who went on pilgrimage to named shrines and contributed money towards
their maintenance. Abuses could arise if monasteries and churches competed to
attract pilgrims by offering ever more generous indulgences, leading to a book-
keeping mentality in which the faithful sought to accumulate ever more
indulgences.[143] The habit of promising a pilgrimage if a saint worked the miracle
– by curing an illness, or by calming a storm – tended to reinforce the
mechanical quality of pilgrimage. A remarkably high proportion of the miracles
attributed to Henry VI followed the bending of a coin in his honour and the
making of a vow to take it as an offering to his tomb.[144] Pilgrimage by deputy

---

[141] W. Stubbs, ed., *Memorials of St Dunstan*, Rolls Series, lxiii (18), pp. 426–39 (I am grateful to
Dr R.R. Sharpe for this reference).

[142] *The Tablet*, 13 February 1993, p. 212.

[143] Williams, *Welsh Church*, p. 520; N. Orme, 'Indulgences in the diocese of Exeter, 1100–1536',
Transactions of the Devon Association, cxx (1988), p. 16.

[144] P.A. Sigal, 'Les differents types de pelerinage au Moyen age', in L. Kniss-Rettenbeck and
G. Mohler, eds, *Wallfahrt kennt keine Grenzen* (Zurich, 1984), pp. 79–80; Spencer, 'Henry of Windsor', p. 248.

again tended to make the relationship between saint and intercessor more commercial than devotional. Erasmus's Ogygius went on pilgrimage to Santiago de Compostela because his wife's mother had vowed that he should do so if her daughter had a son born alive.[145] In September 1526 a servant of Sir Henry Willoughby was paid 12*d* 'by my masters commandment wen he went of paylgramage', probably to the Holy Cross at Garendon.[146] Miles Salley (d. 1517), Bishop of Llandaff, Abbot of Eynsham, offered £10 in his will to an honest and trustworthy man prepared to go on pilgrimage in his name to Santiago de Compostela and a shrine of Our Lady in Castile.[147] If you cannot yourself perform a good work, the next best thing is to encourage someone else to do it; but the risks of abuse are obvious.

A great deal would depend on the spirit in which pilgrims went on pilgrimage. If they went selfishly, as Erasmus mocked, maids praying for handsome and rich husbands, philosophers for a solution to their problems, countrymen for showers, priests for the best benefices, then the whole venture again becomes dangerously mechanical.[148] Of course, pilgrimage had always included an element of tourism and entertainment, and that too offered a target for satire.[149] William Worsley, priest and hermit, was accused in 1530 of having said that no man riding on pilgrimage, having under him a soft saddle and an easy horse, should have any merit thereby.[150] According to John Hewes, draper, the vicar of Croydon had said that much immorality arose from pilgrimages to Willesden and Muswell.[151] Mistress Cottismore of Brightwell allegedly said that 'when women go to offer to images or saints, they did it to show their new gay gear . . . folks go on pilgrimage more for the green way than for any devotion'.[152] Should those pilgrim badges, most of them a cheap alloy of tin and lead, be seen as sacred objects, almost

---

[145] Nichols, *Erasmus*, p. 2.

[146] Williams, *Welsh Church*, p. 504; *VCH, Leicestershire*, ii, 6; HMC, *Middleton MSS*, lxix (1911), p. 384.

[147] R.W. Dunning, 'Miles Salley, Bishop of Llandaff', *Journal of the Welsh Ecclesiastical Society*, viii (1991), 5.

[148] Nichols, *Erasmus*, pp. 5–8.

[149] Cf. Williams, *Welsh Church*, p. 488.

[150] Foxe, *Acts and Monuments*, v, p. 29.

[151] Ibid., v, p. 34.

[152] Ibid., iv, p. 239; A. Hudson, *The Premature Reformation* (Oxford, 1988), p. 469.

'secondary relics', for those who acquired them, or more like the souvenirs that trippers buy today?[153] It is a question of striking a balance: the Brookes compared medieval pilgrimage with modern museums, full of half-comprehending tourists, of young people having a day out, yet with serious and scholarly purposes at their core.[154] Are the experiences of those who go church-crawling, or visit the blockbuster exhibitions in art galleries, or go to concerts at all comparable? Barrie Dobson has suggested as a general rule 'that all flourishing centres of pilgrimage must by definition attract an inseparable if uneasy agglomeration of the genuinely needy, the genuinely devout, and those for whom curiosity is a stronger motive than either need or devotion'.[155] Historians should take care not to be too pietistic. 'Uppermost in the minds of believers who journeyed to Walsingham or Ipswich were the images of the Virgin to be found at those places,' wrote Margaret Aston.[156] Uppermost, no doubt, in the minds of believers, but how many of those who went on pilgrimage were *believers*? How many pilgrims took part in pilgrimages in much the same part materialistic, part sentimental way that many nowadays treat Christmas? A no doubt unenforceable royal proclamation of 1473 claimed that on pretext of pilgrimage far too many people were wandering about in vagabondage: in future no one should go on pilgrimage without a letter of authority under the king's great seal, stating the reasons for the pilgrimage, the pilgrim's place of origin and his destination.[157]

The difficulty for the Church was that pilgrimage was so large-scale and so various an activity, much of it inherited from an obscure past, involving monasteries that were often exempt from episcopal supervision, or informal shrines in remote places, and relics whose authority was based on miracle,[158] that controlling, or even monitoring, it was almost impossible. How much did

---

[153] Spencer, *Medieval Catalogue*, pp. 7–12.

[154] R. and C.N.L. Brooke, *Popular Religion in the Middle Ages: Western Europe 1000–1300* (1984), p. 23.

[155] Dobson, 'The monks of Canterbury', p. 137.

[156] Aston, *Iconoclasts*, p. 21.

[157] *Calendar of Close Rolls 1468–76*, pp. 298–9, cited by Spencer, 'Henry of Windsor', p. 240.

[158] Cf. for last point C. Zika, 'Hosts, processions and pilgrimages: controlling the sacred in fifteenth-century Germany', *Past and Present*, cxviii (1988), 25–64 at 64.

that matter? 'To have a favourite relic or statue, and to honour and cherish it,
and indeed to have a favourite saint – perhaps identified with one's trade or
guild – is, short of obsession, as harmless and indeed congenial as having a
favourite sentimental possession, football team or pop group, providing
comfort, identity, vicarious excitement and inspiration – albeit misplaced, no
doubt, in many cases.'[159] But when in the late 1530s pilgrimage shrines were
subjected to unprecedentedly close scrutiny, as part of the Dissolution of the
Monasteries, what was discovered, sometimes it seems almost accidentally, was
by no means easy to defend. Thomas More had argued that people did not
confuse images and reality: 'I trust there be no man so mad nor woman neyther
but they knowe quycke men from ded stones and tre from flesshe and bone';
'there is no dogge so madde but he knoweth a very cony from a cony carved
and paynted'.[160] All the same, one does wonder about images such as that of
Derfel Gadarn, at Llandderfel, that image of wood of a warrior in arms, on
horseback, carrying a little spear in his hand and a casket of iron about his
neck, who was believed to have the power to fetch the damned out of hell.[161]
Commissioners in 1538 investigated the alleged blood of Christ at Hailes.
Bishop Latimer claimed that pilgrims 'believe verily that it is the very blood
that was in Christ's body, shed upon the mount of Calvary for our salvation,
and that the sight of it with their bodily eye, doth certify them and putt them
out of doubt, that they be in clean life, and in state of salvation without spot of
sin'.[162] The commissioners found it was but honey clarified with saffron, an
unctuous gum and compound of many things (though not duck's blood, as

---

[159] R.G. Davies, 'Religious sensibility', in C. Given-Wilson, ed., *An Illustrated History of Late Medieval England* (Manchester, 1996), p. 122.

[160] More, *Complete Works*, vi (i), pp. 56, 231; cf. Aston, *Iconoclasts*, p. 32.

[161] Wriothesley, *Chronicle*, p. 80; *LP*, XIII, i, 694; Williams, 'Poets and pilgrims', p. 76.

[162] 'Time-honoured frauds' (Dickens, *English Reformation*, p. 158); Finucane, *Miracles and Pilgrims*, pp. 207–8.

[163] PRO, SP1/136 ff. 221–2 (*LP*, XIII, ii, 409); *LP*, XIII, ii, 347, 709, 710; Wriothesley, *Chronicle*, i, p. 90; cf. P. Marshall, 'The rood of Boxley, the Blood of Hailes and the defence of the Henrician church', *Journal of Ecclesiastical History*, xlvi (1995), pp. 689–96 at pp. 692–3. Cranmer had always been suspicious that the blood of St Thomas of Canterbury in the cathedral was 'but a fayned thing and made of some redde okar or of suche like matter' (Cranmer, *Writings and Letters*, p. 378).

some had claimed).[163] Similarly the Prior of Cardigan, examined about the pretended taper of Our Lady there, confessed that he had been deceived by it, saying that he had only seen its nether end.[164]

The commissioners also exposed the mechanical contrivances which worked 'miracles'. The Rood of Grace at Boxley Abbey was an image of Christ crucified. Its singularity was that Christ nodded his head, winked his eyes, turned his beard, moved his eyes and lips and bent his body. According to Foxe, if the gift offered was a small piece of silver, the rood would hang a frowning lip; if it were a piece of gold, then his jaws would go merrily.[165] No doubt these contrivances grew in the telling, yet there is no doubt that the head and eyes of the image did move.[166] It was revealed in 1538 that these miracles were worked by wires through little pipes: 'certen ingynes and olde wyre wyth olde roten stykkes in the backe of the same, that dyd cause the eyes of the same to move and stere in the hede therof, lyke vnto a lyvelye thyng, and also the nether lippe in lyke wise to move as thoughe itt shulde speke'.[167] Was this just 'good propaganda' for Protestants, justifying the Reformation?[168] Surely it provided them with effective arguments precisely because such practices were not readily defensible. It is hard to defend them, and harder still to enter into the mental world of those who operated them. When Jeffray Chamber, who found how the Rood of Grace at Boxley worked, as he presents it, by chance, when the monastery was being defaced, and its images plucked down, he thought 'nott a litle straunge'. He accordingly examined the abbot and old monks, but they declared themselves ignorant of it.[169] Perhaps 'those responsible for the shrines might be as much the dupes of their own contrivances as the pilgrims

---

[164] *LP*, XIII, i, 634 (2); to vindicate my earlier point that these practices can continue, see letter in *The Times* a day before this paper was given (10 July 1996) defending the authenticity of the shroud of Turin written by the priest of the Catholic Church of Our Lady of the Taper, Cardigan.

[165] Foxe, *Acts and Monuments*, v, p. 397.

[166] Finucane, *Miracles and Pilgrims*, pp. 208–9.

[167] PRO, SP1/129/f. 210 (*LP*, XIII, i, 231); *LP*, XIII, i, 348; Wriothesley, *Chronicle*, p. 74; *LP*, XIV, i, 402; XIII, i, 644; XIV, i, 402.

[168] Finucane, *Miracles and Pilgrims*, p. 209.

[169] PRO, SP1/129 f. 210 (*LP*, XIII, i, 231).

themselves'.[170] The clergy and monks described by Erasmus appeared somewhat defensive, evasive and embarrassed when taxed with some of the oddities of the cults and relics over which they had charge. What need to ask such questions, responded a canon showing Ogygius the holy milk of the Virgin when Ogygius asked for proof.[171] The attendant priest at Canterbury could make no answer when John Colet asked whether some of Becket's riches could be taken to relieve the poor.[172] Or perhaps it was all more like the Easter Sepulchres. In the later Middle Ages an image of the living Christ with a host on his breast or in his hands would be secretly inserted into the Easter Sepulchre in order to be dramatically raised from it on Easter morning: 'the "miraculous" appearance of an image of the resurrected Christ displaying a consecrated host in his breast would have increased the impact of the *elevatio*'. It would have looked rather like a tableau from a Corpus Christi procession.[173] It was not exactly deceitful, but it was a set of practices desperately vulnerable to Erasmian, Protestant, or simply common-sense rationalist critiques. And it is understandable that in certain circumstances, such as those of 1538, an abbot such as the Abbot of Hailes might come to take the initiative in promoting an investigation of the relic in his own institution, the blood of Christ.[174]

Such practices could also easily be presented as just a financial racket, monks cynically exploiting the innocent devotion of the faithful people for their own material gain. That would in fact seem exaggerated: the financial benefits of shrines appear somewhat elusive. The by no means unbiased Richard, suffragan Bishop of Dover, claimed that two images at Bangor, including 'the holyest relyke in all Northe Walys' were worth 20 marks a year to the friars, which is not a vast

[170] Williams, *Welsh Church*, pp. 500–1; cf. P. Marshall's suggestion (from *LP*, XIII, i, 348: 'The rood of Boxley', pp. 691–2), 'that the wires were only accessible after the rood had been prised away from the wall. The strenuous profession of ignorance and innocence by Abbot Dobbes and his brethren may thus have been quite genuine'.

[171] Nichols, *Erasmus*, p. 25.

[172] Ibid., p. 52.

[173] P. Sheingorn, *The Easter Sepulchre in England* (Kalamazoo, 1987), pp. 58, 60; cf. Marshall 'The rood of Boxley', p. 692 and n. 13.

[174] PRO SP 1/136 f. 221–2 (*LP*, XIII, ii, 409); *LP*, XIII, ii, 709, 710.

sum.[175] The Canon of Notley Abbey, Buckinghamshire, who served the image of Our Lady at Caversham, had the offerings for his living, which suggests that they were a few pounds a year.[176] If the monasteries did receive a large income from the voluntary gifts of parishioners and pilgrims, it did not appear in the pages of the commissioners' returns in the mid-1530s. Oblations and the income from the church services made up a very small part only of the monastic spiritual budget recorded there. Oblations were very considerable in one case only, that of St Mary's, Walsingham, which had received £260 12s 4d. Becket's shrine at Canterbury had only received £36 2s 7d, and the rood of Hailes £10. Were these figures 'suspiciously low'?[177] It is possible that monks and clergy at pilgrimage centres – except Walsingham – concealed their revenues or received non-monetary gifts or used different accounting practices. The figures for Canterbury, with a remarkable collapse in revenues after 1420, are baffling: £370 p.a. 1390–1439 to £27 p.a. 1440–89 and £14 p.a. 1490–1535.[178] On the face of it, one must conclude that charges that pilgrimage centres were grand financial rackets remain unfounded.[179]

Whatever the truth of the matter, the perception that they had profited, however little, from deceit was obviously damaging. It quickly provoked the charge that the money might better have been spent on the poor. One of the injunctions presented to monasteries in 1535 demanded that abbots and monks 'shall not shew any reliques or feigned miracles for increase of lucre, but that they exhort pilgrims and strangers to give that to the poor, that they thought to offer to their images or reliques'.[180] Was there resentment that people had been duped? According to Jeffray Chamber, who discovered the deceit of the Rood of

---

[175] *LP*, XIII, ii, 200.

[176] *LP*, XIII, ii, 367: Wright, *Suppression*, p. 222.

[177] Dobson, 'The monks of Canterbury', p. 136.

[178] Whiting, *Blind Devotion*, p. 219. Compare Brooke's caution over the decline in pilgrim offerings at some, but not all, shrines ('Reflections on late medieval cults', p. 42).

[179] Savine, 'English monasteries on the eve of the dissolution', p. 104; C.E. Woodruff, 'the financial aspect of the cult of St Thomas of Canterbury', *Archaeologia Cantiana*, xliv (1932), pp. 22–5; *pace* Duffy, *Stripping of the Altars*, p. 164.

[180] Wilkins, *Concilia*, iii, p. 791; cf. Hudson, *Premature Reformation*, p. 308.

Grace at Boxley, when he showed it openly to the people on market day at
Maidstone, 'to see the false craftye and sotell handelyng therof to the dishonor of
god and illusion of the sayd people', they had the matter 'in wonderous
detestacion and hatred'.[181] William Barlow, not a disinterested witness, reported
after the removal of images in summer 1538 that 'the people now sensibly seinge
the longe obscured veryte manyfestly to display her brightnesse, wherby their
inveterate accustomed supersticion apparently detected, all popish delusions shall
sone be defaced, so that erudityon, the parente of certue and unfallible
foundacion of all ordynate pollecye . . . might . . . be planted here'.[182] But not
everyone felt like that: a local woman claimed that the image of Our Lady at
Walsingham had wrought a miracle even after it had been dismantled and sent
up to London (though apparently she was set up in the stocks at Walsingham on
market day, and then sent round the town in a cart, with the boys and young
people throwing snowballs at her).[183]

What makes pilgrimage so tricky to assess is that, as these examples show, the
practice ultimately rested on an act of faith, which many, if not all held, both
educated and ignorant, powerful and powerless, and which it may be something
of an impertinence, perhaps, for a modern historian to call into question.
However, as an act of faith, it was always open to rationalist critiques, whether
from intellectual theologians, or from the homespun down-to-earth first-
principled approach of the unlettered. There had always been a few sceptics, like
Guibert of Nogent in the twelfth century, or Wyclif in the late fourteenth, deeply
suspicious of post-Biblical saints (if 'remarkably silent about image worship and
pilgrimages'[184]), or those accused of heresy in the fifteenth and early sixteenth
centuries, whose alleged wrong beliefs consistently included criticism of
pilgrimages as unscriptural, incredible, mercenary and noisy (and whose
penances when they abjured often included going on pilgrimage). Satirists such
as Langland, Chaucer and Skelton mocked the worldly features of pilgrimage,

---

[181] PRO, SP1/129 f. 120 (LP, XIII, i, 231).

[182] LP, XIII, ii, 111.

[183] LP, XV, 86.

[184] J. Crampton, 'Leicestershire Lollards', *Transactions of the Leicestershire Archaeological and Historical Society*, xliv (1968–9), pp. 11–44 at p. 38.

but one must be cautious in drawing on their satires. Langland hits at fraudulence but pilgrimage is still the symbol of conscience's quest at the end of the poem.[185] Skelton's biting satire of the Church would later be printed by Protestants but was prompted by what was a wholly orthodox, moralizing and idealistic view of what the Church could be. None of that criticism was likely in itself to have brought about the collapse of pilgrimage: pilgrimage had so far rather triumphed over such dissenters, moralists and sceptics as there were. Nonetheless pilgrimage was in two senses vulnerable. First, the more doubtful practices associated with pilgrimage left the Church perennially exposed to criticism, and open to the threat of a more fundamental and systematic attack on the whole system of salvation through the intercession of saints. It is striking that Thomas Bilney, one of the first Englishmen to have been influenced by Luther's doctrine of justification by faith alone, should as early as 1527–8 have preached sermons denouncing pilgrimages at the shrines at Ipswich and Willesden and urging that men should address their prayers instead directly to God.[186] Secondly, pilgrimage, like the Church as a whole, was dependent on the continuing support of the government. Any institution that depends on physical sites and popular participation will find it hard to survive against official disapproval if the government is more or less united and determined. The continued support of the authorities – above all the king, leading ministers and churchmen – is vital to the survival of practices such as pilgrimage. The close relationship between Church and State had in many ways been an indispensable source of strength to the medieval Church, but it left it highly exposed to any change in royal attitudes. Once government policy took the wholly unpredictable turn it did in the 1530s, it was very hard for the Church to resist it.

Henry VIII is in a sense the *deus ex machina* or the *diabolus ex machina* of this story. Although Henry's accounts record routine payments to shrines, although he appears to have gone to Walsingham in January 1511 soon after the birth of his son, and although he was reported to be intending to go on pilgrimage to Master John Schorn at Windsor in gratitude for recovery from fever in 1521, yet

---

[185] Cf. Hudson, *Premature Reformation*, p. 403n.
[186] Cf. ibid., p. 478.

he does not convince as a committed pilgrim – as compared, say, to Catherine of Aragon, that 'indefatigable pilgrim', as David Loades and Christopher Haigh called her, who went to several shrines in the late 1510s/early 1520s, unaccompanied by her husband.[187] It is perhaps suggestive that it was after his accession to the throne in 1509 that the momentum for the canonization and transfer of the body of Henry VI seems to have petered out; in his will Henry VIII wished the tombs of both Henry VI and Edward IV to be made more princely in the same place where they then were, reflecting perhaps a sense of a neglected commitment but also a revealing unwillingness to mark Henry VI out as different from or as more worthy than Edward IV. When in the 1530s official formulations of faith expressed doubts about the value of pilgrimage, and when in the late 1530s pilgrimage shrines were dismantled, that hostility to pilgrimage, not least from the king, was not directly the result of that endemic undercurrent of scepticism (why should a constant now explain a change) nor the result of the adoption of Lutheranism. It reflected more the development of the king's active anti-papalism (itself the somewhat accidental consequence of the divorce) into a rejection of practices seen as associated with Rome, such as indulgences, the idolatrous worship of abused images and anything that might be seen as a potential threat to his rule, such as monasteries, putative fifth columns of papal power, and the shrines they housed.

Since that hostility to pilgrimage came from the top, from the king and his leading ministers, and because it was imposed by force and by pressures, it was irresistible. Abbots and bishops and monks and priests could do very little here. Five bishops – John Clerk of Bath and Wells, John Stokesley of London, John Longland of Lincoln, Cuthbert Tunstall of Durham, William Rugge of St Asaph – tried their best, probably in 1537, when the statement of faith known as the Bishops' Book was being debated. They boldly defended pilgrimage. 'The bodies of saints, and, namely, the relics of holy martyrs, are to be honoured most sincerely, as the members of Christ. The churches builded in their names,

---

[187] E. Hall, *Chronicle* (1809 edn), p. 517; *LP*, II, ii, p. 1449; *LP*, III, i, 1315; D. Loades and C. Haigh, 'The fortunes of the shrine of St Mary of Caversham', *Oxoniensia*, xlvi (1981), pp. 62–72 at p. 67. I hope to explore Henry VIII's piety further elsewhere.

deputed to the service of God, be to be gon unto with faithful and good devotion; and not to be contemened: and pilgrimage to places where Almighty God sheweth miracles, may be don by them that have therunto devotion.'[188] It was a clear expression of conviction, but it was not really an argument, and the critics of pilgrimage, not least the king, proved the stronger. Official hostility to pilgrimage shrines could moreover readily be justified by the abuses now revealed. Physical destruction vividly publicized these abuses, and empty shrines then mocked the impotence of the images to protect themselves.[189] There was, of course, a large-scale popular protest – the Pilgrimage of Grace in 1536 – against religious changes, though it took place before the most important shrines were attacked, and it failed; its failure no doubt on the one hand associated pilgrimage, its declared purpose, with treason in the eyes of the government, and on the other hand helped to deter further rebellion in 1538 and 1539 when the larger monasteries surrendered and the pilgrimage shrines they housed were dismantled. Conformity does not necessarily mean more than acquiescence. In countless ways devotion to the saints survived in popular memory, and even perhaps in attenuated practice, as in the visiting of holy wells in Cornwall or in Wales in search of cures. The disappearance of pilgrimage must have been a shock to many. Some, though they were probably fewer, accepted the criticisms now made of pilgrimage: the spell was now broken. Others, though even fewer still, may have seen the dismantling of the shrines as justifying the plain scepticism they had always felt. How then should pilgrimage be characterized? A flourishing and fervent devotion, merely a social pastime, or a superstitious road to idolatry? It was or it could be seen as all of these. And in its combination of vitality – in its profusion and popularity – and of vulnerability – to criticism and scepticism, and to attack and dismantling by a determined royal government – it epitomizes the strengths and the weaknesses of the late medieval Church as a whole.[190]

---

[188] J. Strype, *Ecclesiastical Memorials* (Oxford, 3 vols in 6, 1822), I, ii, 388.

[189] Cf. M. Aston, 'Iconoclasm in England: Rites of destruction by fire', in B. Scribner, ed., *Bilder und Bildersturm im Spätmittelater und in der frühen Neuzeit* (Wiesbaden, 1990), pp. 175–202 at pp. 185–7.

[190] I should wish to thank Alastair Duke, Peter Gwyn, Margaret Harvey, T.B. Pugh, Mark Stoyle and Greg Walker for their comments on this paper.

7

HENRY VIII AND HENRY V: THE WARS IN FRANCE

Clifford S.L. Davies

May I begin with a disclaimer? I first studied Henry VIII's wars over thirty years ago; and as a would-be administrative historian rather than as a military one.[1] I did not pursue the subject and since then there has been a good deal of important work.[2] While I have lately come back to the world of international relations and have pushed back into the fifteenth century, I claim no expertise on Henry V and am impressed by the plethora of excellent new works.[3]

---

[1] C.S.L. Davies, 'Supply Services of English Armed Forces, 1509–50', unpublished D.Phil. thesis, University of Oxford,1963; 'Provisions for Armies, 1509–50', *EcHR*, 2nd ser., XVII (1964), 234–48; 'The Administration of the Royal Navy under Henry VIII', *EHR*, LXXX (1965), 268–88; 'The English People and War in the Early Sixteenth Century', in *War and Society* (*Britain and the Netherlands*, vol. vi), eds A.C. Duke and C.A. Tamse (The Hague, 1977), pp. 1–18.

[2] S.J. Gunn, 'The Duke of Suffolk's March on Paris in 1523', *EHR*, CI (1986), 596–634; 'The French Wars of Henry VIII', in *The Origins of War in Early Modern Europe*, ed. Jeremy Black (Edinburgh, 1987), pp. 28–51; 'Chivalry and the Politics of the Early Tudor Court', in *Chivalry in the Renaissance*, ed. Sydney Anglo (Woodbridge, 1990), pp. 107–28; 'Henry VIII's Foreign Policy and the Tudor Cult of Chivalry' in *François Ier et Henri VIII*, ed. Charles Giry-Deloison, (Lille and London, 1996), pp. 25–35; R.J. Knecht, 'The Field of the Cloth of Gold', ibid., pp. 37–51; Giry-Deloison, 'Une alliance contre nature? La Paix franco-anglaise de 1525–1544', ibid., pp. 53–62; Giry-Deloison, 'Henri VIII pensionnaire de François Ier', ibid, pp.121–43; David Potter, *War and Government in the French Provinces: Picardy, 1470–1560* (Cambridge, 1993); Potter, 'Foreign Policy', in *The Reign of Henry VIII*, ed. Diarmaid MacCulloch (1995), pp. 101–33; Richard Hoyle, 'War and Public Finance', ibid., pp. 75–99; David Loades, *The Tudor Navy* (1992); Peter Gwyn, *The King's Cardinal* (1990); G.W. Bernard, *War, Taxation and Rebellion in early Tudor England* (Brighton, 1986).

[3] Richard Vaughan, *John the Fearless* (1966); *The Hundred Years War*, ed. Kenneth Fowler (1971); Philippe Contamine, *Guerre, état et Société, 1337–1494* (Paris, 1972); *Henry V*, ed. G.L. Harriss (Oxford, 1985); Christopher T. Allmand, *Lancastrian Normandy* (Oxford, 1983); *The Hundred Years War* (Cambridge, 1988); *Henry V* (1992); Anne Curry, *The Hundred Years War* (1993); *Arms, Armies, and Fortifications in the Hundred Years War*, eds Anne Curry and Michael Hughes (Woodbridge, 1994); *England and Normandy in the Middle Ages*, eds David Bates and Anne Curry, (1994); Michael Prestwich, *Armies and Warfare in the Middle Ages: The English Experience* (New Haven, 1996).

My excuse is that a comparison of the two Henries does at least raise some interesting questions, does tend to pinpoint what is unusual in each case and does supplement the more usual comparison between Henry V and Edward III. It also raises a fundamental question about the responsibilities of historians.

War would seem at first sight to present the classic case of a 'medieval' to 'modern' transition. On the one hand, apparently, a change in the aims of war: from the chivalrous, support of the personal claims of the lord, with sometimes a dash of crusading thrown in, to the pursuit of 'national interest'. On the other, changes in tactics, from an essentially cavalry-based activity, allegedly with little in the way of organization, to a much more 'scientific' approach, with the accent very much on trained infantry, on the use of firepower, both handguns and artillery, on the coordinated use of the different arms, involving increased professionalism and, possibly, a disappearance of 'chivalry'. Of course we all know that such a picture is too crude, that the reality is full of qualifications and nuances. A juxtaposition of Henry V's and Henry VIII's French wars reveals elements both of continuity and of 'transition'. But what emerges even more strikingly is just how extraordinary was Henry V's conquest of Normandy, far transcending any mere 'medieval–modern' comparison.

In terms of war aims, there can be little doubt that, for both Henries, they were conceived largely in terms of the king's personal rights in France, whether possession of areas with a historical connection to the English Crown, Gascony and Normandy in particular, or the claim to the French Crown itself. Of course, this does not rule out an element of 'national interest'. Respect for the person of the king was a necesssary component of successful kingship; respect was perhaps most easily won by military success against the traditional enemy. Nobles and others might win glory and wealth, from ransom, the acquisition of Norman land, or plunder; although one suspects that for ordinary soldiers the proceeds of loot usually finished up in the purses of dealers, provision merchants, tavern-keepers, prostitutes and, indeed, their own captains. And, as Henry V's shipping off of the criminals of Staffordshire and Shropshire indicates, service abroad might provide at least a temporary alleviation of the problems of law and order at home.[4] In the

[4] Edward Powell, 'The Restoration of Law and Order', in *Henry V*, ed. Harriss, pp. 53–74, at pp. 71–2; cf his *Kingship, Law and Society: Criminal Justice in the reign of Henry V* (Oxford, 1989).

case of the conquest of Normandy, relief from attacks by Norman seamen on English shipping and coastal towns was a substantial gain.[5] Nevertheless, the *casus belli* in Henry V's time was undoubtedly the rights of the king, or perhaps, if the two can be distinguished, of the Crown. And, whatever might be true of the conquest of Normandy, the union of the Crowns was hardly likely to be in the English national interest, as indeed the Parliament of 1420 well appreciated.[6]

The situation is less clear cut in the case of Henry VIII. Certainly in his early years there was something of a secular cult of Henry V, along with an abrupt dropping of attempts to canonize Henry VI.[7] Henry VIII, of course, styled himself 'King of France' throughout his reign.[8] He seems to have been eager for war with France from the first days of the reign.[9] He joined the 'Holy League' engineered by Pope Julius II in 1511, buoyed up by the hope that French involvement with the schismatic council of Pisa would result in papal recognition of his claims. The year 1512 saw the landing of an English army at San Sebastian, in the Basque country, just on the Spanish side of the border with Guyenne, but the promised help from King Ferdinand for an invasion did not materialize, the Spanish overran the kingdom of Navarre instead, the English army mutinied and returned home in disgrace.[10] In 1513 Henry himself headed

---

[5] Allmand, *Henry V*, p. 67; Colin F. Richmond, 'The War at Sea' in *The Hundred Years War*, ed. Fowler, pp. 96–121, at pp. 111–12; C.J. Ford, 'Piracy or Policy: the Crisis in the Channel, 1400–1403', *TRHS*, 5th ser., 29 (1979), 63–78.

[6] *Select Documents of English Constitutional History, 1307–1485*, eds S.B. Chrimes and A.L. Brown (1961), pp. 242–3, reaffirming a statute of 1340, ibid, p. 55.

[7] For the cult of Henry V, see Gunn, 'French Wars', p. 37. Henry VIII's 'almost ritualistic imitation of his namesake' did not extend, however, to having the translation and embellishment of Tito Livio Frulovisi's life, made in 1513–14, printed, or even widely copied, although Holinshed used a copy owned by Stow; see introduction to *The First English Life of King Henry V*, ed. C.L. Kingsford (Oxford, 1911). For the dropping of the cause of Henry VI (though briefly revived in 1528), see Bertram Wolffe, *Henry VI* (1981), pp. 351, 358.

[8] C.S.L. Davies, '"Roy de France et roy d'Angleterre": The English claims to France, 1453–1558', *Publication du Centre Européen d'Études Bourguignonnes (XIVe–XVIe s.)* [*CEEB*], no. 35 (Neuchâtel, 1995), pp. 133–49.

[9] *LP*, I, i, nos 5, 17, 156, 230, 264, 278; but cf. no. 413 (ii).

[10] Davies, 'Supply Services', pp. 205–8; James Marshall-Cornwall, 'An Expedition to Aquitaine, 1512', *History Today*, XXIII (1973), 640–7; a study of this episode in the round would be useful.

an invading force of over 30,000 men, which set off from Calais in association
with an army led by the Emperor Maximilian.[11] Henry won a cavalry
engagement against the French ('Battle of the Spurs'), taking a number of
distinguished prisoners including Louis, Duc de Longueville (grandson of the
famous Dunois, bastard of Orléans), and Bayard, the 'chevalier sans peur et sans
reproche'.[12] It was hardly a glorious occasion; a French column attempting to get
supplies into the besieged city of Thérouanne came up against the main body of
the English army, retreated in some disorder and was hunted down. Still, this was
the nearest approximation to a battle that Henry managed to achieve against the
French and, it was thought, the first recorded victory by English cavalry; Henry
made a good deal of it (including making French envoys view a commemorative
picture in 1527).[13] The allied armies then took Thérouanne, destroyed the
fortifications and indeed, whether accidentally or not, the bulk of the houses.[14]
They went on to Tournai, a French city which formed an enclave deep in Habsburg
'Burgundian' territory, and which was protected by a special treaty guaranteeing its
neutrality. That explains Maximilian's eagerness that it should surrender to Henry
as 'Roy de France'. Maximilian hoped that possession of Tournai would keep
Henry in the war and indeed, if their Swiss allies had not been turned back before
Dijon, emperor and king might have descended on Reims or Paris.[15]

[11] C.G. Cruickshank, *Army Royal: Henry VIII's Invasion of France, 1513* (Oxford, 1969); for numbers,
see pp. 28–9. G. Bischoff, 'Maximilien et Henry VIII en guerre contre Louis XII', *CEEB*, 35 (1995),
pp. 163–86.

[12] Cruickshank, *Army Royal*, pp. 105–18. For Longueville, see de la Chenaye-Dubois and Badier,
Dictionnaire de Noblesse (3rd edn, 19 vols, Paris, 1863–76), XII, p. 319. The dukedom was created in
1505. Dunois was a bastard of Louis, Duc d'Orléans, assassinated 1407.

[13] Gunn, 'Henry VIII's Foreign Policy', p. 35; Glenn Richardson, 'Entertainments for the French
ambassadors at the court of Henry VIII', *Renaissance Studies*, IX (1995), 404–15, at p. 411.

[14] Both rulers agreed on the destruction of the fortifications in August 1513; the houses were fired
accidentally; Cruickshank, *Army Royal*, p. 118, Bischoff, p. 178. However, in November Henry asked
the Imperialists to destroy the town completely except the cathedral and canonries, and to expel
remaining inhabitants; *LP*, I, ii, no. 2466; *Correspondence de Laurent de Gorrevod*, ed. André Chagny,
(2 vols, Mâcon, 1913), ii, p. 269.

[15] C.G. Cruickshank, *The English Occupation of Tournai, 1513–19* (Oxford, 1971); C.S.L. Davies,
'Tournai and the English Crown, 1513–19', *HJ*, XL I (1998), 1–26.

As it happened, 1514 saw Henry and Maximilian competing to be the first to make peace. The result was a truce to last while Henry and Louis XII were both alive, the resumption of the French 'pension' or 'tribute' to England under the terms of the 1492 treaty and the marriage of Henry's sister Mary to the French king. Henry insisted on keeping Tournai, and indeed set about an expensive programme to garrison it and to provide a modern citadel. Quite what was the purpose is hard to say. It was represented as the first stage in Henry's reconstituting his kingdom of France; he planned to install there a *cour souveraine* for his French territories, including future conquests, to substitute for the temporarily inaccessible Parlement of Paris.[16] Given the strength of the French monarchy by that date, regaining further swathes of French territory might seem a chimera; on the other hand there was always the possibility that Mary might give Louis XII an heir, thus foiling François D'Angoulême's hopes of the succession. Had that come about (one can understand François' relief when Louis died shortly after his wedding night and Mary was found not to be pregnant), Henry's position in France would have been as strong as it apparently was in Scotland, with an infant nephew as king and a sister as dowager-queen with a claim to the regency. However, situated as it was well within Habsburg territory, Tournai was useless as a base for further operations without Maximilian's cooperation, which, if it were forthcoming, would make a base at Tournai quite unnecessary. Cooperation was not forthcoming and Tournai was eventually sold back to France, for much less than it had cost to garrison and fortify, as part of the 'Universal Peace' of 1518.[17]

Ostentatious peacemaking culminated in 1520 with the Field of Cloth of Gold and 1521 saw negotiations with Charles V for the resumption of the war. In 1522 the Earl of Surrey set off from Calais, spent ten days on an unsuccessful assault of Hesdin, deliberately fired the town of Doullens (30 km north of Amiens) and left a trail of destruction still remembered sixty years later, but failed to provoke a battle.[18]

[16] Ibid.

[17] Cruickshank, *Tournai*, pp. 275–9.

[18] *LP*, III, ii, nos. 2560, 2592, 2595; Potter, *War and Government*, p. 202. Burning of towns and villages was the normal method of warfare on this frontier; see the list of French burnings in Artois, in Louis Brésin, *Chroniques de Flandre et d'Artois*, ed. E Mannier (Paris, 1886), Appendix. pp. 269–334, and Potter, *War and Government*, pp. 200–32.

The Duke of Suffolk did better in 1523, leading a force across the Somme as far as Montdidier, only about 100 km from Paris, swearing the inhabitants to Henry as king of France as he went. Steve Gunn has argued that, had the projected invasion of Champagne by Henry's ally, the rebel Duc de Bourbon, ever got off the ground, Paris would have been in real danger; as it was, the result was once again ignominious retreat.[19] In 1525 Henry's opportunity had come at last, with François captured at Pavia; however, the failure to extract the necessary funds from his subjects in the 'Amicable Grant' foiled his purpose and provoked the 'renversement des alliances' (already being contemplated before 1525) leading in 1527 to an Anglo-French war against Charles V, an initiative once again scuppered by Henry's subjects' resentment, this time at finding themselves at war with their commercial partner, the Netherlands.[20]

War with France did not break out again until 1543. The threat in 1538–40 of François and Charles burying their differences in an invasion of England persuaded Henry that he had to take an active part again in the international alliance game and that an offensive alliance with the emperor was England's best defence policy. Once more the plan was for a joint march on Paris, the emperor via Champagne, Henry marching south from Calais. In 1522 and in 1523 Henry had argued very cogently for a siege of Boulogne, as being more likely to bring tangible benefit than a thrust into the interior, but had allowed himself to be dissuaded.[21] In 1544 Henry followed his instinct, and Boulogne was captured after a spectacular siege; although the Duke of Norfolk (the 'Surrey' of 1522) failed to capture Montreuil, nor, to Henry's annoyance, could he induce the bulk of his army to take up winter quarters at Boulogne. In 1545 a French fleet tried to cut the sea crossing to Boulogne and Calais and to raid the Isle of Wight, leading to a stand-off between the two fleets in the Solent, before plague dispersed them both.[22] Henry's Council argued for peace, which was achieved in

---

[19] Gunn, 'Suffolk's March', esp. pp. 618–19.

[20] Bernard, *War, Taxation and Rebellion*; S.J. Gunn, 'Wolsey's Foreign Policy and the domestic crisis of 1527–8', in *Cardinal Wolsey: Church, State and Art*, eds Gunn and P.G. Lindley, (Cambridge, 1991), pp. 149–77; Potter, 'Foreign Policy'.

[21] *State Papers, Henry VIII* (11 vols, 1830–52), i, pp. 135–40 (*LP*, III, ii, no. 3346).

[22] Loades, *Tudor Navy*, pp. 131–5.

1546, with provision for massive payment of arrears of the French 'pension' and for the return of Boulogne to the French in 1554, after eight annual payments totalling two million *écus* (about 5 million *livres tournois*, or £500,000 sterling). Henry apparently believed he had had the last laugh, and that the French would not afford the ransom.[23] In the event, by taking advantage of the troubled situation in England in 1549, they bought it back for a fifth of that sum in 1550.[24] In 1558 Calais itself, the last vestige of the Crown's French dominion (except the Channel Islands), fell to France.

These events show that Henry VIII, while caring about his 'historic' claims, could be more flexible about them than Henry V had been. Henry VIII lived in a different world from that of his namesake. The French monarchy itself was immeasurably stronger; when the Duc de Bourbon rose in rebellion in 1523 he significantly failed to create a following among his fellow princes, or even to mobilize his own territories against the Crown. Even before the imperial election of 1519 the French were less concerned about the English king than they were about Maximilian, Ferdinand of Aragon and Italian affairs. With the election of Charles V Henry's room for diplomatic manoeuvre became very restricted. In effect, he could ally with Charles, ally with the French, or remain in dangerous isolation. French contempt for the English capacity to harm the interests of the monarchy (as opposed to harming French subjects who got in the way of their armies) was shown by Henry's inability to provoke a battle, and by lack of any sense of urgency on the French side about regaining Calais. Admittedly that was to change in the 1540s with the shift of the main theatre of Franco-Imperial confrontation to the northern and eastern borders of France. Henri II was certainly anxious to recover Boulogne and ultimately Calais, although the actual attack on Calais in 1557–8 was because it was then seen to have become Habsburg territory through Mary's marriage to Philip II. Henry VIII's sense that

---

[23] Giry-Deloison, 'Henri VIII pensionnaire de François Ier', pp. 132–4; J.J. Scarisbrick, *Henry VIII* (1968), pp. 463–4.

[24] 'Documents concerning the Negotiation of the Anglo-French Treaty of March, 1550', ed. D.L. Potter, *Camden Miscellany, XXVIII*, Camden Society, 4th ser., vol. 29 (1984), pp. 58–180, at pp. 63–4.

[25] Potter, 'Foreign Policy', p. 125.

he needed to demonstrate military achievement in the international arena was undoubtedly important. That accounts, I would suggest, for his obstinacy about Tournai, and later about Boulogne. But he was also happy enough when it suited him to forego his claim to territory or the Crown for the symbolic and financial advantages of the 'pension'.[25] In 1528 he contrived to have it both ways when he warned Charles V against destroying the realm of France, 'which is our true inheritance and for the which our brother and ally the French king payeth us yearly a great pension and tribute'.[26] His ministers were generally less enthusiastic than their master. Wolsey used to justify the war policy by quoting Aesop about the dangers of being the only wise man in a world of fools.[27] Thomas Cromwell saw little point in war in France as an end in itself, although ready to advocate it as a means of defence.[28] Henry's councillors at the end of his reign were anxious for peace, even if it meant the surrender of Boulogne.[29]

Henry certainly gave France higher priority than Scotland. His boasting about his exploits in 1513 and perhaps his concern to keep Tournai may be explained by his feeling upstaged by Norfolk's victory at Flodden. The accession of James V to the Scottish throne, aged two, in 1513 saw Henry indulge in a brief bout of 'imperial' pretensions about Scotland, but for the remainder of James's minority, which lasted until 1528, Henry did little more than attempt to limit French influence in Scotland, and none too successfully. James V's death in 1542 and the prospect of the marriage of an infant queen of Scots to the heir to the English throne was too God-given an opportunity to pass by. Henry devoted large resources to getting the Scots to keep their pledge to marry their queen to Prince Edward, and, unwisely, to pressing his own claims to suzerainty. Again, it is remarkable that Henry gave Boulogne apparent priority over this 'British' interest.[30]

---

[26] Edward Hall, *The union of the two noble and illustre famelies of Lancastre & Yorke*, ed. Henry Ellis (1809), p. 746.

[27] Gwyn, *King's Cardinal*, p. 358.

[28] Potter, 'Foreign Policy', pp. 119–22.

[29] Ibid., p. 132.

[30] R.B. Wernham, *Before the Armada* (1966), pp. 153–4, argues that Boulogne was part of a 'British' policy, in that its possession would make French naval links to Scotland difficult, although he accepts that this did not work; however, investment of the money spent about Boulogne directly on Scotland might have paid more dividends.

The arguments surrounding the adoption of the supreme headship of the Church in the 1530s laid their emphasis on England as a corporate entity, with the king as the head of a joint enterprise, appointed for the utility of his people. In these circumstances an emphasis on the king's 'personal' right to his kingdom of France might seem inappropriate. Of course, 'corporate' and 'personal' interpretations of kingship had long been held in conjunction. Nevertheless the emphasis of political discourse in the 1530s was so strongly nationalist, expressed so much in terms of the political self-sufficiency and unity of the English body-politic, as to devalue the alternative concept of the Englishman's duty to support his ruler's personal right to another kingdom. Henry's claim to France did not result in an ecclesiology for his French kingdom. Henry was proclaimed supreme head of the Churches of England and Ireland. Partly as a result, Calais was in effect made part of England in 1536;[31] the Channel Islands were left in ecclesiastical limbo.[32] Justifications of the French war in 1543 emphasize the French threat to English interests and the French alliance with the Turks, rather than the king's right.[33] Statutes enumerating Henry's claims to the gratitude of his subjects list his successful defence of England from invasion, rather than, as earlier in the reign, the glory of his exploits.[34]

In the event the 1530s represent a watershed. Of course, English monarchs styled themselves kings or queens of France until 1801. Elizabeth I in 1562 occupied Le Havre with Huguenot help to use it as a bargaining counter for the recovery of Calais. But she made no attempt to use her patronage of the Huguenot cause, as Henry V had used the French feuds of his day, to assert claims to territory or to the throne; even if the assassinations of Guise and Henri III evoked uncomfortable memories of 1407 and 1419. Of course, dynastic issues inevitably complicated

---

[31] C.S.L. Davies, 'The Cromwellian Decade: Authority and Consent', *TRHS*, 6th ser., 7 (1997), pp. 177–95

[32] I hope to develop this point in a forthcoming paper.

[33] *Tudor Royal Proclamations*, eds P.L. Hughes and J.F. Larkin, (3 vols, New Haven, 1964–9), i, no. 220.

[34] Statutes 32 Hen. VIII c. 50 (1540) and 37 Hen. VIII c. 25 (1545) both stress defence, 34 & 35 Hen. VIII c. 27 (1542–3) Henry's claims in Scotland; cf 14 & 15 Hen. VIII c. 16 (1523), which recalled Henry's 'Royall Viage with puissant army into Fraunce, his victorious Warre there, and his triumphant returne thens' in 1513.

foreign affairs; one could instance the complications for British policy raised by the dynastic union with Hanover in the eighteenth century. (And one could speculate about the consequences for German, and therefore world history, if Hanover had not become detached from the British monarchy in 1837, by a typically medieval inheritance split between heir male and heir general.) Dynastic claims bulk large, even if intermingled with what was perceived to be the national interest, in French policy in the seventeenth century. And it is not inconceivable that had Edward VI lived to be an adult, he might have been tempted into an imperial-Protestant crusade similar to that, later, of Gustavus Adolphus in the Thirty Years War. I am not, therefore, arguing that a retreat from a 'king's rights' view of policy is somehow inherent in the circumstances of the sixteenth century, part of an ineluctable change from a 'chivalrous–medieval' to a 'modern–utilitarian' mode of thought. I would merely suggest that such a change in Anglo-French relations did in fact take place, certainly from 1547, and in essence from the 1530s.

Was there a similar turning point in military technique and military technology? This raises the bogey of the 'military revolution'. It is interesting to see this topic being taken up by medievalists; still more, to see one scholar locating it in the years up to 1350, another in the century or so after.[35] It seems inevitable that war as, by definition, a competitive activity, should see continual striving for advantageous innovation and should tempt rulers to pour whatever resources they can raise into what they hope will be a knockout blow. War is an engine of technological advance and state formation, but also a beneficiary of both processes. Change is therefore endemic. No doubt change is more pronounced in some periods than others. But there seems little point in debating whether any one period saw 'a', let alone 'the', military revolution. Rather we should try to separate out the various elements at play at any one time. The relevant question is not the absolute state of any country's military technology, but rather its quality relative to that of its main competitor. In this sense we could argue that Henry VIII's England, although technically in advance of Henry V's, was, in relation to France at least, much weaker.

---

[35] Prestwich, *Armies and Warfare*; Clifford J. Rogers, 'The Military Revolutions of the Hundred Years War', in *The Military Revolution Debate*, ed. Rogers (Boulder, 1995), pp. 55–93.

Henry V's forces were at least technically the equal of those of his opponents, though obviously in terms of financial resources and the ability to raise numbers the French were, potentially, far superior, and therefore Henry's success depended on political division in France. In the coordination of shot (arrows fired from longbows) and steel (dismounted men-at-arms), the English were superior to the French. Henry seems to have had a state-of-the-art artillery train. That does not mean it was good enough just to smash its way into fortifications; in what Rees Davies calls a David and Goliath contest, Aberystwyth was successfully held for Glyn Dwr against an English siege train for several months in 1407–8.[36] Rouen held out for five and a half months in 1418–19 and capitulated eventually from famine and hopelessness.[37] Melun held out for over four months in 1420, and again food supplies were decisive.[38] Meaux held out for over five months in 1421–2.[39] On the other hand, Caen fell in two weeks in 1417, as did a number of other lower Norman towns, and presumably in those cases artillery bombardment or the threat of it was important.[40] Some other cases seem equivocal; artillery presumably played its part, without producing a decisive breach, either by forcing the defenders to use resources repairing the walls, or by weakening morale by destruction of property within the town – rather like the claimed effect of area bombing in the Second World War. Harfleur, which capitulated in 1415 after five weeks seems a case in point: it suffered a fierce artillery barrage, but disease and the absence of signs of a relieving army were the deciding factors.[41] Artillery, then, was important, but not all-conquering. (Incidentally there seems to be a similar ambiguity about the French recovery of Normandy in 1449–50. Credit is often given to the new French artillery provided by the Bureau brothers; quite what that contributed to the defeatism and

[36] R.R. Davies, *The Revolt of Owain Glyn Dwr* (Oxford, 1995), pp. 124–5. Mr C.J. Spurgeon's exposition during the Aberystwyth conference of the strength of the castle helps makes this episode more comprehensible; nevertheless the fortifications, although massive, were over a century old.

[37] Allmand, *Henry V*, pp.122–7.

[38] Ibid., pp. 152–3.

[39] Ibid., pp. 164–8.

[40] Ibid., pp. 117–18.

[41] Ibid., pp. 79–82.

demoralization, or whether, alternatively, it rekindled patriotism on the part of townsmen who opened their gates to the French army is difficult to estimate.[42]) Nevertheless, Henry V clearly enjoyed the advantage in fire-power, in both infantry and artillery.

In the equipment and training of his infantry Henry VIII was in a weaker position compared to his main enemies. English armies were still essentially equipped with 'bills and bows', with very little in the way of handguns.[43] Bills were the traditional thrust contact weapon, with a pike head and a cutting edge, but with a shorter handshaft than pikes, and therefore less well adapted to the new infantry tactics pioneered by the Swiss, of disciplined mass formations, able (it was hoped) by sheer solidity to withstand the shock of a cavalry charge. By the end of the reign handguns and pikes were kept in central stores in large numbers and issued on campaign, but presumably, with only a crash training course, unlikely to produce the discipline necessary for the new tactics to succeed.[44] In the event this deficiency was less serious than it might have been. At Flodden the two sides were well balanced numerically. The Scots had pikes, as they had had for two centuries, but they did not equal the Swiss in the drill needed for their best use. They advanced in unfavourable conditions and broke formation, giving the English bills a chance to prove their superiority at short quarters.[45] A small number of mounted mercenaries, a better artillery train, a vastly superior fleet, coupled again with bad generalship by the Scots, gave the English victory at Pinkie in 1547; the Scots fled without any infantry engagement taking place.[46] As for the French, various attempts to modernize their infantry had produced disappointing results by Swiss, German, or Spanish standards, although in the

[42] Rogers, 'Military Revolutions', pp. 67–8; Ralph A. Griffiths, *The Reign of King Henry VI* (1981), pp. 515–22; *Histoire Militaire de France* (in progress, 1992–), vol. i, ed. Philippe Contamine, pp. 198–205.

[43] Cruickshank, *Army Royal*, pp. 78–80; David Eltis, *The Military Revolution in Sixteenth Century Europe* (1995), pp. 101–2.

[44] 6,500 handguns and 20,100 pikes in the Tower of London, 1547; see H.A. Dillon, 'Arms and Armour at Westminster, the Tower, and Greenwich, 1547', *Archaeologia*, vol. 51, pt i (1888), pp. 219–80, at pp. 263–4.

[45] Norman Macdougall, *James IV* (Edinburgh, 1989), pp. 274–6.

[46] David H. Caldwell, 'The Battle of Pinkie', in *Scotland and War, AD 79–1918*, ed. Norman Macdougall (Edinburgh, 1991), pp. 61–94.

provision of handguns the French were well in advance of the English.[47] Both French and English relied increasingly on hiring mercenaries, Swiss (on the part of the French) and Germans especially.[48] In competition for mercenaries the French, with superior resources (and perhaps better prospects of continuous service), had the advantage. But in the absence of field engagements, that advantage was not of practical significance. The English were lucky, therefore, that failure to modernize their infantry did not lead to disaster. It was not until the militia reforms of Mary's reign (prompted in part at least by King Philip) and of Elizabeth's that a serious attempt was made to modernize English infantry methods and training.[49] Even then, given that experience and discipline were of the essence for successful European warfare in the early modern period, the English contribution was unlikely to have been significant (except perhaps for the Cromwellian troops at the battle of the Dunes in 1658) until a fair-sized professional army emerged in William III's reign.

Henry VIII took a personal interest in military technology, and enjoyed inspecting the latest guns or finest ships and talking to engineers.[50] Among his proudest possessions in 1513 were the twelve great bombards made by Hans Poppenruyter at Malines.[51] Named for the twelve apostles, they accompanied him on the 1513 campaign; Henry directed that Bartholomew should fire at the cathedral at Tournai and at the houses of the canons, 'to wake them up to be more inclined to serve God'.[52] He also worked hard to foster an English gun-making industry. On the other hand, the art of defence advanced faster than that of assault. Henry built a great series of forts along the south coast from

[47] *Histoire Militaire de France*, vol. i, pp. 230–2; David Potter, *A History of France, 1460–1560* (1995), p. 261; R.J. Knecht, *Renaissance Warrior and Patron: The Reign of Francis I* (Cambridge, 1994), pp. 350–2.

[48] David Potter, 'The International Mercenary Market in the Sixteenth Century: Anglo-French Competition in Germany, 1543–50', *EHR*, CXI (1996), 24–58.

[49] Eltis, *Military Revolution*, ch. 5, pp. 99–135.

[50] A.F. Pollard, Henry VIII (1905 edn), pp. 126–8. For Henry's interest in navigational techniques, see Elizabeth Bonner, 'The Recovery of St Andrews Castle in 1547', *EHR*, CXI (1996), 578–98, at pp. 581–7.

[51] *LP*, I, ii, no. 3613 (178); Poppenruyter also supplied artillery to Louis XII; P. Henrard, *Histoire de l'Artillerie en Belgique* (Brussels, 1885), p. 68; Cruickshank, *Army Royal*, pp. 74–6

[52] Ibid., p. 145; Robert Macquereau (who claimed to be an eye-witness), *Histoire Générale de l'Europe depuis la naissance de Charles-Quint jusqu'au . . . MDXXVII* (Louvain, 1765), pp. 65–6.

St Michael's Mount to Harwich from 1539 to 1542, designed to maximize defensive fire and to present as low a profile as possible to attackers, although, interestingly, these forts missed out on the latest Italian development, the angle bastion, adopted in England only from 1545.[53] These were expensive, but a lot could be done fairly cheaply with earthworks and other improvizations. Certainly Henry was able to put Boulogne into good order to withstand French attack after he had taken it in 1544, while the fortifications of the nearby town of Montreuil were so thoroughly rebuilt by the French after being destroyed by the Imperialists in 1537 as to defeat English besiegers in 1544.[54] No attack on England actually materialized during the crisis years 1538–40, and plague dispersed the French invasion fleet of 1545, so Henry's defence system was not put to the test. Given England's traditional posture as raider, the shift in the balance of advantage to defence worked against English interests. Guns were larger, more of them were needed, supply trains became ever more unwieldy. Henry V had abandoned the *chevauchée* in favour of systematic conquest. By Henry VIII's reign, *chevauchées* were to be much shorter than they had been under Edward III, while conquest had become more difficult than under Henry V. Henry VIII's armies were more advanced technically than those of Henry V, but they had fallen badly behind their opponents in the race for modernity and were lucky not to meet the full force of the French armies.

A similar point can be made about the navy. Henry V was able to establish, by his naval victories of 1416 and 1417, by his occupation of Harfleur and Honfleur, and by continuing patrols thereafter, something like an 'effective command of the Channel'.[55] He owned over thirty ships by 1417, including four great multi-masted ships, apparently in imitation of the great Genoese carracks the French were in the habit of hiring.[56] However, Henry directed in his will that

[53] J.R. Hale, 'The Defence of the Realm, 1485–1558', in *The History of the King's Works*, ed. H.M Colvin (6 vols, 1963–82), vol. iv, pp. 367–401; esp. pp. 377, 387, 393–4.

[54] Pierre Héliot, 'Les Fortifications de Boulogne sous l'Occupation Anglaise', *Revue du Nord*, XL (1958), 5–38; Héliot and Alphonse Leduque, 'Les Fortifications de Montreuil-sur-Mer au Moyen Age', ibid., XXX (1948), 157–83; H.M. Colvin, 'Boulogne', in *King's Works*, vol. iii, pp. 383–93.

[55] Richmond, 'War at Sea', pp. 114–15.

[56] Allmand, *Henry V*, p. 226; Ian Friel, 'Winds of Change? Ships and the Hundred Years War', in *Arms, Armies, and Fortifications*, eds Curry and Hughes, pp. 183–93.

some of his ships were to be sold after his death; in the event most of them were, while the great ships which were kept gradually decayed through neglect. Presumably, the conquest of Normandy made a royal fleet unnecessary.[57] Henry VIII, on the other hand, faced a Brittany as well as a Normandy firmly in French hands (with a new fortified naval base at Le Havre). Following his father's lead he built warships adapted to be essentially gun-platforms, able to ship a powerful complement of artillery, involving not merely large size, but expensive armament, specialist crews and an inescapable requirement therefore for a permanent royal navy, complete with elaborate docking facilities and ongoing administration.[58] The French fleet in the Ponant (Atlantic) was slightly smaller than the English one and the new base at Le Havre, begun in 1517, took some years to become fully operational, but Henry faced formidable opposition – not least in that the use of galleys to supplement warships gave the French the advantage in manoeuvre and in flexible deployment.[59] Henry VIII created a permanent navy; Henry V on the other hand enjoyed a far more effective command at sea.

In military technology, then, the England of Henry VIII was in advance of that of Henry V in artillery, fortification and naval strength, though hardly in infantry technique. (Indeed lack of practical experience sapped English proficiency even at massed archery.) But in terms of comparative advantage Henry V was clearly in a much stronger position than Henry VIII. Technically, he was the equal or

[57] Richmond, ' War at Sea', pp. 114–15; cf. Susan Rose, 'The King's Ships in the First Half of the Fifteenth Century', introduction to *The Navy of the Lancastrian Kings*, ed. Rose (Navy Records Society, vol. 123, 1982), at pp. 29–56.

[58] Loades, *Tudor Navy*, pp. 39–42, 48–50, 72–102; in spite of the development of a 'royal' navy, both Henries depended on the impressment of merchant ships for transport, and indeed for fighting. N.A.M. Rodger, 'The Development of Broadside Gunnery, 1450–1650', *Mariner's Mirror*, XLVI (1996), 301–24, emphasizes the technical difficulties which still impeded the widespread adoption of broadside fire for much of the sixteenth century, severely limiting therefore the effectiveness of artillery and ensuring the continuation of traditional close-grappling and hand-to-hand fighting.

[59] Michel Mollat du Jourdain, in *Histoire Militaire de France*, vol. i, pp. 286–90; *Histoire du Havre*, ed. André Corvisier (1987).

superior of France in all respects, at least after knocking out the French naval bases in the Seine. Of course, the French had potentially much greater resources. But the inability of Charles VI to control the literally murderous feuding of the French princes put Henry V in a totally different situation from that faced by Henry VIII after eighty years which had seen the French monarchy successfully face down the internal opposition.[60] Are these two factors – Henry V's forces being better placed in relation to the enemy in terms of military technique, and the political situation in France – sufficient to explain the contrast between the achievements of the two Henries, the contrast between the purposive, systematic conquest by Henry V, and the somewhat random and apparently not very successful strategies of Henry VIII?

Certainly Henry VIII never contemplated repeating Henry V's strategy of a direct sea-borne attack on Normandy. All his campaigns, except the attempted invasion of Guienne from Spanish territory in 1512, set off from Calais. Even when, in 1525, in the aftermath of Pavia, a royal invasion of Normandy was mooted, the army was to set off from Calais, treading the path of 1346 and 1415 in reverse (securing the Somme crossing at Blanchetaque was to be crucial).[61] Calais had the advantage, not only of the short sea crossing, but of the availability of supplies (food, and also transport, horses and carts) from the Netherlands, now ruled by the Habsburg successors of the Valois dukes of Burgundy. Netherlands shipping, too, was invaluable in transporting supplies and equipment from England.[62] Setting off from Calais, the alternatives were either conquest of nearby French territory, or of a *chevauchée* into the French interior. The conquest of Tournai had a possible historic resonance, as revenge for Edward III's failure there in 1340 (though I am not aware that this was ever invoked). But, as an enclave in Habsburg territory, Tournai too obviously

---

[60] Steven Gunn seriously underestimates the extent of French disarray in 1413 when he suggests that the English position then was 'not much stronger than that in 1509'; 'Henry VIII's Foreign Policy', p. 34.

[61] *Calendar of State Papers – Spanish*, vol. III, i, nos 39, 79; *LP*, IV, i, no. 1249 (MS original quoted in Bernard, *War, Taxation and Rebellion*, p.35).

[62] Louis Sicking, 'La Maîtrise de la Mer. Coopération navale entre l'Angleterre et l'Empire des Habsbourg pendant la première moitié du XVIe. siècle', *CEEB*, 35 (1995), pp. 187–97.

suggested that England's role was as the emperor's subordinate, and did not provide a base for further conquest. There was no historic English resonance about Boulogne and the Boulonnais, although their acquisition might make Calais itself more secure.[63] It might be possible to re-acquire Ponthieu (the coastal region between the Canche and the Bresle, straddling the Somme estuary, and extending about 50 km inland, including the town of Abbeville) – a historically 'English' area but not one of very obvious attraction, or likely to win Henry much in the way of renown[64] – or, more ambitiously perhaps the 'Somme towns', including Amiens. None of these potential acquisitions, except possibly the Boulonnais, were likely to please Henry's Habsburg allies. *Chevauchées* into the French interior, as attempted in 1522 and 1523, neither provoked the French to battle nor set off rebellion in France. On both occasions the result was a humiliating break-up of the English army with the onset of winter and the failure of supplies. Any military action depended on supplies from the Netherlands. The apparent advantage enjoyed by Henry VIII over Henry V in the availability of such supplies may in the end have been a snare. All of Henry's campaigns were dogged by arguments with the Brussels government about food, horses, carts, carters and exchange rates, and by a clash about strategic objectives. The one exception was in fact in 1513 when Henry was, arguably, duped into doing Maximilian's work for him by taking Tournai. The refusal or the inability to adopt the Norman option, understandable as it was, condemned Henry VIII's campaigns to apparent futility.

Henry VIII's hesitations about Normandy highlight the extraordinary nature of Henry V's conquest. However, the Norman strategy was in no sense an easy option for him either. Why did he adopt it?[65] In part, no doubt, because of tradition: the ancient but by now remote historical claim to Normandy. There was also the precedent of Edward III's campaigns. More recently, in 1412,

[63] Gunn, 'French Wars', p. 33.

[64] Oddly Ponthieu was not included in Henry's demands in 1525, though Thérouanne, taken in 1513, destroyed and abandoned, was; Bernard, *War, Taxation and Rebellion*, p. 33.

[65] Anne E. Curry, 'Lancastrian Normandy: The Jewel in the Crown?', in *England and Normandy*, eds Bates and Curry, pp. 235–52.

Henry's brother Thomas, Duke of Clarence, had landed an army at St Vaast-la-Hogue and had ravaged the Cotentin before setting off for the heart of France.[66] Given the scale of French privateering in the Channel, it is possible to see Henry's attack on Harfleur and the conquest of Normandy (including the closure of the *clos des galées* at Rouen) as part of the defence of the English coasts.[67] Henry had the further advantage of a long-term truce concluded with Brittany in 1414.[68] Moreover, Harfleur could be a base for an overland route to Gascony. Calais on the other hand was in the sphere of Henry's accomplice, the Duke of Burgundy; territorial acquisition in Picardy was therefore inopportune, while the country itself was less fabulously rich than Normandy.[69] The Norman strategy therefore made sense, especially (although this is disputed) if Henry was already thinking of vindicating his claim to the French throne.[70]

Edward III and Clarence seem to have had no difficulty in landing armies in Normandy. Edward had allies in Normandy. Clarence was invited by the Armagnac party among the French princes. The Armagnacs were being besieged by royal and Burgundian forces at Bourges. Clarence could therefore land in Normandy and march unopposed as far as Blois until the French composed their differences and paid him off to proceed to Bordeaux.[71] Clarence's experience

---

[66] J.H. Wylie, *The Reign of Henry IV* (4 vols, 1884–98), iv, pp. 73–81; for a convincing revaluation of the scale and importance of the expedition, and of Henry's disapproval of it, see J.D. Milner, 'The English Enterprise in France, 1412–13', in *Trade, Devotion, and Governance*, eds Dorothy J. Clayton, Richard G. Davies and Peter McNiven (Stroud, 1994), pp. 80–101.

[67] See n. 5, above.

[68] G.A. Knowlson, *Jean V, duc de Bretagne et l'Angleterre (1339–1442)* (Archives Historiques de Bretagne, no. 2, Cambridge and Rennes, 1964), p. 82.

[69] Vaughan, *John the Fearless*, p. 5 (map). When in 1416 the county of Boulogne was seized by John, Calais was completely surrounded by Burgundian territory; ibid., p. 237.

[70] Curry, 'Lancastrian Normandy', pp. 239–41. Whether Henry seriously aimed at the crown before Montereau (September 1419), or whether his conquests in the Île-de-France were intended only to strengthen his bargaining position over Normandy is a moot point; cf. John Palmer, 'The War Aims of the Protagonists', in *Hundred Years War*, ed. Fowler, pp. 51–74, at pp. 68–9, and Allmand, *Henry V*, pp. 133–5. Given Henry's tendency to increase his demands with each success, it seems unlikely that he would have refrained from a serious attempt at the crown if Paris were at his mercy.

[71] W.M. Ormrod, 'England, Normandy, and the Beginnings of the Hundred Years War', in *England and Normandy*, eds Bates and Curry, pp. 197–213; Wylie, *Henry IV*, iv, pp. 73–81; Milner, 'English Enterprise'.

may have determined Henry not to depend on the vagaries of alliances, even for the provision of supplies, although he may have had a tacit agreement with Burgundy.[72] In 1415 he therefore acquired a safe base, a second Calais, at Harfleur. Two years later he set about the systematic, painstaking conquest of Normandy, town by town, fortress by fortress, a campaign of over two years involving successive winter sieges at Falaise and Rouen, followed immediately by two years hard fighting in the Paris region.[73]

Keeping open the sea lanes, keeping up the flow of supplies from England and from the conquered territory itself, conducting a whole series of difficult but successful sieges, maintaining the discipline which so impressed opponents, garrisoning his conquests, above all keeping an army in being so long (Henry VIII failed in his two attempts, in 1523 and 1544, to keep a field army in winter quarters[74]), all underline the familiar point that Henry V was a wholly exceptional commander, meticulous in planning and inspiring in the

[72] Vaughan, *John the Fearless*, pp. 204–7 for a projected agreement for joint military action which was never concluded; pp. 207–8 for Burgundy's absence from Agincourt. What was concluded at Henry's talks with John at Calais in October 1416 is conjectural, but it seems that John refused to support Henry publicly until Henry had acquired 'a notable part' of the kingdom; 1417–18 was to see separate but parallel campaigns; Vaughan, pp. 213–15, 219–24; Allmand, *Henry V*, pp. 110–12. Milner, 'English Enterprise' for lessons drawn by Henry from Clarence's campaign.

[73] Curry, 'English Armies', p. 39, on 'earlier English involvement in France' providing 'nothing which truly compares with the comprehensive nature of Henry's campaign of conquest and occupation'; the same could be said of later English military efforts in Europe up to the Peninsular War.

[74] For 1523, see the vivid account by Ellis Gruffydd, a soldier in Sir Robert Wingfield's retinue, translated by M.B. Davies as 'Suffolk's Expedition to Montdidier, 1523', in *Bulletin of the Faculty of Arts, Fouad I University, Cairo*, VII (1944), pp. 33–43, at p. 40; 'some said that it was too much for them to be there lying on the earth under hedges and ditches dying of cold, another said he wanted to be at home in bed with his wife. . . .'; Gruffydd berates the soldiers for unprofessionalism in not making themselves 'a snug warm hut'. Cf also Hall, *Union*, pp. 670–2, and Bernard, *War, Taxation and Rebellion*, pp. 5, 16. It is hoped that Gruffydd's mostly unpublished chronicle, written in Welsh (National Library of Wales, formerly Mostyn MS 158, now MS 3045 D), may soon be edited and printed. For Henry's unsuccessful attempt to have Norfolk's troops stay on at Boulogne after their failure at Montreuil, *LP*, XIX, ii, nos 374, 383, 402, 415, 436.

field.[75] He was determined to be his own man, to carve out a domain for himself in Normandy, independent of Burgundian military or logistic. In Monstrelet's words, he 'estoit moult sage et expert en toutes besongnes dont il se vouloit entremetre; et si estoit de trés haultain vouloir'.[76]

Even so we must recognize that Henry's strategy was one of immense, if calculated, risks. The conquest of Harfleur could easily have gone wrong. It needed heroic resistance by the garrison as well as Bedford's naval victory to prevent its being recaptured by the French in 1416. Breton goodwill could not be taken for granted; indeed the Duke of Brittany led a contingent to the French army in 1415, though getting no nearer to Agincourt than Amiens.[77] Henry's march to Calais in 1415 seems not so much risky as positively suicidal. Again, quite what was he hoping for? It seems generally assumed that he had to do something with his army, but surely the taking of Harfleur was, as most of his Council evidently thought, sufficiently honourable in itself?[78] He did not, I take it, positively seek a battle with a massed French army. Rather, he was trying to cock a snook by marching to Calais unchallenged, or at most by fighting the much smaller army under Boucicaut which was shadowing him. Finding the ford over the Somme estuary at Blanchetaque fortified against him, he was forced to march a sick and hungry army 100 km inland before finding a crossing place over the river, with the massed French army now between him and his destination. The actual crossing was a moment of extreme danger.[79] In the event the very size of the French army at Agincourt turned out to its disadvantage. But Henry could hardly have foreseen that. He gambled. His success obscures the point that it was a gamble against extraordinarily high odds and, soberly considered, an unjustified gamble.

---

[75] For food supplies, see Allmand, *Henry V*, pp. 119, 124, 217–18, 223–4; R.A. Newhall, *The English Conquest of Normandy, 1416–24* (New York, 1924), pp. 247–58. Monstrelet singled out the respect Henry extracted from 'ses princes et capitaines' by enforcing discipline with stern punishment; *La Chronique d'Enguerran de Monstrelet*, ed. L. Douet-d'Arcq (Société de l'Histoire de France, 6 vols, 1857–62), iv, p. 116.

[76] Ibid., iv, p. 116.

[77] Knowlson, *Jean V*, pp. 94–6.

[78] Allmand, *Henry V*, p. 84, quoting *Gesta Henrici Quinti*, eds Frank Taylor and John S. Roskell (Oxford Medieval Texts, 1975), p. 61.

[79] Prestwich, *Armies and Warfare*, p. 260 for food supplies; for the danger of the crossing, see *Gesta*, pp. 71, 73.

Whether he was in fact reckless, or whether he believed, as is sometimes suggested, that Providence was on his side, can only be a matter for speculation. There is a general assumption that he was a man of high religious principle, convinced of the rightness of his claim both to the 'historic' English lands in France, and to the French throne itself. He invoked Deuteronomy 20, and his actions do seem to be modelled on God's battle-orders to the people of Israel as they went forth to conquer.[80] It may be as well to remind ourselves just what this entailed. The Israelites were assured that the Lord was on their side and that they should not be disheartened by the superior numbers of the enemy; indeed, they should send home those of their number whose enthusiasm for the fight might be diminished by recent betrothal, the building of a new house, or the cultivation of a new vineyard.[81] When they besiege a city they should proclaim the justice of their cause and give the inhabitants the opportunity to become their subjects; if they refuse the city is to be assaulted and the men killed, although women, children and cattle were to become the property of the conqueror, and the plunder was to be shared out in orderly fashion. However, in cities close to the existing heartland, all the inhabitants were to be killed, lest they contaminate their conquerors with false worship. Fortunately this last consideration did not apply in fifteenth-century Normandy, though Henry was prepared, at Harfleur and at Caen, to expel the poor, women and children, their condition rather than unreadiness to swear fealty, apparently the deciding factor.[82]

Henry certainly succeeded in creating the impression of himself as the epitome of Christian kingship. Whether he did this by projecting a false or exaggerated image of himself as a paladin of righteousness, the better to inspire his followers, win over

[80] *Gesta*, pp. xxx, 35, 48, 155.

[81] Henry's repudiation of Sir Walter Hungerford's wish that the army were bigger, invoking God's favour 'in hac humili paucitate' seems to echo Deuteronomy, although the author of the *Gesta* invokes Judas Maccabeus; ibid., p. 78. Cf. the version in Frulovisi's 'Life', 'Verum nollem huic exercitui meo solum virum addi' (*Titi Livii Foro-Juliensis, Vita Henrici Quinti*, ed. Thomas Hearne, Oxford, 1716, p. 16). Interestingly, Shakespeare diverged from his source, Holinshed, by changing the context from Providence to honour ('God's peace! I would not lose so great an honour / As one man more, methinks, would share from me'), while reintroducing the Deuteronomic permission for 'he which hath no stomach to this fight' to depart: *Henry V*, Act iv, 3, and Geoffrey Bullough, *Narrative and Dramatic Sources of Shakespeare* (8 vols, 1957–75), iv, p. 394.

[82] Allmand, *Henry V*, pp. 81, 117; *Gesta*, p. 55 for women, poor children, and infants. Frulovisi has the bland statement that 'tam milites quam oppidani' were allowed to depart; *Titi Livii*, p. 10.

waverers, and intimidate enemies, or whether he actually schooled himself to fulfil that ideal to the best of his ability, we cannot know. Sixteenth-century historians have taken to talking about 'self-fashioning'. That can cover, as I understand it, either the deliberate creation of one's own personality, or the projection of an image. There seems no need to see 'self-fashioning' as a peculiarly 'Renaissance' concept; medieval hagiography provides plenty of examples. Stephen Greenblatt sees 'self-fashioning' as a particularly 'bourgeois' phenomenon, something not necessary for those who 'inherit a title, an ancient family tradition or hierarchical status that might have rooted personal identity in the identity of a clan or caste'.[83] Henry V was no bourgeois. But it might be reasonable to suggest that his emphasis on righteous kingship reflects unease on his part about his own position.

One fundamental point must, surely, have worried him, namely, the disparity between the historic claim to the French throne by Edward III in the right of his mother, and the realities of the English dynastic situation since 1399, when such legitimist principles were blatantly disregarded. Whatever may be argued about the succession to the English throne, the rightful claimant to France on the Edwardian principle was Edmund Mortimer.[84] Henry could not but be extremely

---

[83] Stephen Greenblatt, *Renaissance Self-Fashioning: From More to Shakespeare* (Chicago, 1980), p. 9.

[84] Among the few historians to raise this point, see John W. McKenna, 'How God became an Englishman', in *Tudor Rule and Revolution: Essays for G.R. Elton from his American Friends*, eds DeLloyd J. Guth and McKenna, pp. 25–43, at p. 35, and T.B. Pugh, *Henry V and the Southampton Plot* (Gloucester, 1988), p. 72. John Watts draws my attention to Powell, *Kingship, Law, and Society*, p. 133: 'there is more than a hint of dynastic insecurity in this stress on the king's performance of his duties, a sense of striving for legitimacy, which is also evident in the unremitting drive with which Henry applied himself to his French campaigns'. Theodor Meron, *Henry's Wars and Shakespeare's Laws: Perspectives on the Law of War in the Later Middle Ages* (Oxford, 1993), discusses Edward III's claim at length, while ignoring the question of how Henry could derive a valid claim from it. French controversialists concentrated on the defence of the Salic law and on the inability of French kings to alienate sovereignty, whether at Brétigny or Troyes, but also mentioned the illegitimacy of Lancastrian rule in England, in terms of the usurpation and the killing of Richard II, and occasionally the superior claims (in the absence of a Salic law) of the Mortimer line; see *Écrits Politiques de Jean Juvenal des Ursins*, ed. P.S. Lewis (Société de l'Histoire de France, 3 vols, 1978–92), i, pp. 175–7, 182–3, ii, 155–6. More generally see Lewis 'The English Kill their Kings' and 'War propaganda and Historiography in Fifteenth-Century France and England', in *Essays in Later Medieval French History* (1985), pp. 191–2 and 193–213, and Nicole Pons, 'La guerre de Cent ans vue par quelques polémistes français du XVe siècle', in *Guerre et Société en France, en Angleterre et en Bourgogne XIVe–XVe Siècles*, eds Philippe Contamine, Charles Giry-Deloison and Maurice H. Keen (Lille, 1991), pp. 143–69, at pp. 144, 148.

conscious of this point, and indeed the Southampton plot on the eve of his departure for Harfleur was an unpleasant reminder of it.[85] Could it be that his Norman gamble was a challenge to God to vindicate his right and appease his conscience? Or was it rather a desperate and cynical throw – one is tempted to say a Machiavellian one – by a man who believed it the only way to buttress an uncertain hold of his throne?

So far, I have been arguing that Henry V was much more conspicuously successful than Henry VIII, and that he pursued a much more systematic political strategy. He was much more single-minded in his concentration on France. Where Henry VIII gave France priority over Scotland, Henry V seems to have totally subordinated Scottish policy to his French interests in spite of having the king of Scots as his prisoner.[86] Historians generally make a virtue of Henry V's concentration on his objectives in France, whereas in Henry VIII's case, French policy is not usually counted among his more notable achievements.[87] That may be unjust. The viability of Henry V's policy in the longer term is surely questionable. Admittedly there is one 'God-given' possibility which might have made the dual monarchy a permanency: that is the death of the dauphin Charles without male issue, leaving Charles, Duc d'Orléans, a prisoner in England since Agincourt, as the Valois claimant. As long as the dauphin lived, however, the Treaty of Troyes committed Henry's French and English subjects to a long, hard, and extremely expensive struggle to win territory inch by inch. The argument that Henry, but for his death in 1422, could have carried it through successfully must be questioned. Henry's failure to capture a Loire crossing at either Beaugency or Orléans in 1421 because of extended lines of communication emphasizes just how

---

[85] Pugh, *Southampton Plot*, pp. 125–8.

[86] Michael Brown, *James I* (Edinburgh, 1994). Henry did, however, send a spy to Scotland in 1418 (the chronicler John Hardyng), to spy out the land and collect evidence for English claims to sovereignty; Antonia Gransden, *Historical Writing in England* (2 vols, 1974–82), ii, p. 275, 285–6; Patricia J. Bradley, 'Henry V's Scottish Policy – a study in Realpolitik', in *Documenting the Past: Essays in Medieval History presented to George Peddy Cuttino*, eds J.S. Hamilton and Bradley (Woodbridge, 1989), pp. 177–95.

[87] Gunn, 'Henry VIII's Foreign Policy', p. 35 draws attention to the the capture of Boulogne as the event of Henry's reign most frequently cited in seventeenth-century almanacs.

far success would have to depend on systematic piecemeal conquest; how remote, therefore, was the chance of recognition throughout France.[88] It may be that his acceptance of the inheritance of the French throne at Troyes followed ineluctably from the extraordinary circumstances of French politics in 1419, but even Henry's narrower aim, of Normandy (and Aquitaine) in full sovereignty, was an unlikely recipe for long-term peace. Given the strategic and commercial stranglehold over Paris conferred on the English by possession of Rouen and the Seine estuary, it is inconceivable that a French regime installed in the capital would not have set about the reconquest of Normandy at the earliest opportunity. No wonder that the aged Adam of Usk ended his chronicle with a prayer that Henry should not follow the famous conquerors of the past and incur the wrath of the Lord.[89]

Henry V did not pursue the claim to the French Crown inflexibly. He did, however, set his claims in France at a level which the French were almost bound to reject; at least the Brétigny terms for Aquitaine in 1414–15, Aquitaine and Normandy in full sovereignty in 1418–19.[90] By contrast, Henry VIII, it could be argued, achieved what he sought, namely recognition as a player on the international scene at the cost of relatively limited intervention. By making his alliance desirable he ensured that, except in 1538–40, England was not left isolated and therefore a target for invasion. He also safeguarded an English national interest in keeping the Netherlands independent of France.[91] His flexible policy, enormously expensive as it was, leading to tax rebellion in 1525 and massive sales of capital assets in the 1540s, created grave difficulties for his successors. But Henry VIII never locked himself into a commitment from which he could not retreat with honour. (He was a master at the art of declaring victory in unpromising circumstances.) While Boulogne was a distinctly awkward legacy for Edward VI, it did not equal the burden of obligation bequeathed to his son by Henry V.

---

[88] Allmand, *Henry V*, p. 163; Pugh, *Henry V*, pp. 137–8.

[89] *Chronicon Adae de Usk*, ed. E.M. Thompson (2nd edn, 1904), pp. 133, 320.

[90] Palmer, 'War Aims', pp. 66–70. Maurice Keen believes that Henry was aiming for more than the Brétigny terms, notably Normandy, as early as 1414, and criticizes Henry for lack of skill at 'the strategic level, in diplomacy if not in war', a lack of 'sense of the limits of the possible'; 'Diplomacy', in *Henry V*, ed. Harriss, pp. 181–99, at pp. 187, 198–9.

[91] Gunn, 'French Wars', pp. 31–2, 46–7.

Henry V was single-minded, perhaps ruthless, in the pursuit of his goal; he also clothed his activities in a cloak of righteousness. His invocation of divine approval, however hollow, had solid political advantages – the capacity to inspire others, perhaps a laying aside of internal quarrels in the common cause. The disadvantages are less often considered, at least in Henry's case – the taking of unjustified risks, the sacrifice of one's own and one's subjects' goods and lives (not to mention those of the enemy) for an end which, I would argue, was unobtainable. The point is commonly made in mitigation that there was no judgement available but God's in disputes between sovereign princes and that God's judgement was best shown in battle.[92] The problem with God's jurisdiction is that the losing party is reluctant to accept the apparent verdict as final. Defeat is commonly seen as a punishment for sin and as a trial of faith rather than as a judgement on the issue as such. So, from one viewpoint, God upholds Henry's right at Agincourt. From another, Joan of Arc is God's true messenger.[93] Henry's reputation for righteousness, by limiting his options, may not have been an unalloyed political advantage.

Military history raises in acute form a dilemma faced by all historians. Total scientific detachment, even if it were possible, would be dehumanizing. Value judgements creep into our discourse in all sorts of ways. Perhaps the best we can do is to be aware of their presence. Oddly, 'judgementalism' is considered a heinous professional sin when the historian's judgement is negative; a positive verdict, on the other hand, is seen as permissible, indeed evidence of success in understanding the person under discussion. I am always amazed at the rhetorical praise heaped on Henry V (involving as it does an extraordinary piece of teleology) by the normally coolly appraising K.B. McFarlane:

---

[92] Allmand, 'Henry V, the Soldier, and the War in France', in *Henry V*, ed. Harriss, pp. 117–35, at pp. 120–1.

[93] See Christine de Pisan, *Ditié de Jehanne d'Arc*, eds A.J. Kennedy and Kenneth Varty (Medium Aevum Monographs, new ser., vol ix, Oxford, 1977), composed immediately after Charles VII's coronation. I owe this lead to Colin Richmond. Jean Juvenal des Ursins, *Écrits Politiques*, i, pp. 196–7, argued that Henry's victories were a punishment for French sin, but did not give Henry a right to the kingdom: 'souvent Dieu punist les gens pecheurs par pires pecheurs que eulx'.

By whatever standards he is judged Henry was superlatively gifted: his only weakness was the physical one from which he died. He was born to rule and to conquer. . . . Take him all round and he was, I think, the greatest man that ever ruled England.[94]

Slightly less extravagant, perhaps a shade ambivalent, is Gerald Harriss' view that Henry aimed at bringing 'reconciliation out of hate, unity out of conflict, justice out of wrong-doing, legitimacy out of usurpation', and that these aims were 'neither unworthy nor wholly impossible'.[95] The sting surely lies here in 'nor wholly impossible'. A utilitarian argument that war may be justified in pursuit of peace is only tenable if peace seems a reasonably likely outcome. That, I suggest, is not the case in this instance.

The image of Henry V is a compelling one, the more so as he died in his prime, the classic tragic hero. That image was deliberately created, and its successful creation was itself a political achievement, bringing advantages in terms of greater political stability to England. Recognizing that achievement does not, however, mean accepting the image uncritically. Neither in terms of right, nor in terms of long-term viability, do Henry's claims to the French throne or to the duchy of Normandy seem convincing; although arguably the Brétigny terms for Aquitaine could be regarded as legitimate and, after 1415, perhaps obtainable and even sustainable.[96]

More generally in trying to understand the ethos of a ruling group, we may distort the picture as a whole, passing too lightly over what that ethos entailed. We understand that military prowess was considered a virtue in rulers, indeed

[94] 'Henry V: A Personal Portrait', in *Lancastrian Kings and Lollard Knights* (Oxford, 1972), pp. 114–33, at pp. 132–3.

[95] 'Conclusion', in *Henry V*, ed. Harriss, pp. 209–10. Harriss seems to be echoing *Gesta*, p. 181. Interestingly those English historians who have studied Henry from an overseas vantage are less enamoured; Vaughan, *John the Fearless*, pp. 204–5 ('one of the most aggressive and shifty products of an age of violence and duplicity'), and Knowlson, *Jean V*, pp. 78–9, who sees him as a self-obsessed actor.

[96] My point here is that Henry's would-be legitimist claim to the French throne was invalidated by the events of 1399, while any claim to Normandy had been legitimately abandoned in the 1259 Treaty of Paris. Brétigny, however, was an attempted settlement of the unresolved Gascon problem; while its terms were obviously unpalatable to the French, Gascony was a less vital interest to them than Normandy.

that it was an indispensable element in kingship and that to pursue one's right was a positive duty. There is no point in facile moral condemnation; the two Henries were doing in their different ways what was expected of them. But to go further, to indulge in positive praise, is to disregard the equally valid claims of the victims of their wars for a hearing. Without labouring the point, numbers of innocent peasants and townspeople endured robbery, the burning of their houses and fields, the loss of livestock, rape, mutilation and murder, as rulers pursued their rights. In Henry VIII's case the victims were mostly the people of Picardy and the Scottish borders, whose property was systematically torched; in Henry V's, the inhabitants of besieged towns. I see little sign that chivalry, as practised by the two Henries, had much to do with Maurice Keen's 'hereditary and honourable duty to be ready to draw the sword to defend the weak and the oppressed'; the weak and oppressed in both periods were treated with callous indifference when they fell foul of the 'rights' of their betters.[97] Indeed the laws of war accepted the wholly unreasonable proposition from Deuteronomy that it was the fault of the inhabitants of a town if they failed to be instantly persuaded by a claim of right issued by their besieger.[98] The author of the *Gesta Henrici Quinti*, and innumerable other English clerics, could therefore justify Henry's Christian warmaking by an absurd reference to the 'more than adamantine obduracy of the French, which neither the tender milk of goats nor the consuming wine of vengeance, nor yet the most thoroughgoing negotiations could soften'.[99]

Perhaps the best comment remains Shakespeare's:

KING HENRY (*incognito*): Methinks I could not die any where so contented as in the king's company, his cause being just and his quarrel honourable.

WILLIAMS: That's more than we know.

---

[97] *Chivalry* (New Haven, 1984), p. 253. Keen is, of course, acutely aware of the dichotomy; see his *Nobles, Knights and Men-at-Arms in the Middle Ages* (1996), *passim*.

[98] M.H. Keen, *The Laws of War in the Middle Ages* (1965), p. 123; Meron, *Henry's Wars*, pp. 22, 103, 193–4.

[99] *Gesta*, p. 181. F.W. Russell, *The Just War in the Middle Ages* (Cambridge, 1975), pp. 304–7, makes the point that just-war theory depended on an unrealistic assumption that one side was unequivocally in the right, and that to oppose the right was to deserve punishment. The result was a chorus of clerics applauding their rulers and, *de facto*, a slide into the view that 'might made right'.

BATES: Ay, or more than we should seek after; for we know enough if we know
we are the king's subjects. If his cause be wrong, our obedience to the king
wipes the crime of it out of us.

WILLIAMS: But if the cause be not good, the king himself hath a heavy reckoning
to make; when all those legs and arms and heads, chopped off in a battle, shall
join together at the latter day, and cry all, 'We died at such a place'; some
swearing, some crying for a surgeon, some upon their wives left poor behind
them, some upon the debts they owe, some upon their children rawly left.[100]

The discussion veers off at a tangent, to the improbability that soldiers dying in
battle will be in a state of grace, so giving Henry the chance to disclaim
responsibility for those who have neglected to make their peace with God
beforehand. But Williams' initial point remains unanswered: how can the king
know that the suffering he has caused is justified by the righteousness of his
quarrel?[101] That, of course, applies equally to both Henries. Quite what arguments
were used by Henry V to silence the qualms of Vincent Ferrer, or by Henry VIII
those of John Colet, we do not know.[102] It is perhaps reassuring to realize that these
problems were sometimes raised and to read (admittedly in a French source) of Sir
John Cornewall who concluded, when he saw his son killed at the siege of Meaux,
that whatever the justice of the Norman campaign, the attempt to deprive the
dauphin Charles of the crown of France was against all reason and justice.[103]

---

[100] *Henry V*, Act iv, 1. I hasten to make clear that I quote Shakespeare not as a primary source but
as an informed and sensitive commentator.

[101] A point made notably by Wycliffe, among others; see C.T. Allmand, 'The War and the Non-
combatant', in *The Hundred Years War*, ed. Fowler, pp. 163–83, at p. 176.

[102] *First English Life*, pp. 130–2; Scarisbrick, *Henry VIII*, p. 33

[103] Allmand, *Henry V*, p. 166, quoting Jean Juvenal des Ursins. Philippe Contamine, *War in the
Middle Ages* (trans., Oxford, 1984), p. 293, alleges 'numerous French chronicles' for Cornewall's
resolving never again to fight Christians. He certainly departed precipitately from Meaux, but his
later career as custodian of the Duke of Orléans, peer (Lord Fanhope) and regular member of the
royal council, hardly suggests principled opposition to royal policy; C.G.S. [Foljambe], Earl of
Liverpool, and Compton Reade, *The House of Cornewall* (Hereford, 1908), pp. 179–83, and A.C.
Reeves, *Lancastrian Englishmen* (Washington, DC, 1981), pp. 139–202.

CONCLUSION
John L. Watts

D o these essays bring us any closer to a view of when, or how – or even if – 'the Middle Ages' ended? At first sight, perhaps, the answer may be 'no'. Questions like these are *questions mal posées* – indeed, they are questions no one writing now would seriously pose at all, although the objection may be one of language more than of substance. None of the contributors argues that the decades around 1500 saw a wholesale and concentrated series of changes from one great system to another. Instead, their essays reflect many of those features of modern writing discussed at the outset: the explicit rejection of older grand narratives; greater recognition for the specific and the circumstantial; more extensive factual knowledge and social understanding; a sharp eye for continuities and echoes where earlier generations emphasized difference. Our picture of the fifteenth and sixteenth centuries has become so complex that it defies summation, let alone summation in terms which scholars have been attacking for almost a century. To echo Maitland's famous witticism about the introduction of knight-service into England, the Middle Ages (which began, perhaps, in the seventeenth century), were well and truly over by the 1950s, let alone the 1990s.

But the possibility of some large-scale discussion of the problems raised in the introduction remains open. The contributors have gone far beyond the substitution of a simple narrative of 'continuity' in return for one of 'change'. George Bernard and Cliff Davies show that the pilgrimages and French Wars of Henry VIII's reign took place in a different environment from that of their fifteenth-century equivalents. It is clear from Steven Gunn's article that Sir Thomas Lovell was a different kettle of fish from the 'new men' encountered in the twelfth century, or under the house of Lancaster: his authority in the localities was more complete, and more completely provided and maintained by his royal master – and he was one of a group, a group analogous (perhaps) to King John's Poitevins or Richard II's chamber knights, but also clearly different in its attributes and functions. While, as Richard Britnell shows, the size and vigour of the economy changed much less dramatically than older accounts suggest, there were clearly quite striking developments in some of its sectors. Today's historians are mostly reluctant to talk in terms of systems, and we are conscious that – notwithstanding the influence of everything on everything else – things may change at different rates or times, that they may change for different reasons and that these changes are not made once and for all. The essays in this collection do not fall into Elton's neatly identified error, of opposing to the untenable notion of the Renaissance an equally untenable notion of stasis.

Do they do more than that? After all, 'change' has always been accepted at some level; protestations of continuity have always been partly rhetorical, calls for a shift of emphasis rather than literal statements of fact. Perhaps they do. A striking feature of many of these essays, as of other works dealing with the phenomena of the period, is the dialogue which they present between elements of continuity and elements of change. On the one hand, we have old forms in new clothes: in 1511, John Skelton writes a 'speculum principis', but, unlike the many fourteenth- and fifteenth-century versions of the genre, it is written in a showy Latin, it drips with classical allusions and the moral advice is perfunctory, an excuse for an exercise in style;[1] in 1528, Henry VIII warns the emperor against destroying the realm of France, on the traditional grounds that it is his by right, and the altogether more novel ones that the 'French king' is his 'brother and ally' and 'payeth us yearly a great pension and tribute'; meanwhile, Wolsey justifies his master's war in the strikingly unmedieval terms of Aesop's fable about the folly of being the only wise man in a world of fools.[2] On the other hand, there are new forms in old clothes: Thomas Lovell and Robert Dudley seek the status and accoutrements of medieval magnate lordship, even though they are operating in significantly different judicial and governmental contexts; the multi-faceted and multi-layered rising of 1536 presents itself under the name, and partly in the forms, of a pilgrimage. In a way, of course, these examples simply call to mind the all-too-familiar problem of the fifteenth-century mixture of 'new' and 'old',

[1] Above, p. 33.
[2] Above, p. 242.

which was mentioned in the introduction and which is partly a product of the Renaissance paradigm and its slow disintegration in the course of the present century. At the same time, however, the familiarity of the problem does not mean that it is irresoluble or unworthy of attention. In some ways, indeed, the historiographical developments of the last few decades have extended our means of addressing it.

To a certain extent, one's position on the prominence of change in the period around 1500 depends on the kind of attention given to what we might call the outward forms of social and political phenomena: on the one hand, the ways in which these phenomena are conceived, represented and discussed; on the other, the formal apparatuses of such diverse structures as government, justice, publishing, complaint or the various kinds of economic activity. Inasmuch as the nineteenth-century case for Renaissance and New Monarchy was more than the working out of a series of *a priori* beliefs about the course of human development, it rested on the identification of significant changes in these areas – and in particular in the arts, in the language of written sources and in the institutions of politics. To some extent, as we have seen, this Renaissance paradigm was dissolved by a wave of empirical discoveries which demonstrated that its constituent changes were actually less unprecedented or concentrated than had been claimed. But scepticism also arose from a series of shifts in the philosophy and methodology of history which challenged the long-presumed links between language and reality, between institutional forms and social practice, between the activities of élites and the experience of peoples, in fact between the historically privileged zones of high politics, high culture and constitutional development on the one hand and the larger workings of society on the other. Even where they defied empirical correction, therefore, the kinds of changes registered by nineteenth-century historians were often seen as either epiphenomenal or documentary.

These trends are visible in the essays printed above. For one thing, those contributors working on the deeper structures of society, or from less artful sources, are generally less struck by an atmosphere of change than those working nearer the surface and from more complex, or public, texts. For another, there is clearly a measure of disagreement among today's historians concerning how we should evaluate the materials on which the Victorians bestowed such unsceptical attention. As a result of the so-called 'linguistic turn', the historiographical developments mentioned in the previous paragraph have, in their turn, been challenged. Interest in ideas, and in language as a means of conveying and enacting ideas, has revived, and there is a greater readiness to attribute socio-political significance to such phenomena. While this remains a controversial matter (as Colin Richmond's paper demonstrates), it does open up some new ways of looking at data from our period.

In particular, the notion of a political culture, defined by a common acceptance of certain principles and practices and made real by a necessary deference to these in public statements and other behaviour, provides a framework into which otherwise miscellaneous features of public life may be fitted and treated as something of an aggregate. This is particularly valuable for the understanding of our period, since the detailed exposure of precedents for many individual features of mental and social life at the turn of the century has had an atomizing effect on the evidence. As A.B. Ferguson noted in relation to the political ideas of the period, it has been much easier to demonstrate continuities from earlier precedents than to document the 'change of texture', the '"feel" of the Renaissance'.[3] One obvious retort is, of course, that this 'feel' is an artefact of historiographical tradition, but another is that the problem arises not because there *was* no 'texture', or 'change of texture', but because of the difficulties twentieth-century historians have had with finding a satisfactory analogue for the nineteenth-century sense of collective consciousness as a key element in the making of society. We cannot use terms like 'the nation' or 'the medieval mind' with conviction; we cannot talk about 'the constitution' or the 'public' without being provocative, or at least needing to explain what we mean. Yet there can be few of us who doubt that there were some kinds of collectivity in the past we study, some shared manners and rules, some propensity for words and ideas to become grouped together and to play off one another, and some relationship between these groups and the behaviour of individuals. An approach which takes language to be, in Jean-Philippe Genet's words, 'the most important

---

[3] 'Renaissance Realism in the "Commonwealth" Literature of Early Tudor England', *Journal of the History of Ideas*, 16 (1955), 287–305, at p. 305.

of social institutions' provides a way forward. It blurs the lines between the ideal and the real, presupposing – on grounds which can be justified – that there are links between what people say, what they think and what they do. It underpins the notion of a political culture and, since changes in both language and culture can to some extent be documented, it helps to resolve the kinds of question posed in the introduction. It gives us another way of measuring the impact and causation of formal, or institutional, change by looking at the mental world in which such change became possible and the linguistic world in which it was negotiated and expressed. Finally, it draws our source material together in different ways and, in particular, it helps us to see how the conjunction of phenomena which are not all, in themselves, unprecedented could nonetheless create a new socio-political environment.

As Genet's paper makes clear, the analysis of political language is not a task to be entered into lightly. The analysis of political culture, if pursued with a similar kind of scientific rigour, would be all the more complex and time-consuming. Even the comparatively impressionistic interpretations that have begun to appear, particularly for the early sixteenth century, have to rest on substantial research. Nonetheless – in the interests of drawing attention to some of the possibilities of this approach and, indeed, of rounding off this volume – it is tempting to make some broad suggestions about how English political culture may have been affected by certain cultural developments in our period and what this may have meant. The powerful impact of law and of bureaucratic literacy on the political society of the thirteenth century is now well understood. It seems plausible to argue for a similar conjunction at the end of the fifteenth, and that developments in the worlds of thought and language were indeed instrumental in the making of a new polity.

It is hard to deny that, in this period, the facilities for communication were improving rapidly in both width and depth. The emergence of printing coincided with a longer-term trend in favour of spreading and deepening literacy. There were more schools and colleges; more groups within society received extensive education; the curriculum of common knowledge was widening. It does not particularly matter that Caxton's early publications were romances, histories and handbooks of a completely traditional kind, or that many of them were translations of older works long available in manuscript. What is important is that more people were being more directly and continuously exposed to language, to a sense of shared knowledge, to oft-repeated modes of description and expression. And the language itself was changing too: as English became the medium for a widening range of administrative, political, social and religious discourse, so its vocabulary grew and its structures became clearer and more expressive. Ideas could move about more easily, both within a wider social space and across the boundaries of different specialisms. Alongside this, new modes of historical and political analysis were developing. Part and parcel of the rise of the Inns of Court in late fifteenth-century England was a growing interest in legal sources and a sharper perception that knowledge of laws and institutions was the key to political understanding. The analytical categories used in the discussion of politics were becoming more diverse and complex: classical models were used with greater sophistication and precision; polities – not types of constitution, but actual states – were coming to be compared with one another; princely morality was presented in a more subtle light; a relatively static and reactive sense of the purposes of government was replaced by a more dynamic interest in reform and a more positive concern with the problem of maintaining obedience within a fickle populace. Histories began to explain more. If the fate of humanity was still shaped mainly by the divine plan and the consequences of personal immorality, the agencies of retribution were becoming more multi-faceted and realistic: in the Crowland chronicle as much as in Vergil, Richard III's crime is not only that he betrays his family, but that he nourishes the factionalism and ungovernableness of the people; Edward IV's achievement, conversely, is that he succeeds in governing, not that he does so virtuously, or on the basis of the rightful claim.

All this, of course, is well known, but its impact on the public and on politics – at least before Henry VIII's reign – has been little explored. What did it mean for the curiously unselfconscious political system of the medieval kings to have the arc-lights turned on? It was not that the system had never been examined before: recurrent political crises had provoked attempts at definition; the complex mixtures of formal and informal authority must have been well understood by the many who used them, even if their understanding was more instrumental than articulate. What was different was that kingship, lordship, justice, the social structure, the economy, history, law, religion, morality had never before been opened up to such searching and extensive comment. This kind of information explosion cannot have been without political and social consequences – consequences as major, in their way, as the rise of mass politics in the modern age, or of the spread of information technology in the present decade. We know that to rewrite the relations of twelfth-century warriors in legal and tenurial language was to alter those relations; we have not yet completely grasped what it did to the largely unaccountable monarchy of the Edwards and Henries to have it written up as 'dominium politicum et regale', or how the king's place in government was modified by the spread of senatorial imagery on the one hand and of handbooks for the courtier on the other, or how lordship was affected when its central role in the provision of justice was consistently presented as malign. Nor, perhaps, have we thought enough about the impact of institutional growth in an environment like this – an environment which must, with its interest in legal and bureaucratic structures, have played a part in stimulating that growth: once-comparatively-informal relations of petitioning, of counsel, of attendance, of justice were becoming routinized long before the 1530s; what did it mean that government was, in a sense, becoming both more bureaucratic and more personal at the same time?

Clearly enough, socio-political structures are not instantly reshaped by words, nor – as the historians of bastard feudalism know all too well – are they destroyed by changes to the institutional environment. It must be as valuable for historians to indicate (often unverbalized) continuities as it is for them to demonstrate articulate differences. Even so, the way to resolving what I would suggest is a common quandary – that mid-sixteenth-century England looks pretty substantially different from mid-fifteenth-century England, but we cannot quite say how it got there – must be to look again at the well-attested changes in the common mental life of that society and their relationship to the social, political and governmental environment with which most of us are more familiar. In the later fifteenth century, where progress in this area has perhaps been most limited, we shall see a society with a fuller, richer, more diverse and more critical sense of itself, a society which does not instantly discard its dissonant features, but which cannot experience any of them quite as it did before, a society in the early stages of a Kuhnian paradigm shift. We cannot see this as the 'End of the Middle Ages' because we know that similar periods of new awareness, of changing political culture, have occurred before. Following this, we may be tempted to argue that change of this kind is constant, rather than periodic, though it is difficult to avoid a feeling that there *are* times of change, times when a concatenation of factors produces a significant impact. Equally, it would be hard to deny that, rather as the weight of the historiography suggests, the sense of a shift from one age to another is strongest at the level of the social super ego and weakest at the level of the id. But, as we are coming once again to believe, the ways in which people thought and spoke about what they were doing are an important way into the evaluation of their society. Perhaps there is something in the notion of a 'Renaissance state' after all.

INDEX